YOU CAN DRAW

YOU CAN DRAW

BRUCE ROBERTSON ARCA

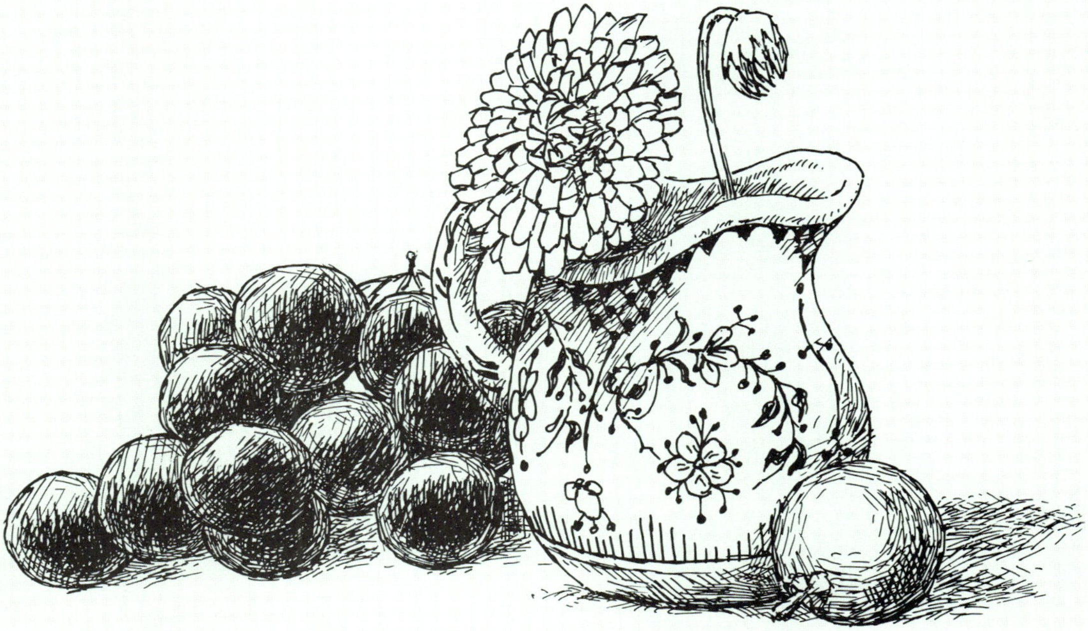

PRENTICE HALL PRESS • NEW YORK

Dedicated to Patricia

The Diagram Group
Editor Moira Johnson
Editorial assistance Maureen Cartwright, Denis Kennedy
Art staff Joe Bonello, Alastair Burnside, Richard Czapnik, Brian Hewson, Richard Hummerstone, Philip Patenall, Paula Preston

Contributing artists Robert Chapman 29, 53
Stephen Dhanraj 45, 50, 65, 68, 71, 116, 125, 126, 152
Janos Marffy 69
Anne Robertson 54, 56, 62, 75, 77, 126, 135
Jane Robertson 8–9, 88, 114, 132, 148, 149
Michael Robertson 52, 63, 74, 154
Paul Robertson 57, 63
Graham Rosewarne 10, 13, 24, 25, 26, 27, 28, 29, 32, 33, 64, 65, 66, 67, 69, 75, 83, 91, 105, 125, 153, 164, 165, 166, 167, 169, 170, 171, 172, 173, 175, 177, 185, 186, 188, 189

Published by Prentice Hall Press
A Division of Simon & Schuster, Inc.
Gulf + Western Building
One Gulf + Western Plaza
New York, NY 10023

Originally published in Great Britain by McDonald & Co. (Publishers) Ltd.

Library of Congress Cataloging-in-Publication Data

Robertson, Bruce, ARCA.
You can draw.
Includes index.
1. Drawing—Technique. I. Title.
NC730.R55 1986 741.2 86-42525
ISBN 0-13-972613-6

Manufactured in the United States of America

10 9 8 7 6 5 4 3 2 1

First Prentice Hall Press Edition

foreword

Drawing is 'thought with a line round it'. It does not require a fluent 'hand', the easy drafting skill of a professional, or years of practice.

You can draw. Unfortunately you may feel your efforts do not match the standards of work you see in books and galleries. This comparison reduces your confidence, weakens your resolve to continue, and ends in your not enjoying an activity that could bring years of pleasure.

Drawing is simply recording what you see. Look – try to capture the observations – and you have a drawing. Begin with simple tasks – copying from a photograph, drawing an old shoe, a bunch of flowers, a tree – and always try to finish each drawing.

Careful observation, perseverance and a will to enjoy the task are all you need to produce your own drawing. The equipment is inexpensive, the opportunity for pleasure infinite, and with continued practice you will exceed your own ambitions and startle your friends.

Drawing is fun, and it gives you pride in your achievements.

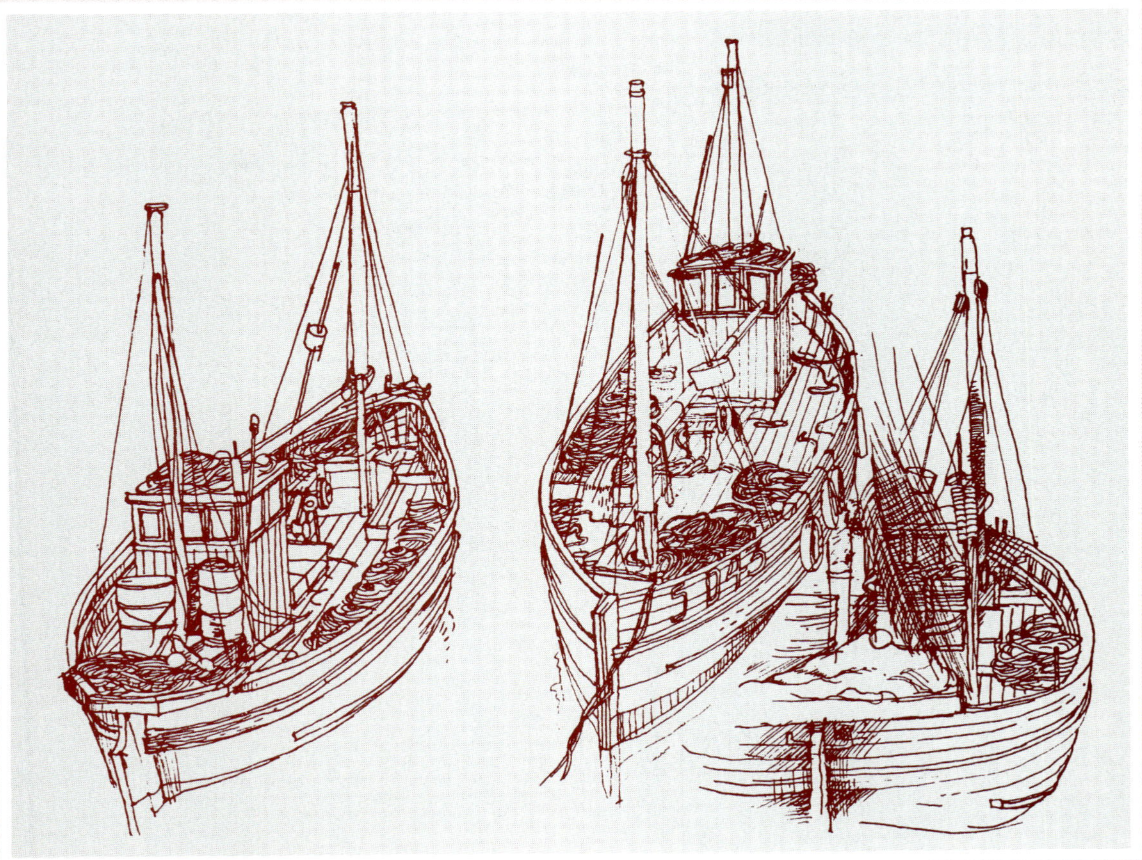

contents

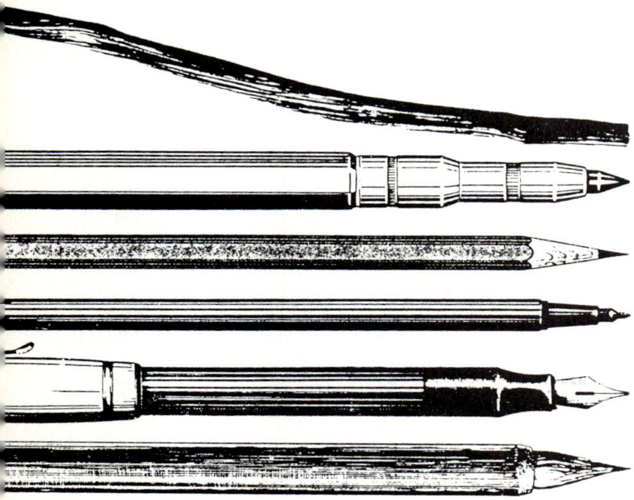

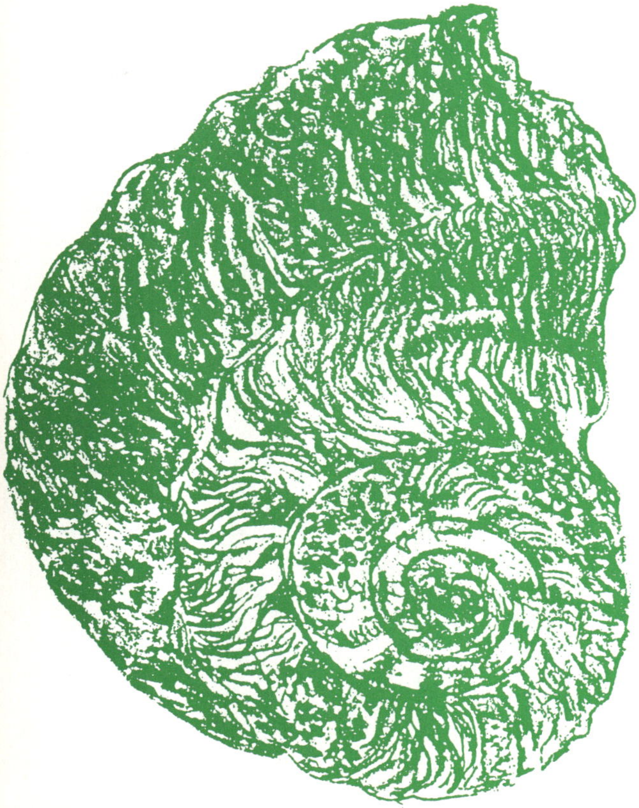

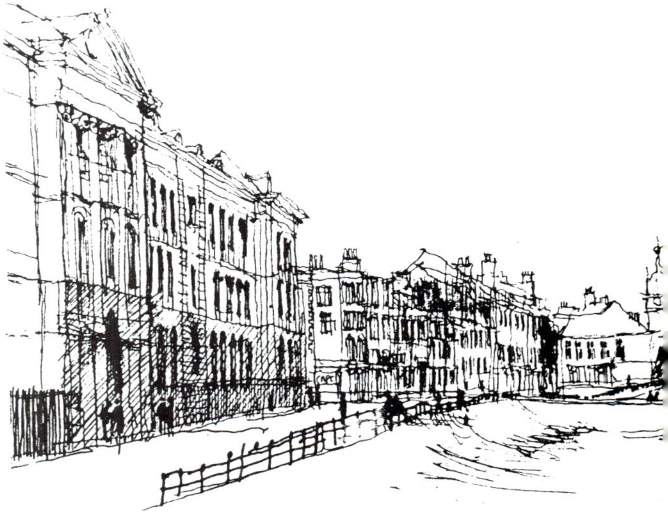

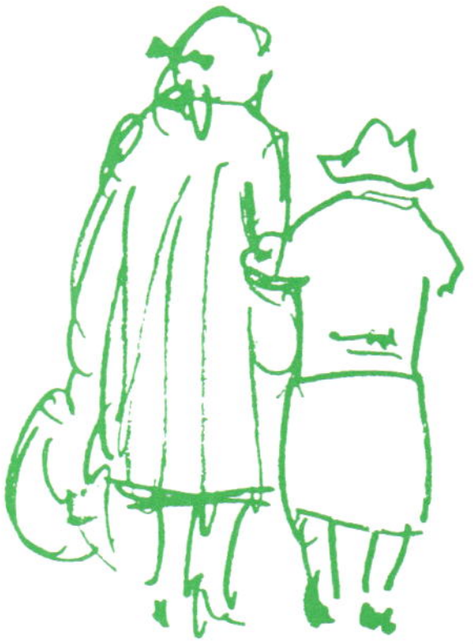

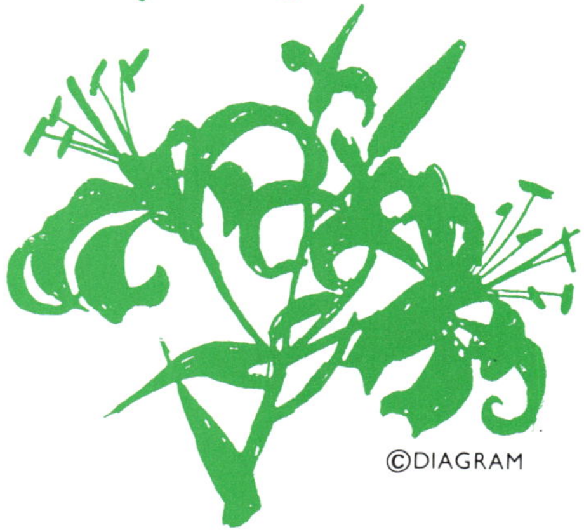

Part One

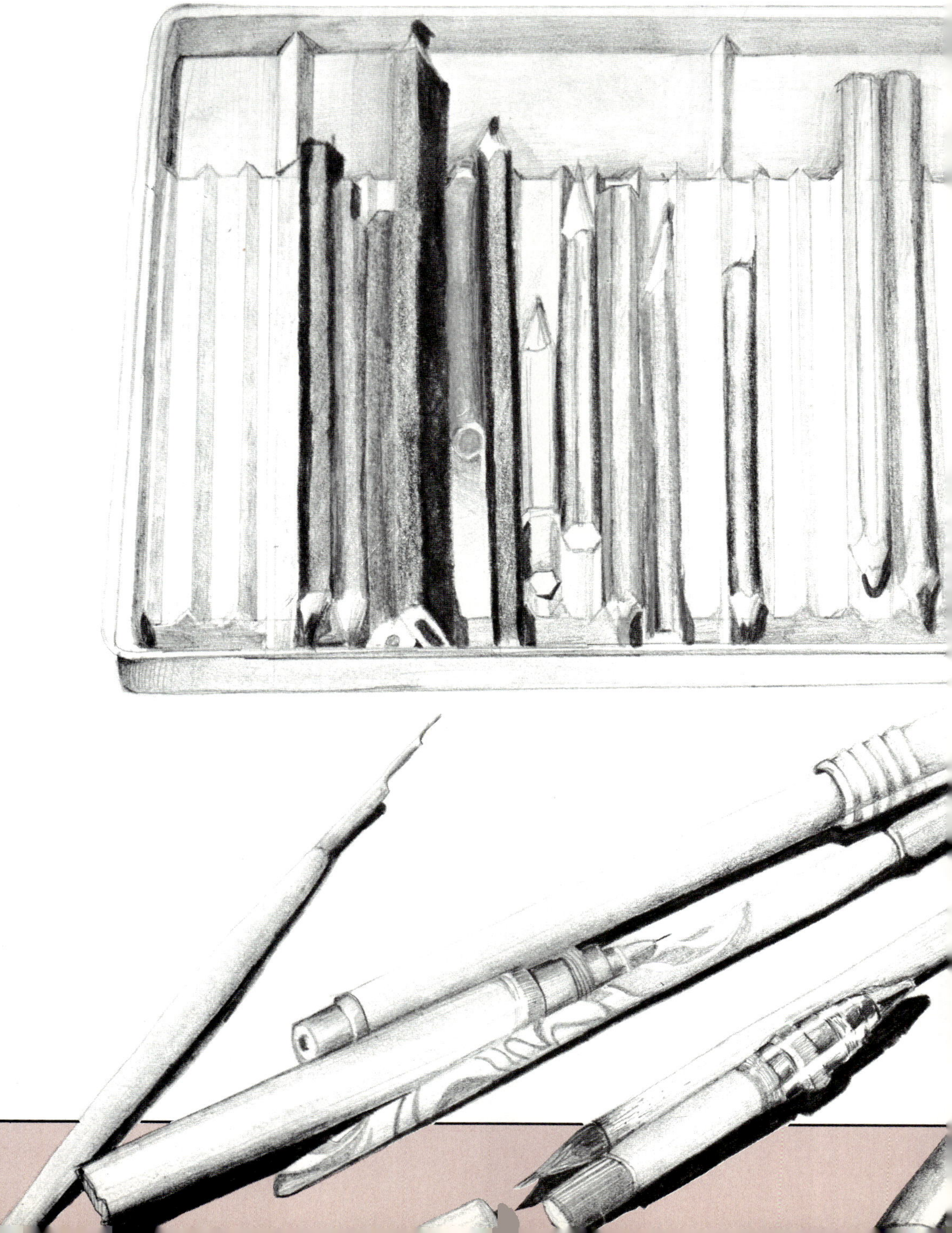

THE EQUIPMENT

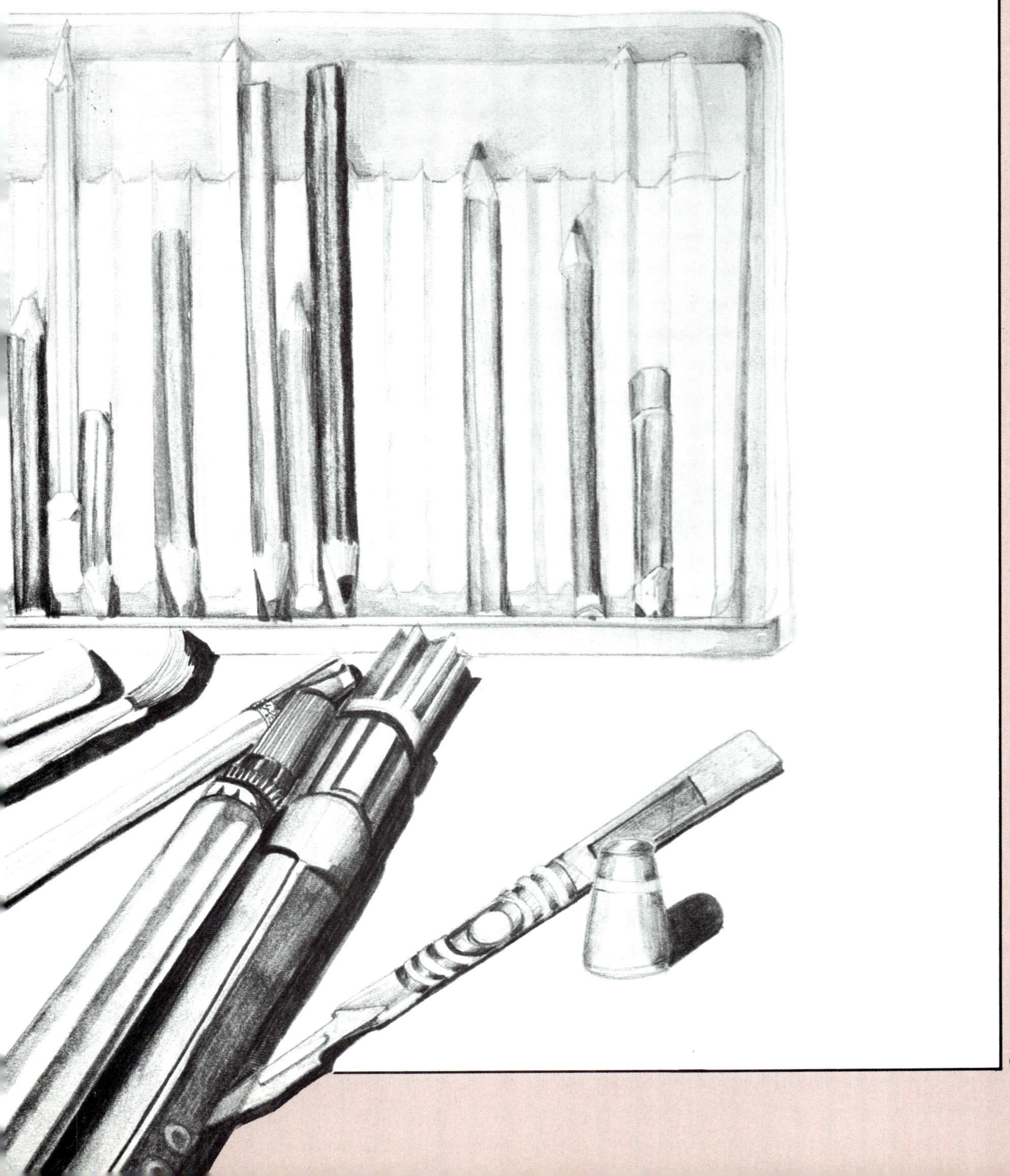

where you work

Sketching outside is exciting and valuable. Selecting subjects, collecting information and impressions, filling sketchbooks with experiences and observations – all this helps your study of reality, which is the heart of drawing. Make sure you will be comfortable. You may sit or stand for long periods, so take warm clothing, or, in the heat, wear a hat or perch in the shade. Take along a shoulder bag to hold your favourite pencils, pens, ink and sketchbook. Don't give room to untried tools. In a wind secure your paper firmly to a board. Keep alert for attractive views and colourful atmosphere; sketch your general impressions and all intriguing details.

You get out only what you put in, so spend time observing the world. Don't be put off by onlookers. Only you can truly judge what you draw; you can never do a bad drawing, only one that doesn't quite catch what you intend.
Never despair. Work with care.
Drawing is fun.

Where you sit
You can usually find somewhere to stand or sit so that you are in a fixed position for looking at your subject; but without a movable seat you may be limited in your choice of view because of the lack of a suitable place to sit.

a Sit on a wall or tree or any comfortable perch

b Carry a small collapsible stool or chair

c For careful work take a light portable easel. It may be difficult to handle in wind, however.

a

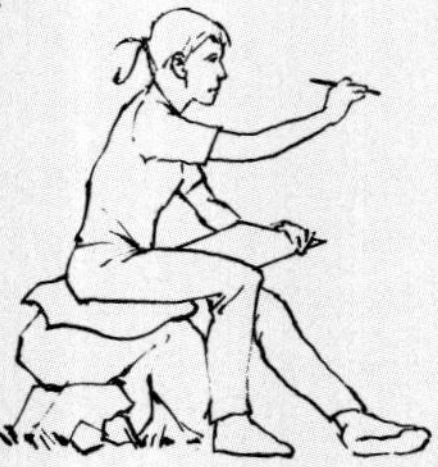

b

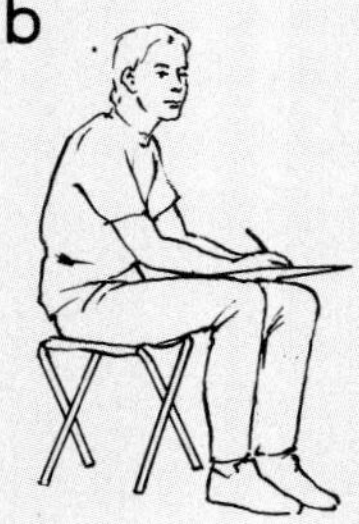

c

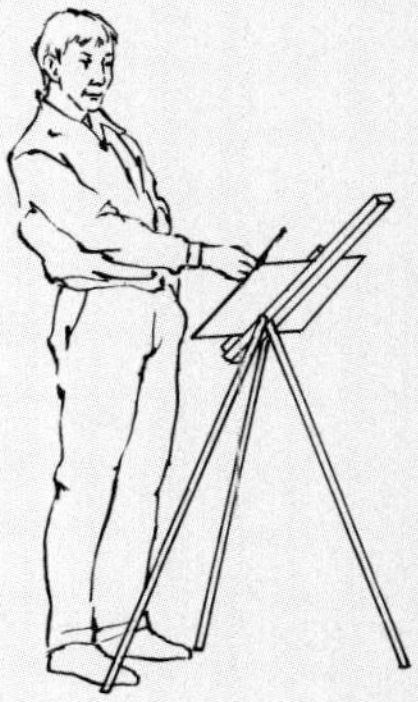

How far from the subject?
Leonardo da Vinci said, '*When you have to draw from nature, stand at a distance equal to three times the size of the object you wish to draw.*'
Your choice of a site at which to draw will be governed by such factors as your composition, the aim of your drawing, or how long you can observe the events or view. Try to put yourself 6m from the object, your drawing surface 50cm from your eyes, and record a 2m-high object 16cm on the paper.

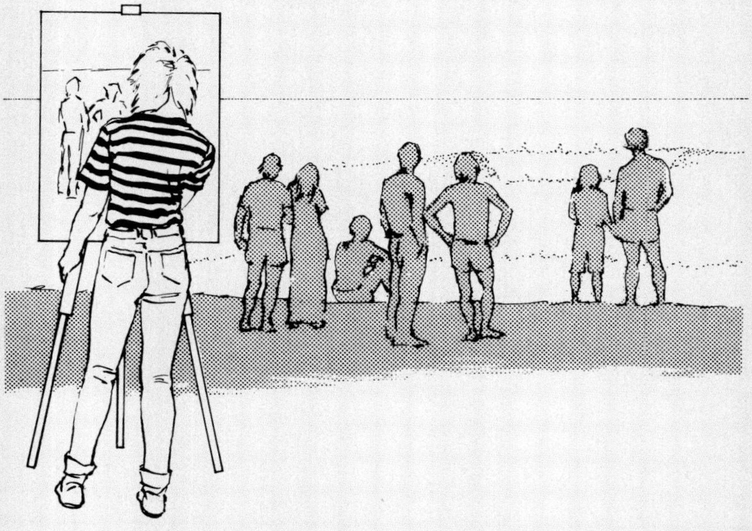

19th century vicarage
(Pencil drawing)
This page examines the close detail of a vicarage (*right*), whose basic forms were recorded earlier. When out sketching you are collecting information on the special nature of reality, which cannot be invented without a vast knowledge of many particulars. Detail of the actual size of sketch (*below*).

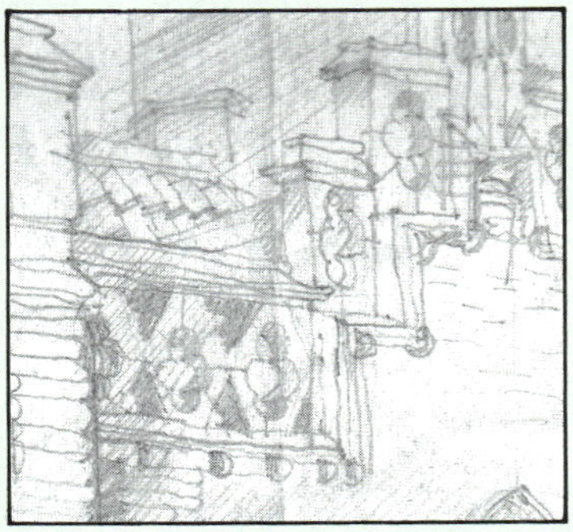

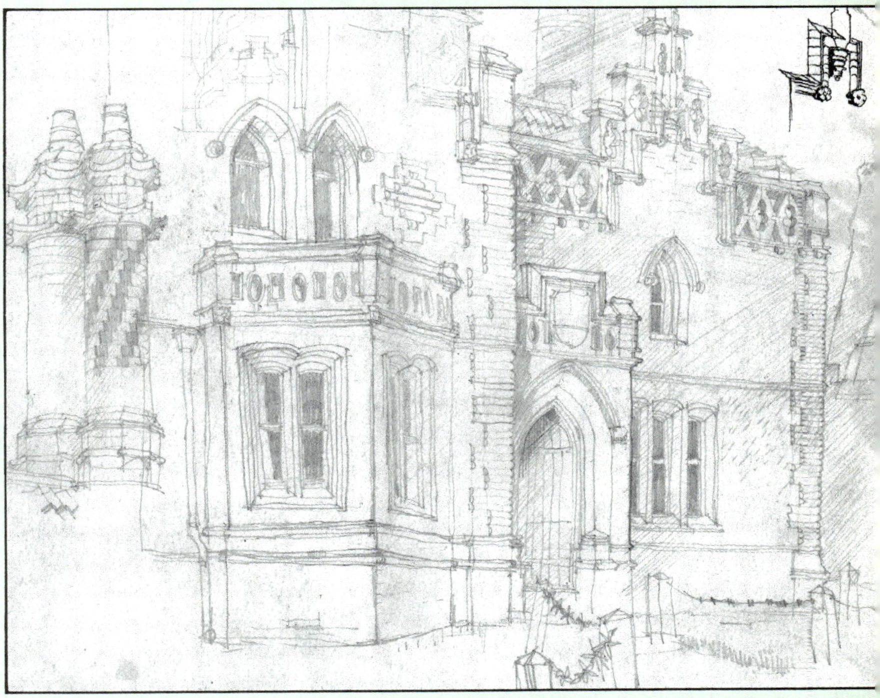

Winter funeral, Milan
(Pen, brush and ink drawing)
Capturing atmosphere, the feel of a place, how it encloses space, and light, is the exciting task of outdoor sketching. Later these images will evoke clear memories of events, such as the funeral (*right*) and will also reveal, unlike a photograph, how you felt at the time. Detail (*below*).

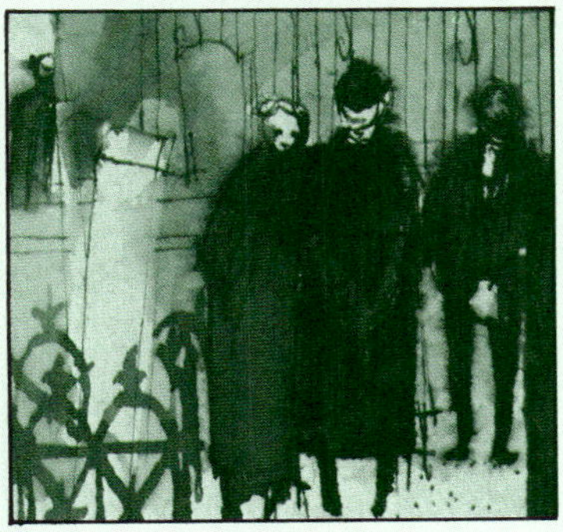

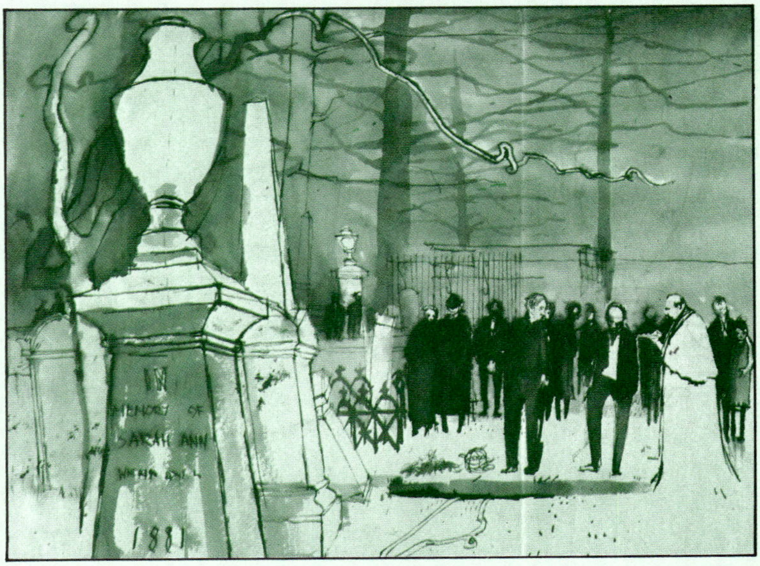

where you work

Grow into your working space and find out what is most convenient. Some basics:

- Light should fall from the left and in front (if you are right-handed).
- Chairs must be comfortable for many hours.
- Work surfaces should be clean, replaced if worn, and inclined slightly towards you with flat surrounds to hold pens, etc.
- Pencils, pens, brushes should be stored upright in jars or horizontal in drawers. Discard all old, unusable ones.
- Paper must be kept flat, but picture frames and glass upright. Store drawings in a plan chest (buy secondhand), but don't overload it.
- Everything should be within easy reach.
- A clean environment makes clean drawings.
- A clean surface equals clear results.
- Allow no distractions; face a wall or a window with a quiet view.
- Vary your work to avoid tiredness and errors.
- Buy serviceable tools, not glamorous ones.
- Care for your tools and work space.

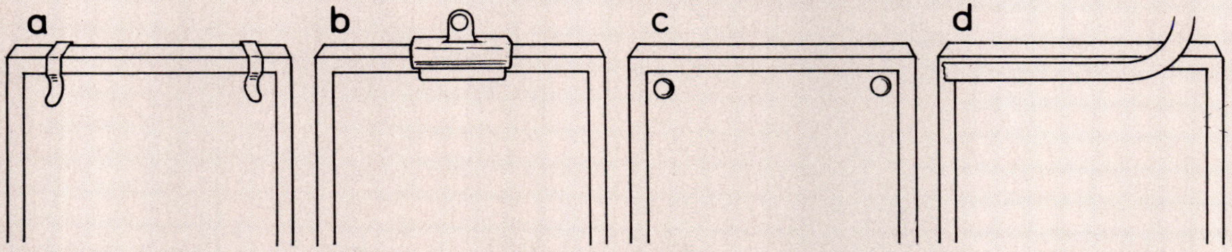

Never be seduced by costly equipment. Great drawings can be done with simple materials, and expensive tools need care in handling. Don't use worn-out brushes, pencils with broken leads, rulers with nicks in them, or a dirty drawing board surface. Enjoy and experiment with the different marks tools make. Develop your skills with them.

Your drawing surface
Paper is the commonest drawing surface and it can be fixed on a board in several ways:
a Board clips; leave board and paper surface undamaged.
b Stationery clips; equally good, but can become too weak.
c Pins; most commonly used, but can damage board surface.
d Adhesive tape; can affect paper so stick across corners.

Points of cleanliness
If you can maintain clean, tidy conditions around your work it will not be marred by stains and smudges.

1 Keep water out of the way so that it cannot be spilled
2 Never sharpen pencils over your work
3 Discard old scraps of paper
4 Protect your work by resting your hand on paper
5 Avoid sliding objects across your work surface
6 Never use your work surface as a cutting board
7 Put all unused tools away
8 Cover your work when complete or while you rest
9 Keep your work area clean and clear of unwanted objects
10 Change the top surface of your drawing board regularly by working on a large piece of card pinned or stuck to it

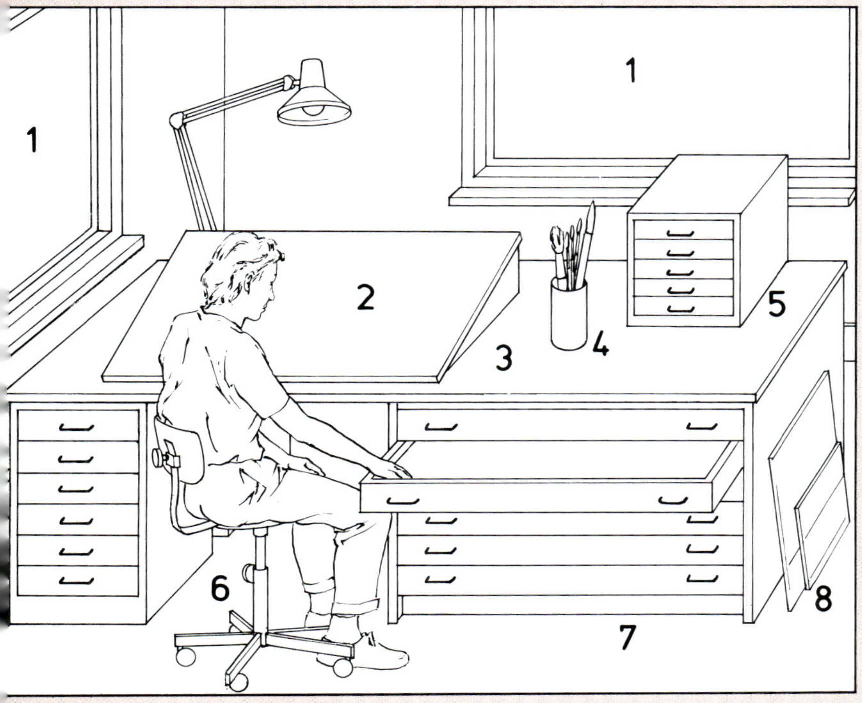

A permanent work space

Shown (*left*) are some basics about working at a desk:

1 If right-handed, light source at front and left.
2 Steady drawing board slightly raised on blocks to prevent having to lean over too far.
3 Flat work space at the side on which to put down pens, etc.
4 Jars and other drawing tool holders within easy reach.
5 Store for tools and small objects.
6 Comfortable chair with back rest, and easily movable so that you can review your work.
7 Plan chest for storing drawings and paper flat.
8 Space for storing frames and glass upright.

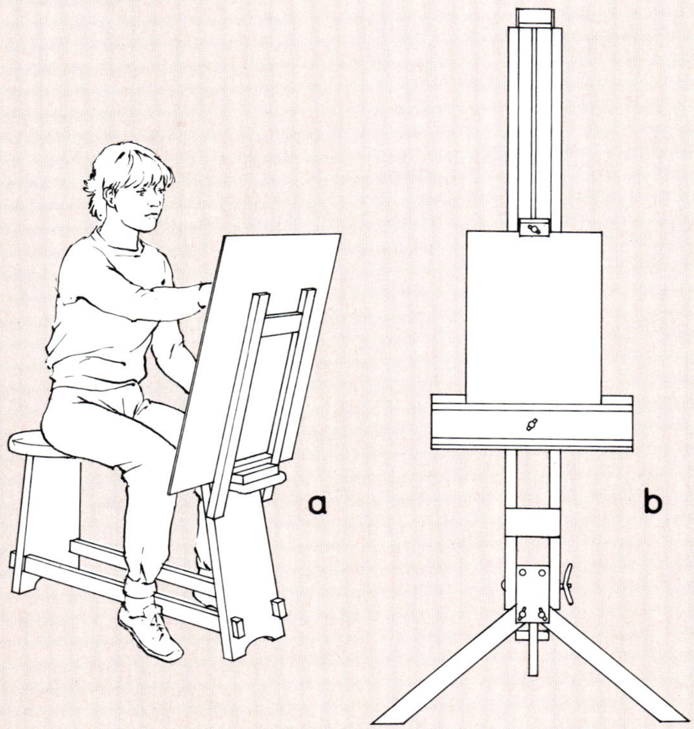

Drawing in a studio

To record a static composition (a model or still life) artists sit or stand at an upright drawing surface.
a A donkey (*far left*) is often available in a life class. It can be tiring because your back is unsupported.
b An easel, invented to hold a canvas while you paint, (*left*), is also used for life drawing but provides no rest for your hands.

pencils

Pencils are the most common drawing tools, and have been in use for several hundred years. They are readily available and convenient to work with, and the drawing can easily be altered with an eraser. Pencils can be used for many styles of drawing, from precise technical plans to smudgy freehand sketches.

Various factors control the mark that the pencil makes on the paper. These include the texture of the paper itself, the pressure exerted on the pencil, the grade of the pencil, and whether the tip or the side of the point is used. Pencil is not a permanent medium as it smudges easily; drawings need to be fixed with a coating of spray.

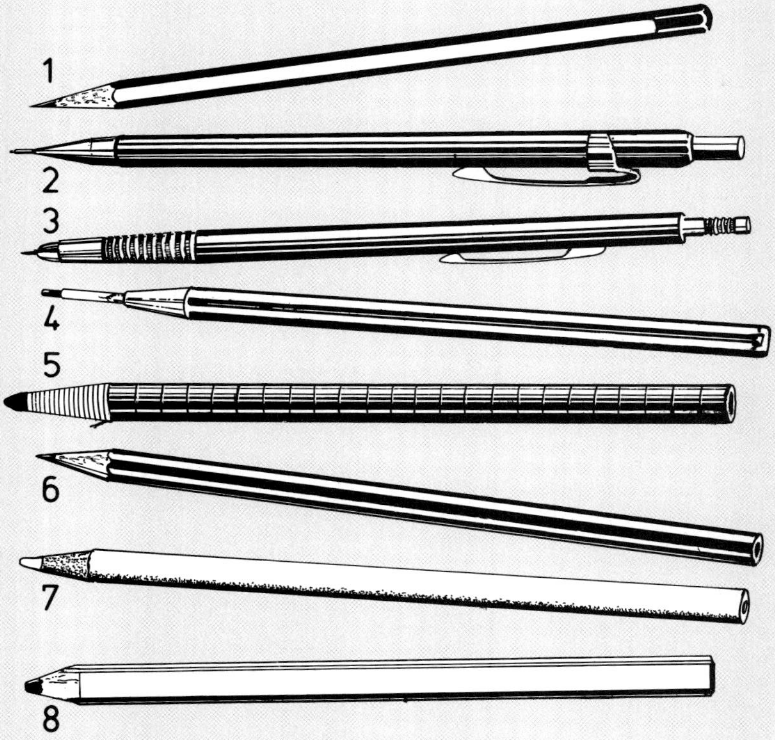

Types of pencil
Pencils are available in various forms, simple and sophisticated, for different uses.
1 Ordinary lead pencil with a casing of juniper wood to protect the lead.
2 Propelling pencil with a screw mechanism to move a separate lead through the holder to the required length.
3 Clutch pencil with teeth to hold the lead.
4 Engineer's pencil: a propelling pencil with a broad, flat lead.
5 Lithographer's pencil with a 'lead' of wax protected by paper.
6 Coloured pencil with a pigmented lead.
7 Wax pencil for writing on very smooth surfaces.
8 Carpenter's pencil with flat lead.

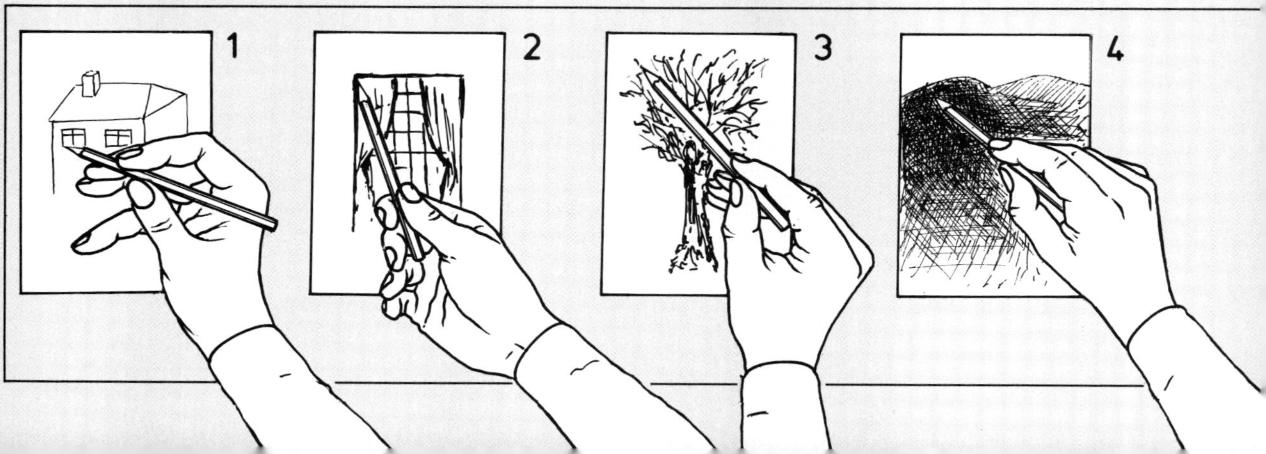

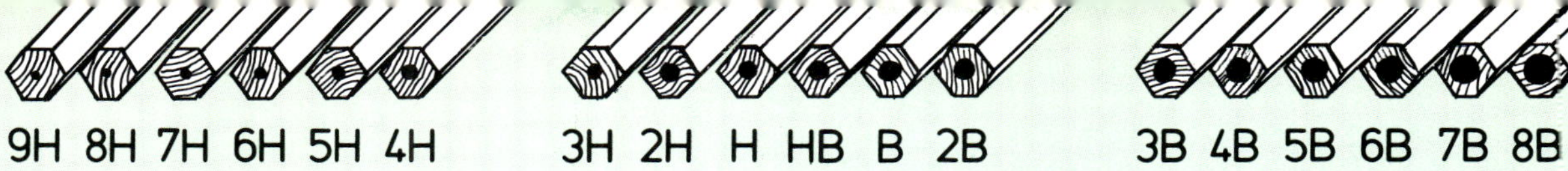

Pencil grades (*above*)
Pencils used to be made of sticks of soft metal – hence the name 'lead' for the pencil's core. These days leads are made from graphite, usually encased in wood. The hardness and thickness of the lead determines the pencil's grade: 9H is the hardest, 8B the softest. Hard pencils range from 9H to 4H; they are used for extremely accurate plans and drawings. Medium grades are 3H to 2B; these are the most commonly used pencils. Soft grades range from 3B to 8B.

Sharpening pencils
The way you sharpen your pencil will affect the kind of mark it produces on the paper. Always sharpen the opposite end from the grade mark so that the pencil grade is still identifiable. Make sure that you don't sharpen pencils over your work area, as graphite dust falls on the paper and causes smudgy marks. Sharpen your pencil frequently during use so that the line it produces is regular. Conserve your pencil by sharpening sparingly. Ordinary pencil sharpeners tend to be rather wasteful; a penknife is preferable (**1**), as it can cut a long even point that can then be repointed on a sanding block (**2**). Keep your sanding block in an old envelope to contain the graphite dust (**3**). Don't drop your pencils as this breaks the lead; store them point up in a tin or pot for protection.

Points
Hard pencils should be shaped to a long, sharp point of even or gently tapering thickness. The hard leads are strong enough to be shaped this way to produce the fine, even lines necessary for technical drawings (**A**). Soft leads are used for broader strokes and should be sharpened to a rounded tip; wider leads can also be bevelled into a chisel shape with a penknife (**B**).

A

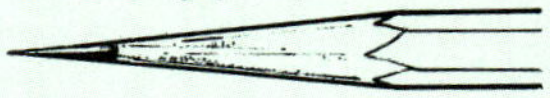

B

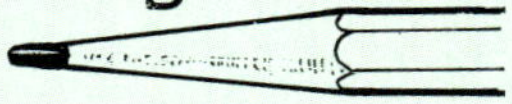

1

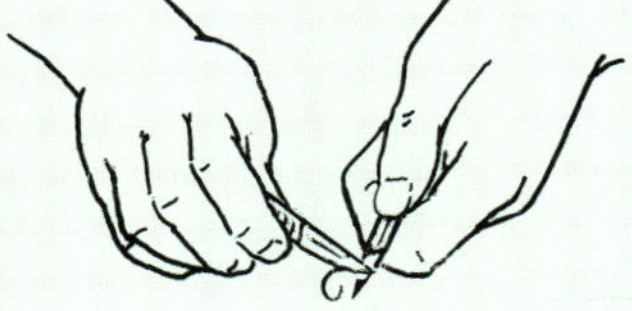

2

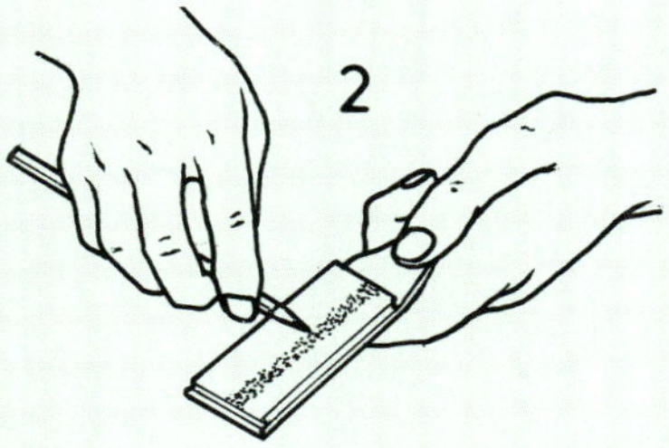

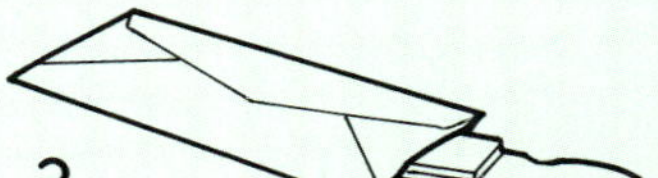

3

Working with pencils
When you are drawing, the pencil acts as an extension of your finger, your hand, or even your arm, following the movement made by your muscles. The way in which you hold the pencil will determine the kind of lines that you can produce.

1 In the writing position the pencil is held close to the tip, and the hand is rested on the paper. This gives maximum control over fine detail.
2 The sketching position gives more freedom; the pencil is held near the end, with the fingers curling toward the palm.
3 The pencil can be held near the end with the fingers pointing along the shaft; this position does not allow a great deal of control.
4 If the pencil is held with the first finger along the shaft, this gives good control for exerting gentle or firm pressure for different weights of line.

chalks

These drawing tools can be used to make a wide range of marks, and are especially useful for adding tone or when working on a dark-toned paper. Use a rough textured paper to capture all the particles of colour. Handle the surface carefully to prevent smudging, and protect the finished drawing with a fixative spray.

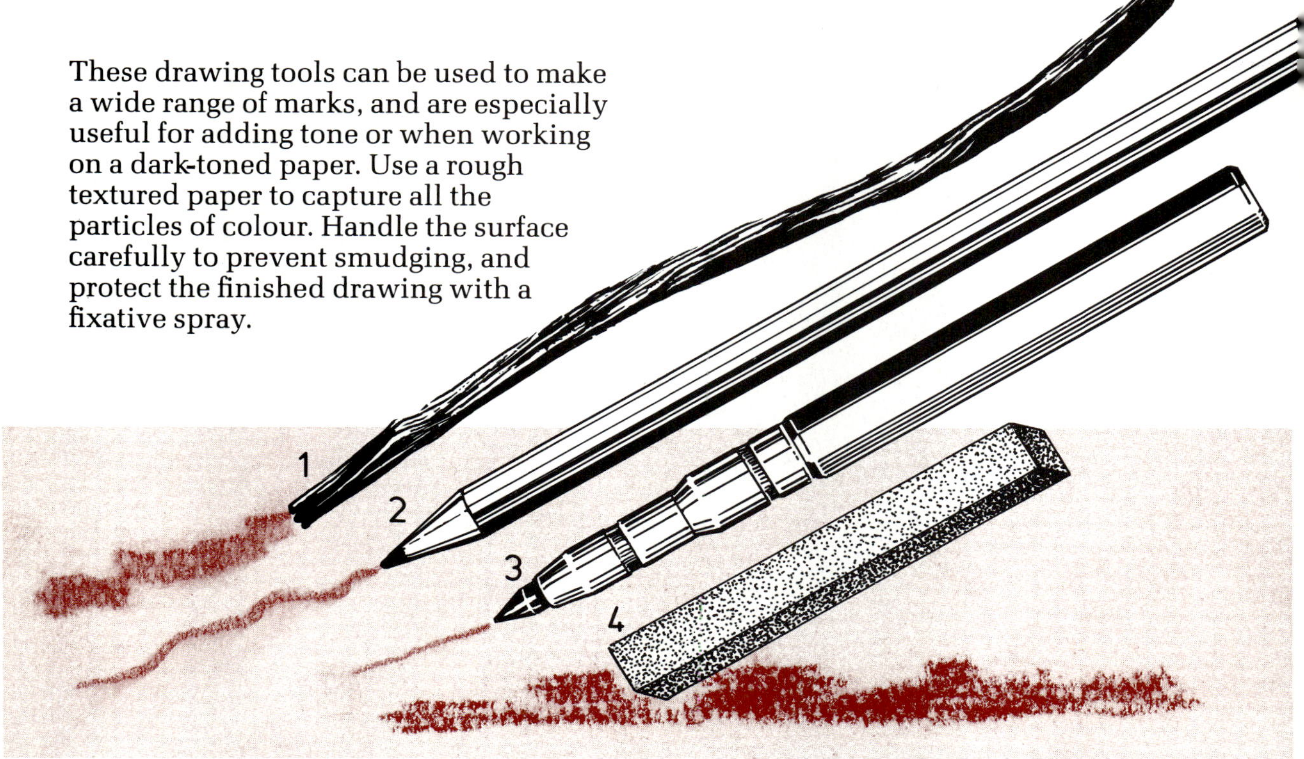

Charcoal and graphite (*above*)
1 Natural charcoal is made from charred willow, beech or vine. The sticks are brittle, difficult to handle, and unsuitable for detailed work.
2 A charcoal pencil is less messy but is also less versatile.
3 A graphite pencil is best suited to outdoor sketching.
4 A graphite stick is useful for working large areas of tone.

Working with charcoal, chalks, and pastels (*below*)
A Use the point to produce uneven fine lines. The point can be kept sharp on a piece of sandpaper.
B Use the side for large areas of tone, graded from dark (nearest to the main point of contact) to soft grey.
C Use a finger to soften lines into forms or shadows.
D Use a putty rubber to dab at the work to make corrections, pick out highlights, or soften lines. A ball of soft bread may be similarly used on charcoal.
E Highlights in dark areas may be added with white chalk or crayon.
F Highlights can also be produced by removing colour with skilful erasing.

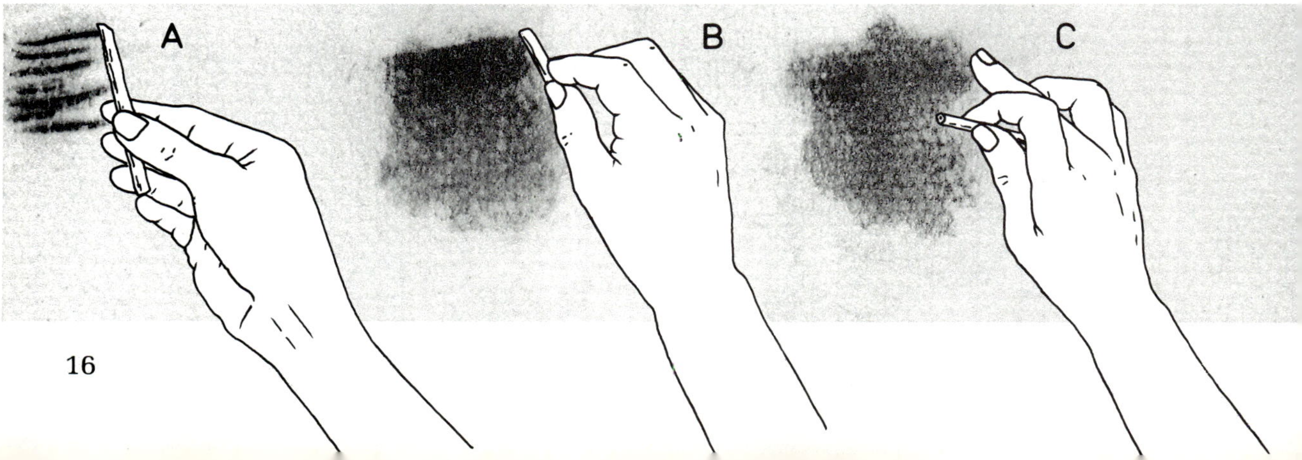

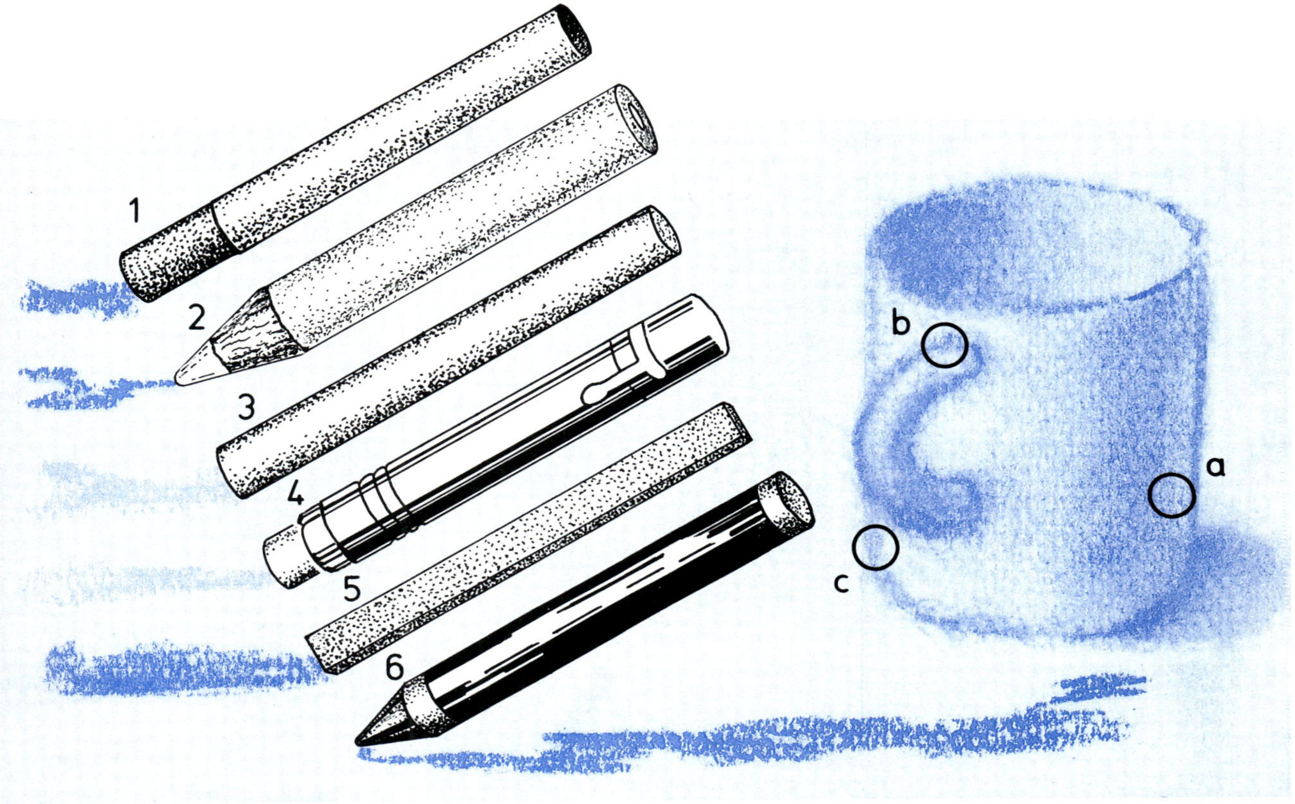

Pastels, chalks, crayons (*above*)
These are available with chalk, oil, or wax bases, in three grades (soft, medium and hard) and in over 600 shades. The paper covers protect your fingers.

1 Pastel stick
2 Pastel pencil
3 Chalk
4 Chalk holder
5 Conte crayon
6 Wax crayon

Fixing and storing
All pastel, charcoal and crayon drawings need to be sprayed with a fixative or they will smudge and eventually rub off. Use several light coats of fixative as a heavy coat will discolour the paper. The fixed drawings should then be stored between sheets of thin tissue paper.

Charcoal sketch
In the example of a charcoal drawing (*above*), notice the smudge areas (**a**), the highlights (**b**), and the softening edges (**c**).

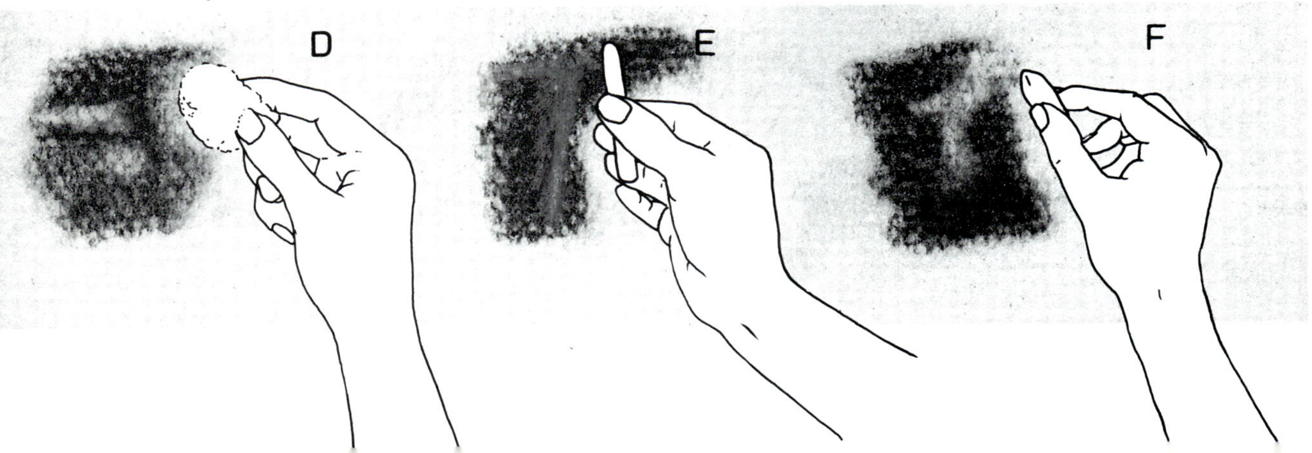

pens

Pens are very useful for preparing work which is to be printed or photographed. Ballpoints and felt tips are excellent for sketching because they give immediate and permanent results. The exact marks made by a pen depend on the nib, ink and paper chosen, and on the direction and pressure of the stroke used.

Pen and ink drawing
The drawing (*right*) shows how the flow of garments can easily be captured using a traditional pen. Downward strokes or strokes made with hard pressure produce thick lines; across strokes or strokes made with soft pressure produce thin lines.

Pens, ballpoints, felt tips
1 The traditional pen uses a wide selection of nibs to produce a rich variety of lines of differing thicknesses. The line qualities compensate for the need to carry ink. The nibs should be removed from the pen holder and stored in a box when not in use.
2 A mapping pen is a variation on the traditional steel-nibbed pen. The finer range of nibs make it useful for small detail work.
3 A fountain pen can be useful for sketching outdoors.
4 A ballpoint pen can be used for sketching, but is not really suitable for reproduction work, as it can produce blotchy and inconsistent lines.
5 Felt tip pens are available in a wide variety of thicknesses, colours and degrees of hardness. The top must be replaced or the pen will dry out.
6 Marker pens are useful for covering large areas rapidly as an alternative to water colour. The marks may spread or seep through the paper.

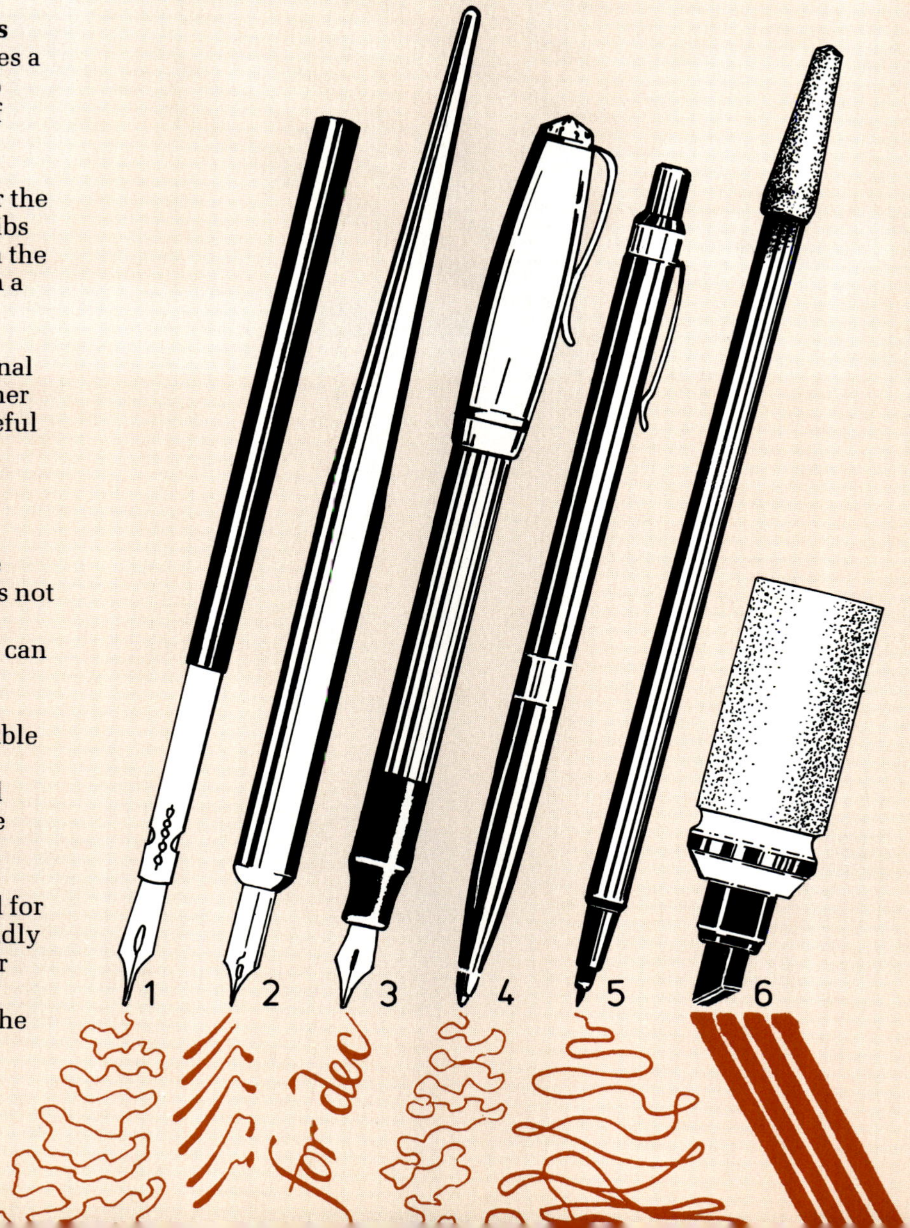

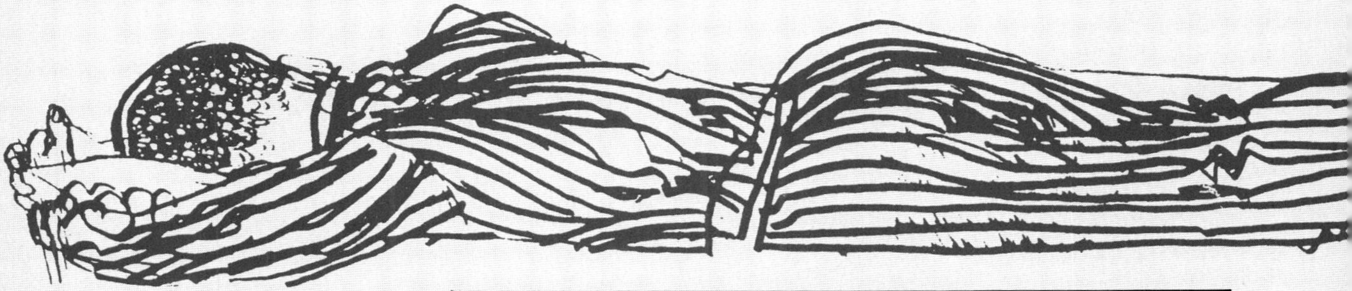

Ink
Good-quality inks produce clean, permanent lines of reproducible quality that do not soften or smudge. The inks can be diluted with water to produce a softer line. Poor-quality inks tend to flow unevenly and to dry too quickly. Always replace the cap on the bottle to keep your ink clean and prevent it drying out.

Paper
Pen marks are affected by the quality, thickness and texture of the paper used. Pen nibs can catch on rough paper, or tear through thin paper. Ink can soak through thin paper onto the next page. Get the best results by using a smooth, good-quality paper – you will then also be able to scrape off the ink if you make an error.

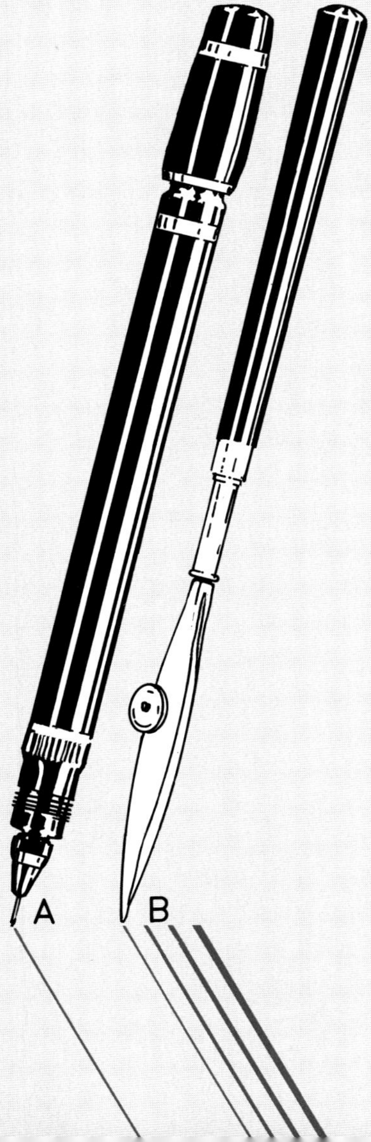

Technical pens (**A**)
For best results, these should only be used indoors on a smooth drawing surface, as the ink flow is affected by air pressure and temperature. The nibs wear down easily and can be damaged if heavy pressure is used. Each nib produces only one thickness of line: a variety of nibs is needed when lines of differing thicknesses are required.

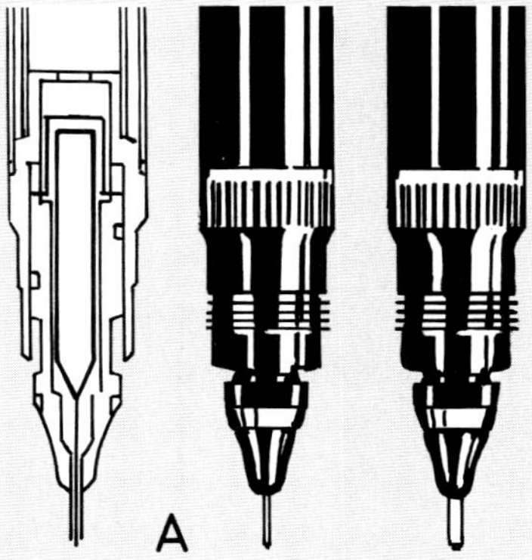

Ruling pens (**B**)
These are used with a rule to draw lines or may be fitted to a pair of compasses for drawing arcs and circles. They are filled using a pipette or small brush which releases the ink onto the insides of the pen blades. It is important that the ink does not get onto the outer edges of the blades or the line will smudge.

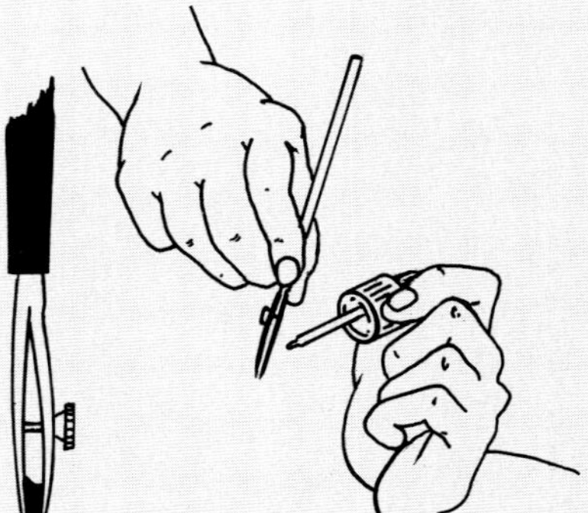

brushes

Brushes are not normally thought suitable for drawing; they are the instruments of a painter, whether used for watercolour or oils. But if you explore the energy in the line created by a brush you can produce startling results. Always keep water well away from your work, and when working out of doors be sure you have a good supply of clean water in which to wash your brushes after every use. Buy sable-haired brushes because they last longer and produce beautiful lines. Use a brush with *bounce*; dead ones produce poor lines. Experiment using an oriental brush which is shaped differently and is used in a different way from ours (see *opposite*). Through experience in linework you will gain a mastery that will bring you undiminished enjoyment.

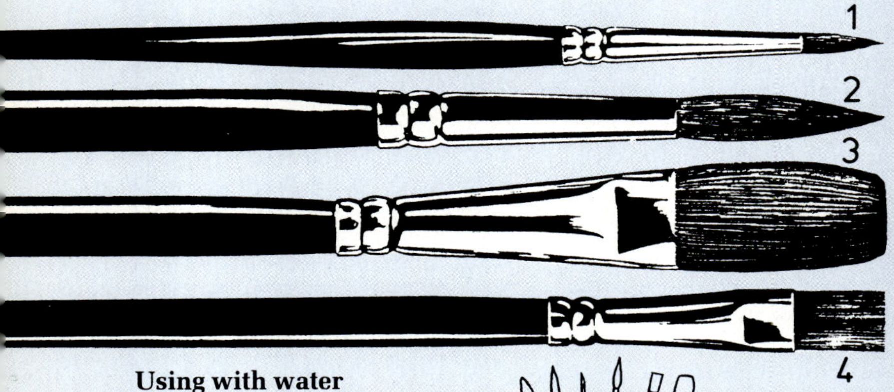

Selecting brushes
Brushes come in a variety of thickness, length and quality:
1 Short-headed, for detail; must be constantly refilled.
2 Long-headed, for expressing energy; produce both fine and very thick lines.
3 Flat-headed, for filling in tone.
4 Bristle, unsuitable for drawing; create broken lines.

Using with water
Store your brushes upright. Try to keep them free of thick inks or oily paints and always wash them out well. Discard old ones when they fail to make the marks you want. Keep water jars away from your work. Mix your inks on a china palette and clean it often. Screw on firmly the tops of commercial ink bottles.

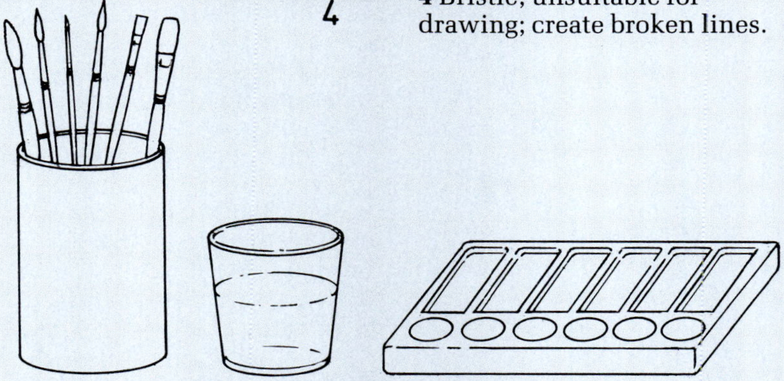

Brush marks
A brush is hard to control. If you need steady, straight lines rest your hand on a malling stick, or run it along a ruler. A brush responds to the least pressure so is best used for drawing quickly. Brush lines take longer to dry than pen and ink lines. Practise constantly to draw evenly. Brush lines, actual size (*right*).

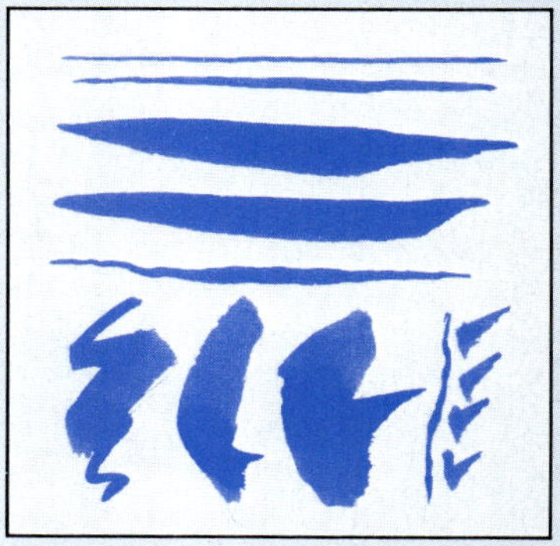

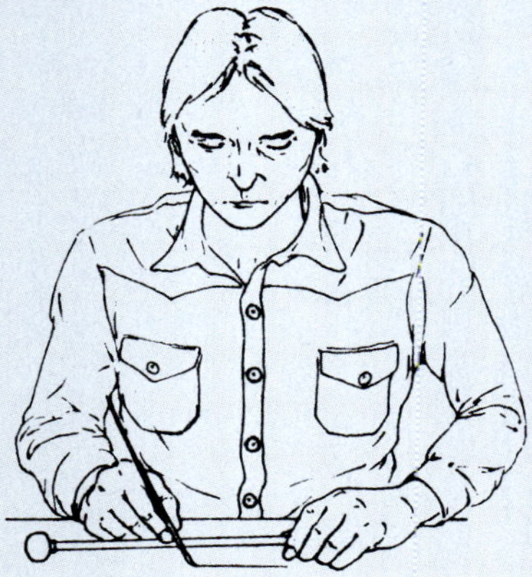

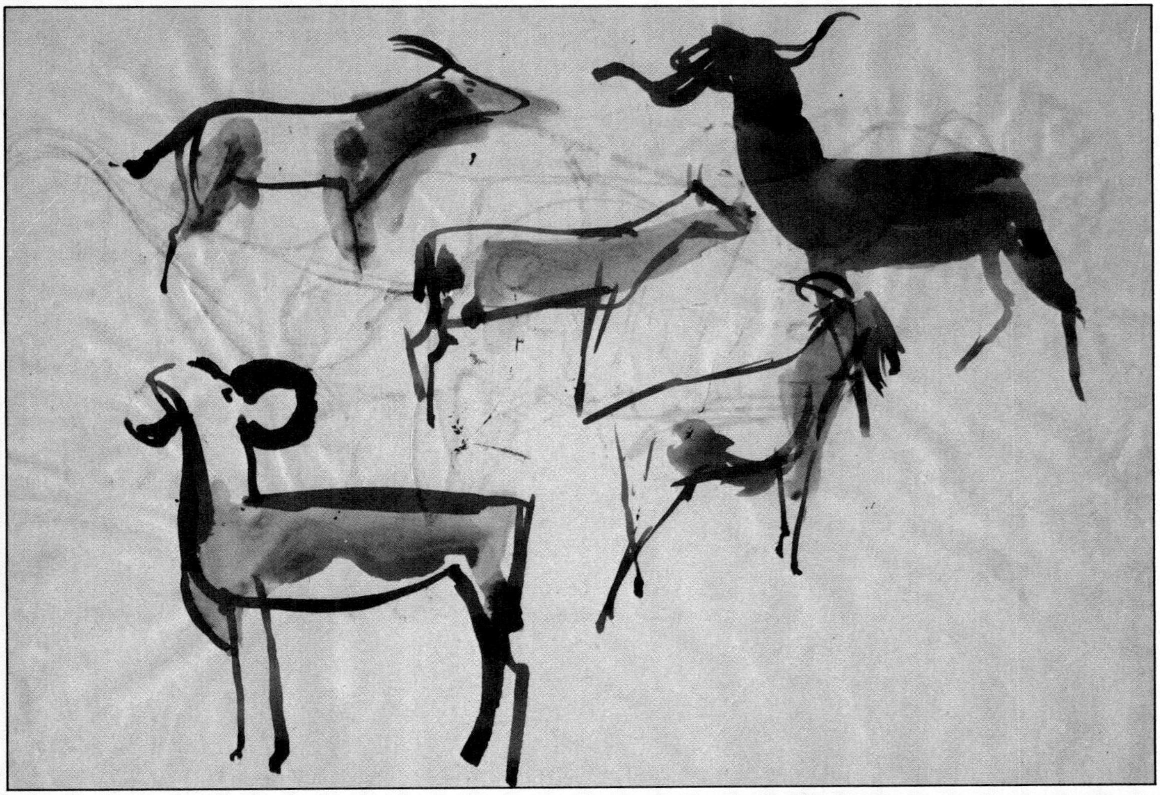

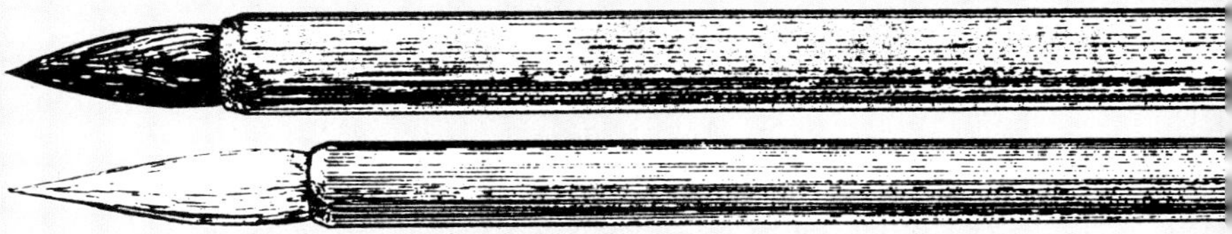

Deer and goats, London Zoo
(Brush and ink drawing)
For fast sketching, brushes can be handled quickly and their line width can be varied with minimum pressure. Once mastered, the brush breathes life, tension and atmosphere into sketches of plants and animals (*above*).

Oriental brushes
The fat-throated Chinese brush is most effective where fine lines must widen suddenly. The brush is held vertical (*right*), pressure being applied from the wrist. The Chinese use blocks of ink, ground up with water.

Bamboo leaves
(Brush and ink drawing)
Each leaf (*right*) was made with one brush stroke. Such work needs much practice.

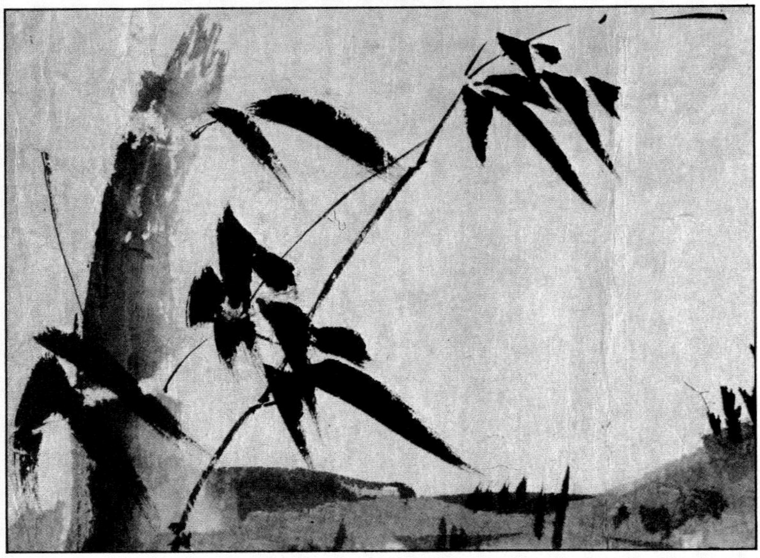

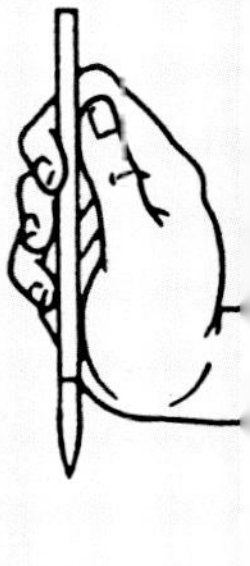

technical drawing instruments

Technical drawing instruments are precision-made professional tools and should be chosen and maintained with great care. They should be cleaned regularly and stored properly with the working edges well protected. Working edges should never be used as cutting edges. The work surface should be kept clear and clean, and covered with a piece of card or paper that is changed regularly. The work surface needs to be larger than the drawing surface, and should preferably be fitted with side benches or shelves where materials and spare equipment can be stored.

Drawing guides
1 Drawing board
2 T square, used for drawing horizontal lines
3 Set squares, used for drawing vertical lines or lines at regular angles. Available as 30/60/90° and 45/90° fixed triangles (**a**, **b**) or as adjustable triangles (**c**)
4 Rules, used for measuring in various units
5 Parallel rules, used for drawing parallel lines
6 Proportional dividers, used for making proportional increases or reductions in size
7 Protractor, used for measuring angles

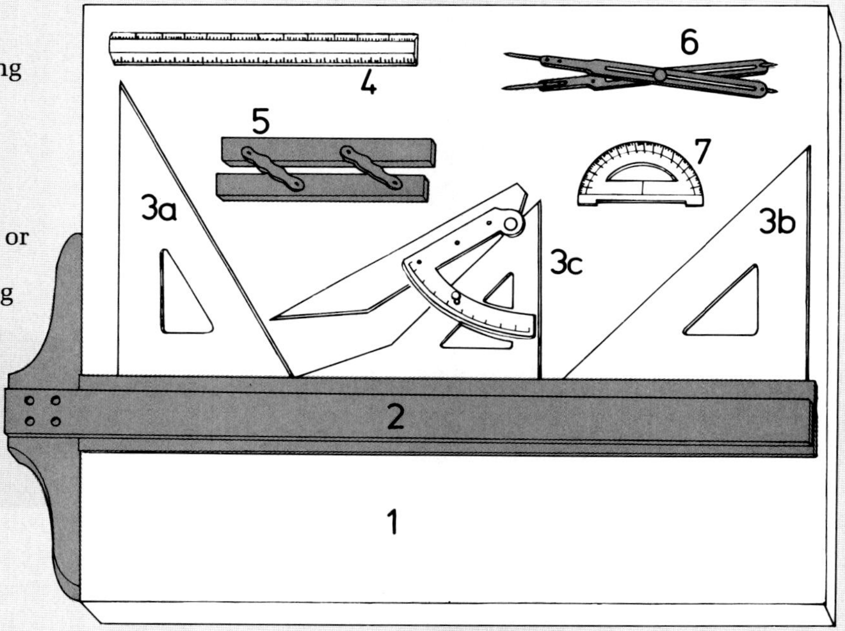

Drawing a straight line
It is important that the rule should be held firmly in place. For stability, rest some fingers on the rule and some on the paper itself (**1**). Keep your eyes on the line you are drawing.
If using a pencil, make sure that it is sharp, and rotate it slowly as you move it along the edge of the rule. The pencil point must be kept very close to the rule. If the pencil is angled outwards from the ruler (**2**), the drawn line will be separated from the intended line. If the pencil point is angled into the corner between the rule and the paper (**3**), the drawn line will be where it was intended to be. If using pen and ink, use a rule with a raised bevelled edge (**4**), or the ink will flood under the rule and ruin the line.

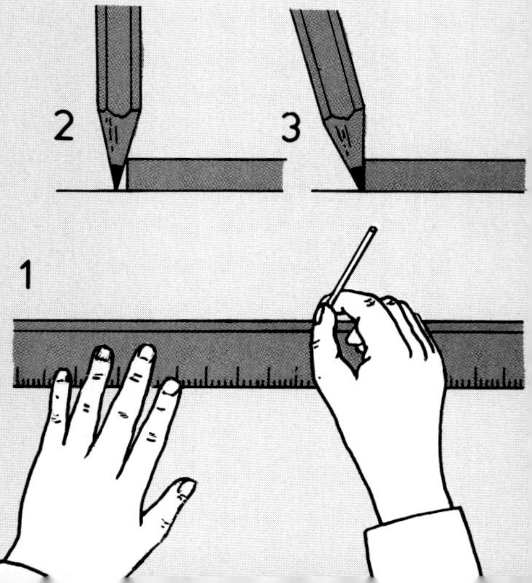

Circles

For a cleanly drawn circle, hold the compasses from the top and keep your wrist loose. Avoid making a large hole in your work by sticking a small square of low tack adhesive tape over the centre of the circle before inserting the compass point. A springbow compass (**1**) is useful for drawing small, precise circles, as the adjustable screw fixes the circumference size. Drawing compasses (**2**) have extension arms for drawing very large circles. Both compasses are available with a choice of writing attachments and accessories.

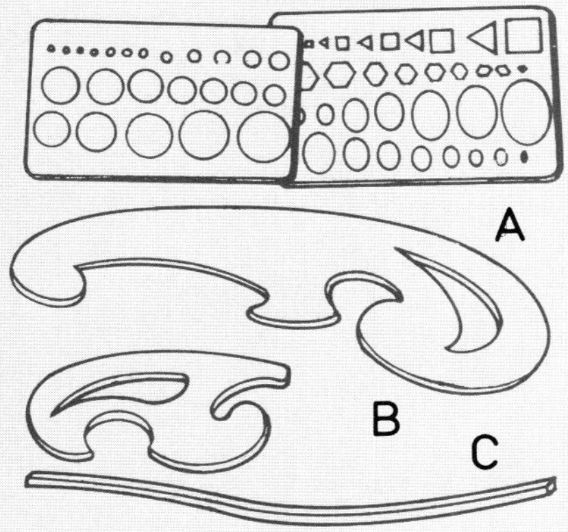

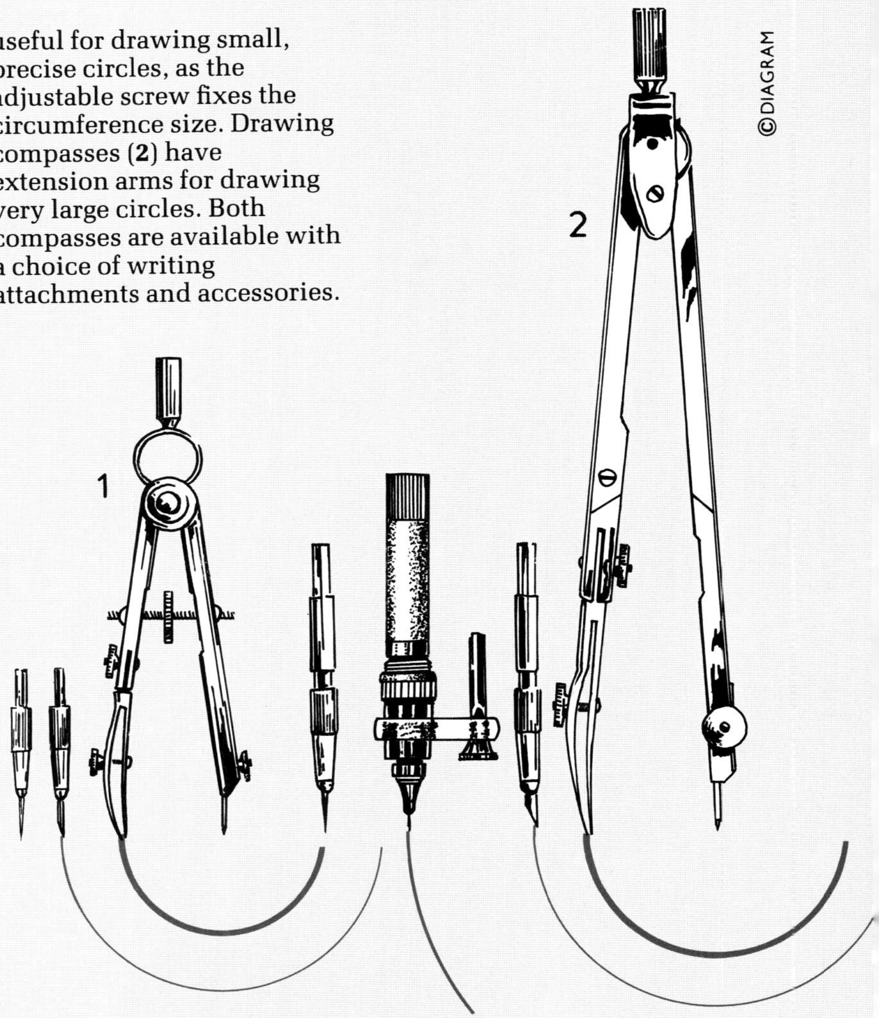

Curves (*above*)
A Templates can be used to draw circles, curves and ovals quickly and accurately.
B French curves are templates for drawing selected irregular curved lines.
C A snake curve is made of plastic covered wire and can be bent to form any curve required.

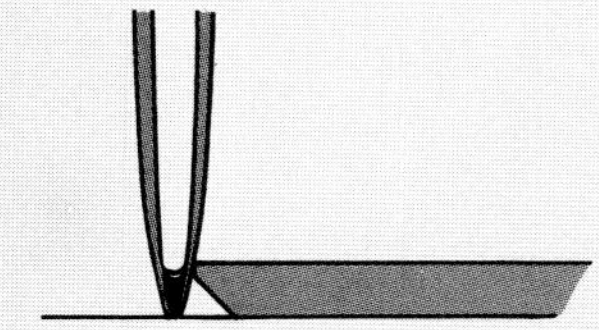

4

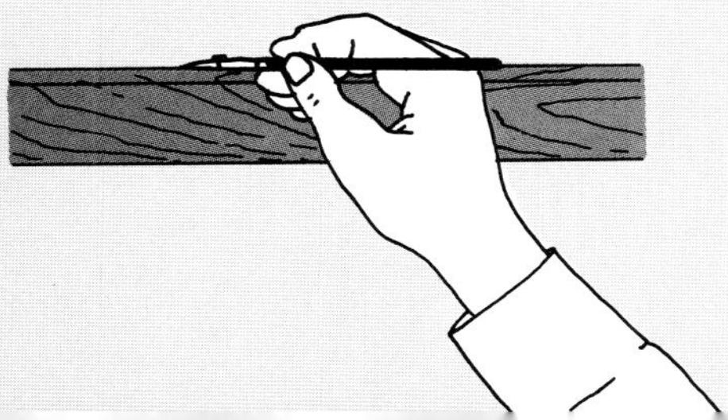

Painting up to an edge

When filling in a shape or painting up to an outline, the brush or pen should always be inside the boundary line (**a**), i.e. the point of the brush or pen should always point towards the line from inside the shape. Make sure that the brush is never on the outside by turning the paper around as you work (**b**).

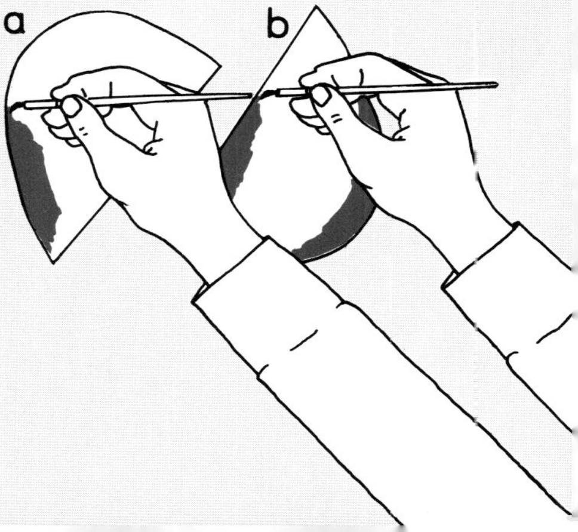

textures and tones

If a drawing is to be reproduced, you can add mechanically applied textures put on reprographically, but if you apply tone yourself you can control the tonal values. Textures come in sheets: one is self-adhesive and, after cutting to roughly the right shape, it is stuck down; the other is rubbed onto the drawing. Store sheets in closed, horizontal drawers; they spoil quickly and gather dust which makes them unusable.

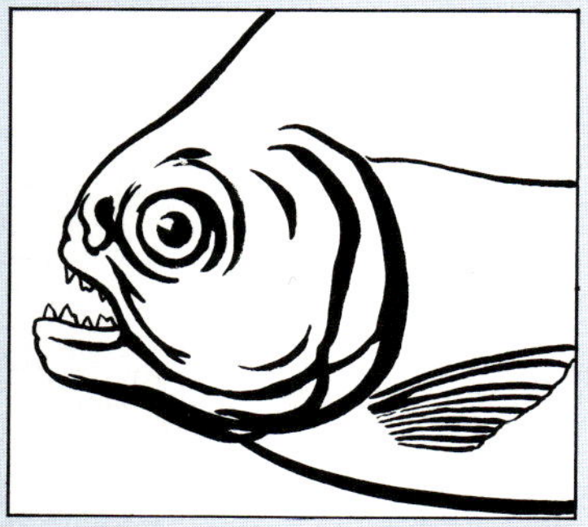

1

Selecting a texture
You can buy a large range of textures, both regular and irregular, but they are costly. Store unused parts carefully. Unless you know you will need particular designs, it is expensive to collect tones just because of their interesting appearance. A few of the available range are shown (*below*): **A** rub on **B** mechanical overlay.

Applying the overlay film (*below*)
1 First complete your drawing.
2 Lay over it part of the texture sheet with its backing between your work and the film tone. With a scalpel cut out roughly but not wastefully the area required.
Remove the backing sheet and the unused parts of the tone with care. Put the shaped area of tone over your work and gently rub down in the centre only. Do not get dirt on the film.
3 Carefully cut around the area of tone you want.
4 Burnish all over, using a strong, clean, smooth tool such as the edge of a plastic rule, rubbing down on spare paper between the film and the rule.
5 Establish the absence of dirt, and begin to overlay a second, different film texture. The final result (*far right*) will have strong black containing lines and a variety of tones in positions you want.
Avoid laying down over large areas.

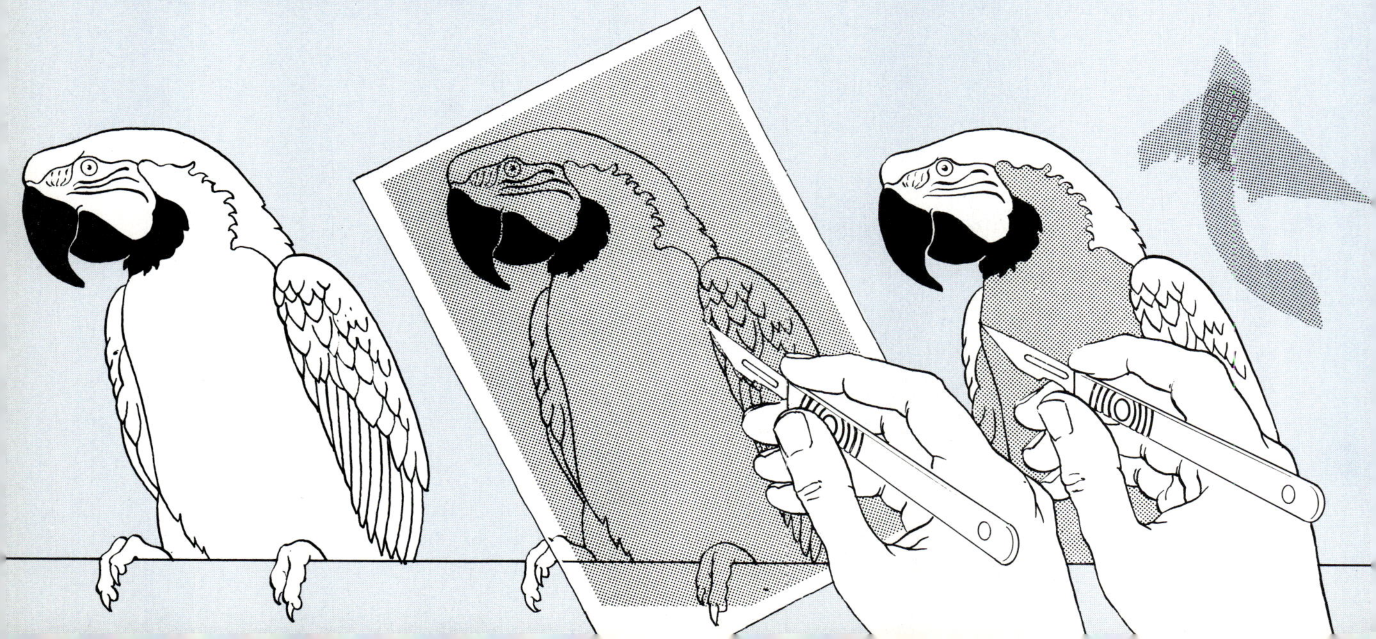

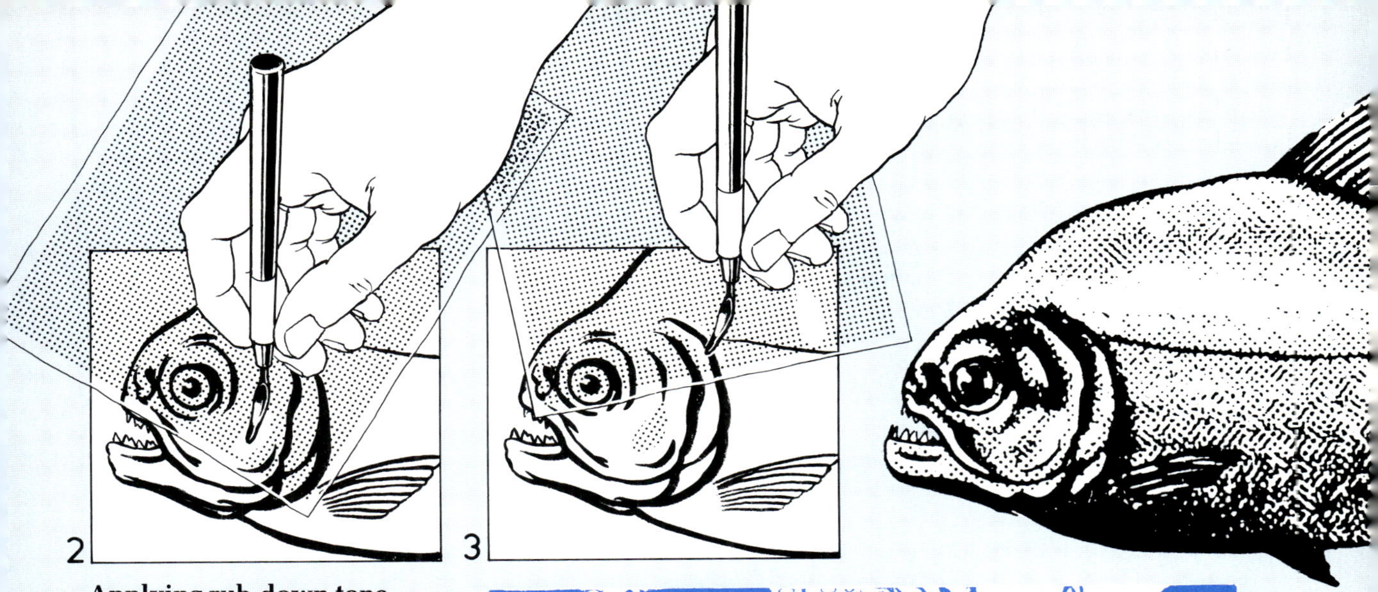

Applying rub-down tone
(*above*)
1 Complete a line drawing.
2 Lay the film tone over your drawing and rub using a blunt tool. Lift the overlay often to examine your work because you cannot judge its effects through the film.
3 Move the unused tone to another area and apply again. If you use an irregular tone you can lay one over another.

Chinese game players
(Pen and ink drawing and mechanical tone)
The Chinese players (*right*) show the result of sticking a mechanical tone over a drawing and then working with a scalpel to remove the tone and to expose the highlights.

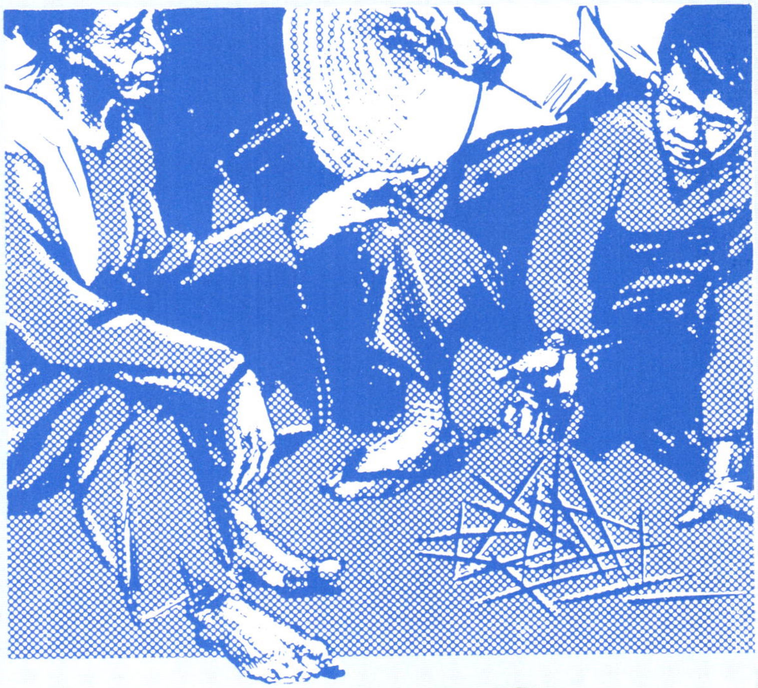

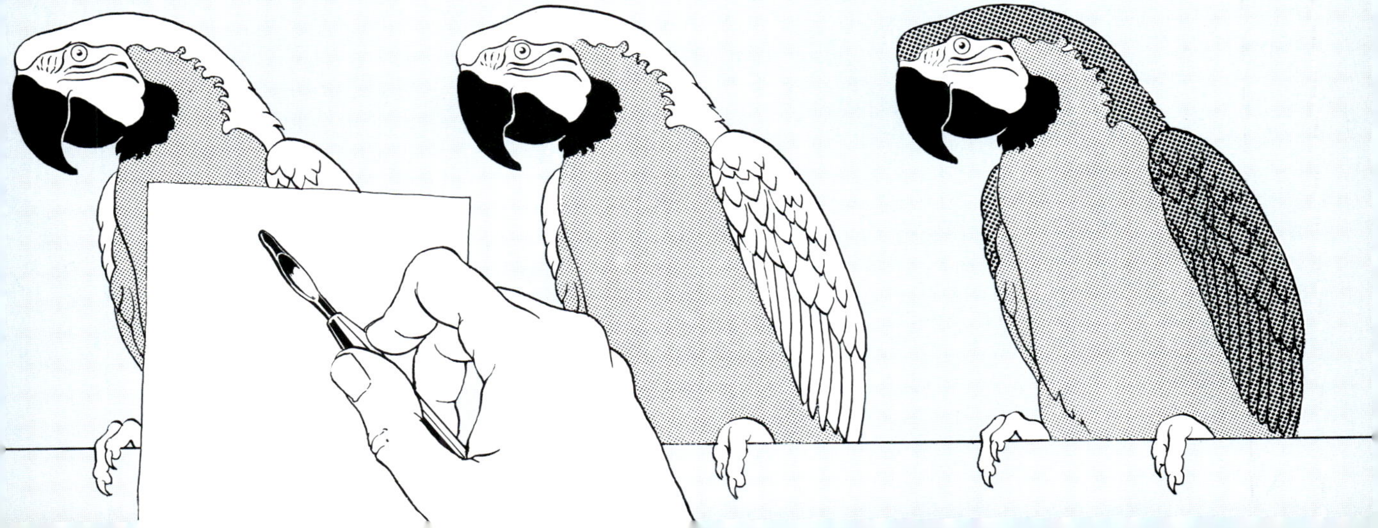

textures and tones

Drawings can accommodate a wide variety of unusual textures. Explore the possibilities. Often the use of several techniques leads to exciting discoveries which become valuable in later drawings. Textures should not be employed for their own sake; they should be an integral part of the drawing and blend with the line work. Do not use any textures which might damage the drawing surface. Control the areas of application within the space of the drawing. All the examples on these pages are of primitive, coarse textures which, if correctly applied, can give your drawings life and vitality.

Stipple
Regular textures can be obtained by using a large blunt-ended brush and stippling in the tones (as *below*). Protect the other areas with a mask, and do not use thin ink or paint, as this causes blotches. Always test the effect of a freshly loaded stencil brush on scrap paper before applying.

Frottage
'Frottage' is used to obtain a pattern by rubbing your outline sketch over a coarse-grained surface (see *below*). Be sure to keep your work still. Either tape it onto the rough surface, or hold firmly. Use only pastel, crayon, or pencil and the side of the drawing lead.

Smudging
A very common technique, but take care to avoid a messy result. The end of your finger (see *below*), a putty rubber or soft material can be used to spread the tone. Afterwards fix or otherwise protect the surface to stop the smudge from spreading.

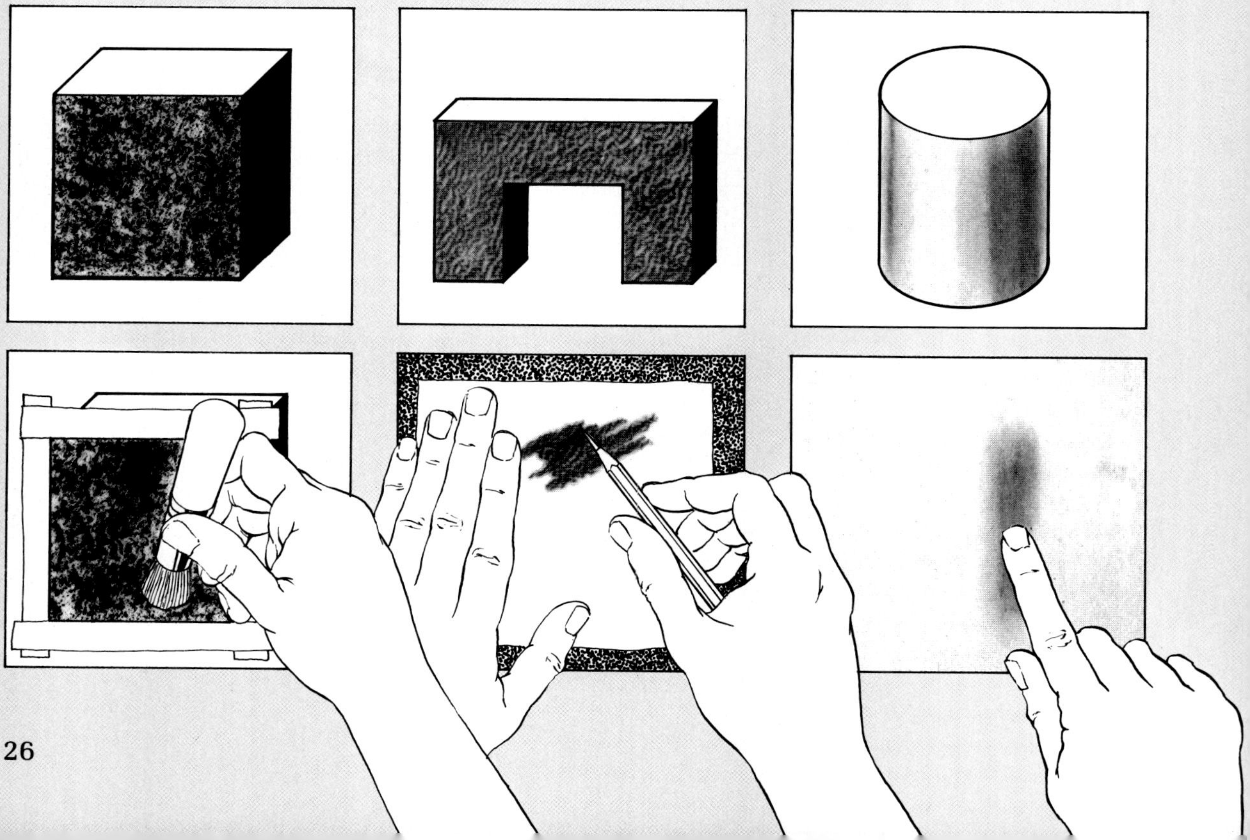

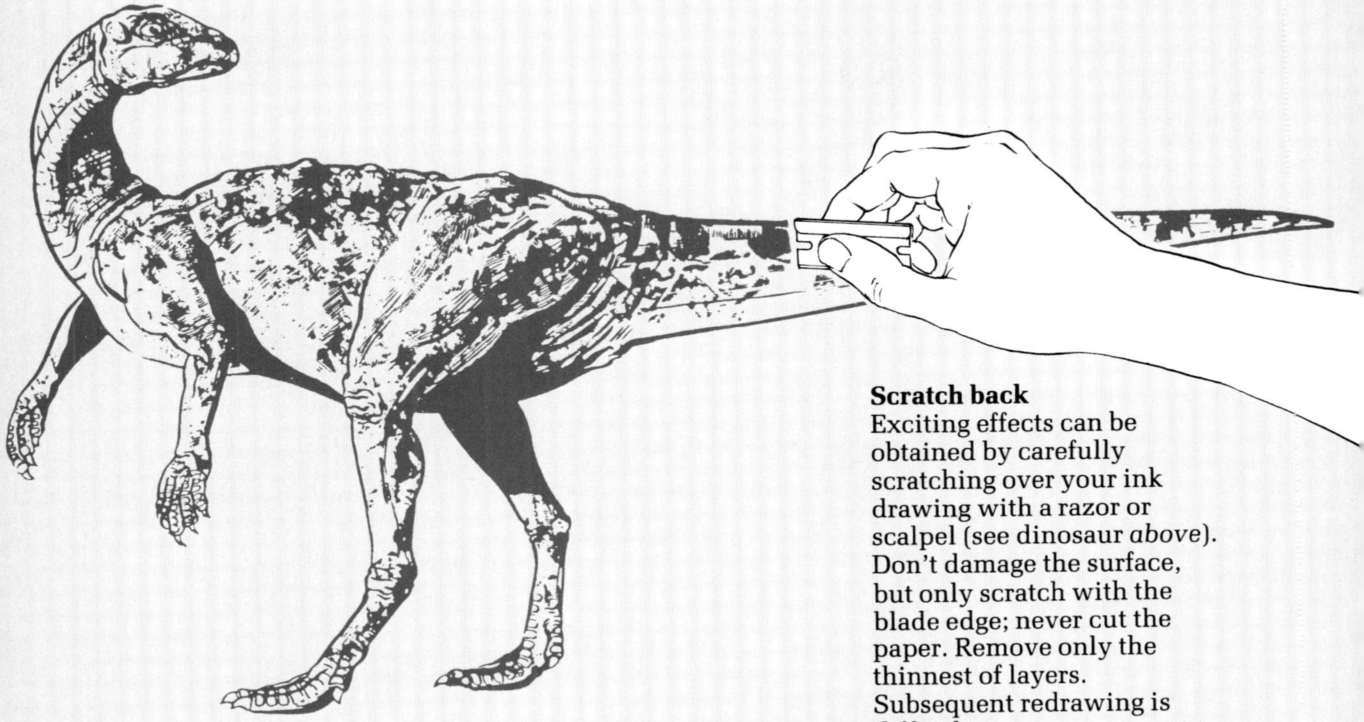

Scratch back
Exciting effects can be obtained by carefully scratching over your ink drawing with a razor or scalpel (see dinosaur *above*). Don't damage the surface, but only scratch with the blade edge; never cut the paper. Remove only the thinnest of layers. Subsequent redrawing is difficult.

Resistant materials
Wax and water do not mix. You can investigate the effects of drawing part of your illustration with wax crayons (**a**) (*below*), candle or liquid wax applied with a brush. Subsequently add a wash of tone (**b**) which will not adhere to the wax surface and will thus expose your earlier drawing (**c**).

Indentations
Using strong paper, draw outlines, for example of fruit (*right*) with a hard pencil which leaves only faint marks. Rubbing over tones later reveals the pencil marks as fine white lines.

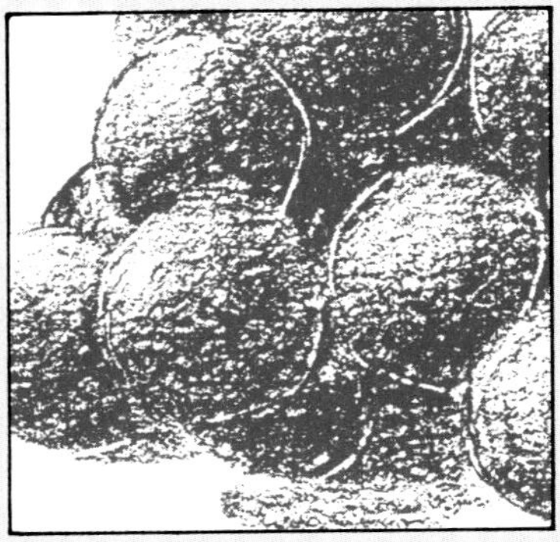

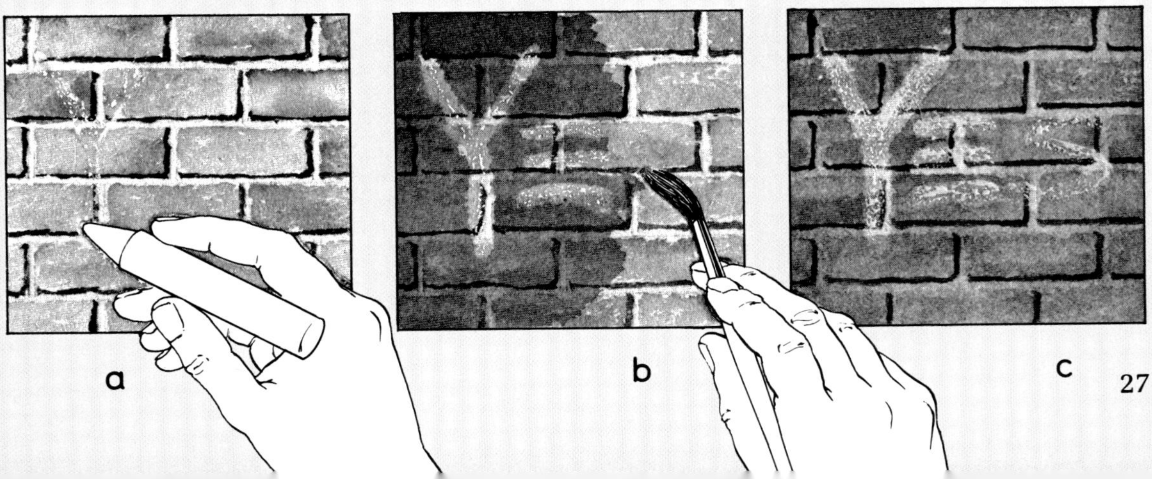

a b c

textures and tones

Expert use of an airbrush produces a professional appearance but it is a skill which cannot be mastered quickly. The brush is easily damaged and judging the tonal values against the masked areas requires experience. Airbrushing is often done on work that is to be reproduced; ink is not always absorbed by the paper so drawings for display are easily spoiled. It is wise to plan all airbrush drawings before beginning to spray. With practice, even, flat tones, graduated tones and soft-edge borders can be achieved. Always test on scrap paper before spraying your work as the brush may splutter. The liquid in the brush must be free of hardener, oil or dirt – all cause spitting and bad results. Try building up tone by overspraying frequently to get the right strength. Always spray-fix drawings after completion and protect with overlays.

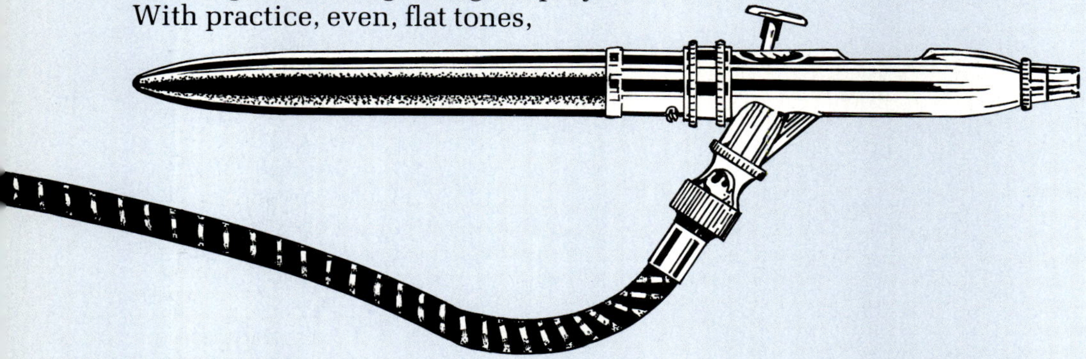

Applying spray tone (*below*)
First prepare your drawing so that the edges of the areas to be sprayed are clearly defined. If you wish to have gradually fading margins, where the tone disappears into other backgrounds, you will have to protect all those parts on which the spray should not appear.
1 Cover the drawing completely with masking material – usually transparent film or tracing paper – stuck down with low-tack sellotape.
2 Carefully cut out from the mask the area to be sprayed. This is an exacting task, but inaccurate edges will mean incorrect margins on your work.
3 Remove the cut – out area, and spray the tone slowly. Practice on spare paper, building up gently to the density you want, spraying lightly all over at first. You can gingerly lift up the edge of the mask to check your tone. Never spray thickly; the paint dries slowly and can congeal into unpleasant blotches.
4 Build up forms by increased spraying on darker areas.
5 Repeat procedures for subsequent areas.

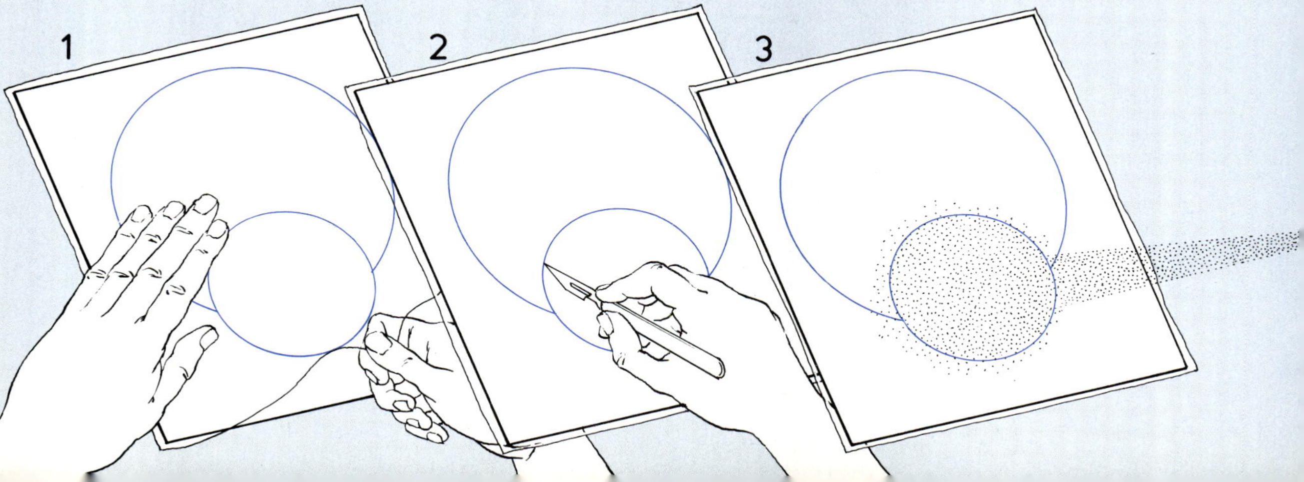

Tooth brush spray
The variety of textures on the tree (*right*) was achieved by running a match across the top of an ink-filled tooth brush. Practice first.

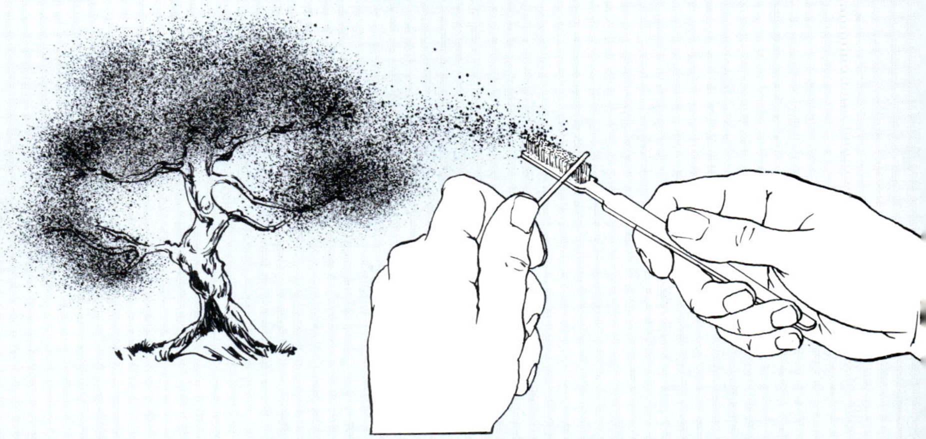

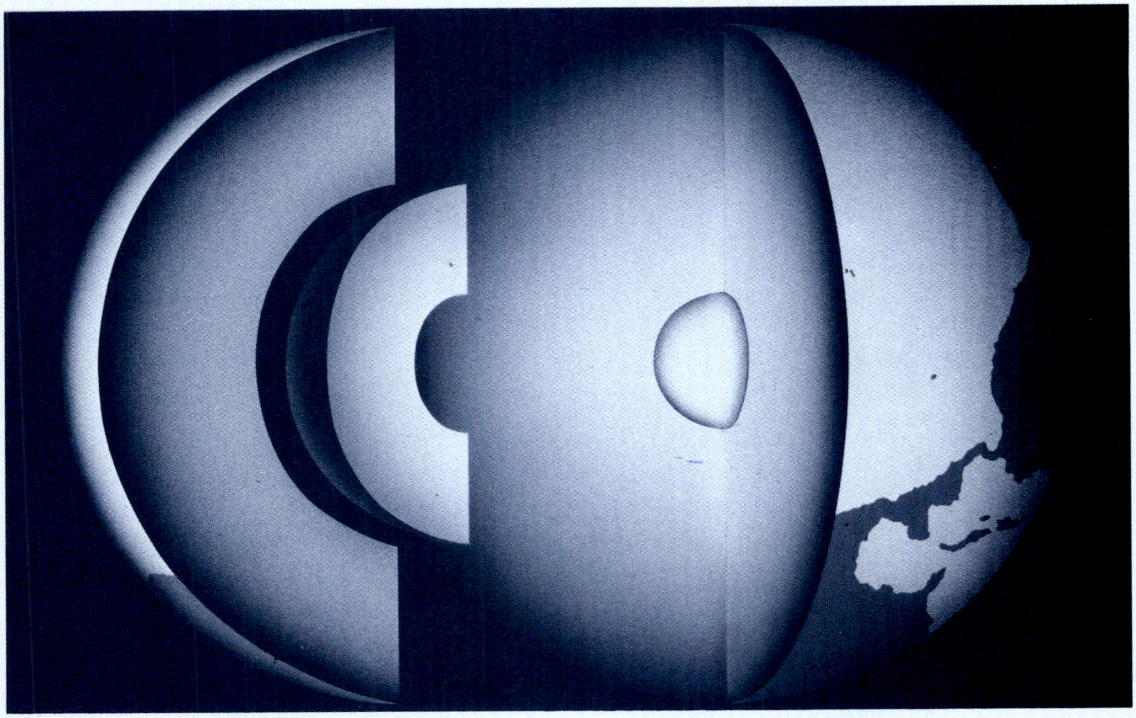

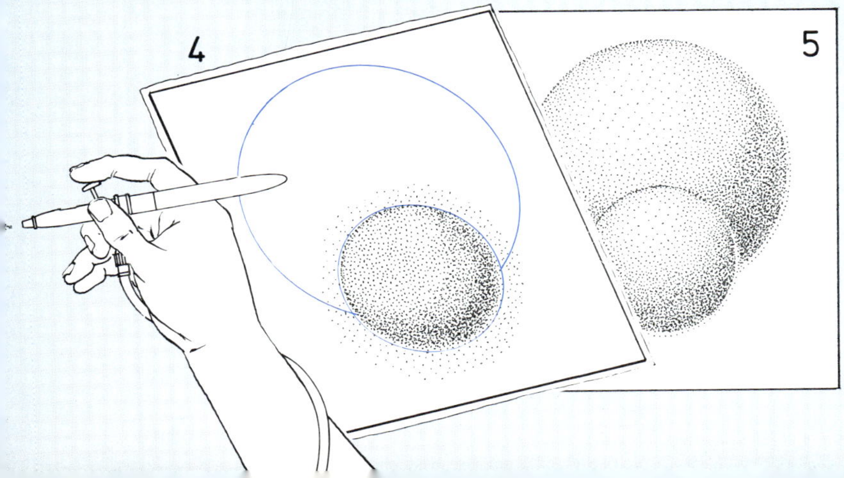

Earth's interior
(Airbrush drawing by professional artist)
Subtle tonal changes, like those (*above*), require long experience. Experiment first with flat, hard-edge tones.

the drawing surface

The choice of correct working surfaces is as vital as the range of your implements. An inappropriate paper can cause bad results. Your options will be influenced by the texture you need for the tools you pick; the strength or durability necessary to achieve the aim of your work; expense (costly papers inhibit use); translucency (if you want to rework); colour, if you like background tone; and finally the paper with which you feel comfortable.

Selecting your surface
(Six examples reproduced actual size, *below*)
The quality of a surface, and its texture or smoothness, cannot be illustrated in a reproduction. But qualities of linework on different surfaces can. Always try to work on the paper which is most suitable for your intentions.

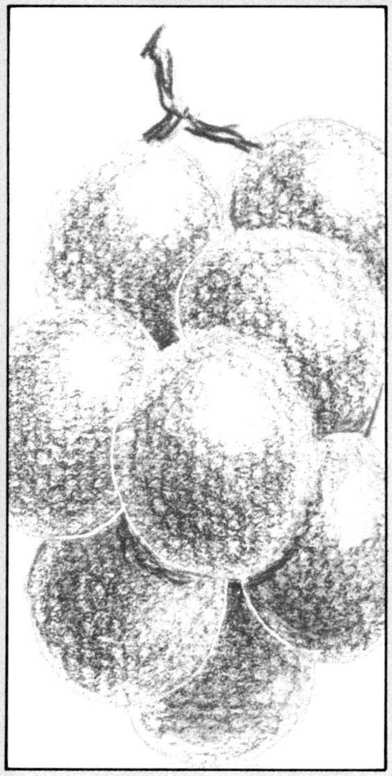

Coarse-grained paper
(Grapes: coloured pencil drawing)
Usually thick; regular surface texture; best for chalk, crayon, pastel, not for pen; strong so good for overworking; often in colour. Mottling (*above*) is due to clumps of colour on the raised surfaces. The white line was made by a hard pencil (see p. 27).

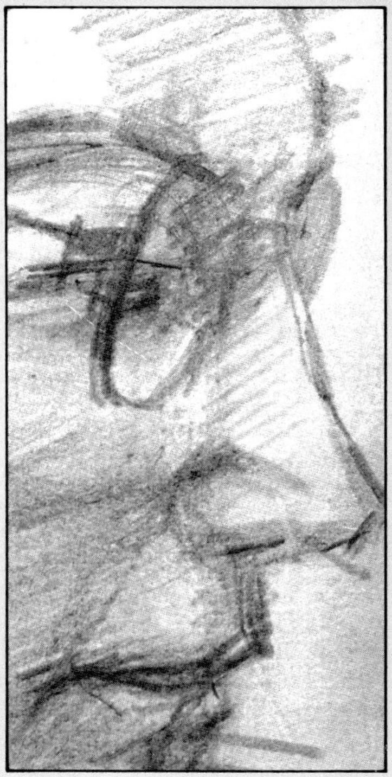

Normal cartridge paper
(Detail of head: pencil drawing)
Available as sheets and in sketchbooks; most common and versatile surface for drawing; strong, so takes erasing well; good for brushes, ink, water colour; holds pencil lines and takes smudging for tone, see face (*above*); paper ages well but pencil and chalk need fixing.

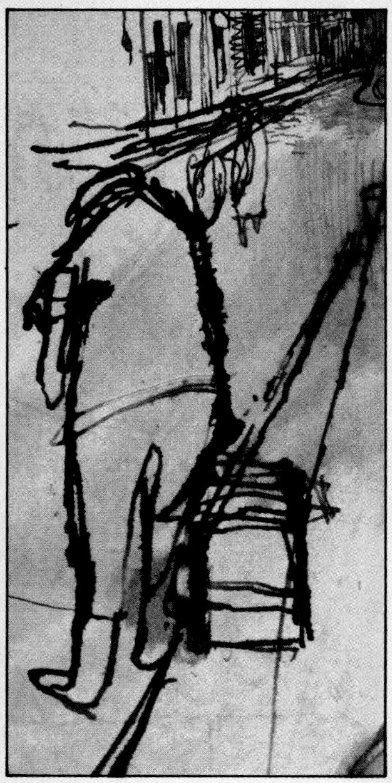

Fine detail paper
(Street scene: pen and brush drawing)
Best for pens but unsuitable for adding watercolour; buckles, tears easily, becomes worked out quickly and allows ink through to the next sheet; but coated, smooth surfaces are ideal for outdoor sketching (*above*).

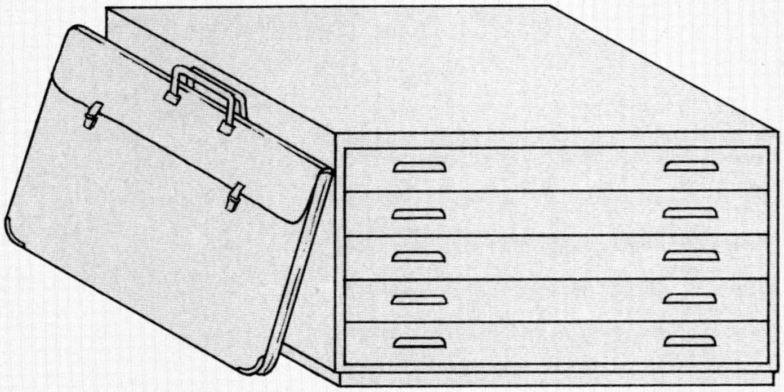

Storing
Store drawings horizontally in a plan chest or in a portfolio, perhaps kept under the bed. Avoid storing chalk and crayon drawings facing each other. Protect with interleaves of tissue paper or by putting each drawing against the back of the next.

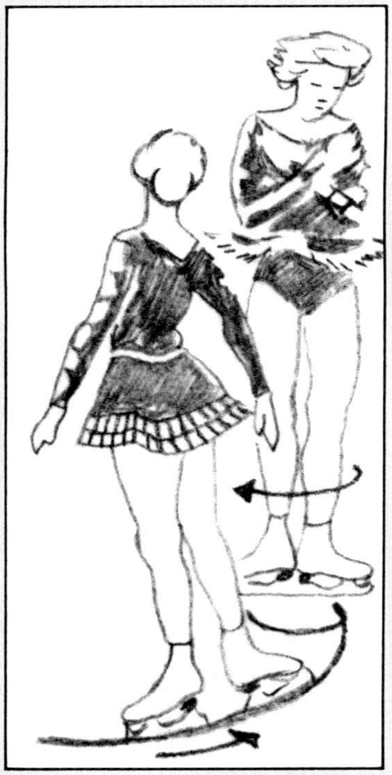

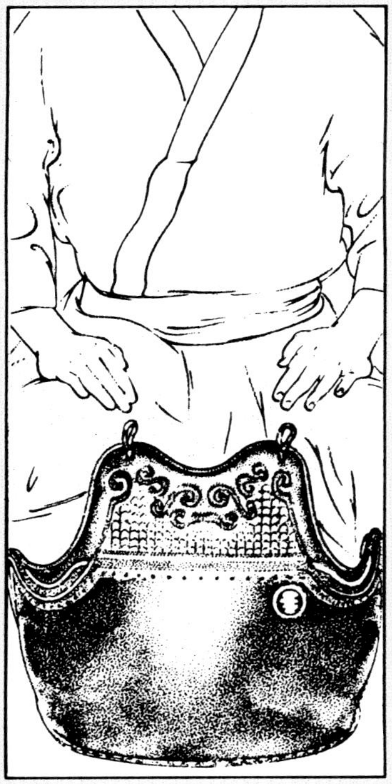

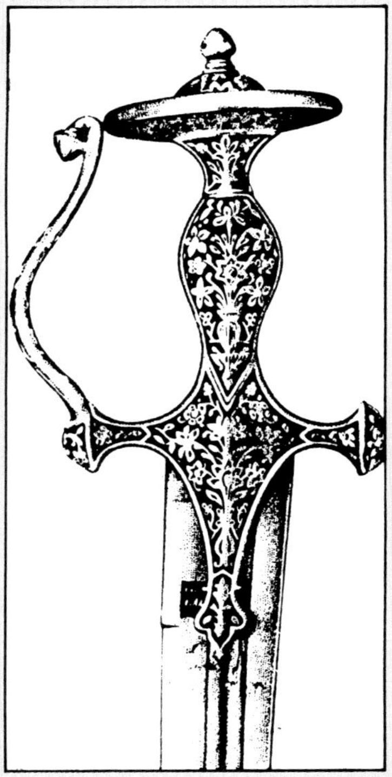

Tracing paper
(Skaters: pencil drawing)
Rolls or pads essential for studio work; transparency permits working over previous drawings; takes hard pencils well; one rough side for pencil, one smooth surface for pen; cannot take water; best used for preparing drawings; unsuitable for finished work because of grey effect (*above*).

Smooth art card or board
(Japanese Kendo fighter: detail of pen technical drawing)
Necessary to construct your drawing (perhaps on tracing paper) before starting; can cope with very fine rules and lines of varying thickness (as *above*); corrections possible by scraping back or overpainting and reworking; ideal for reproduction.

Plastic surface
(Persian sword: detail, pen drawing)
Very glossy back, very fine grained working face; takes reworking over earlier lines and correcting by scraping; permits close detail in ink; easily reproduced; affected by changes in temperature and humidity; cannot take water; for technical work and line (*above*).

the drawing surface

The surface on which you work is the most permanent element in your drawing. Near invisible corrections and stabilizing your marks are vital in preparing clean, finished work. Try to make few mistakes as corrections are never entirely satisfactory. The method you choose for making alterations depends upon the surfaces and tools you employ. Lines can be erased, tone seldom can. Always alter cautiously since speedy revision can destroy a drawing. The surface of sketches done in granular tools (pencil, chalk, crayon) needs to be fixed to avoid losing particles. Unfortunately all preservative methods have drawbacks: they may discolour the paper, be difficult to use and perhaps cause damage if applied badly.

Always store your drawings away carefully.

Methods of correcting (*right*)
Take great care when drawing. Poor surfaces hinder revision, so try out different papers.

1 Rubbing: pencil, crayon and charcoal lines can be erased carefully and then redrawn but damage may occur. Test rubbers and remove dirt. Use india or putty rubbers and try soft bread. *Shake* off all bits.

2 Scratching back: scratch back the incorrect lines with the side of a sharp razor or scalpel. Scrape, do not cut. Redrawing is difficult.

3 Painting out: remove lines with white watercolour. Overdrawing is impossible.

4 Patching: if your linework is to be reproduced photographically, patch big areas with paper stuck down. Shadows on the film negative can be adjusted.

Working on surfaces
To produce careful studies and finished drawings before reproduction, work with a piece of paper beneath your hand for protection (*right*). Skin secretes oils which affect the paper surface. Odd scraps of paper should be used to try out marks made by pens or brushes.

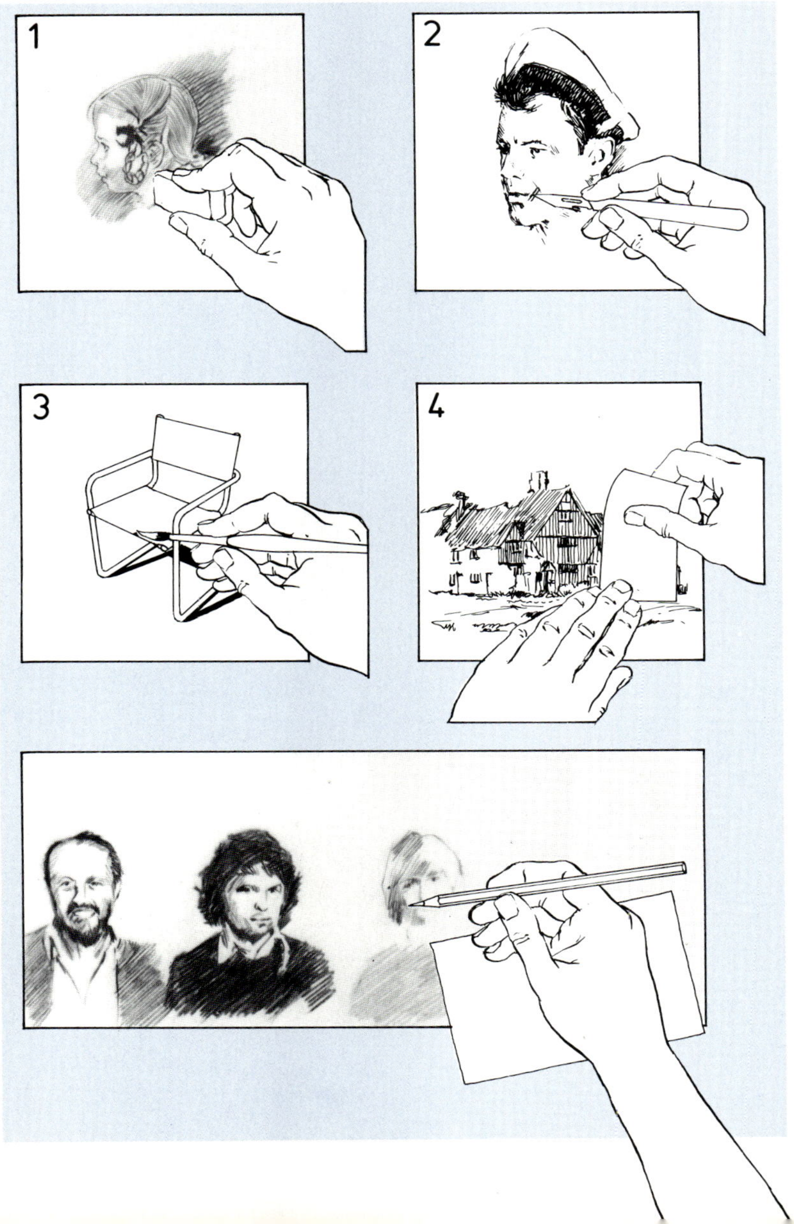

Protecting the surface
Finished charcoal, pencil and crayon drawings should first be fixed and then stored interleaved with layers of tissue paper. When displaying these drawings you can protect their surfaces with a covering of clear plastic film (see *right*).

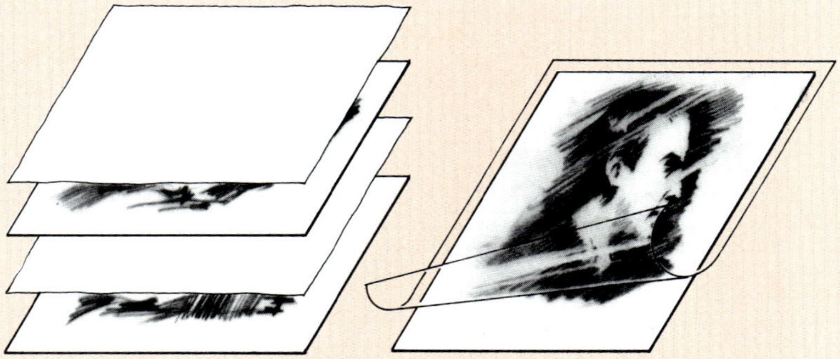

Stick-on film
For permanent protection (*right*), cover your drawing with clear self-adhesive film laid on the paper and cut to size. Application is not easy: it can crease, cause your paper to buckle, enclose air bubbles, become marked with dirt or fingers, or, if put down wrong, it can spoil your work. Removal without damage is impossible.

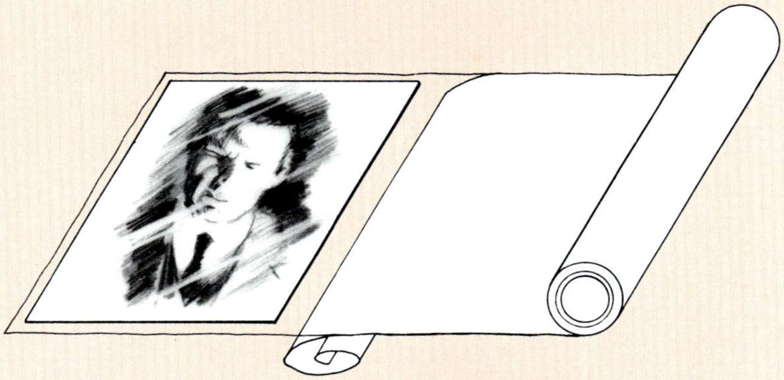

Spray fixing
Drawings can be protected with spray-on fixative. Inhalation of the spray is dangerous so use sparingly and in an open space. Hold your drawing upright and direct the spray onto it from about 40 cm away (*right*). Always spray lightly, allow to dry and spray again. Discoloration of the paper will take place in time.

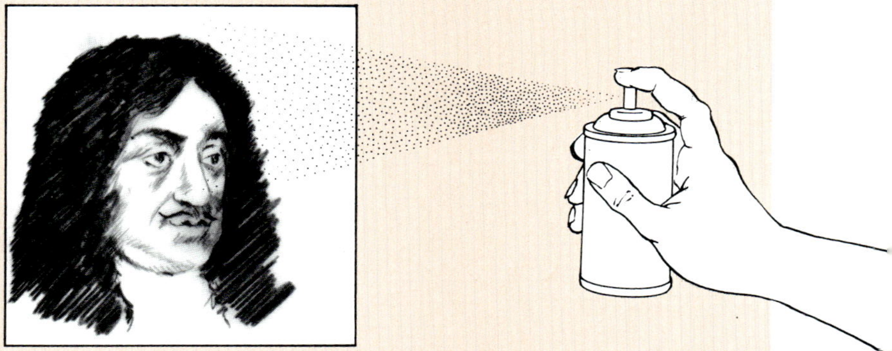

Blow fixing
Bought as a solution, this fixative is applied from a small mouth-held spray (*right*). Control of the dispenser is not easy as breathing can affect the amount of fixative ejected. Hold the paper 40 cm from your mouth. Overspraying by both methods (see *above*) can lead to coagulation with ugly, opaque results.

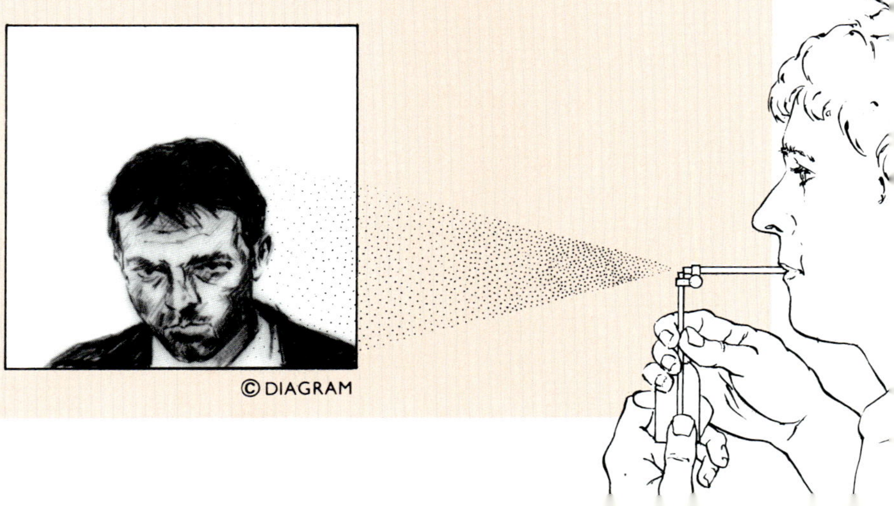

Part Two

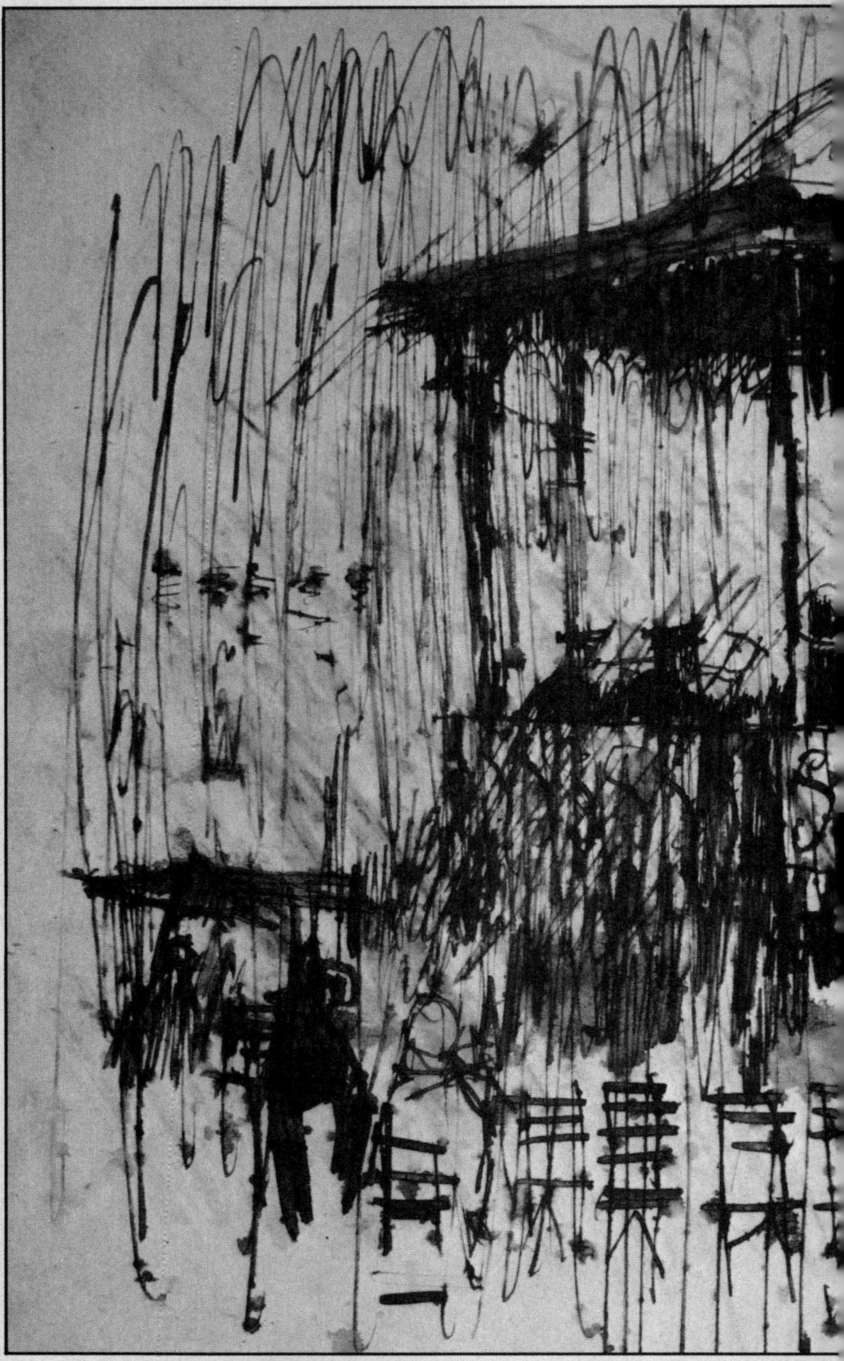

THE TREATMENT

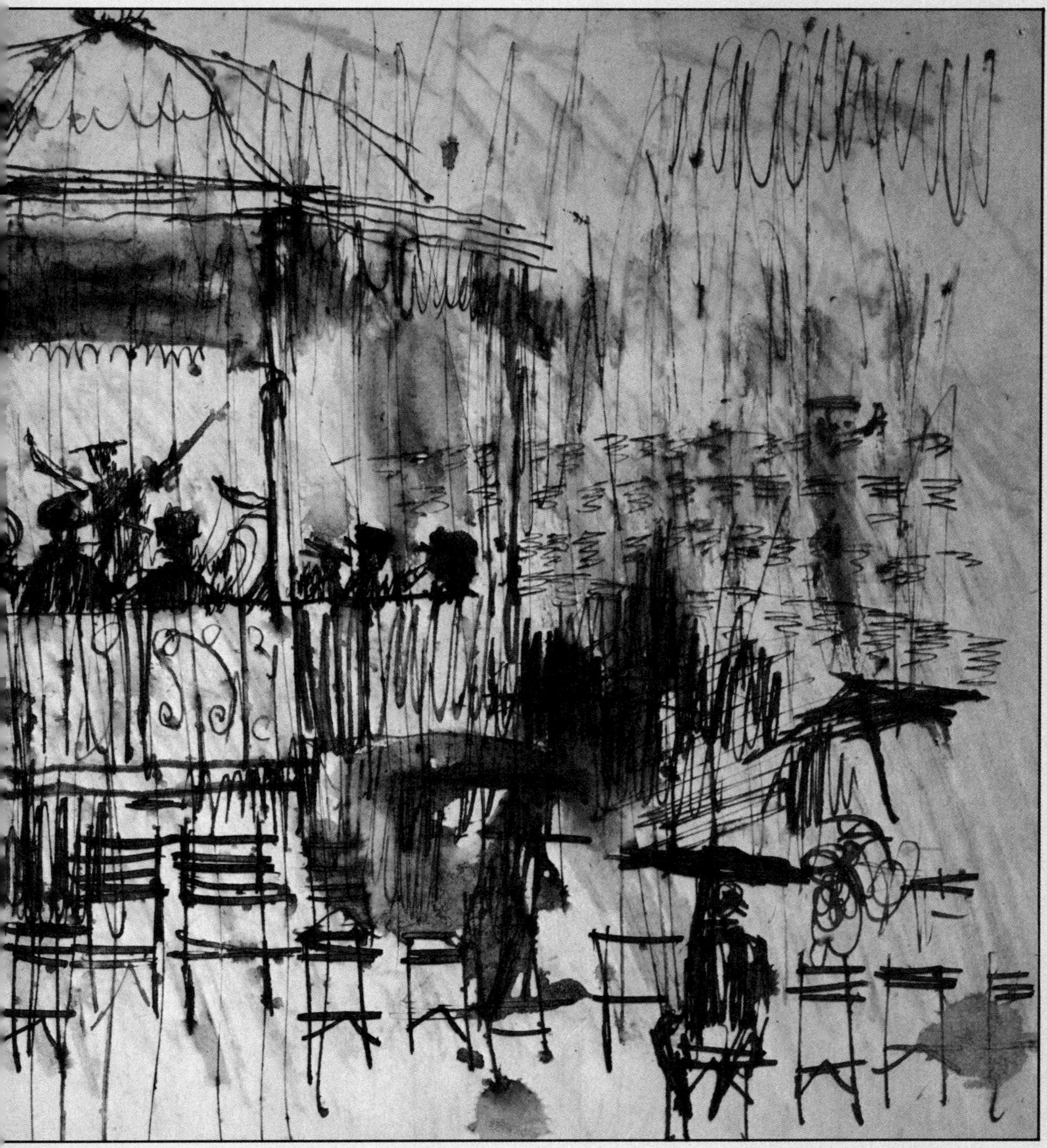

©DIAGRAM

understanding drawing

Drawing is a convention and, like writing, it has developed a grammar of its own. It is a means to convey on a flat surface our surrounding world made up of a complex mixture of forms and surfaces, all of which reflect or absorb light to lesser or greater extents to reveal edges, textures, colours and tones. By drawing we usually mean line drawing since pictures with a major element of tone are considered paintings. But some of the basic principles involved in depicting the physical world are the same for drawing as for painting. Drawings are usually done on a light surface, normally white or cream, and you must compensate for the fact that the world is rarely seen against such a pale background.

Drawing in line
(Pen drawing)
The line drawing (*right*) on a light background, is of objects which are: yellow (the flower), reflective (the tomato), dull (the grapes), rough (the flower's stem) and smooth (the jug's side). **Remember your drawing is not copying reality but describing it.**

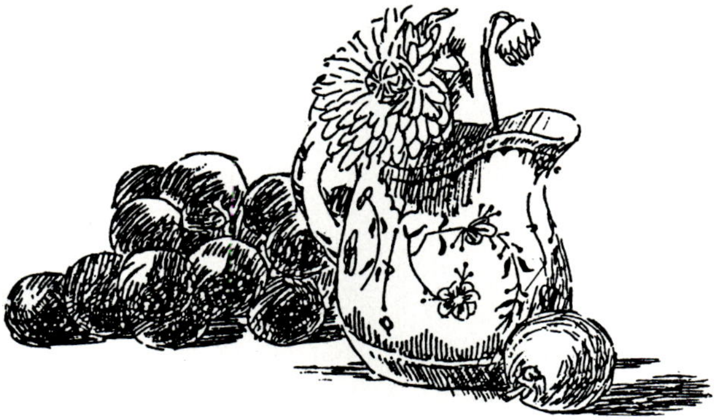

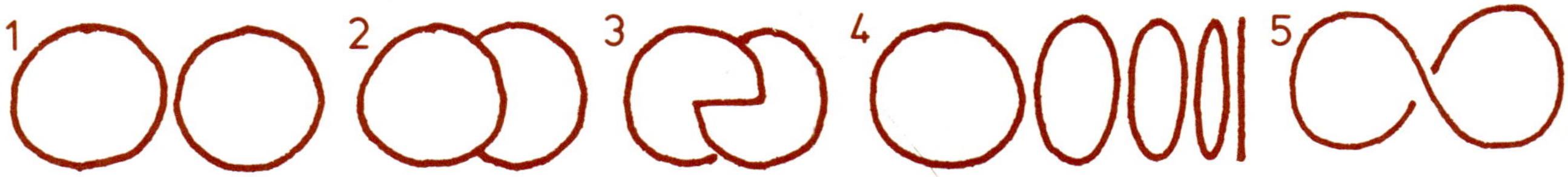

Distinguishing areas
Your line divides areas and shows the edges of forms. The lines indicate the different qualities of the areas they enclose (*above*):

1 Two separate discs on a similar plane to the viewer.
2 One opaque disc overlapping another.
3 Two interlocking discs at different angles.
4 Four separate discs each turning progressively farther away from the viewer.
5 A single, curled object like a potato whirl.

Ambiguities in volume
Three views in line of two solid objects are shown (*right*). Can you guess what they are? (Answer page 39). Because we accept that drawings describe reality, when we are faced with apparently conflicting views of an object, we are confused.

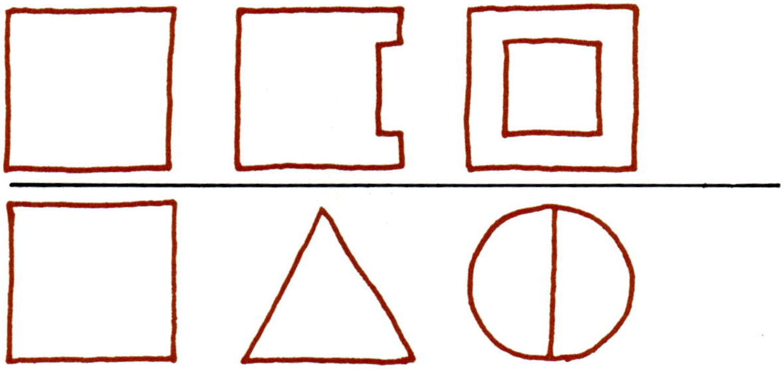

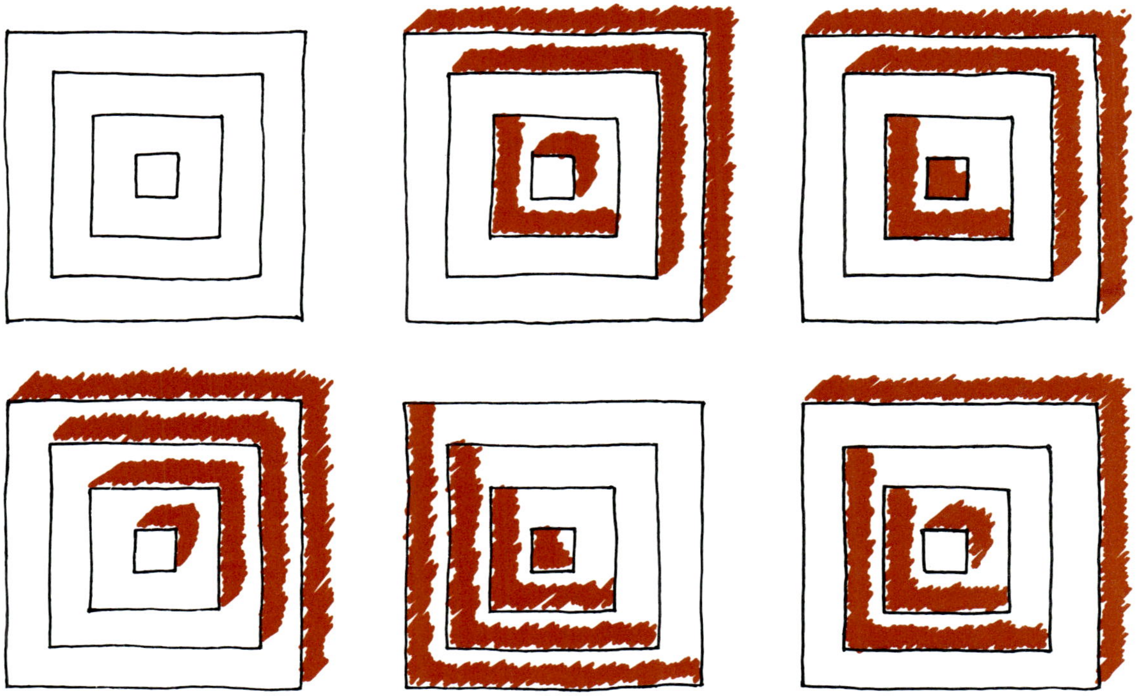

©DIAGRAM

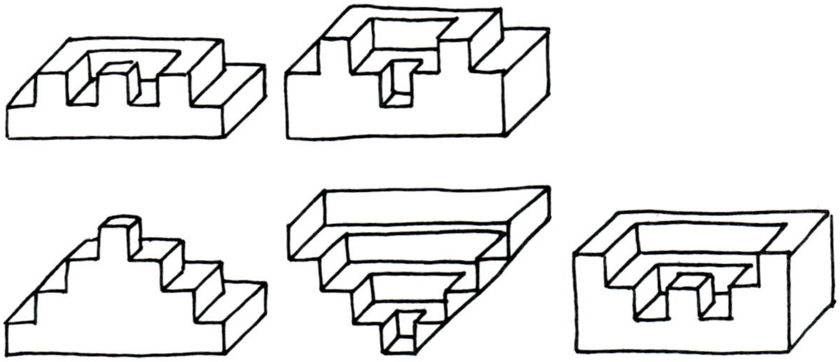

Projecting and receding forms
Often it is only because an object is lit from one main direction that we can identify it. Draw two rows of boxes within boxes (*above*). Now add shadow to describe different possible forms by imagining the light falling from above and from either side. Match the five solids (*right*) to the drawings (*above*).

Space and ground
Recognising that we are looking at the inside or the outside of an object depends on first identifying its form: We begin seeing shape (**A**) and end seeing shape (**B**). Looking at ambiguous forms like this helps to train you to see the shapes between the more obvious forms.

A

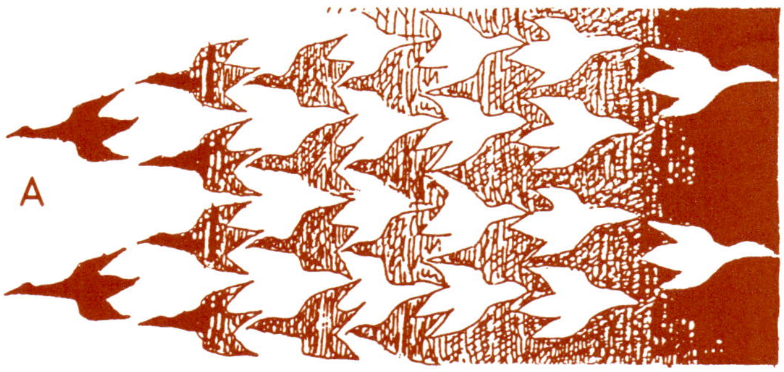

B

composition

You can discover the basic structure of any picture by tracing off the major features. When you are doing a drawing yourself (and it will normally be inside a rectangle), keep in mind how the separate elements relate to each other in your two dimensions. Always maintain an overview of the whole picture, which is more than just the sum of the parts. There is really very little need to learn composition formally – classical structures are fundamentally only observed relationships selected in a particular way. There are no absolute rules, but you should consider the balance of the elements, the tensions created between them and the effect they produce by their location within the composition.

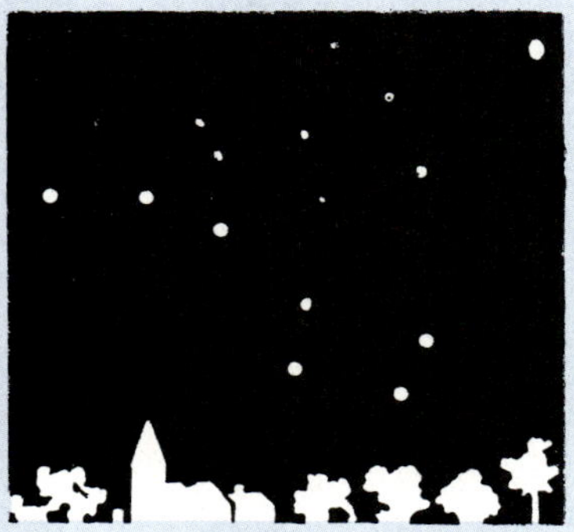

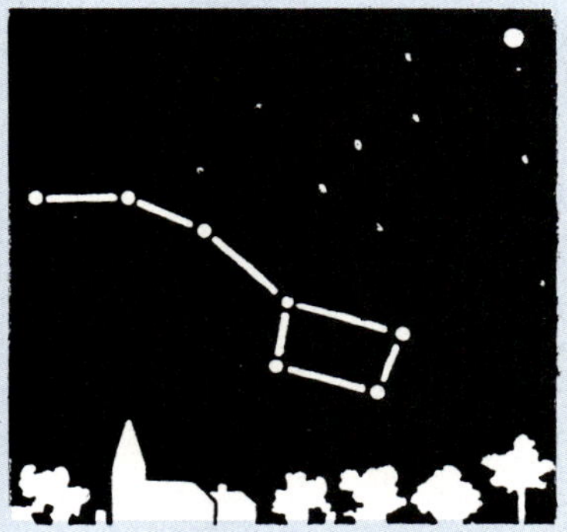

Superimposing patterns
The stars in the sky (*above*) appear to be on a flat black background. Because of this we can imagine them as points, which if joined by lines, form a memorable shape; for instance, the Plough, (*above*). Such a plan ignores the differing distances between the stars and between them and earth.

The golden section or mean
The golden section is an age-old harmonic proportion based on a line or area which is divided in such a way that the smaller part is to the larger as the larger is to the whole. Used intuitively by great artists, it can be found in many works of art. You can construct your own grid as a guide.

Constructing a golden mean rectangle (*right*)
1 Draw a square with sides the height of your projected rectangle.
2 Construct diagonals within it. Where they cross, project to **a**, base line centre.
3 Setting a compass at **a**, draw an arc from the top right **b** to cross an extended base at **c**. This gives you the golden mean on the base.
4 Complete the rectangle to **d**.
5 With your compass at **d**, draw an arc to cross the vertical at **e**. Draw a line through **e** parallel to base. You now have golden means on horizontal and vertical lines (**A** & **B**) which divide the rectangle into smaller areas whose proportions are golden sections.

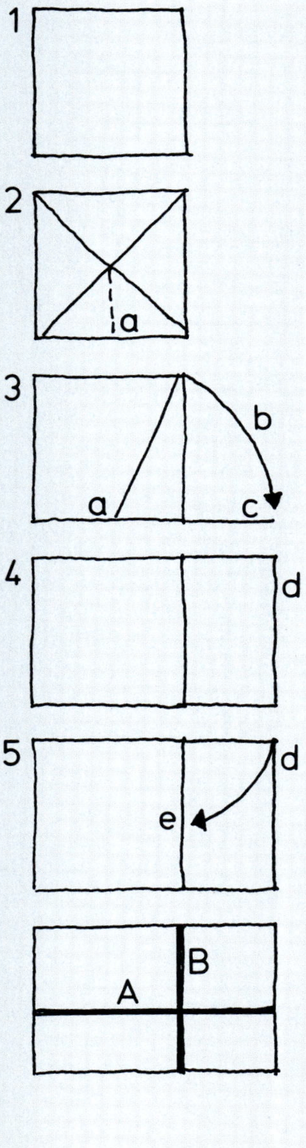

Inner space

Where you put objects within a picture is a result of your understanding of their scale and relationship to each other. Explore your responses to scale and possible relationships by experimenting with silhouettes of different shapes and scales.

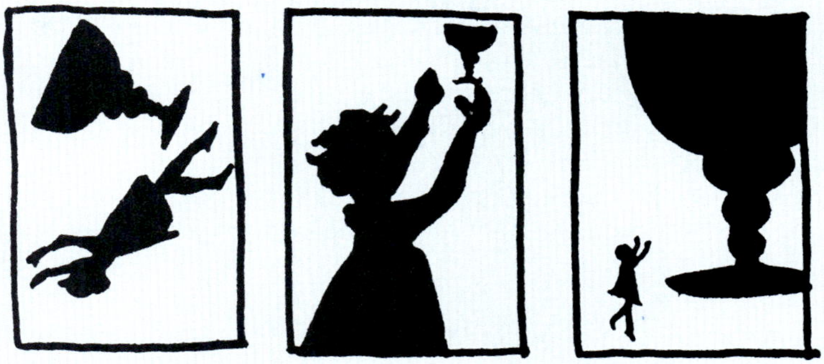

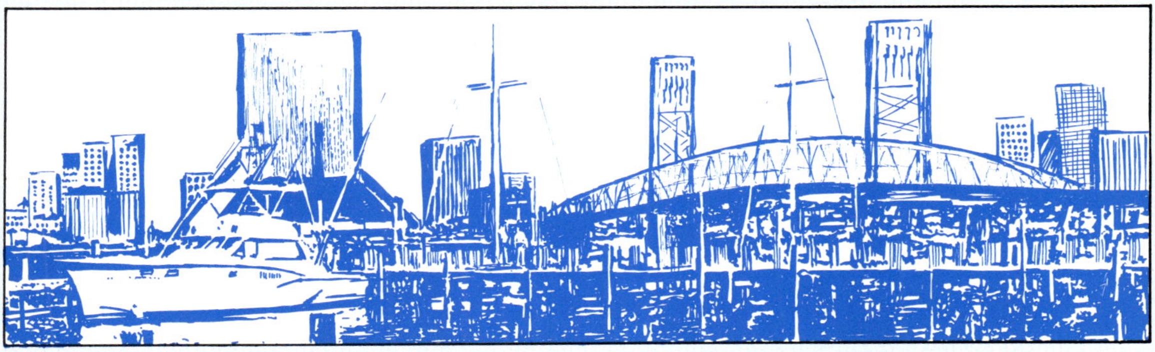

Selecting a composition

When you have a scene with fixed relationships (*right*), explore the range of effects of bordering it with different sizes and shapes of frame. Notice the variety of results you can achieve by selecting only parts of the picture and finding dramatic groupings.

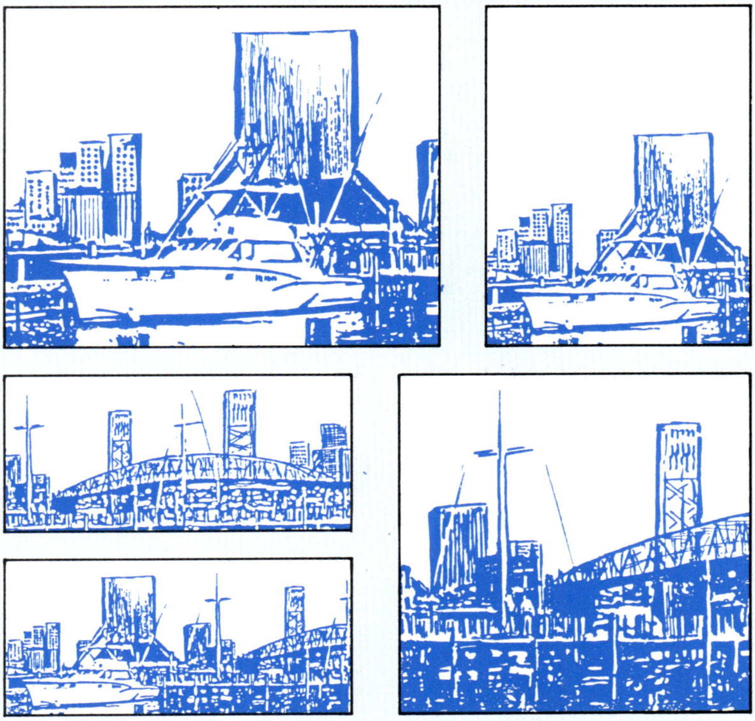

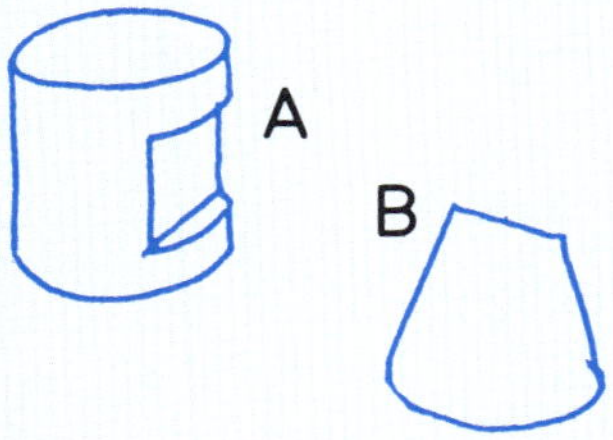

The two objects drawn on page 36 sketched from a view which makes their form clear.

dynamics

Good drawings possess movement within their compositions. This is because the eye, after absorbing an overall impression, then moves around the picture following the lines of structure. In this way the observer is involved in the inner space, almost as if he or she had become part of the subject.

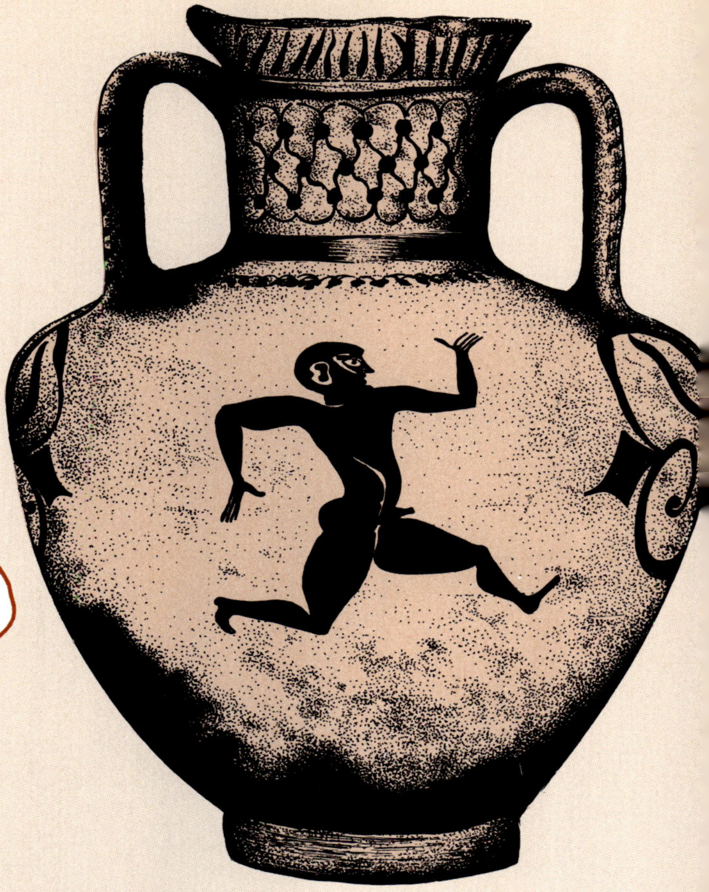

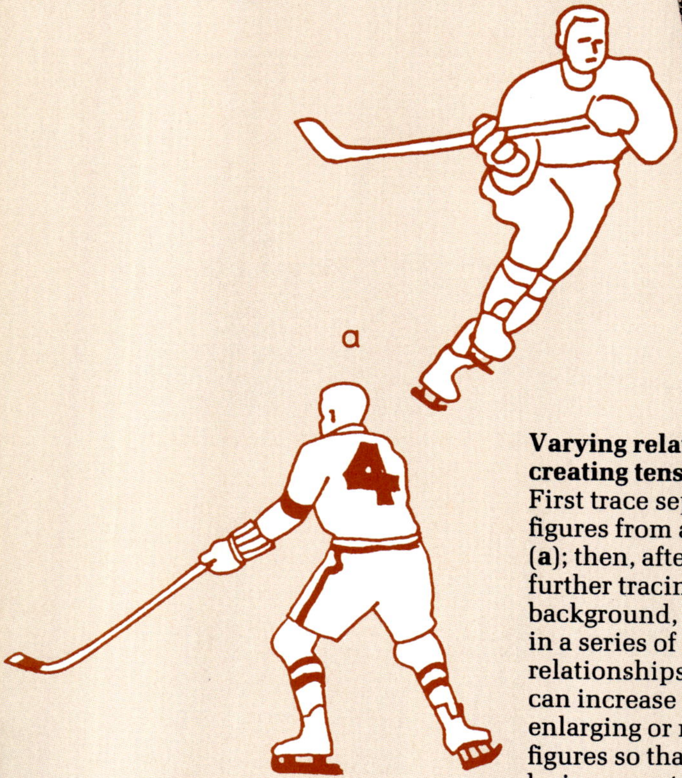

a

Varying relationships and creating tensions
First trace separately two figures from a photograph (**a**); then, after doing a further tracing of the background, put the figures in a series of different relationships (**b**, **c**, **d**). You can increase the tensions by enlarging or reducing the figures so that they appear to be in separate planes.

Greek vase
The drawing of the vase (*above*) is accurate, static and describes the volume and the surface features. The drawing of the running man on the side of the vase is distorted but has energy and dynamic tension.

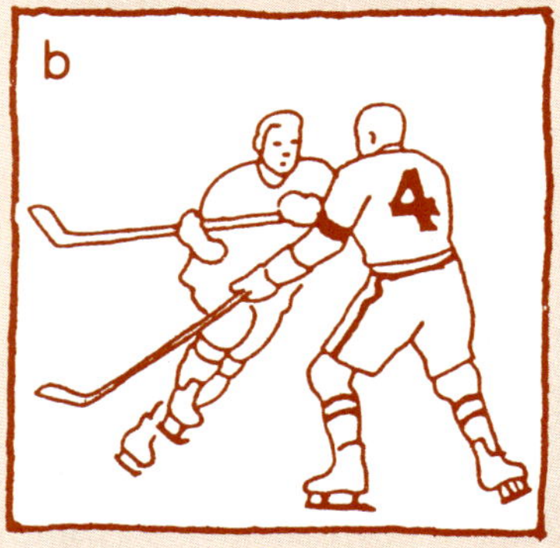

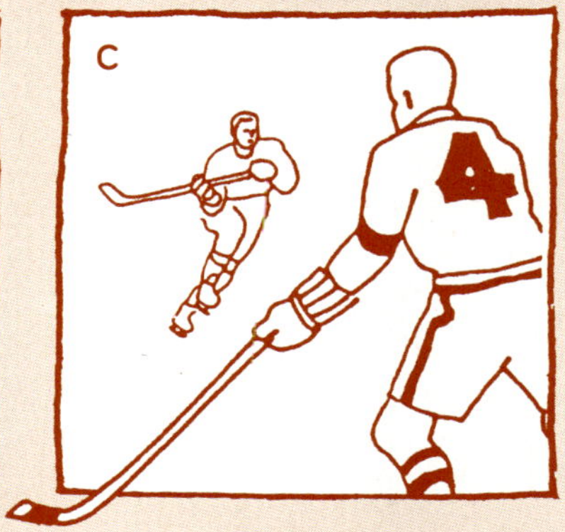

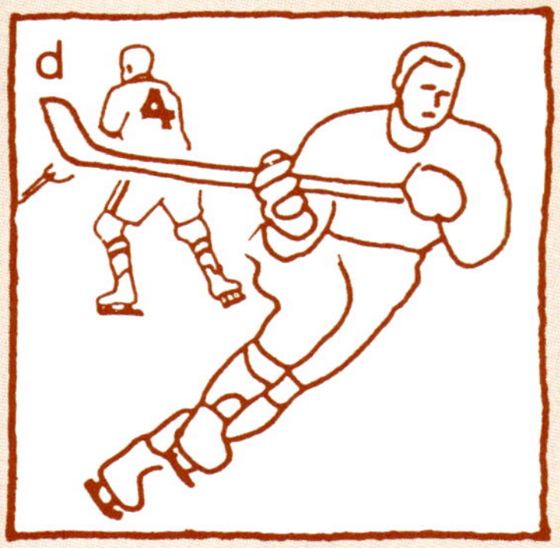

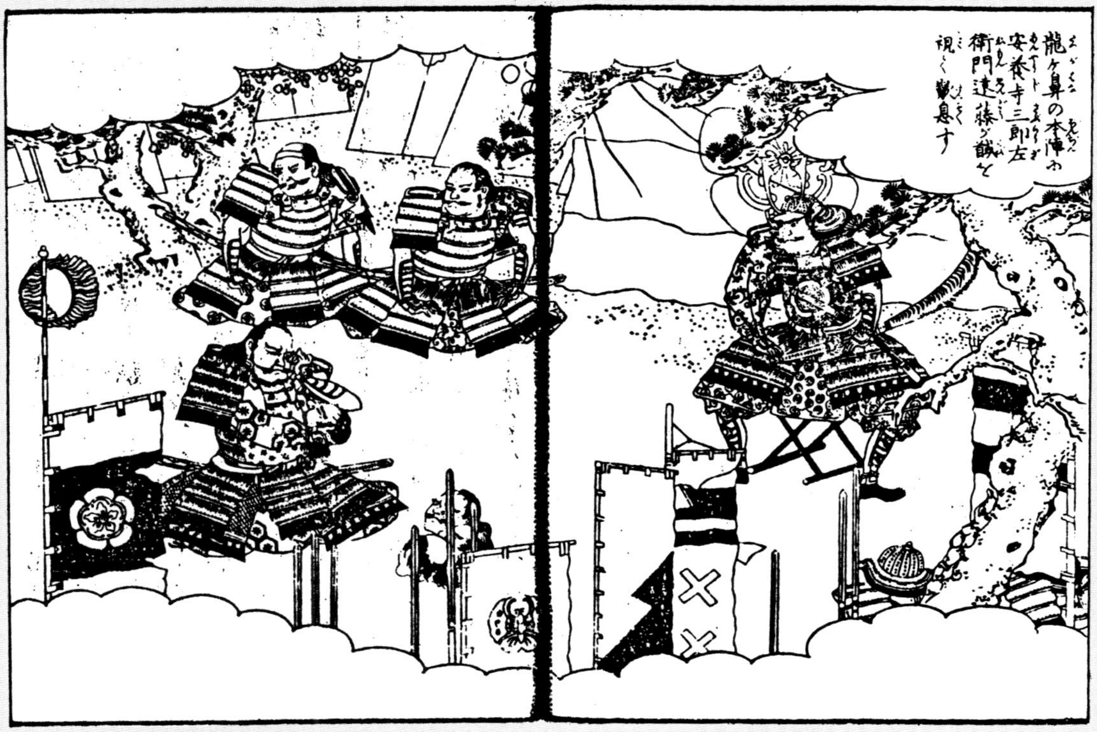

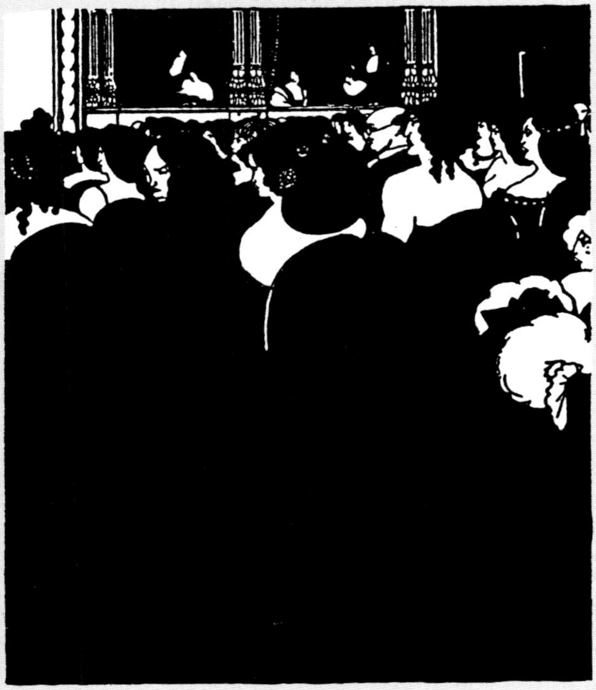

Japanese woodcut, 19th century
Discover the spatial relationships between the elements of a drawing (*above*); the figures form a triangle set within a circle (see *below*).

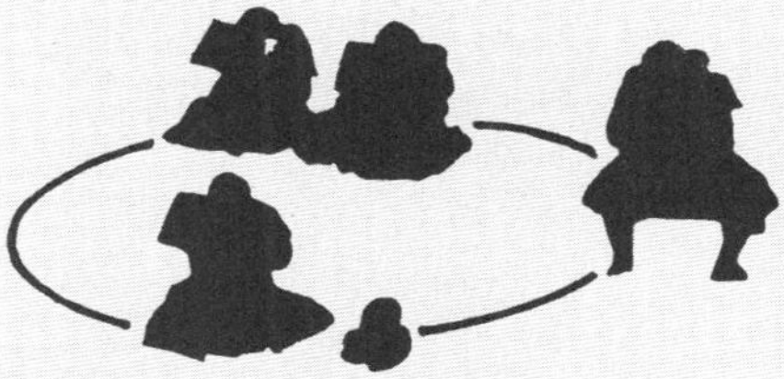

Theatre audience
(Pen and ink drawing by Aubrey Beardsley)
Using any artist's drawings, e.g. the Beardsley (*left*), describe the positions and relationships of the figures within the space.

perspective

Beginners tend to worry that their drawings "do not look right". They usually mean they "do not accurately describe what they see". Improving your accuracy will improve your confidence, and understanding the basic principles of perspective helps you to check your observations.

Perspective is the means by which you achieve a convincing spatial relationship between the parts of the drawing. The laws of perspective are like the laws of grammar: to be learned and then used to help you express yourself – they should not dominate your subject. Normally vertical edges are drawn as verticals on your drawing and horizontal edges are drawn as converging lines which meet at either a distant central or vanishing point, or at two points at either side of the object.

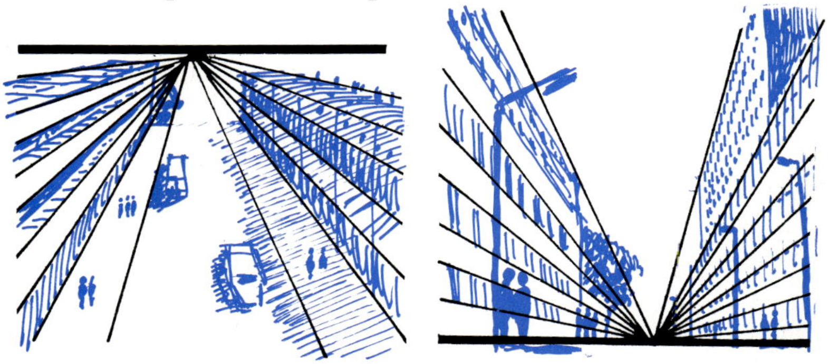

Eye level
The vanishing point of the horizontal lines depends on the height at which you observe the subject: the higher you are the higher the vanishing point, and the lower you are the lower the vanishing point. The eye level is at the level of the vanishing point.

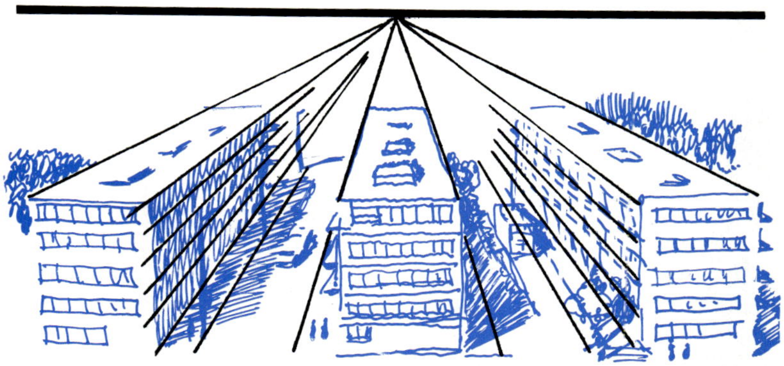

One vanishing point
Imagine three blocks of flats standing side by side. The roads, windows and roofs all have parallel horizontal lines. When viewed side by side, their receding edges will appear to converge on a common vanishing point (*left*).

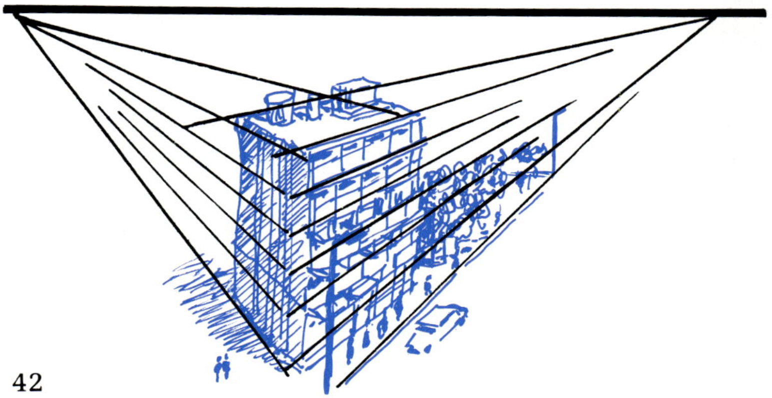

Two vanishing points
If you are drawing boxes or corners of buildings, each side will produce converging lines which meet at two separate vanishing points (*left*). In both single and double vanishing point drawings the distant point is always at your eye level.

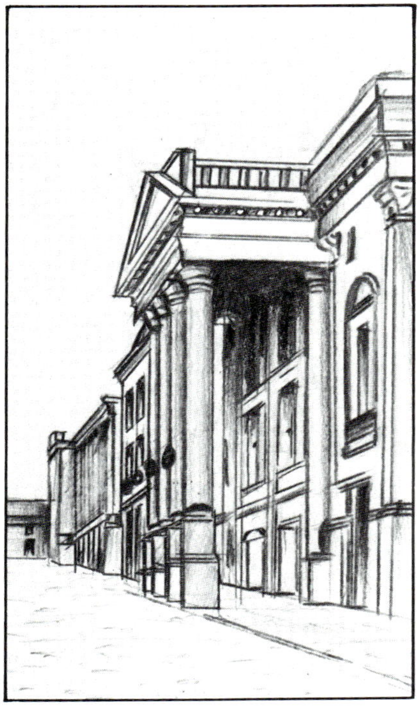

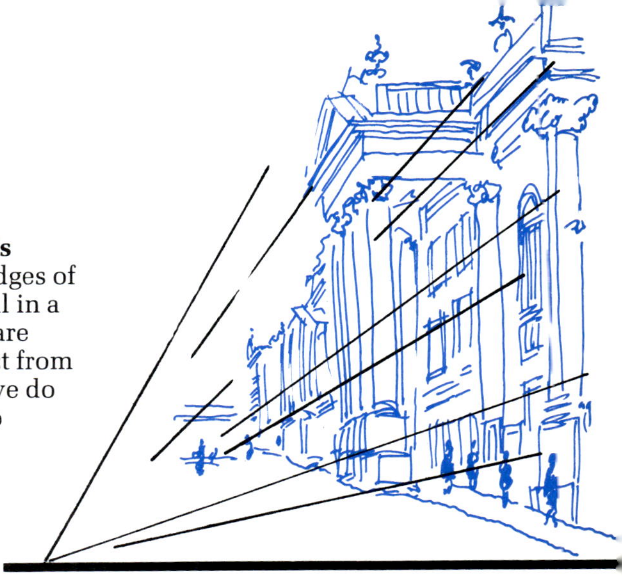

Watching the verticals
Usually the vertical edges of objects remain vertical in a drawing. Only if you are looking at your subject from directly below or above do the verticals appear to converge.

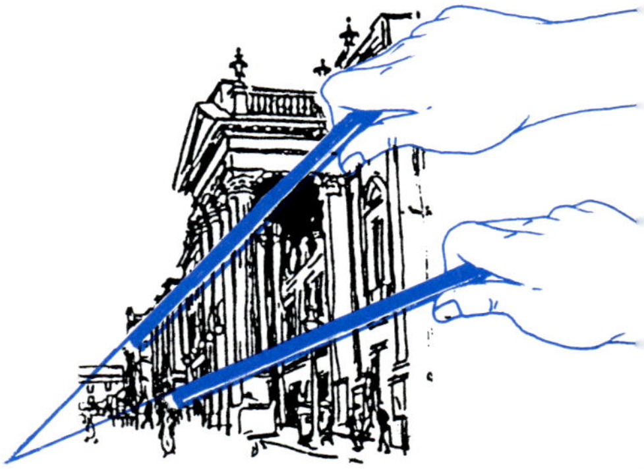

Low eye levels
If you are lower than your subject (see the pencil drawing *left*), all the converging lines will slope downwards. Establish the direction and point of convergence by holding your pencil along the lines and copy down the direction.

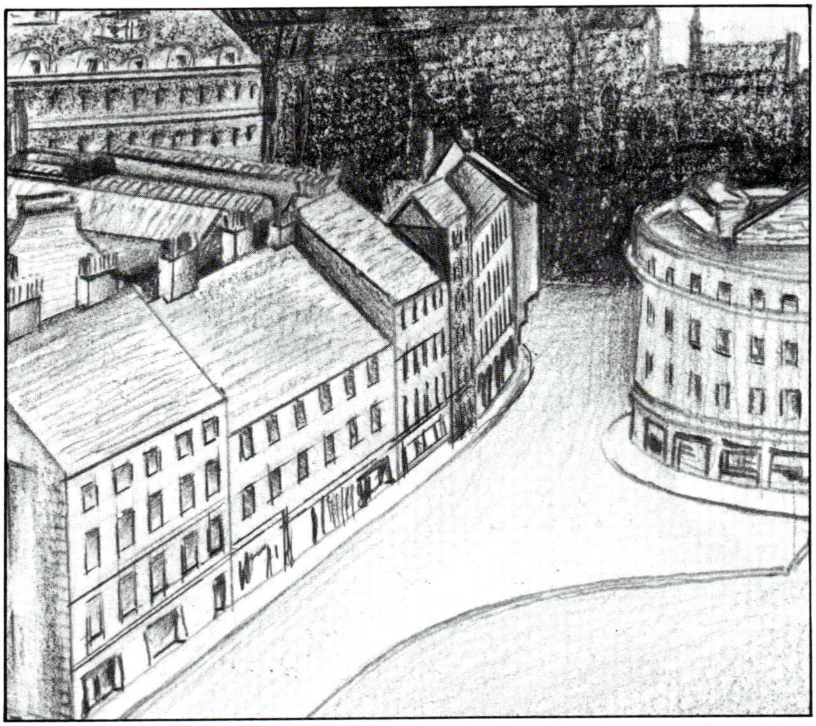

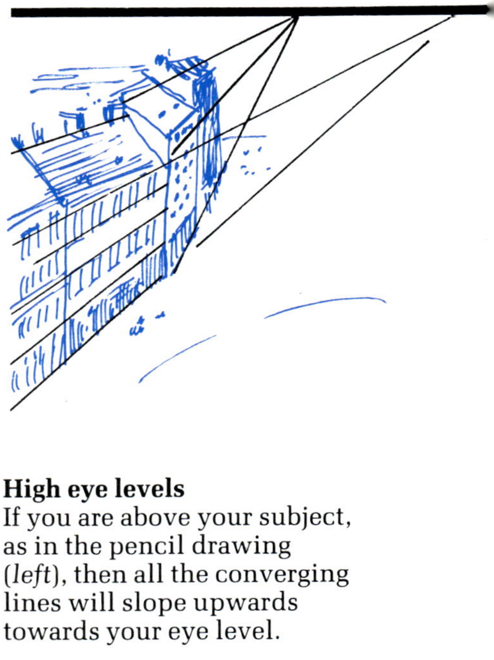

High eye levels
If you are above your subject, as in the pencil drawing (*left*), then all the converging lines will slope upwards towards your eye level.

perspective

Two of the main aims of any drawing are to recreate in two dimensions the space and volumes present in the world, making the more distant features appear to be farther away than those in the foreground; and making objects seem solid. Careful observation of space and volume is essential if you want to achieve accuracy.

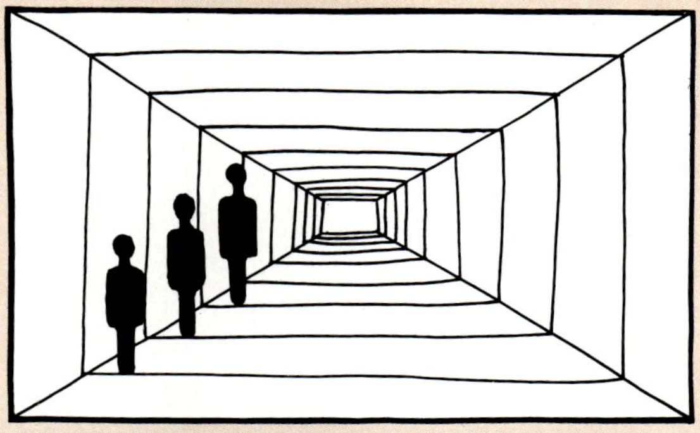

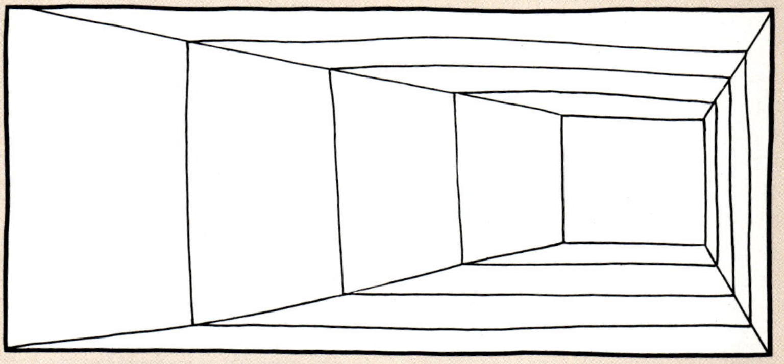

Recession
The interior of the box (*left*) appears to recede. Superimpose several identical figures along one side – and they seem to grow larger. Trace off a figure, place it in the drawing of a room (*above*). and see its scale change as its position within the room changes.

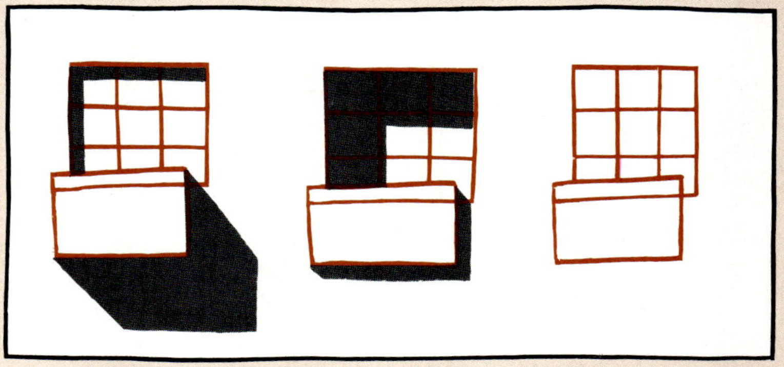

Projection
Of the first two window balconies (*left*), one seems to project farther out than the other. Superimpose a tracing overlay on the third and experiment with shadow until it looks right.

Unusual view
Some objects are multi-directional, like the plant (*below*), whose structure is revealed better from above.

Overlapping
A sense of distance can be created by overlapping objects, as in the design (*left*); all the figures are the same size. Trace your own images and by overlapping rows build up a feeling of depth.

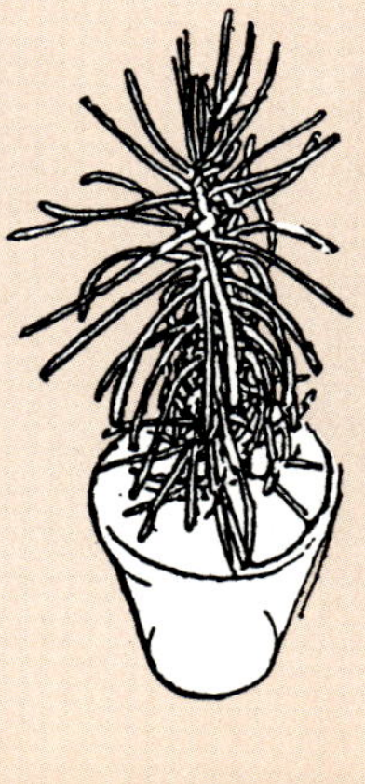

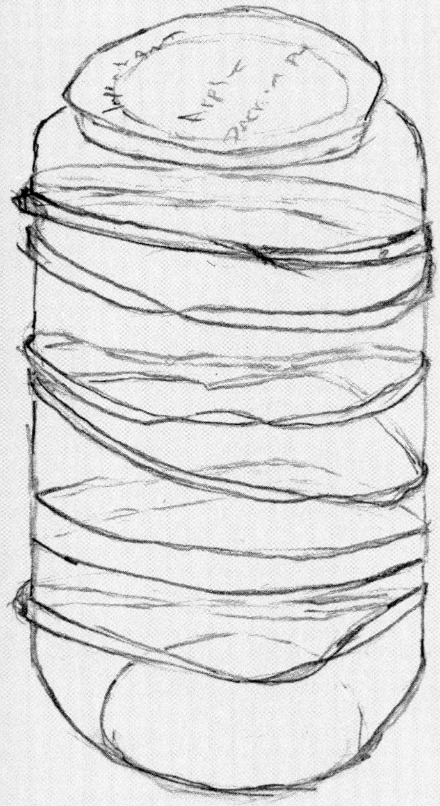

Volume
(Pencil drawing)
Every object has volume. To demonstrate the volume of a jar, encase it in rubber bands which, if drawn accurately, will show its "roundness", (*above*).
Note how when your eye level changes, so does your view of the bands.

Scale
(Pen and ink drawing)
All the grass in the field (*right*) is about the same height, but by carefully recording the diminishing scale of the blades the field appears to recede into the distant landscape.

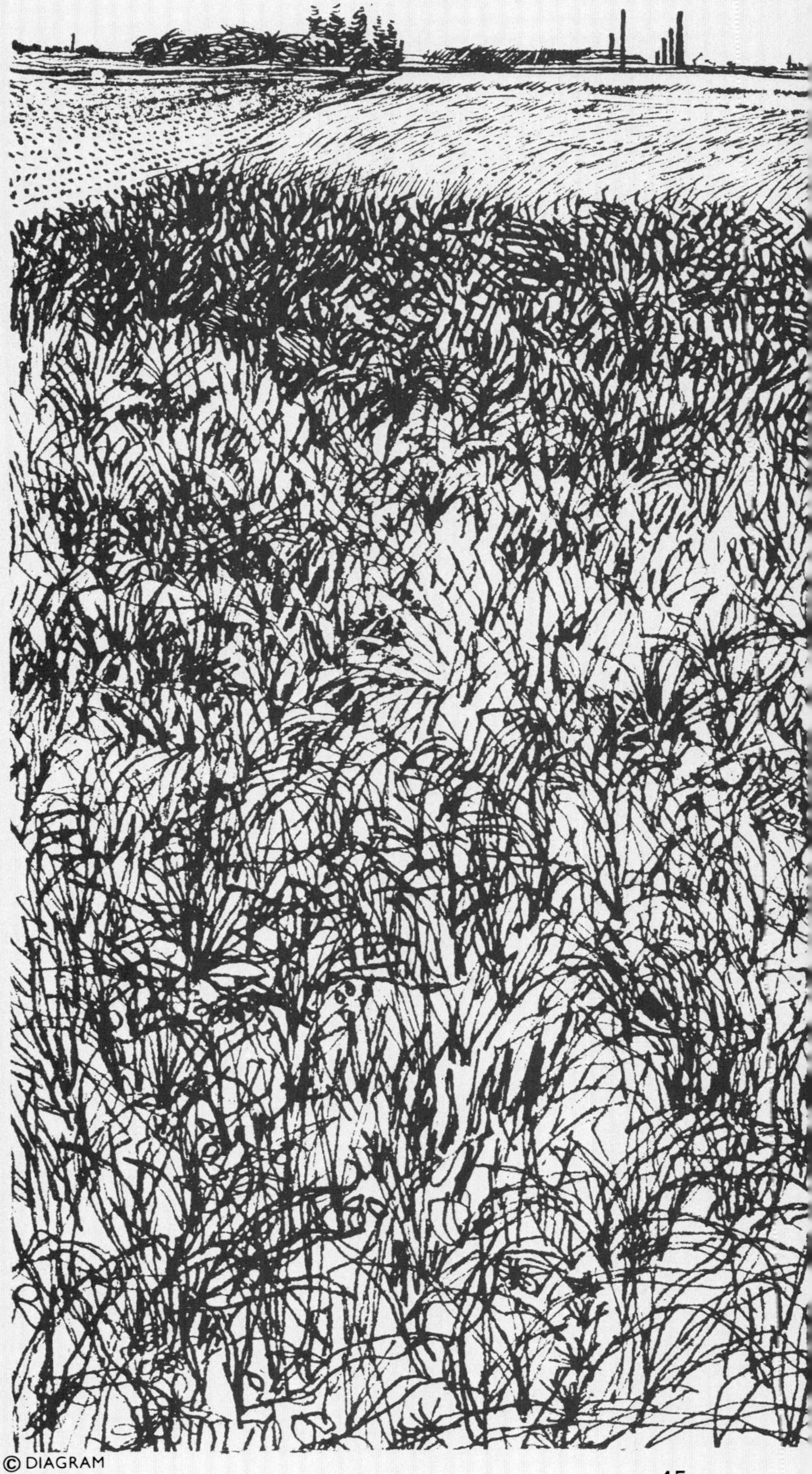

improving your accuracy

Many people feel that their drawings of the objects they see are not quite accurate, that the shapes and sizes are somehow wrong. To draw is to transfer what you see onto the paper in front of you, but the eye is easily deceived. There are a number of simple techniques and checking devices that you can use to make sure that you draw what is actually there, not what you think you see. Try to position the object you wish to draw in the centre of your field of vision – widening your field of vision unnecessarily only increases the possibility of inaccuracy.

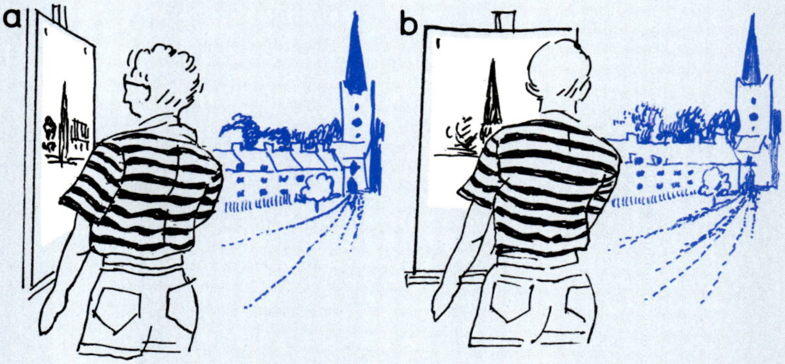

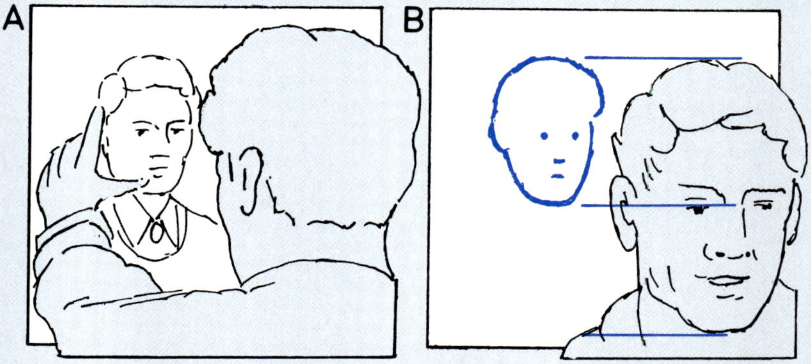

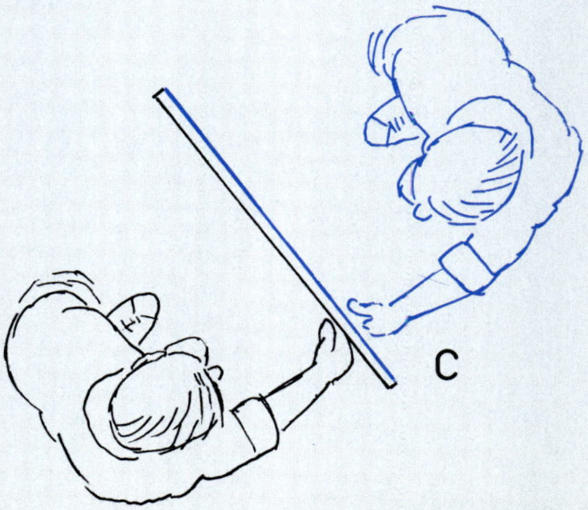

Parallel positioning
How you stand in relationship to the object you are drawing is very important. The object and your paper should be as close to parallel as possible, so that you can just flick your eyes from one to the other.
a Poor position: the head must turn each time a line is drawn.
b Correct viewing position: the head can remain still.

Check what you see
Objects are not necessarily the size that we think they are. For example, what size is your reflection in a mirror? Look in a mirror and estimate the size, then use a wax crayon to actually draw the outline of your face on the mirror's surface (**A**). When you measure it, you will find that the outline you have drawn is half the size of your head (**B**), although most people would have expected it to be the same size. The eye has seen what it believed to be there: the optical image that is the same size as your head is as far behind the mirror as you are in front of the mirror (**C**), not on the mirror surface itself.

Checking devices
Most artists use some sort of checking device to help them test their judgement of horizontals, verticals, and angles. A plumb line (**a**) is a simple device for checking vertical alignments, while a pencil held out horizontally (**b**) can be used to check angles or distances across. If you have a composition that contains a number of difficult features (**c**), you can check it through a right-angled frame marked out to show distances. View the object through the frame (**d**) and note down where the points touch the edges of the frame.

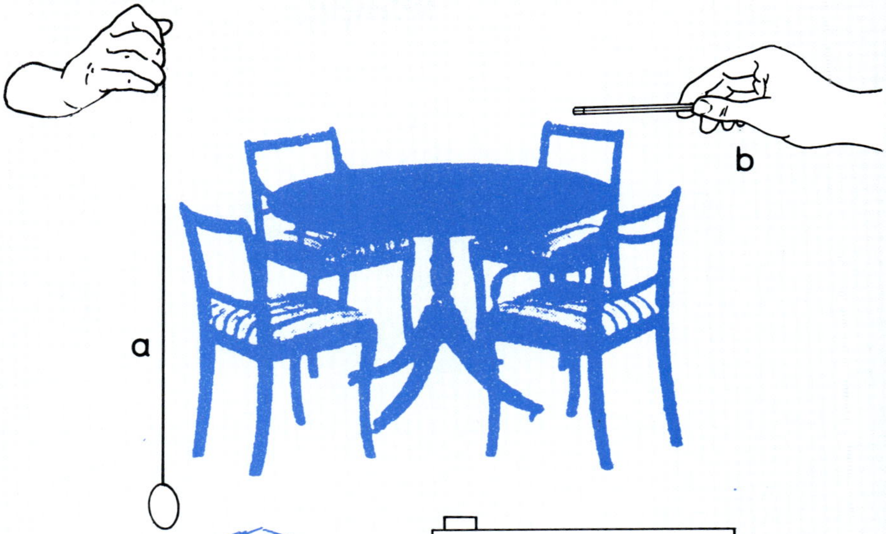

c
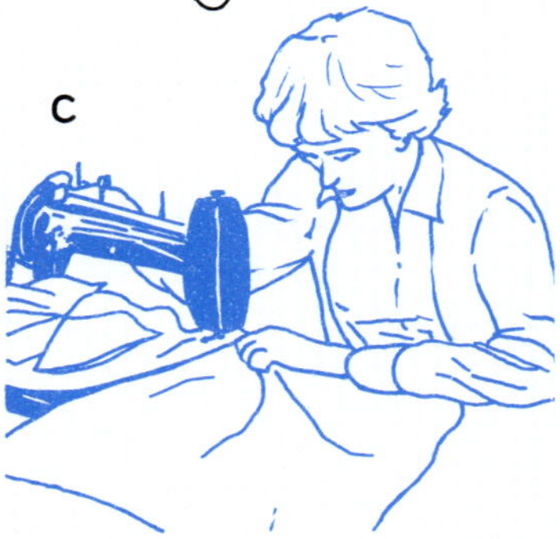

d
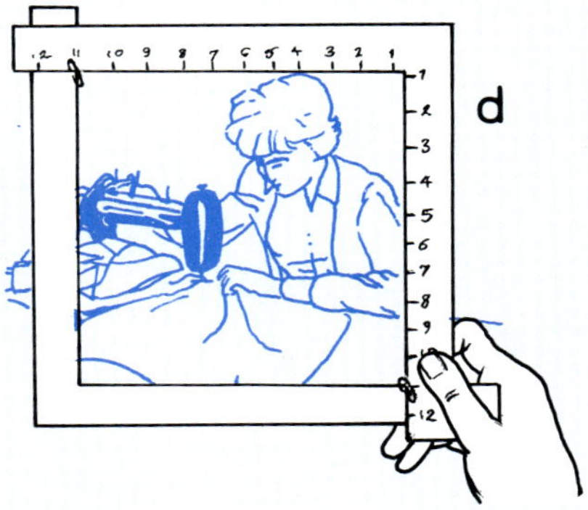

Using grids
The most direct way to transfer shapes accurately is to stand the object you are drawing in front of a grid (**A**). You then record the irregular shapes against a similar grid drawn on your paper (**B**), working through square by square. Artists very often sketch on graph paper (**C**), as the accurate grid helps to guide their judgement of shapes and sizes.

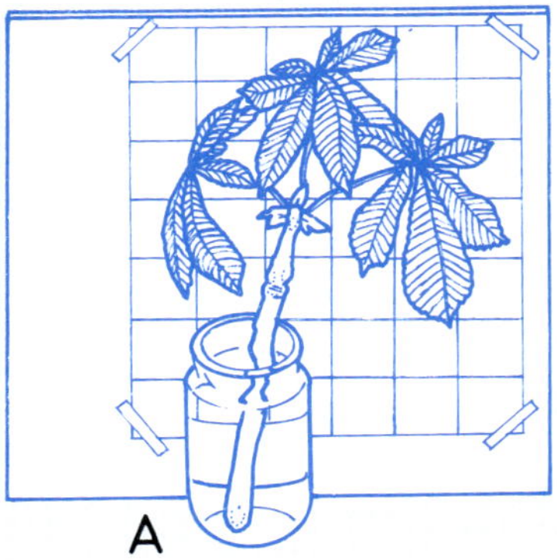
A

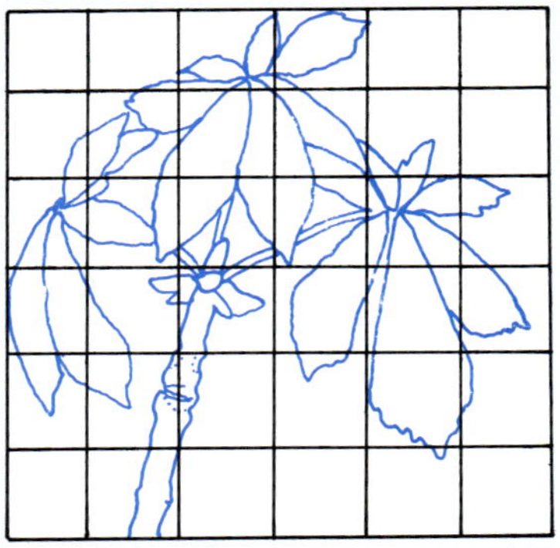
B

C
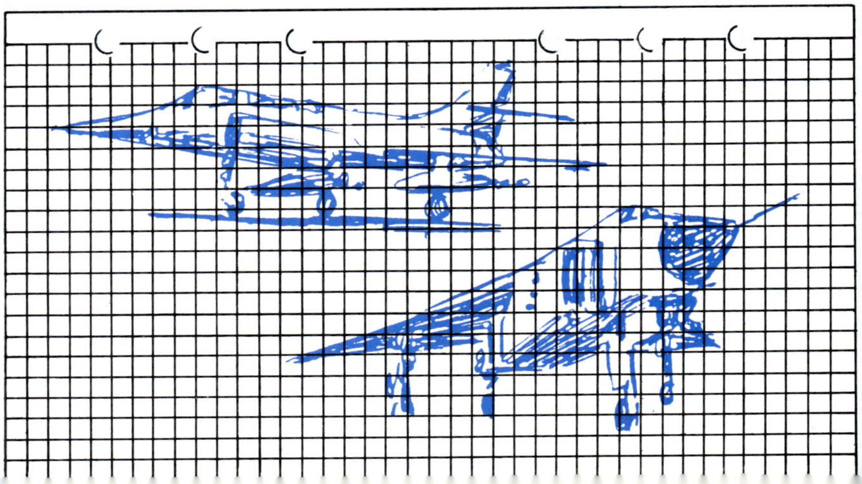

shapes

Another drawing exercise that will teach you a great deal is the art of drawing the shapes between the objects. This will show you how objects relate to each other; for instance if you are sketching a group of plants, drawing the shapes between all the leaves will show you how all the shapes interact. Every angle you look from will give you different shapes; as you practise you will learn to look with a fresh eye at the objects you are drawing.

1

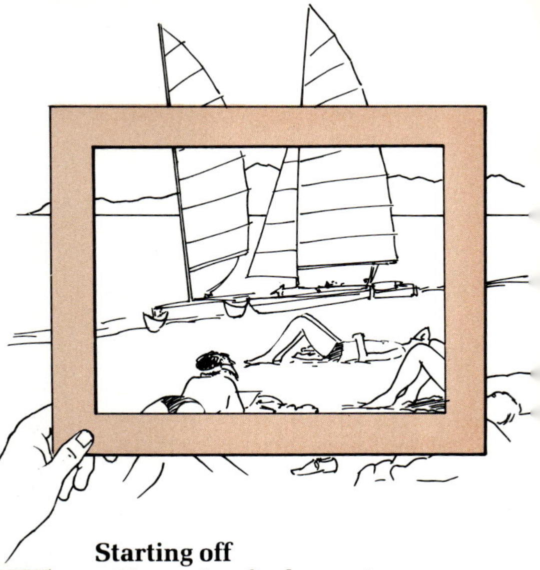

Starting off
1 Use a viewfinder, a piece of card with a hole cut in it, to select a pleasing composition.

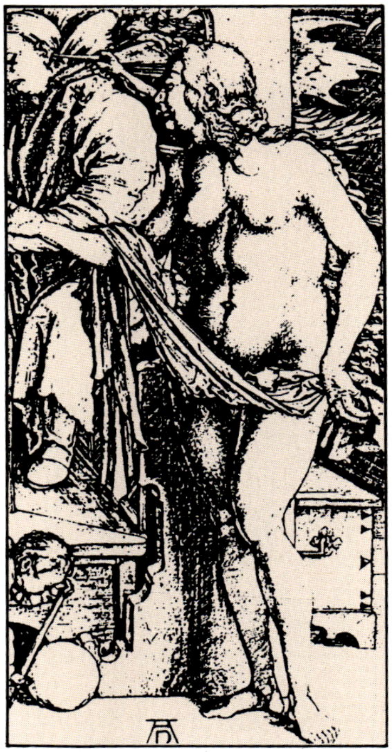

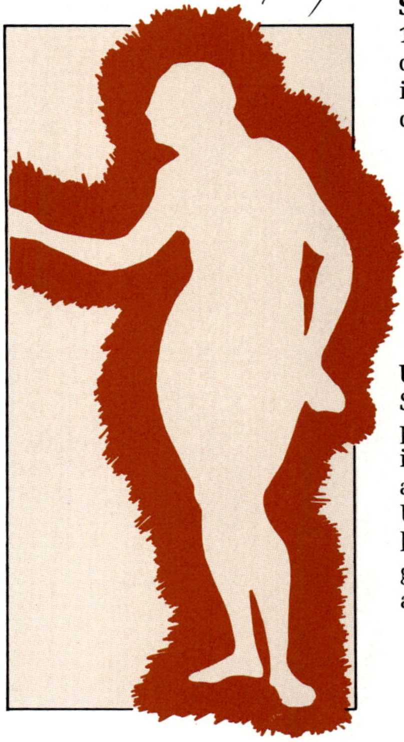

Using other sources (*left*)
Select a clear picture or a photograph, and convert it into a drawing of the shapes around the objects portrayed. Using this approach on well-known paintings will often give you an insight into the artist's unique view.

Changing views (*right*)
Move your viewfinder around the same objects so that you get a completely different view each time. The drawings show the spaces between and around an ordinary chair, and each viewpoint is unique; some views are more immediately recognisable than others.

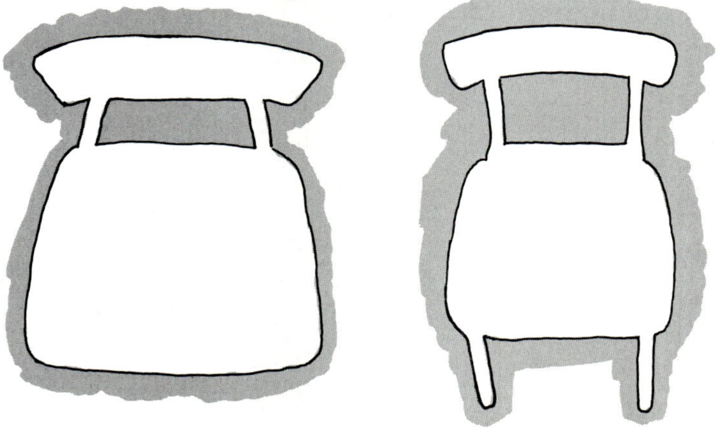

2

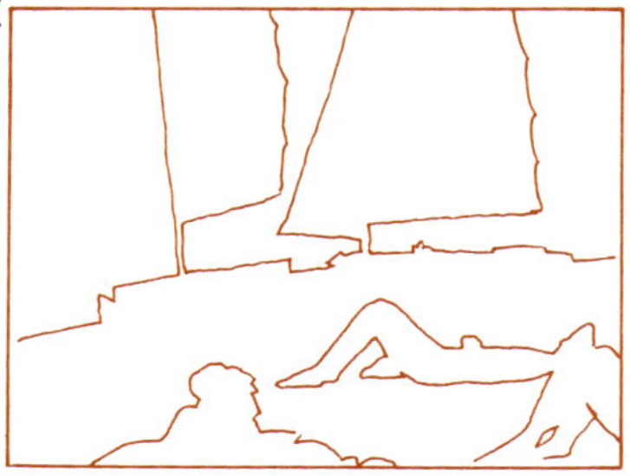

3

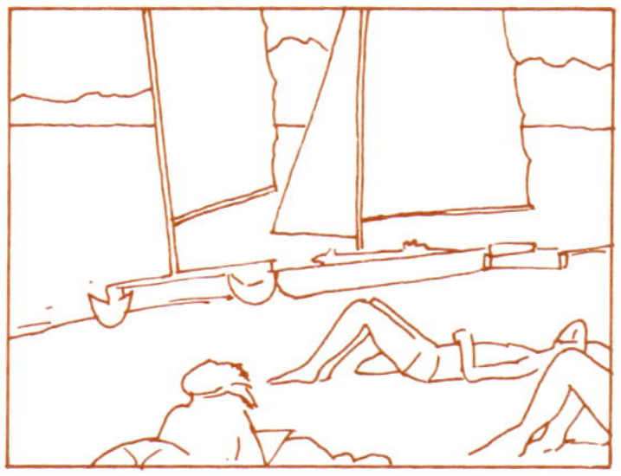

4

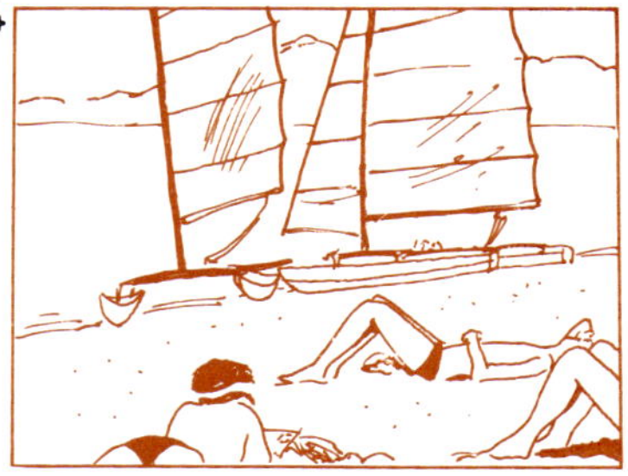

2 Looking through your viewfinder, draw on your paper very lightly the major areas of space between the objects.

3 Now draw the smaller areas lightly; this should give you an accurate basic composition.

4 Gradually rework these shapes one by one with a strong line, putting in all the details.

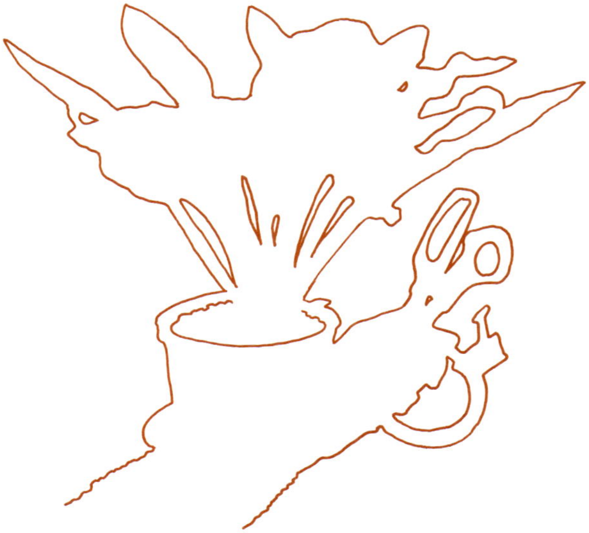

Practising from life
Drawing the shapes between living objects will improve your skills and also teach you how plants grow, and how animals and people stand or sit or move. Try this exercise on a pot plant or a bunch of flowers, and on a hand holding different objects (*right*).

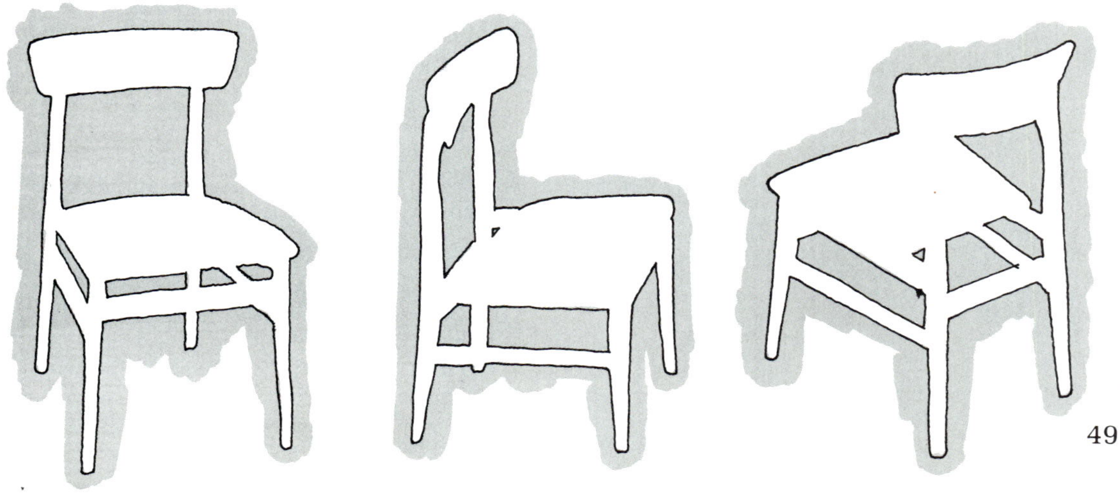

shapes

Drawing silhouettes is an easy exercise that will train your eye to represent shapes accurately. By concentrating on the outline you will learn to cut out distracting details and also gain confidence in your own skills. You can obtain a good silhouette by drawing the shadow cast by an object held between a strong light source and white paper, or by tracing around shapes in pictures and photographs. Silhouettes make very attractive and striking illustrations.

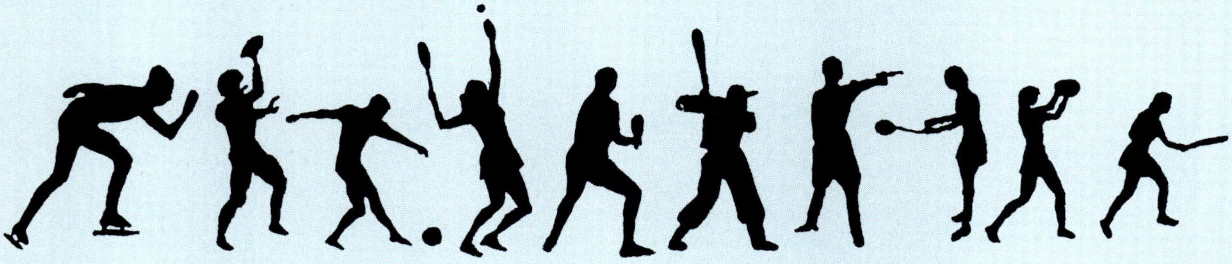

Silhouettes from photographs
Use tracing paper over a photograph to obtain a convincing silhouette of people in action, animals, trees, flowers or buildings. Follow the outline of the shape with a pencil, then fill in with dark ink to make a strong contrast. The drawings (*above*) were done by a 15-year-old, with no art training, working from a sports encyclopaedia.

Landscapes
Landscapes can provide beautiful silhouettes when the sun is strong and shining from behind shapes. Trees, walls, chimneys, lamp posts and scaffolding all make very satisfying shapes; move around until you find a pleasing composition.

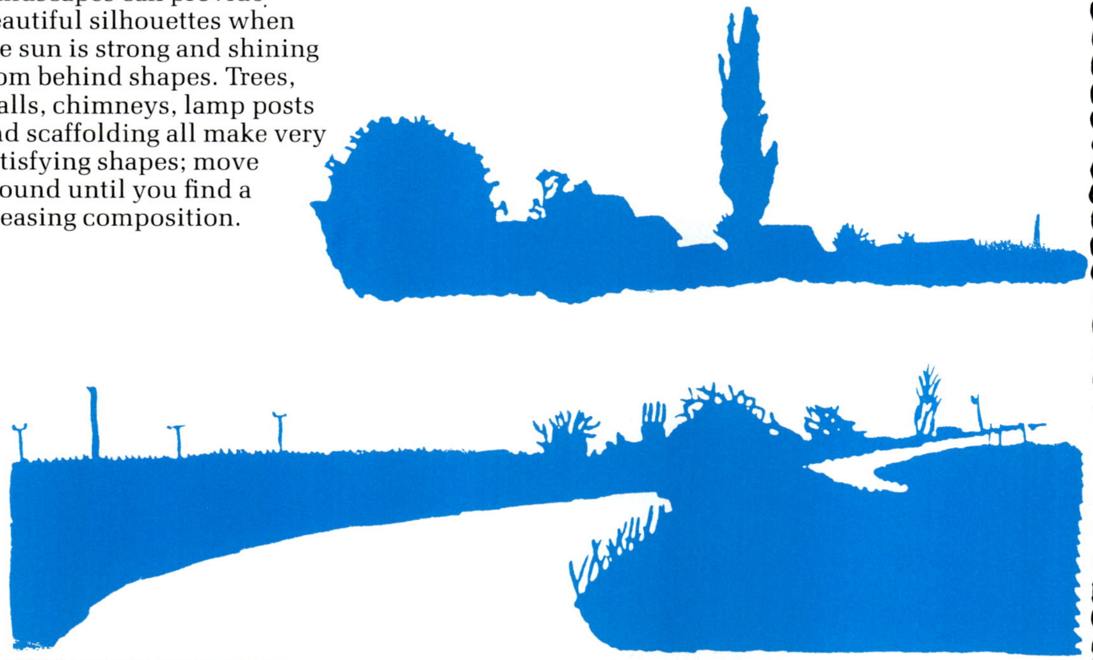

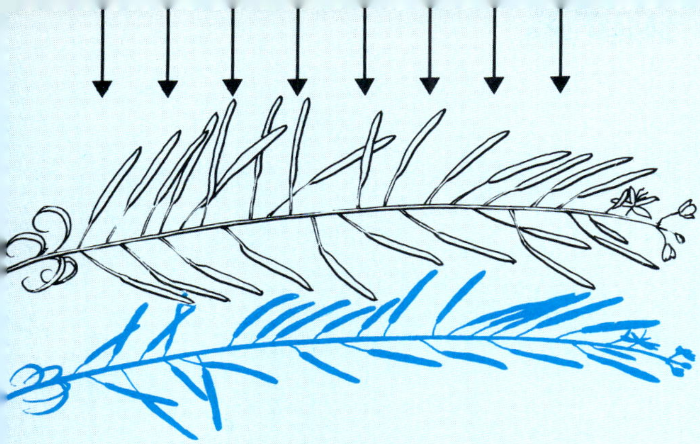

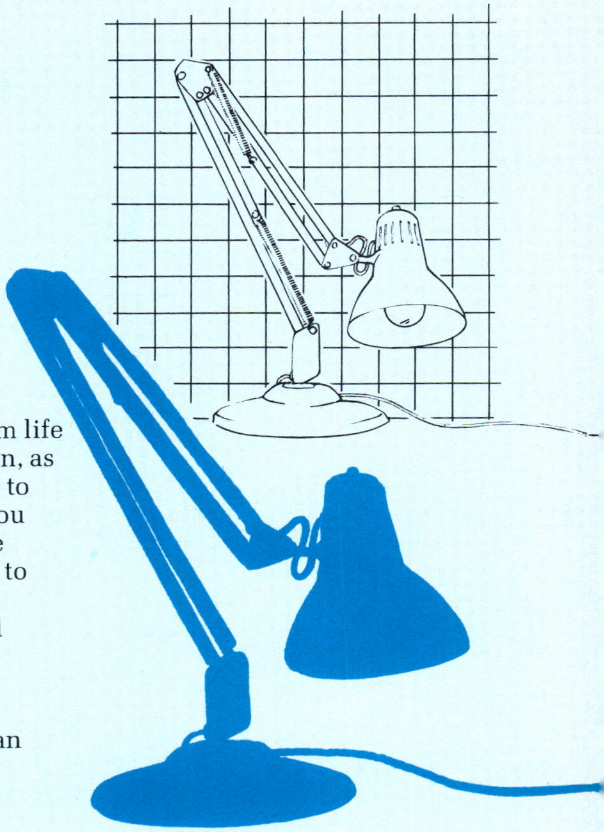

Shadow Silhouettes
Arrange a strong light so that it throws shadows onto a piece of paper – don't bring the light too close or the shadow will be very distorted. Using thick fibre-tipped pens or a brush and ink, paint the shapes of the shadows. Remember that this is not the same shape that you see if you look at the object directly, but the projection of light past the object.

Working from life
Drawing silhouettes from life takes more concentration, as you do not have a shape to trace around directly. You can begin by placing the object on a squared grid to help you draw more accurately. A successful silhouette will contain enough information to identify the object; for instance a side view of an elephant will be more understandable than an aerial view.

Silhouettes from life
People and animals are the hardest silhouettes to do successfully. They require more practice, and also a retentive memory so that you can capture the shapes as they move. Make lots of quick sketches of a pet, and see if you can capture its distinctive characteristics.

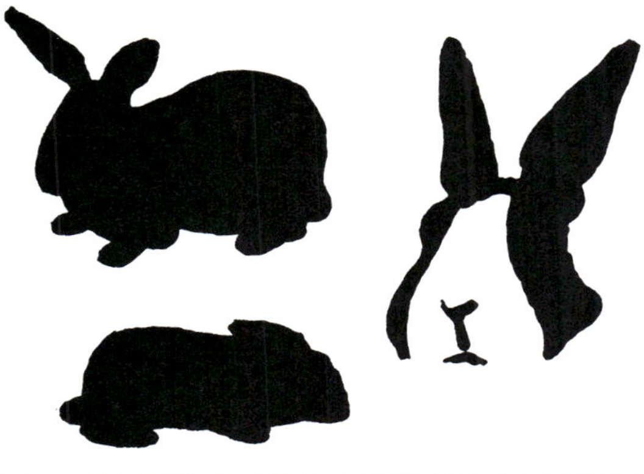

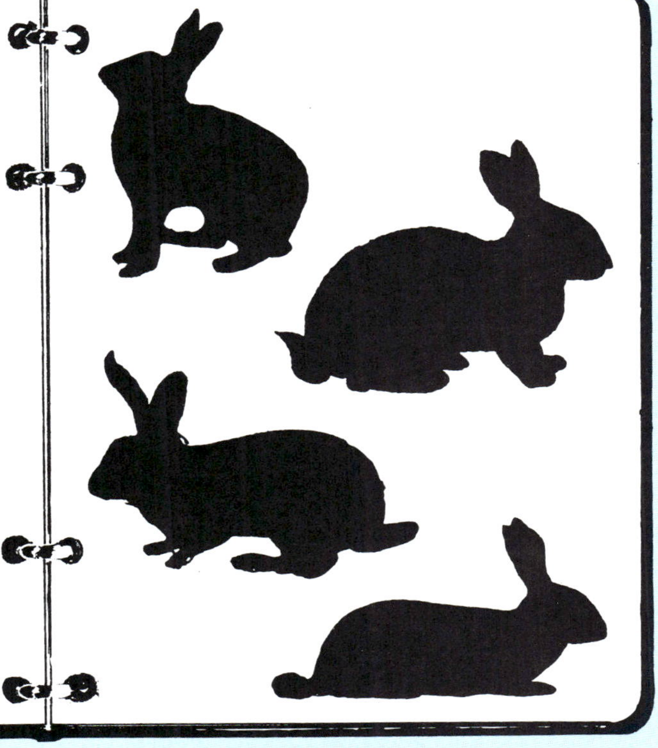

light and shade

Light and shade are the two ranges of tone which are most used by artists to describe the form of objects. Light normally falls from above and from either the left or right side, producing shadows and highlights. By observing carefully the direction of light, you will be able to judge the extent to which surfaces protrude or recede.

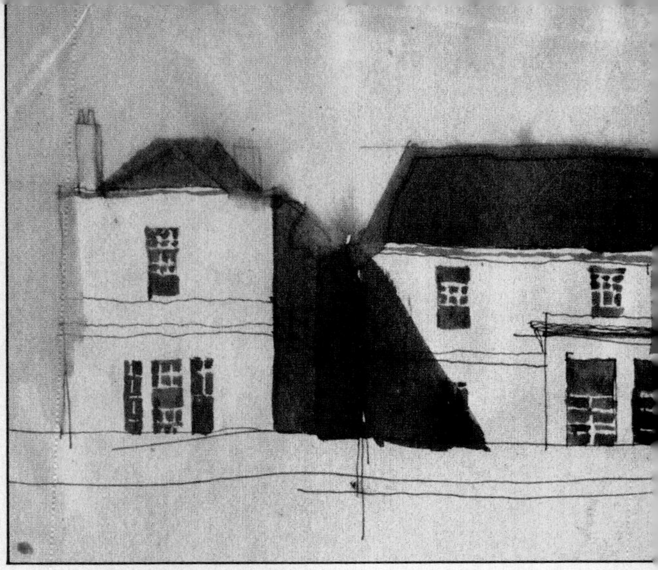

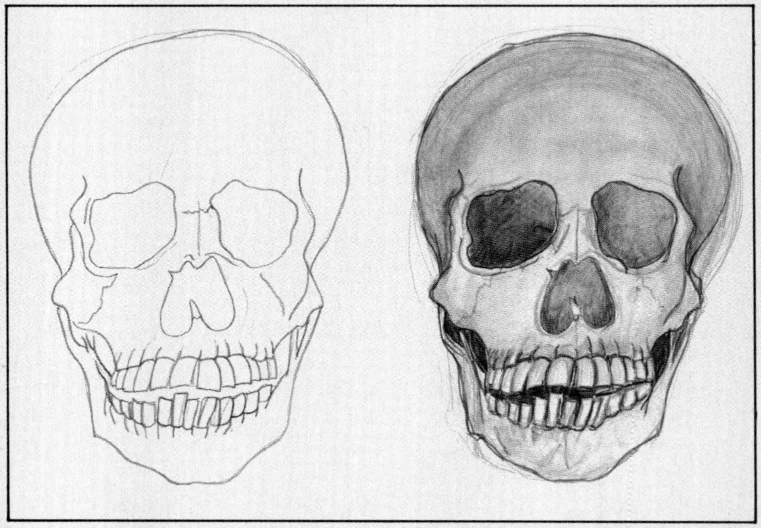

Skull studies
(Pencil drawings by Michael, aged 16)
The line drawing of an object (*far left*) seldom enables you to describe accurately the form, i.e. which shapes are hollow or which are bumpy. By the addition of tone and description of the darker areas, the form becomes more easily understood (*left*).

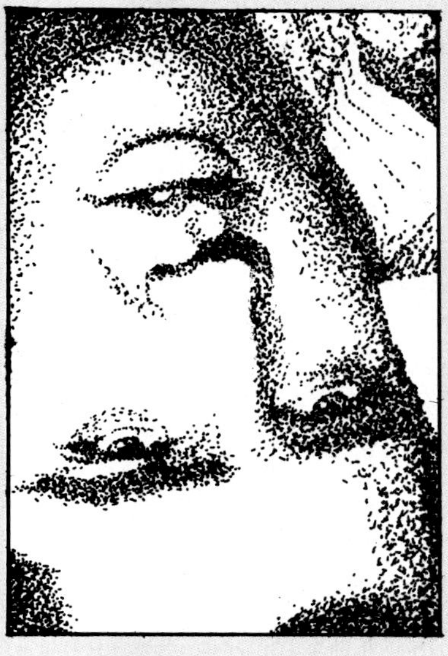

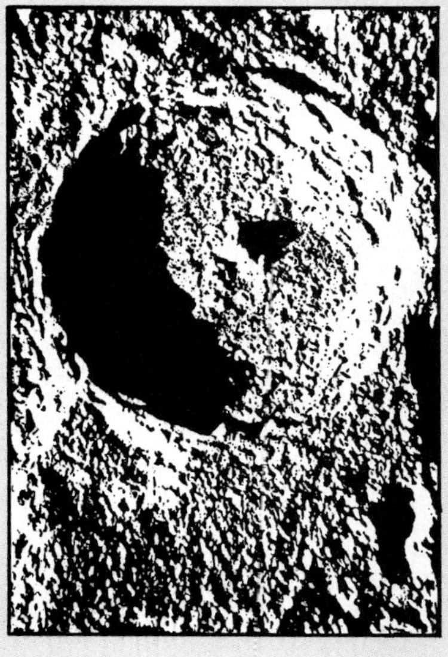

Recognition
(Pen drawing of a head)
Everyone uses the natural existence of light and shade to interpret identities, and if we look at images upside down we find it hard to recognise a face. Turn the picture (*far left*) upright and the person is more easily identifiable.

(Pen drawing of the moon's surface)
The identification is particularly difficult when we observe objects in unusual contexts, where the direction of light is not immediately apparent. The drawing (*left*) could describe a crater or a mountain

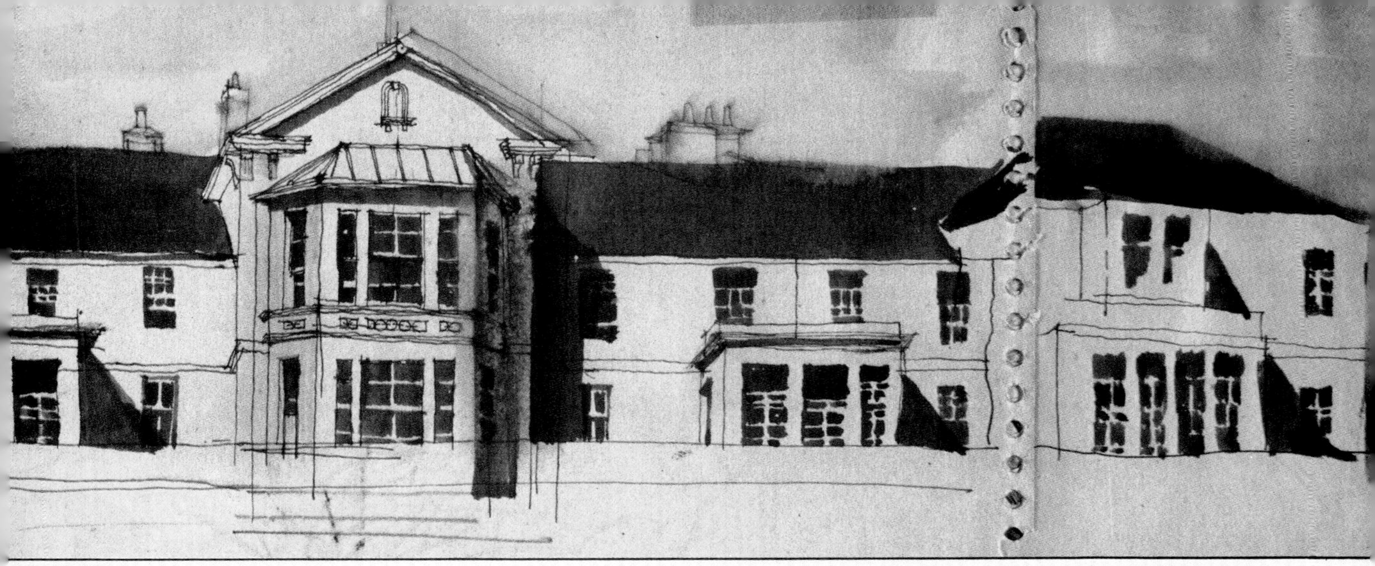

19th century buildings
(Pen and wash drawing)
The buildings (*above*) offer excellent subjects for practising your light and shade technique. Clear directional shadows help describe the parts of the building which protrude or recede.

Drawing exercise
(Six crayon drawings)
The knowledge we already have of how shadows describe surfaces helps us to interpret these surfaces. The drawings (*below*) describe forms illustrated in the sections. Try drawing a simple shape in outline then imagine how the light would cast shadows if it were projecting or receding from the page surface.

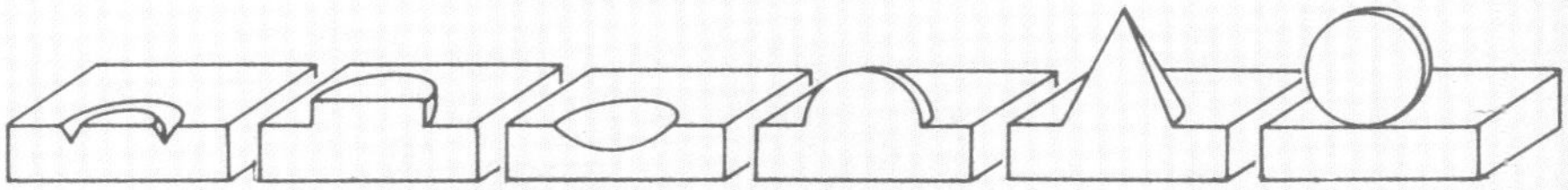

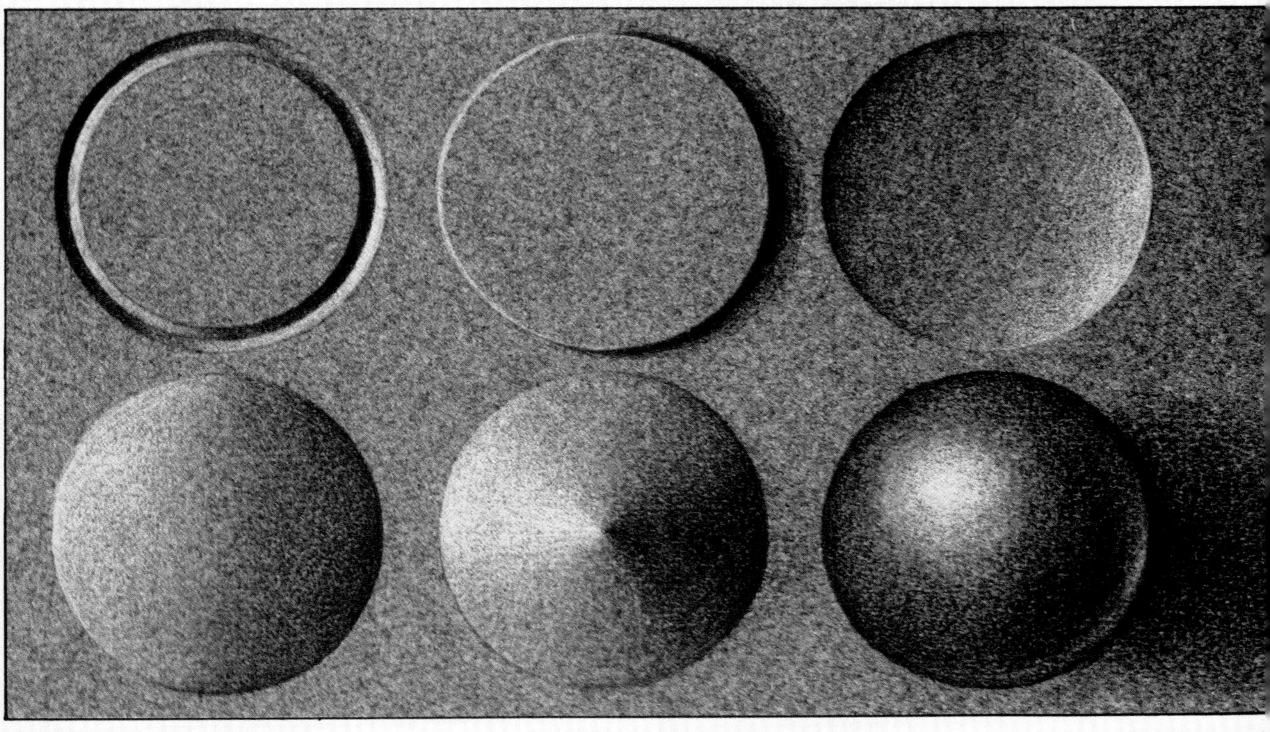

colour

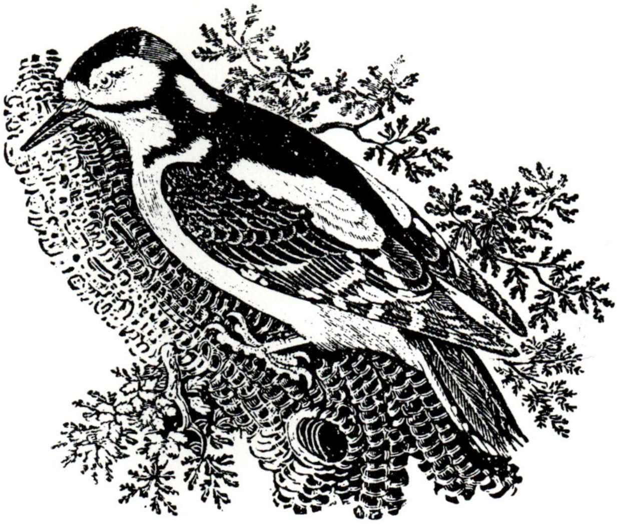

When drawing, if you want to convey a sense and range of colours using only one, you should describe the reflective qualities and tones of each object as compared to the others and to the surroundings. Darker tones, which absorb more light, should appear darker, and bright, reflective colours should be lighter. Practise drawing flowers or coloured fabrics to develop your sense of colour.

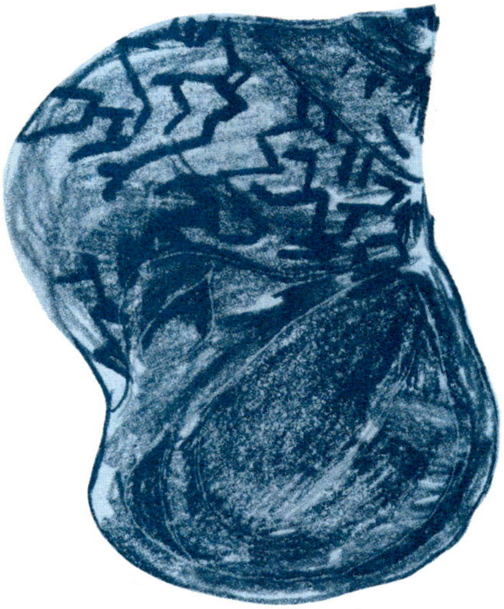

Shell
(Drawing in coloured pencils, by Anne, aged 17, *left*)
Although we show them in one colour only, Anne copied the pinks, browns and blues of the shell – a range of colours you can easily recognise.

Old sports shoe
(Pencil drawing by Michael, aged 15, *below*)
If you are working only in black and white, the contrasting qualities of colour and texture must be carefully reproduced, as in this old shoe.

Pied woodpecker
(Wood engraving by Thomas Bewick, 18th century)
Bewick's knowledge of woodcut tones enabled him to describe with great accuracy the hues and colours of the living world, especially birds (*above*) .

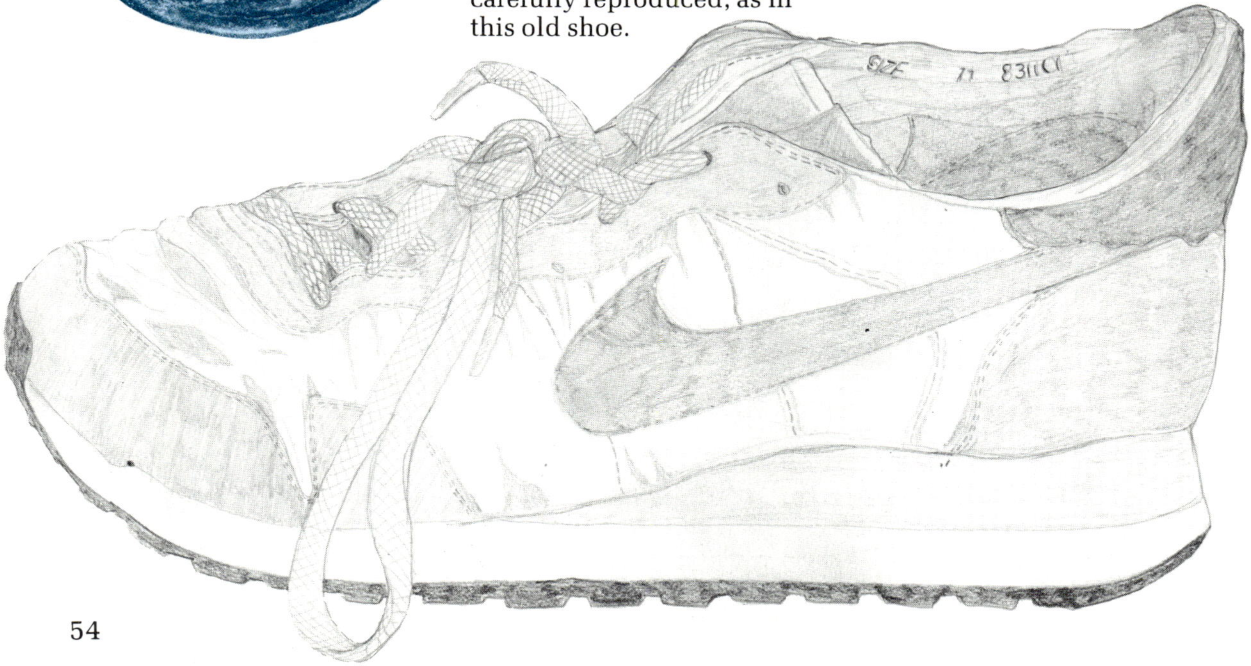

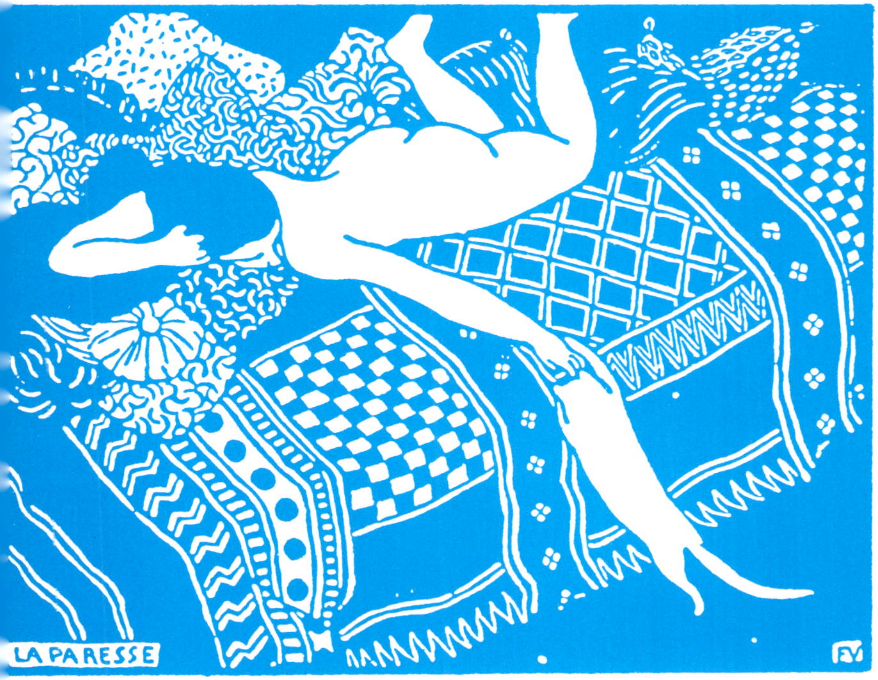

La Paresse
(Woodcut by Felix Ballotton)
The qualities of the bright patterns on the bed rug and cushions are beautifully captured by a careful manipulation of the tones of the drawing (*left*).

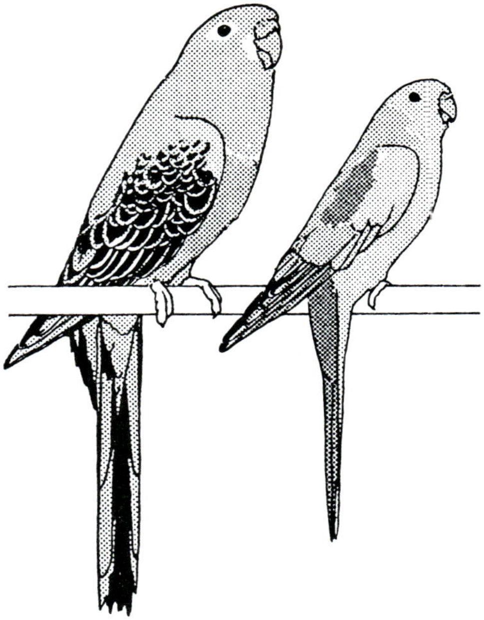

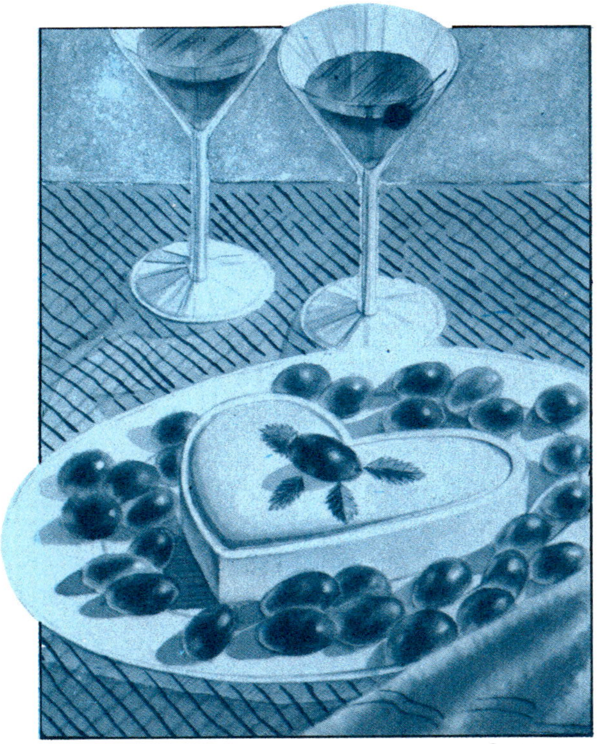

©DIAGRAM

Caged birds
(Line drawing with mechanical tints)
The use of flat mechanical tints over blocks of area can convey a sense of differing colours (see the birds, *above*), but choose tints of medium value so they do not overpower your drawing.

Pudding and grapes
(Pencil drawing and watercolour)
Choose your colours carefully. Try to "lay off" bright against dull objects, the reflective beside the absorbent and the dark against the light (*left*).

texture

If we look carefully, we can see that the surfaces of the objects around us exhibit a wide variety of textures. These textures and the contrasts between them – rough/smooth, glossy/dull, fine/coarse – help us to describe the characteristics and form of the world around us.

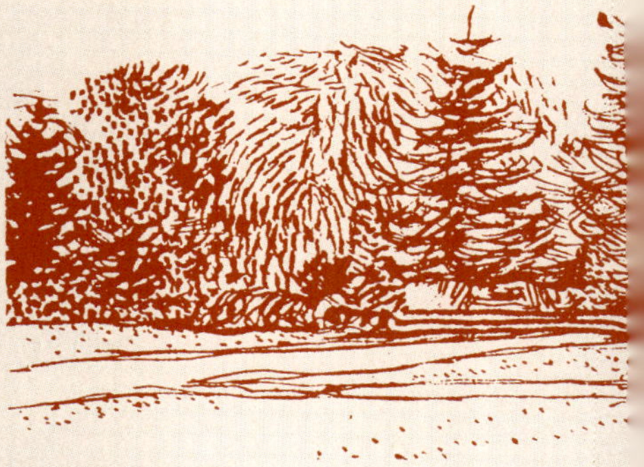

Trees in the park
(Pen drawing, actual size)
Here the contrasts in texture show us the individual trees of different species in this mixed woodland. This effect is easily achieved by varying the pen marks, as shown in the enlarged detail (*right*).

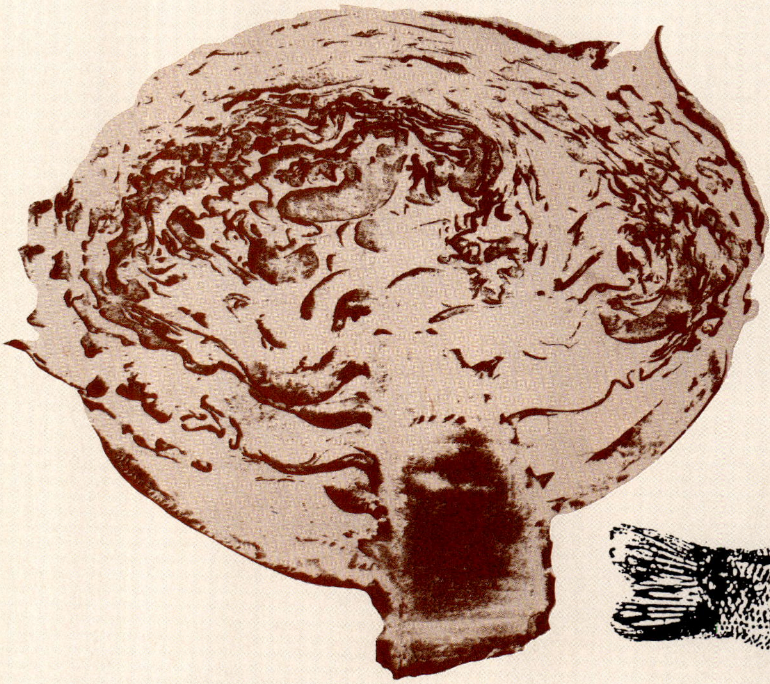

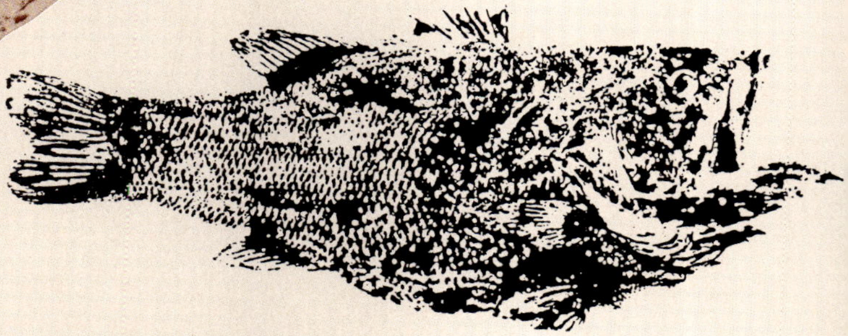

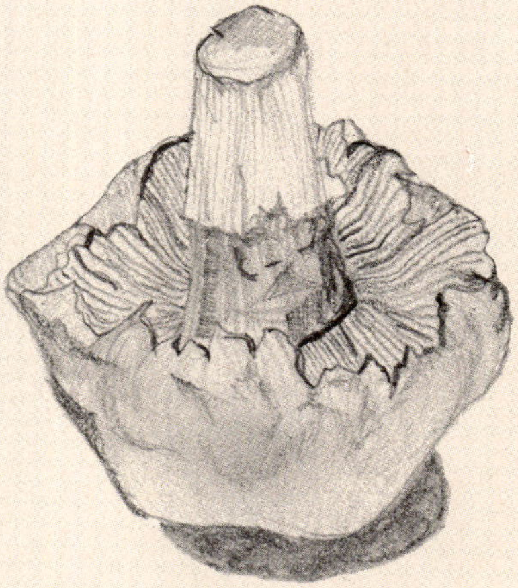

Mushroom
(Pencil drawing by 16 year old girl, shown actual size)
The artist has conveyed the texture and quality of the skin on the mushroom's cap by smudging the pencil lines with a finger.

Cabbage and fish
The pictures of the cabbage (*above left*) and the fish (*above*) are not drawings, but prints made directly from the objects themselves. Both show their texture very clearly. Other objects with a characteristic texture could be used to make prints in the same way.

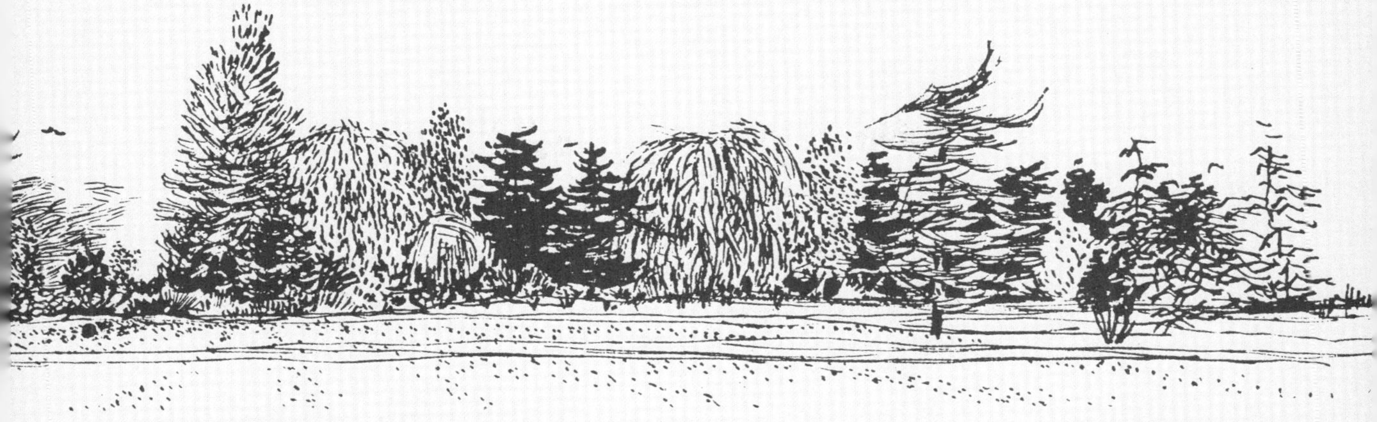

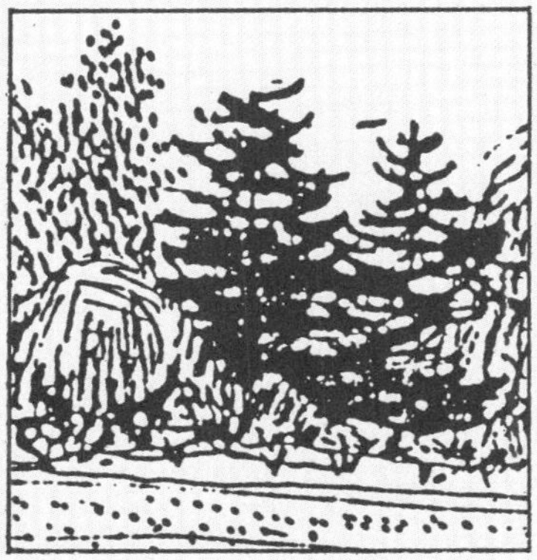

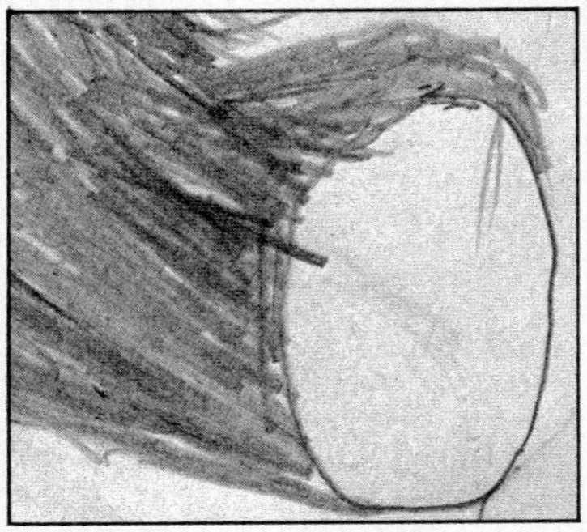

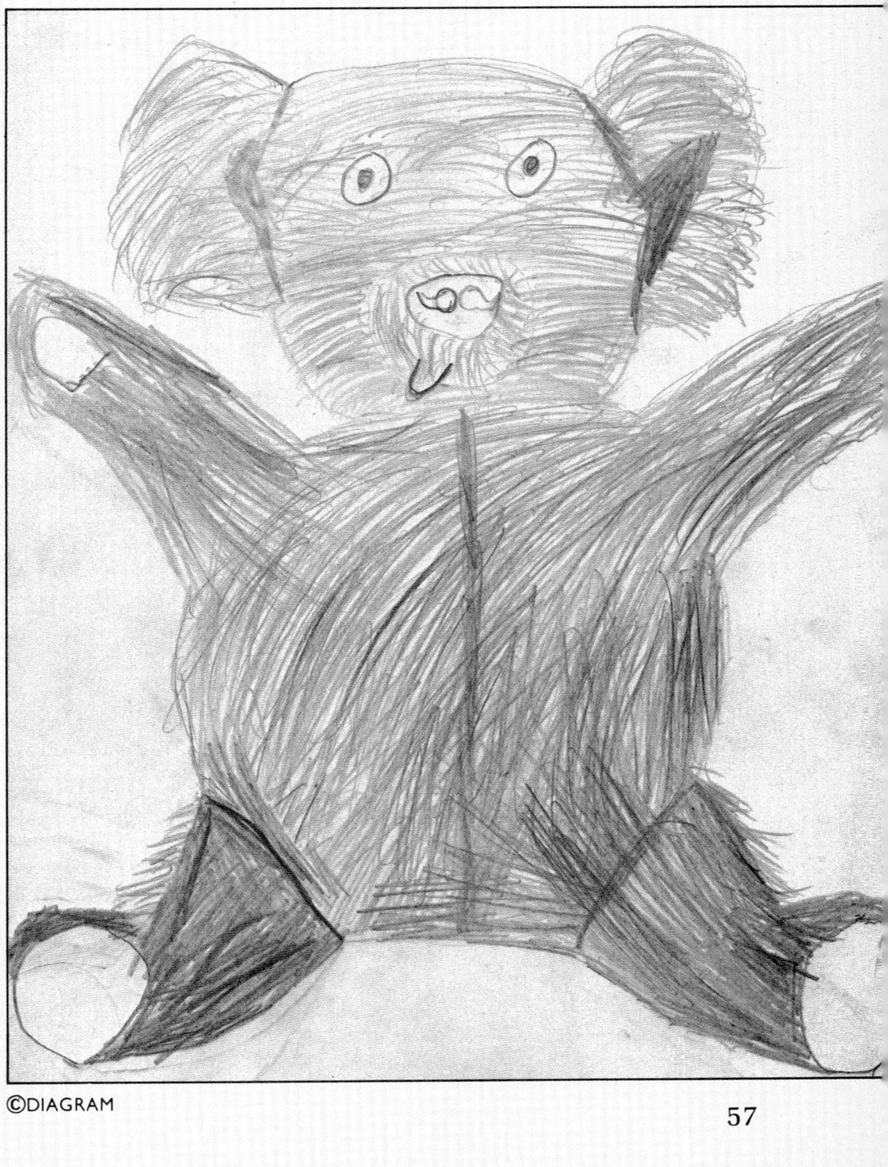

Teddy bear
(Pencil drawing by Paul, aged 10, shown reduced in size (*right*) with detail (*above*) shown actual size) The smooth surfaces of the paws, the soft furry fabric of the body, and the reflective glass of the eyes are all clearly visible in this drawing.

sketching

Keeping a sketchbook is one of life's most enjoyable activities. Think of it as talking to yourself about your view of the world and be totally subjective. Draw whatever detail, whatever aspect, whatever qualities you see as you stand in front of the subject. Look for what interests you and draw it. Forget about other people: don't think about what they may think of your sketches, or let the thought of them looking over your shoulder deter you from sketching exactly what you want to record. Your sketchbook is the source for your future pictures and (like a bank account) you can only take out of it what you put in. Every sketch is an individual record, so note down the date, the quality of the sky, the weather, how you feel, or any other details that will help you recreate the picture in later years. Jot down notes about colours, surfaces, and so on. Don't attempt to produce a finished piece of work or a complete statement: that stage will come later when you produce your final picture.

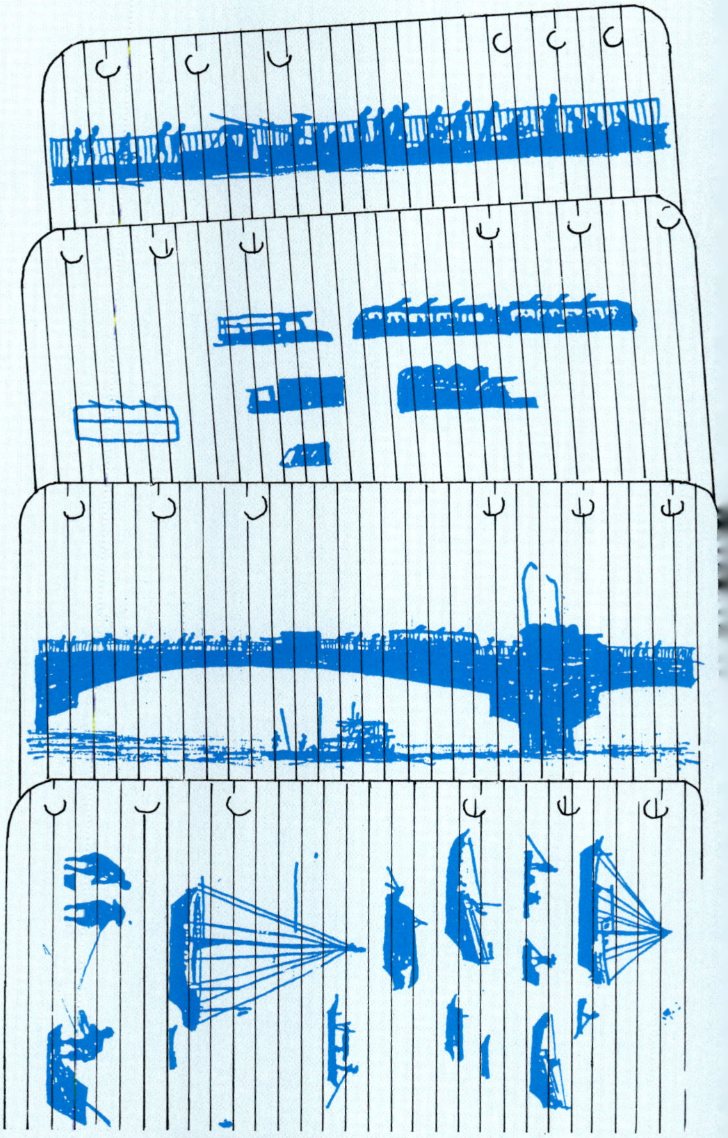

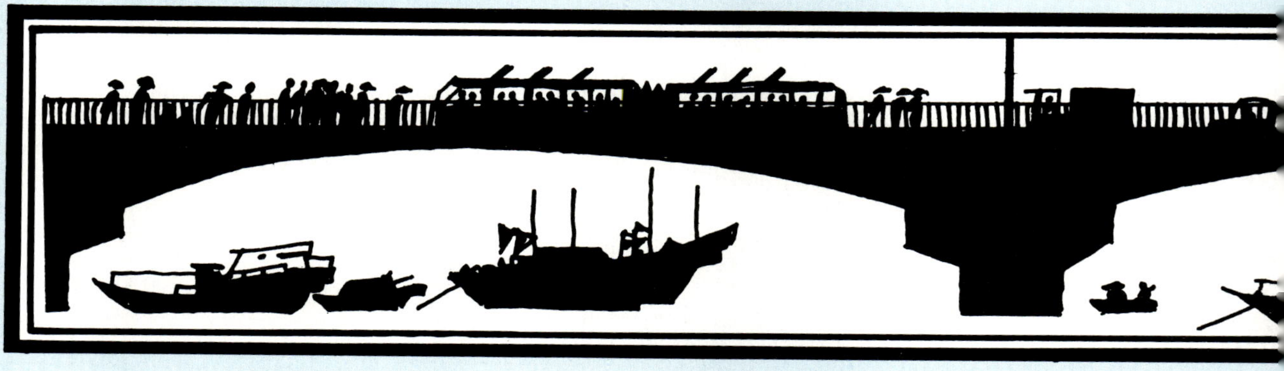

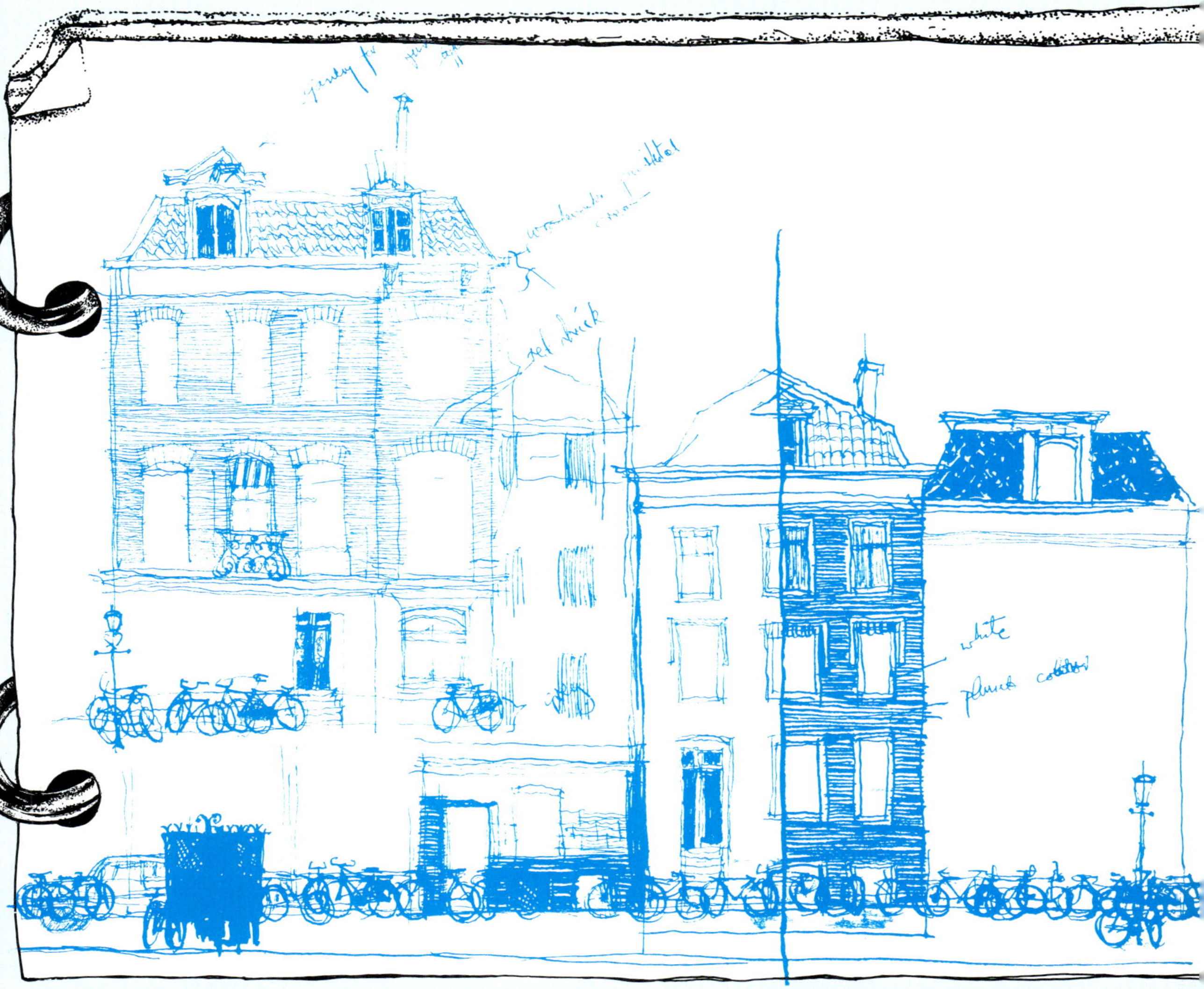

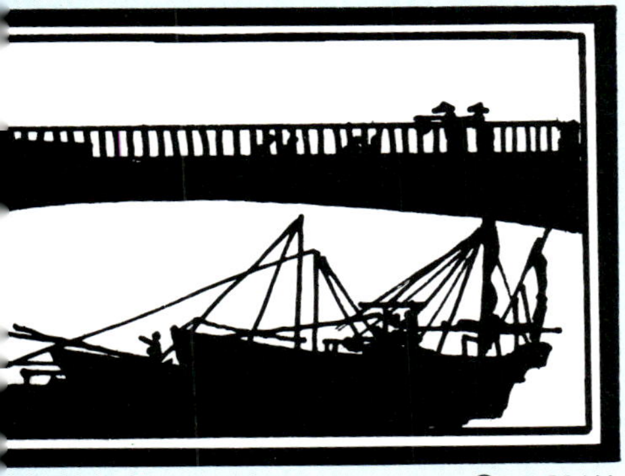

Bridge over a river, China (Pen drawing *left*, created from pen sketches, *above left*)
The finished drawing is based on dozens of separate sketches of the people and vehicles crossing over the bridge and of the boats passing underneath it. The sketches are the vocabulary from which the finished statement of the picture is assembled.

Houses, Singel Canal, Amsterdam (Pen sketch, *above*)
No attempt has been made to produce a finished picture. Only parts of the roofs, walls, and windows have been drawn, but there is enough information for the whole to be recreated. Notes of colours and textures have been added as memory aids.

sketching

Sketching people presents one particular problem – they move. Unless you are deliberately sketching people in action, try to pick subjects who are in fairly static poses – lying down, sitting down, waiting for something or someone – or who are preoccupied with another activity – reading, for example, or watching television. They are then likely to remain in the same position for long enough for you to capture their pose. When you sketch action figures, concentrate on the general shapes and the basic movements of the forms, and forget the detail. Each sketch should capture the moment's unique gesture or movement. These incomplete sketches will all contribute to your total view of how people place and move their bodies.

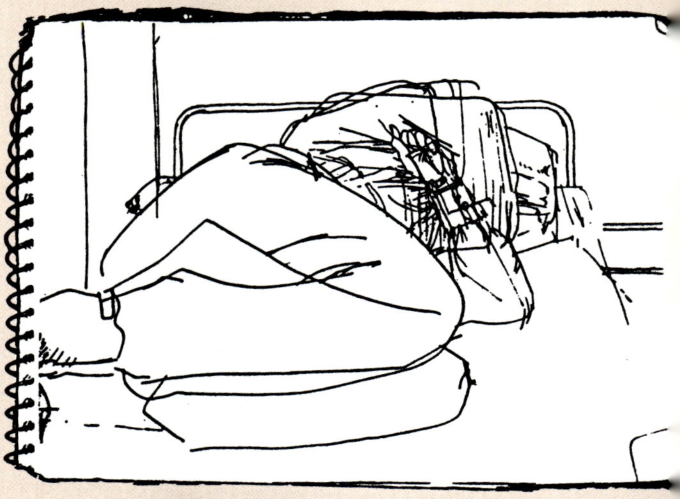

Sleeping soldier, Germany
(Pen sketch)
A sleeping person is a perfect subject for sketching. Your subject will both stay still and ignore you, so you have the chance to move around until you find the most interesting view.

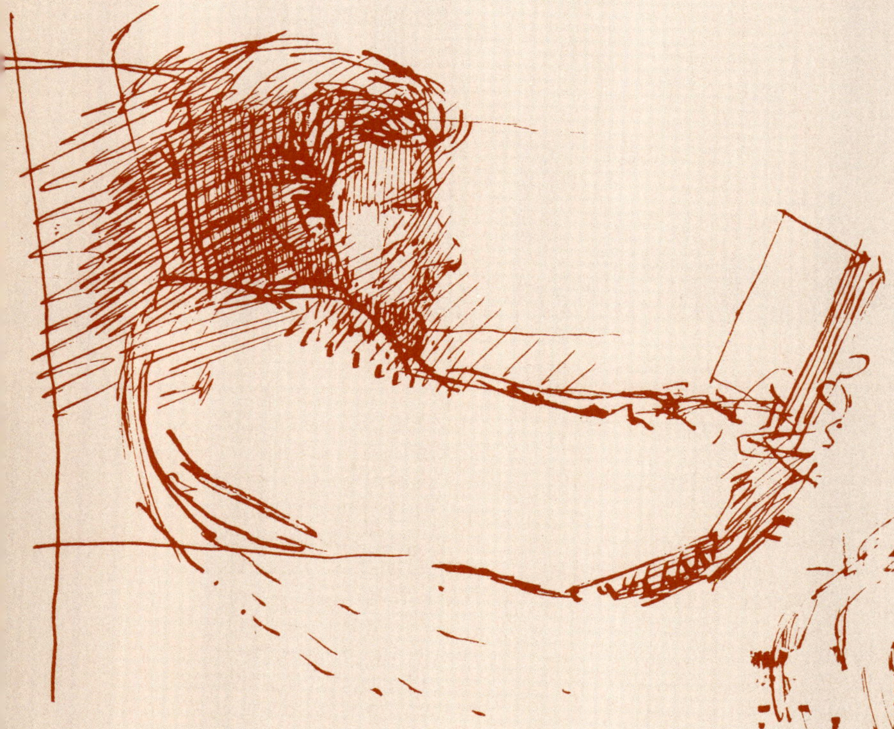

A reader
(Pen sketch)
It is always preferable to start a sketch knowing that the subject will not move away or change position. Suggest to your friends that you sketch them while they are occupied with some other activity, such as reading, sunbathing or ironing.

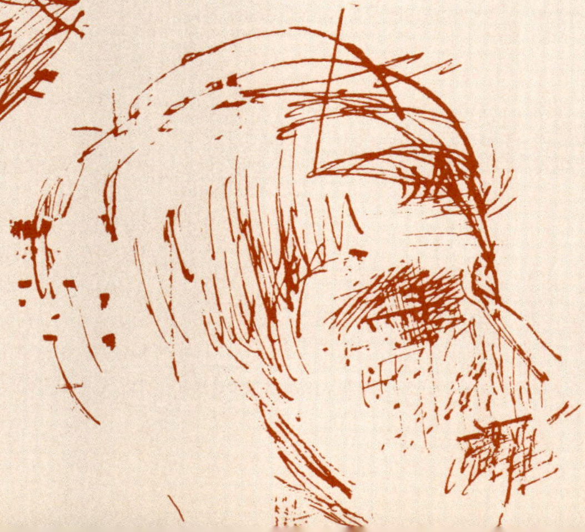

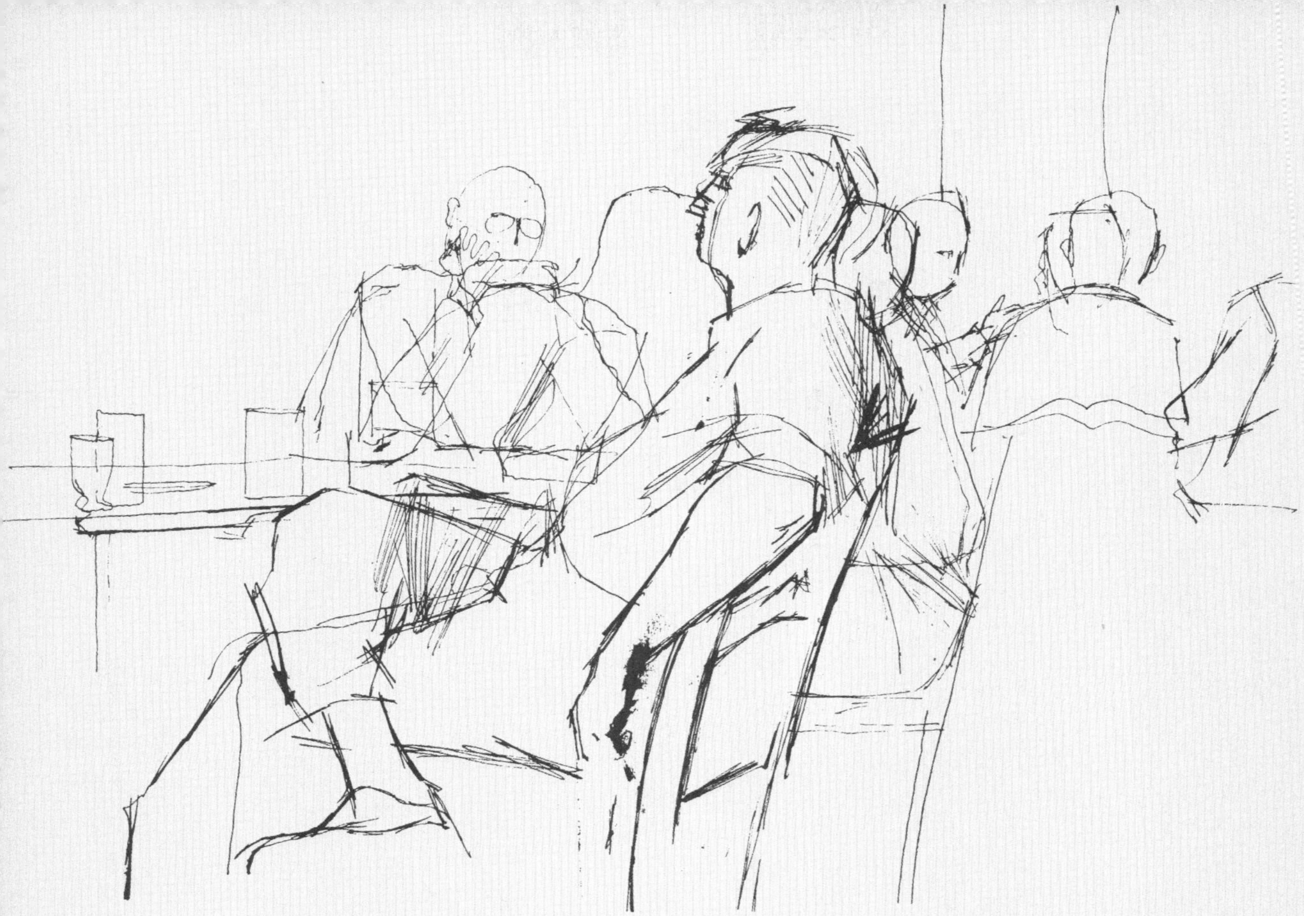

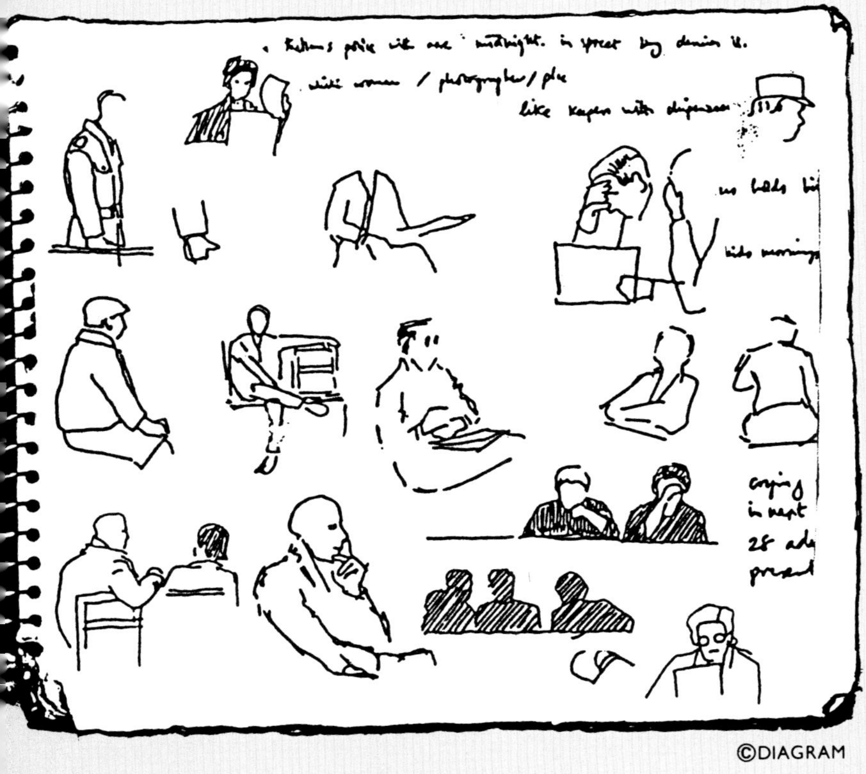

Greek café
(Pen sketch)
Groups of people eating and talking together offer a good opportunity to capture strong shapes and forms. You will probably have the chance to record interesting details, such as how an arm hangs from a chair.

Notes at a trial
(Pen sketches)
Court rooms, waiting rooms, libraries and churches are all good places to study people. If the person you are sketching moves away or changes position, switch your attention to another subject. Put together, your studies will help you recreate the characters of the figures.

drawing from memory

I once made the mistake of asking a child what she was drawing. She replied, "I don't know yet as I haven't finished." Drawing from imagination or memory can be very exciting. An exacting test of your observational powers, it will make you look around properly when you are not drawing. You will gradually build up a memory bank of useful images. Try drawing the view from your window with the curtains closed. Draw the objects in your bedroom when you are in the living room. Try drawing events in a novel which stimulated your imagination. Attempt to remember in memory sketches places you have visited recently or know well. At all times enjoy your drawing. **Do not concern yourself with failure.** The more you practise recalling images the more observant you become when you are out sketching from life.

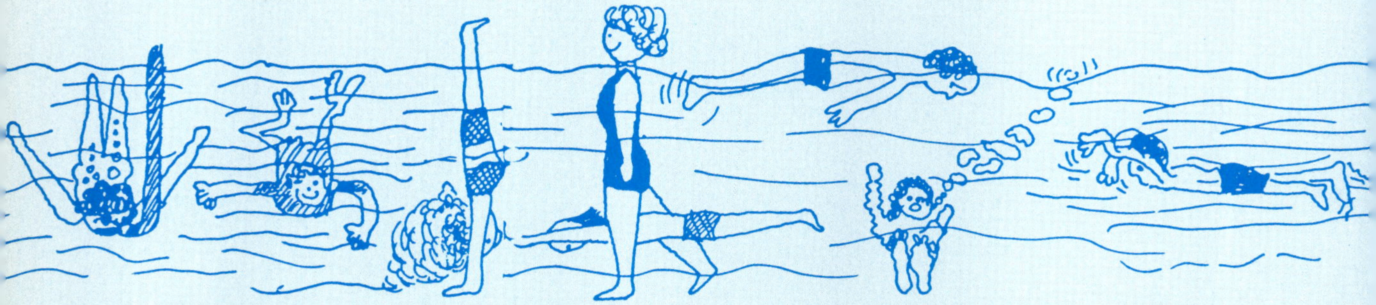

Public baths
(Pen and ink drawing by Anne, aged 10, *above*)
Drawing people from recollection you often catch unusual and memorable poses.

Practise drawing
Take any chance you can to sketch from memory and draw whatever pictures your mind throws up, trying to record the details accurately. As a suggestion, select from the following list:

Cat	Policeman	Telephone
Dog	Nurse	Violin
Horse	Skier	Typewriter
Fish	Soldier	Motorbike
Elephant	Old man	Hairdryer
Bear	Viking	Pushchair
Beetle	Red Indian	Bus

Railway station
(Pen and ink drawing by Bruce, aged 14)
Memory exaggerates detail: the individual items in the drawing (*right*) are out of proportion.

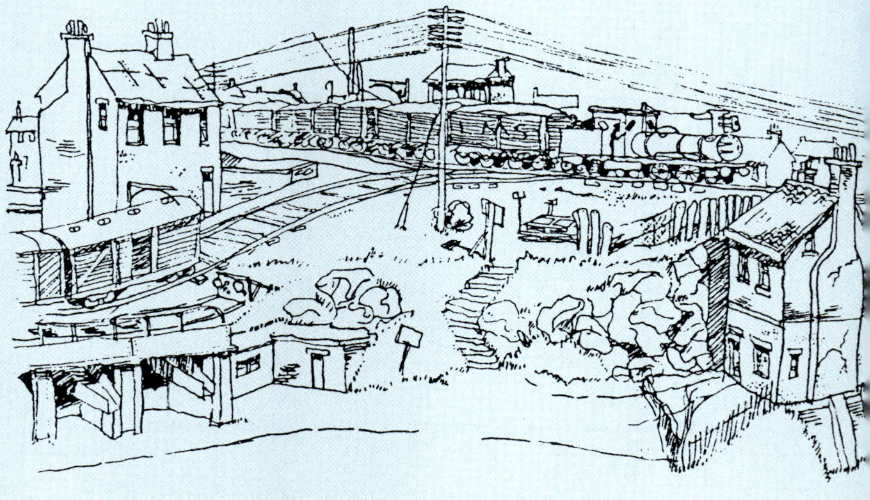

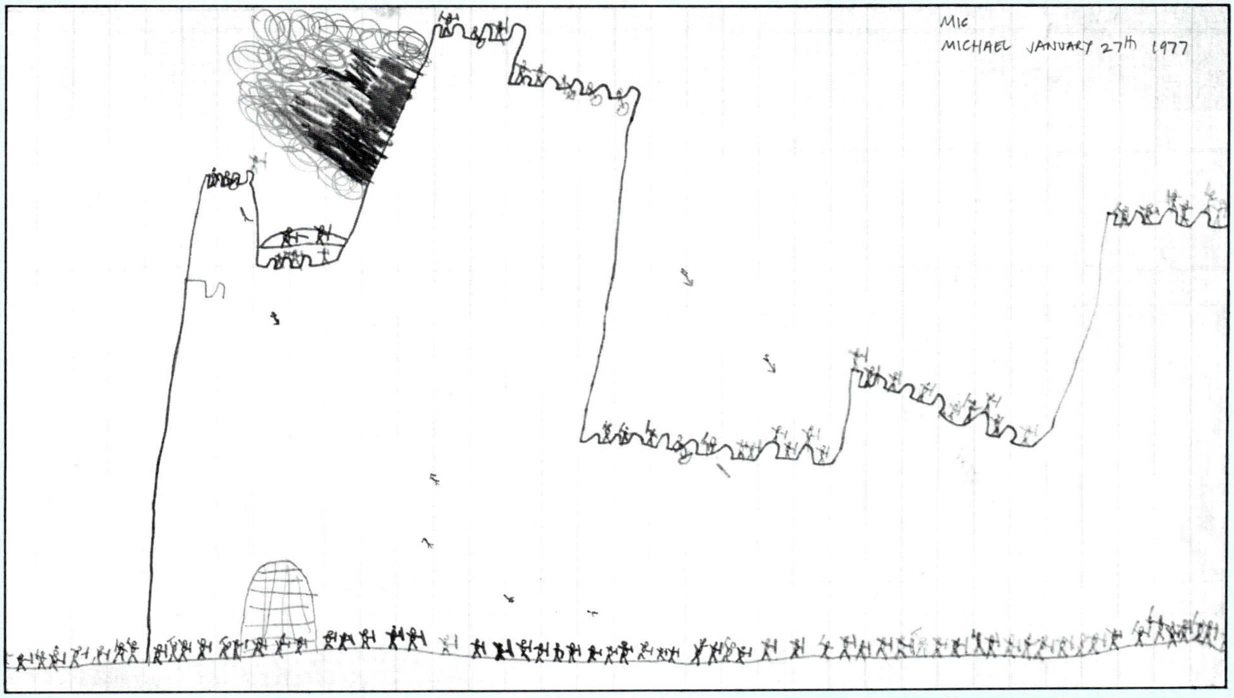

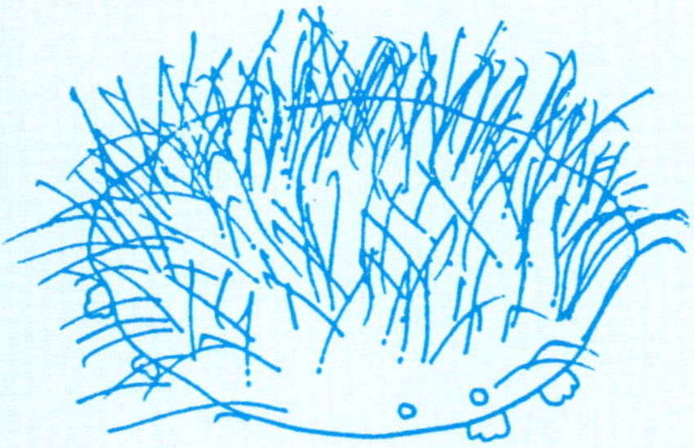

Nervous hedgehog
(Pencil drawing by Paul, aged 5, *left*).
Paul remembered the main feature of the creature, its prickliness. A hedgehog's eyes are not clearly visible but Paul included them because he must have felt they would help to portray the hedgehog's fear as he tried to pick it up

Besieged castle
(Pencil drawing, by Michael, aged 8)
Although the scale of the figures to the castle (*above*) is incorrect, and the soldiers' simplicity tends to be repetitive, the sense of activity and excitement is accurately depicted. Try drawing a scene from a film or an incident in a book.

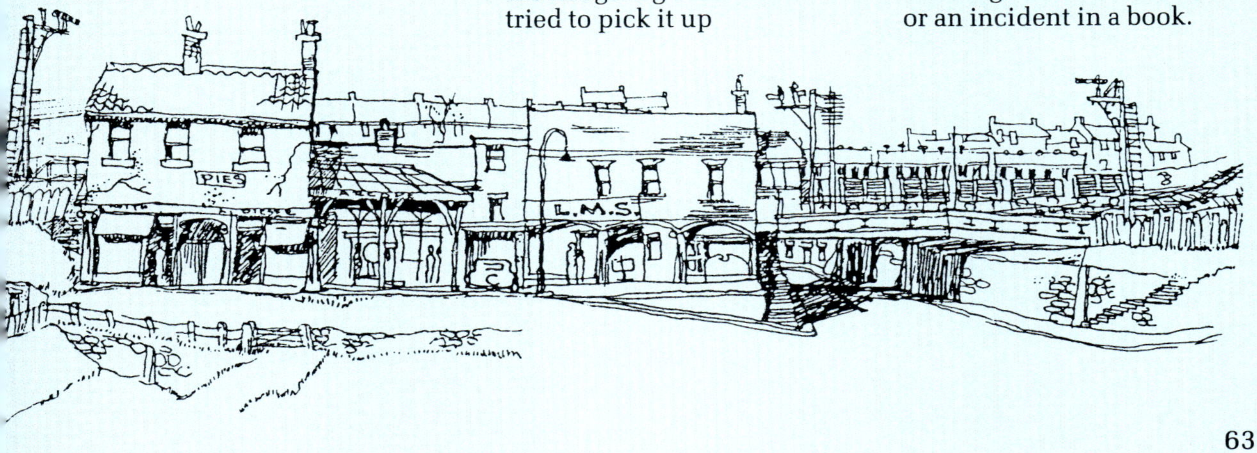

working from photographs

Artists have always used pictorial sources in their pictures for information. Before photographs, many used book illustrations or other artists' paintings which they copied and adapted. A drawing is not less valuable because its source was other than observed reality. You can achieve excellent results as a beginner from copying photographs because almost every drawing you produce increases your confidence and your knowledge of reality. When copying from photographs it is important that you adapt what you see. Direct, faithful copying will never produce a satisfactory drawing; modifying the original will improve your personal aptitudes.

Remember you are not a human camera – you are a creative, intelligent and subjective human being.

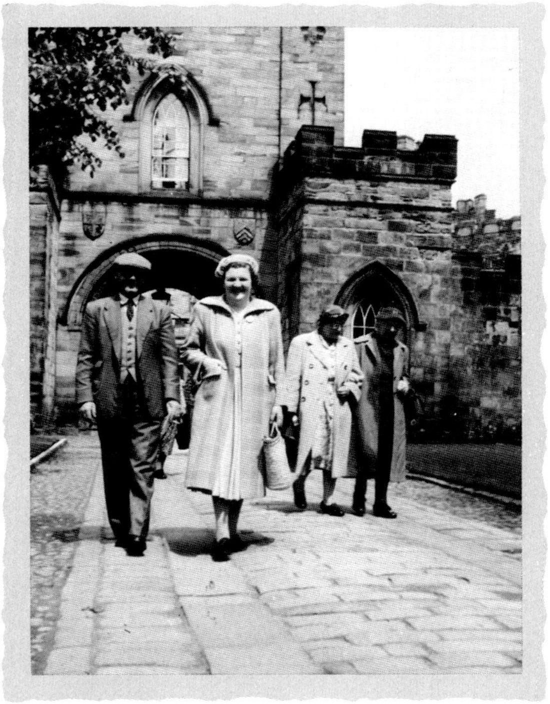

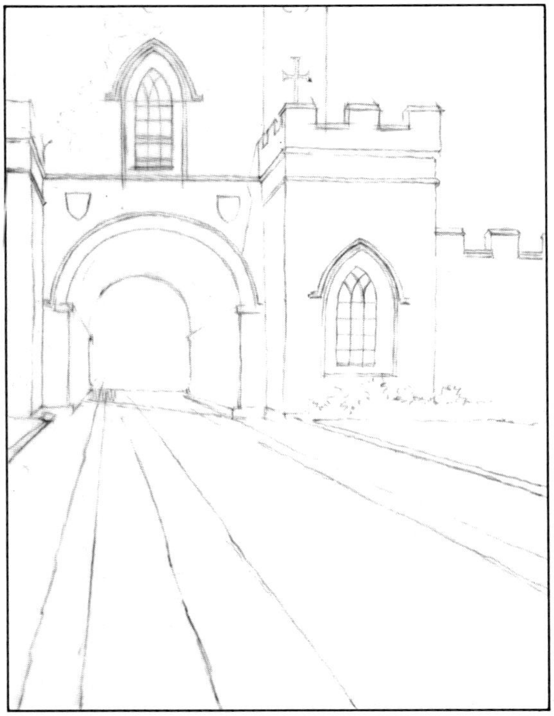

Producing a drawing

1 The photograph (*above*) provides a very good basis for a drawing; it is sharp and the lighting is excellent. But the planned main focus, the foreground figures, is poorly positioned against the background and the other couple spoil the composition.

2 Trace the setting.

3 Trace the figures required.

4 Enlarge the figures.

5 Reposition the figures.

6 Carefully render the detail so you produce a harmonious final drawing.

If you compare the photograph to the drawing you will notice:

a The photograph has an overall grey tone; the drawing is made up of tiny grey lines on a white background.

b The repositioned figures are now the real focus in the drawing; they are framed and joined by the arch.

c The drawing seems to contain more information; it broadens and directs you to detail – for example, see the shields on each side of the arch.

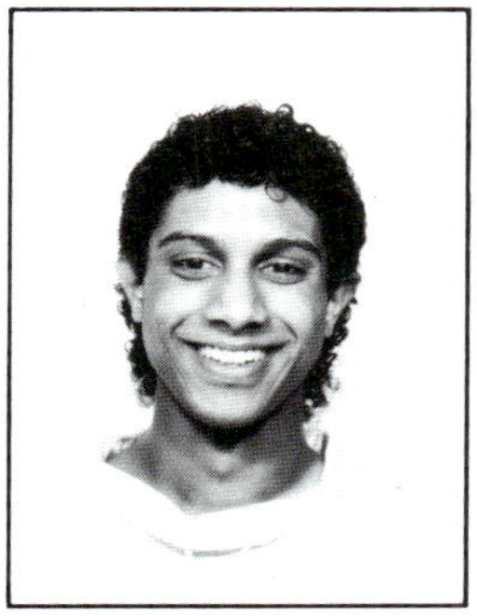

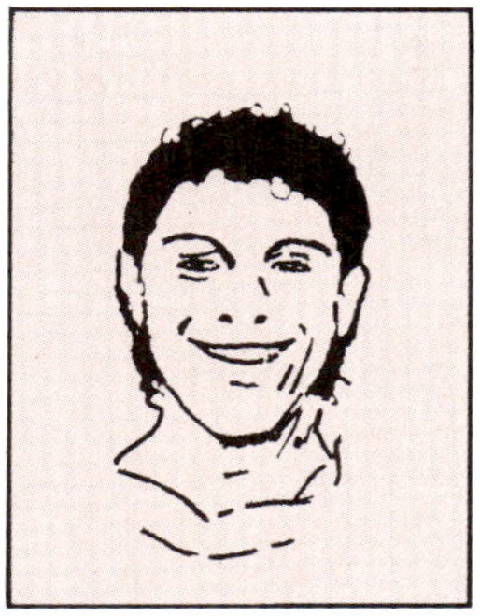

Simple conversions
(Pentel drawing by Steve, aged 16)
Using a passport photograph, Steve simply traced off the dark areas (*left*). This technique produces clean, effective results, and you can adapt the details from an original photograph many times.

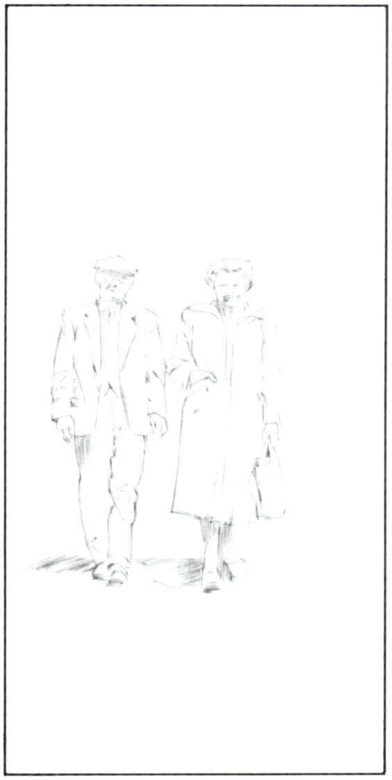

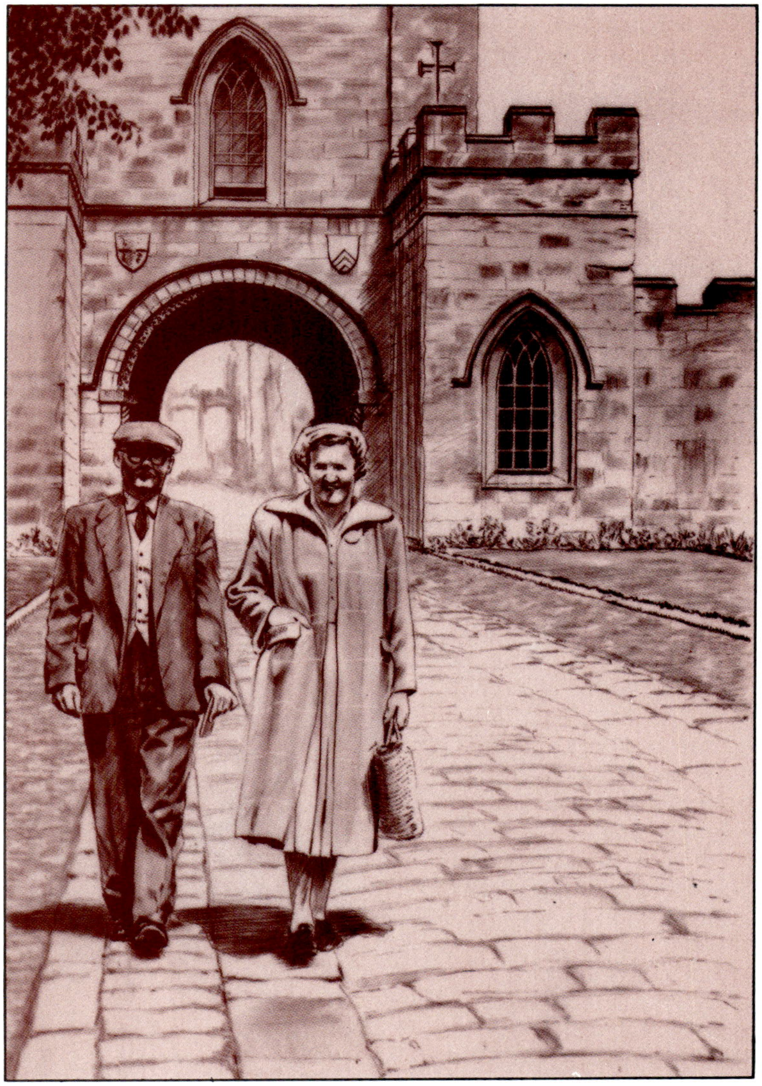

Points to remember
When copying from photographs don't exactly duplicate the tones of the image – this is better achieved by having the photograph rephotographed. A drawing of a photograph is not a copy of it. You have the opportunity to improve the composition, lighting, surfaces and content.

working from photographs

Improving reality
Old photographs may be damaged, or of poor quality; the selection of information may be accidental, resulting in a poor composition. By drawing and adapting you can improve on the original. The photograph (*right*) has a number of defects:
1 A severe crack across the face of one of the figures.
2 A faded background.
3 Cropped-off legs.
4 Merging tones rendering detail hard to read.

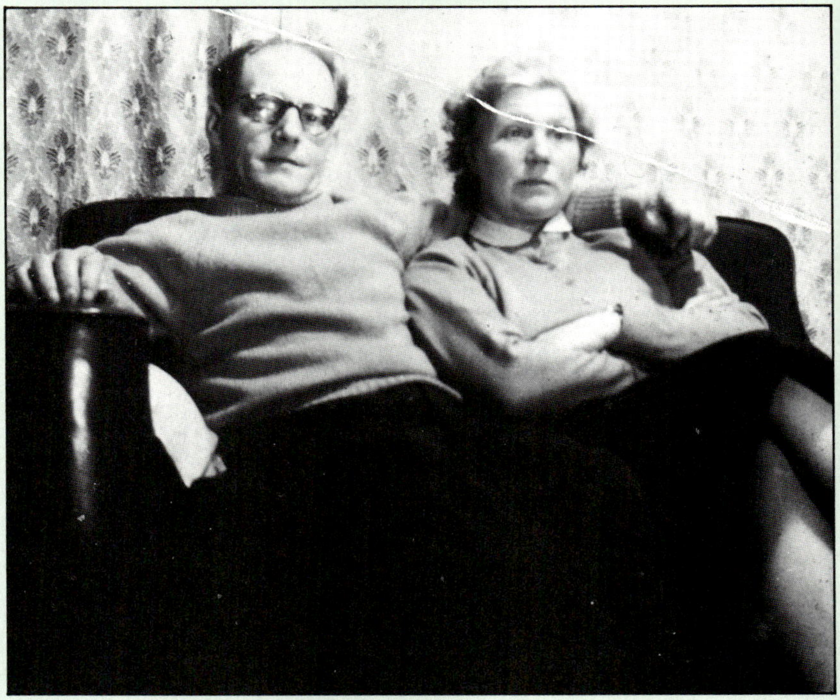

Parents when young
(Pencil drawing from an old photograph)
The photograph (*above*) was used as the basis for the drawing (*right*). First the photograph was traced onto paper larger than it was. Then the couple's legs were carefully constructed and extended beyond the original photograph area. Next the lighting on the figures was copied and adjusted to clarify the areas where the darkness obscured detail, and the textures of the curtain and pullover were stated more clearly where they were faded.
Finally, a thin line was added as a frame to a composition which lacked the negative features of the original photograph.

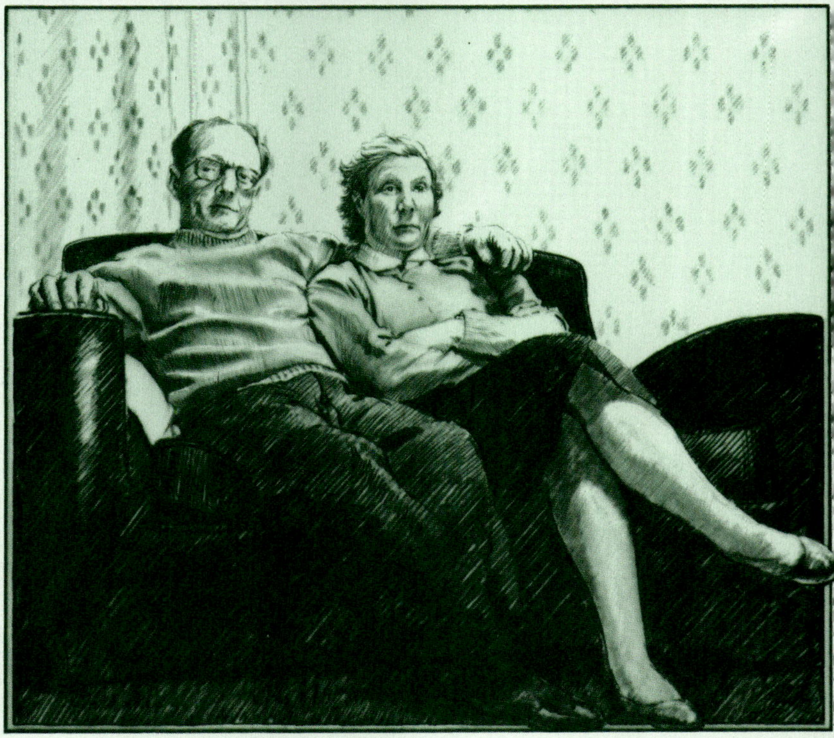

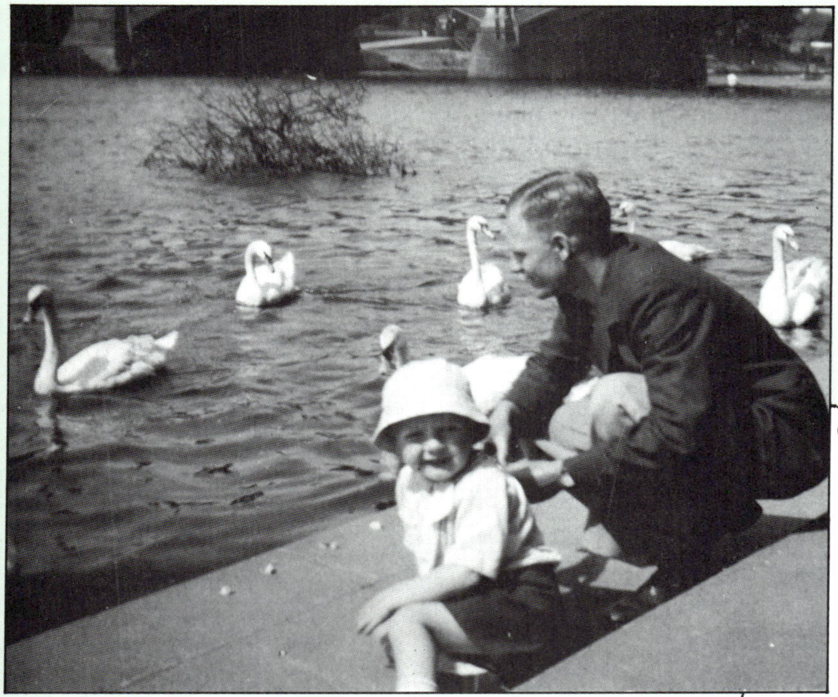

Composing from photographs
Photographs can be a useful starting point for an idea, and a source of information when you are composing a picture. But you can draw additional detail and extend the area of the image to include other features.

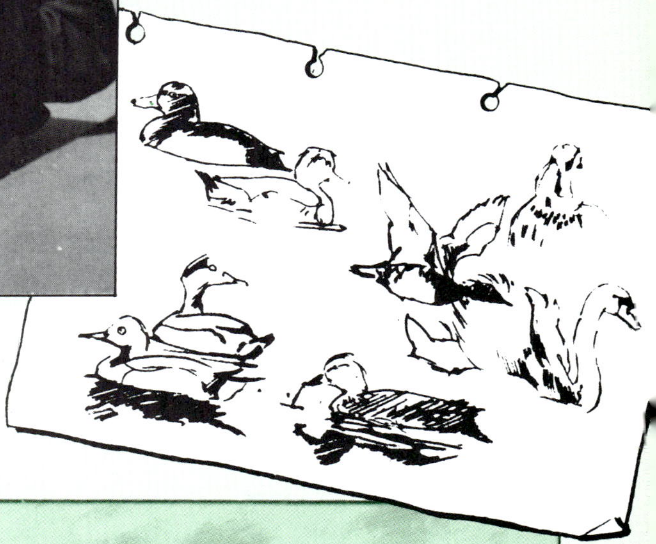

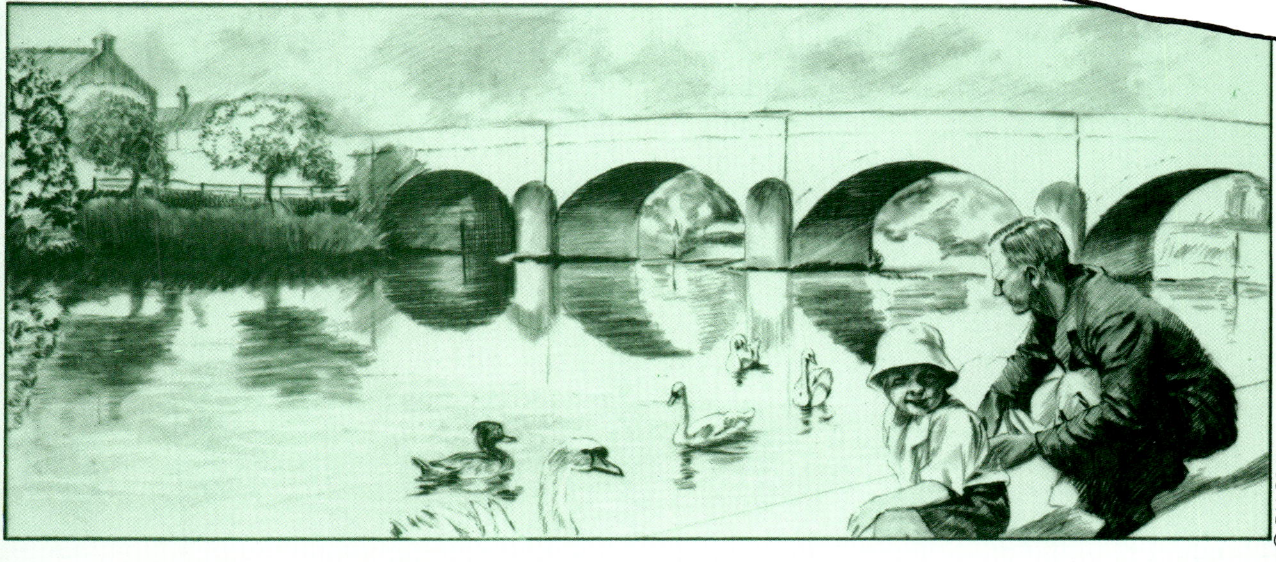

working from photographs

Special effects
(Pen drawing by Steve, aged 18)
Very attractive results can be achieved by simply putting tracing paper over a photograph and inking in all the dark areas. When Steve produced this drawing he adjusted for form, volume and space. He either missed out grey areas, or if they seemed to be dark, he filled them in as black. Although it may appear sometimes to be confusing, this type of drawing is ideal for simple reproductive methods so can be used for local magazines or your own cards.

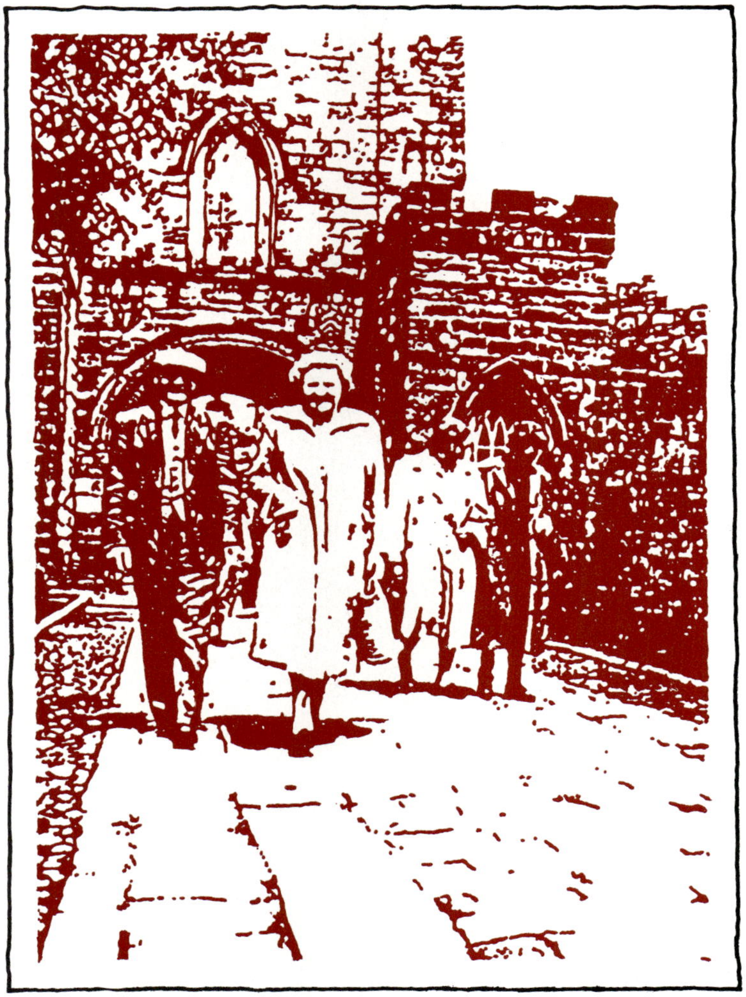

Embellishing
Racing cyclists
(Pen and ink drawing by Joe, aged 19)
It would require great skill and knowledge to draw motor cyclists in detail. The drawing (*below*) was copied over a photograph and lines and scratches added to create the effect of speed.

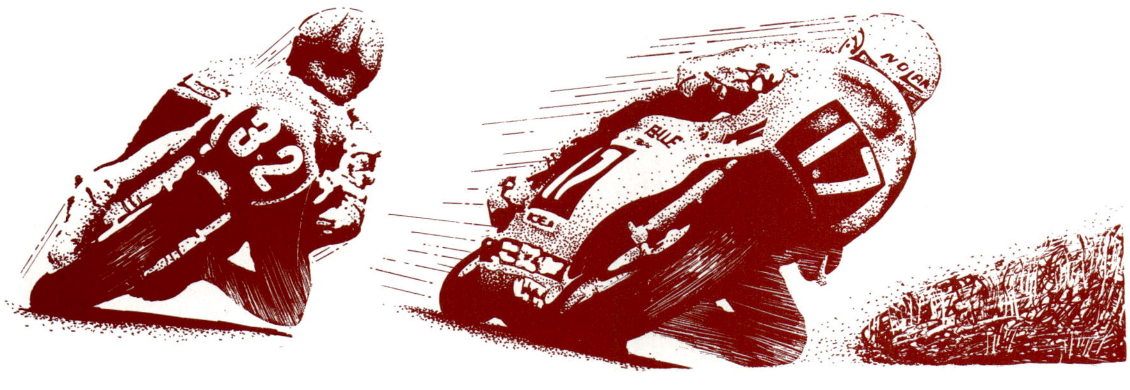

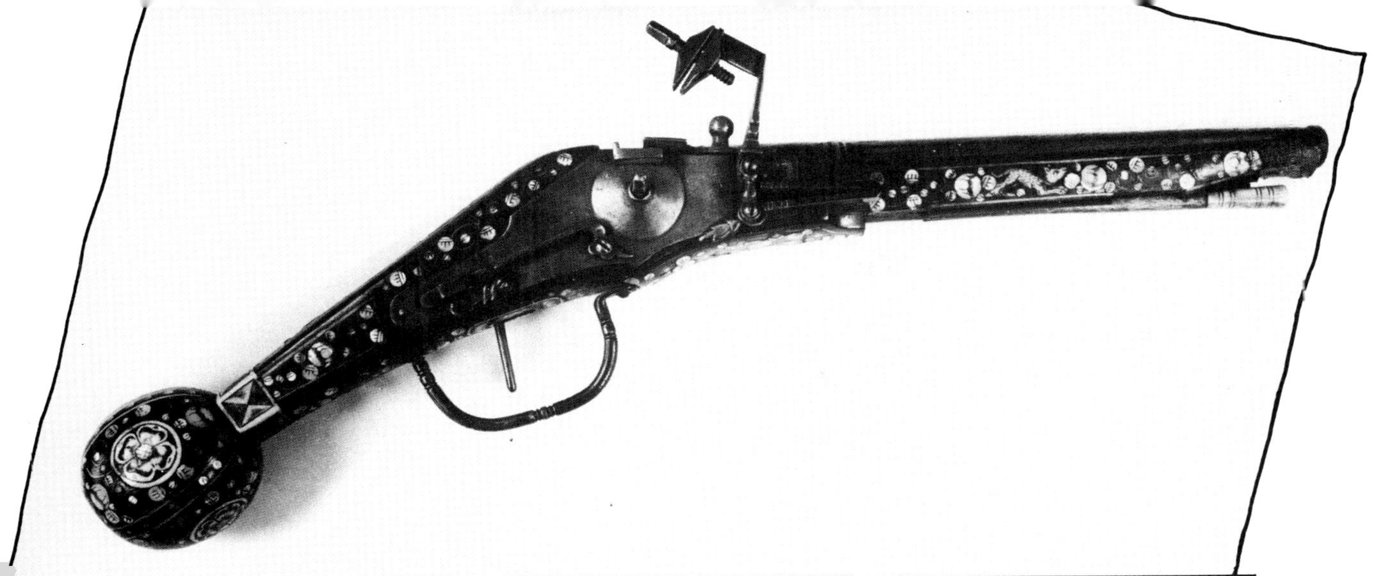

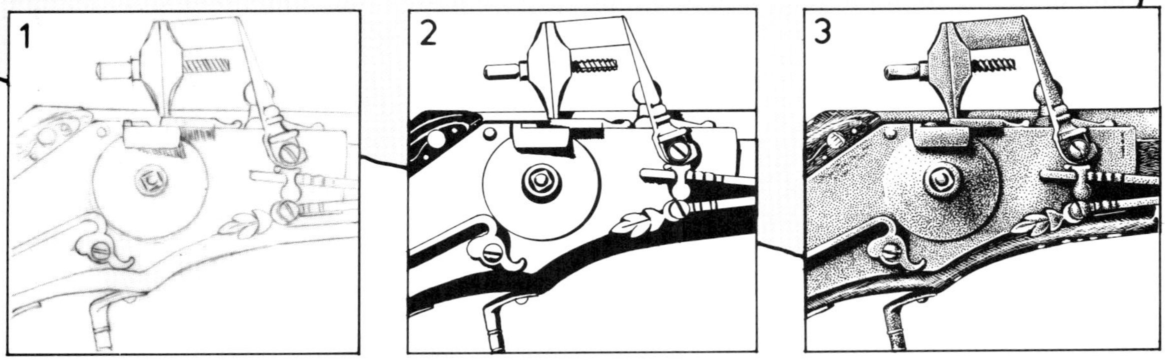

Professional illustration
This photograph of a 16th century pistol (*top*) is not sharp. The edges of forms are soft, the lighting does not help to clarify the structure and the print quality makes colour and texture confusing. A professional illustrator does not copy a photograph; he uses one like this for reference.
1 Working on smooth-surface, clear plastic, he first traces the photograph using a soft but sharp pencil. He often lifts the plastic covering to examine the photograph closely to check how the parts are made.
2 Removing the covering, he then paints on it the major dark areas.

3 Finally, he applies thousands of tiny pen dots, building up carefully the tonal values. The sequence (*above*) is shown in the original size, but usually such an illustration is reduced in reproduction (*below*) so as to enhance its detail.
4 An enlargement of one area revealing the dot technique.

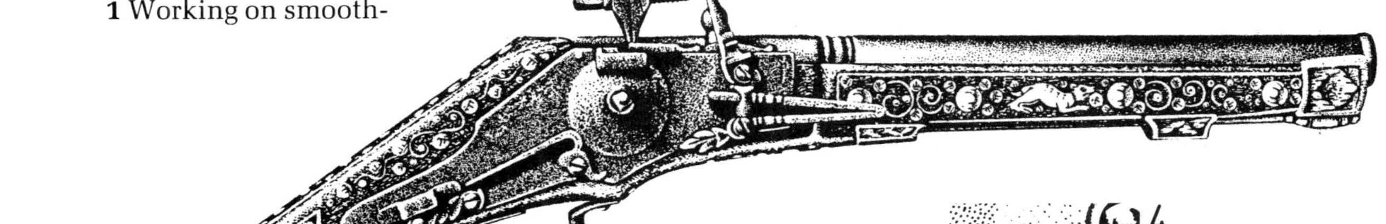

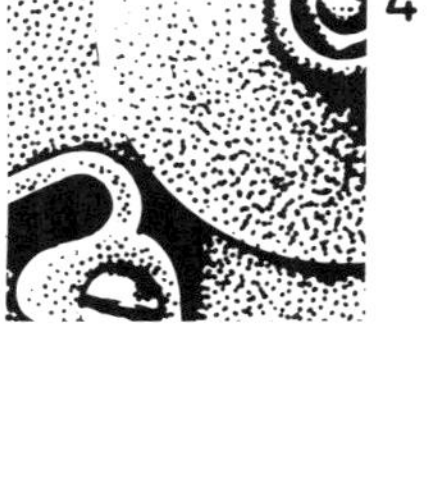

techniques

Whatever you draw the implements and surfaces will influence the results, and your style will suffer if you use uncongenial materials. There is a great variety of equipment, from the simple pencil on white paper to wax crayons overlaid with watercolour. But your drawing does not depend on your tools, only on the care and experience you put into it. Never let the equipment dictate your style. Familiarise yourself with simple tools and then explore the possibilities with new types. You are master of your drawing; make your equipment serve your needs.

Pencil drawing
Railway engine sheds
The soft lead pencil drawing on cream paper (*right*) offers ideal media for conveying the soft light and smokey atmosphere.

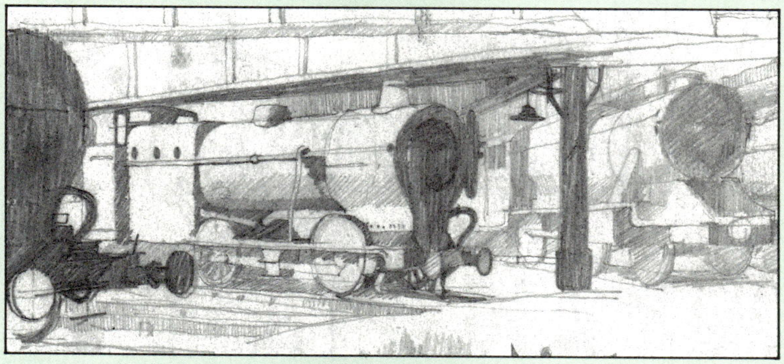

Pen and ink
Düsseldorf in the rain
The immediacy of working out of doors is apparent in the drawing of a rainy day (*right*), rendered by the variable thickness of a pen nib on smooth, fine paper. The odd drop of rain on the page has added to the effect.

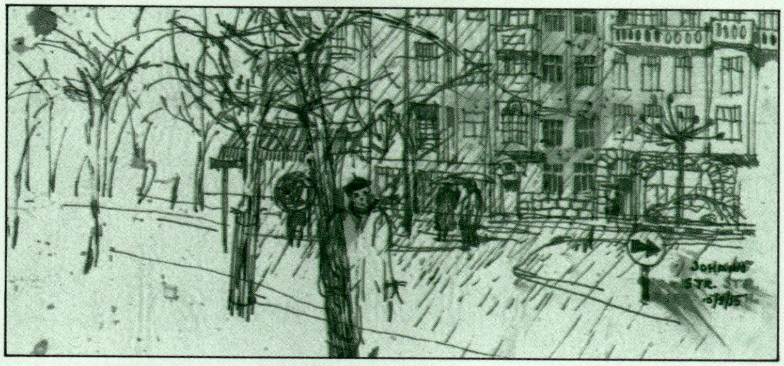

Pen and ink on plastic
Professional illustration of a saxophone
This pure but sterile description of a saxophone (*right*) has been achieved by accurate copying, using photographic references, in the clean environment of a commercial studio.

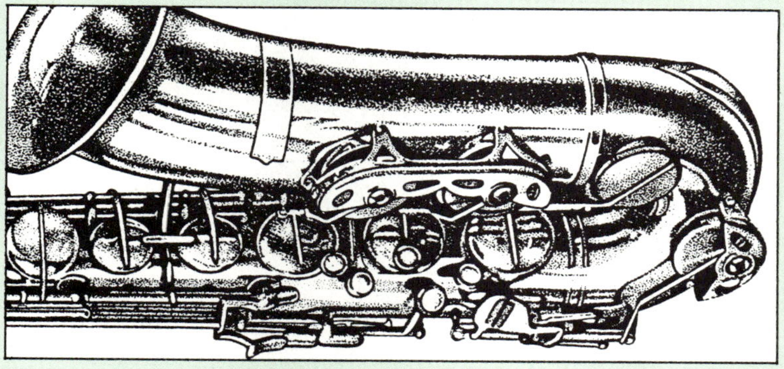

Exploring techniques
Same subject, different media:
1 Hard pencil/tracing paper
2 Soft pencil/cartridge paper
3 Charcoal/rough paper
4 Crayon/coloured paper
5 Pastel/rough paper
6 Technical nib/tracing paper
7 Pen/cartridge paper
8 Felt tip pen/smooth paper
9 Brush/smooth paper

Some simple do's and don'ts
- Have available a selection of equipment
- Do not use worn implements, as this can cause frustration
- Apply broader tools for large, dark tonal areas, not fine, linear ones
- Meaning and vision are much more important than your marks, however attractive they are
- Experiment to find the tools most suitable for the particular needs of your drawing

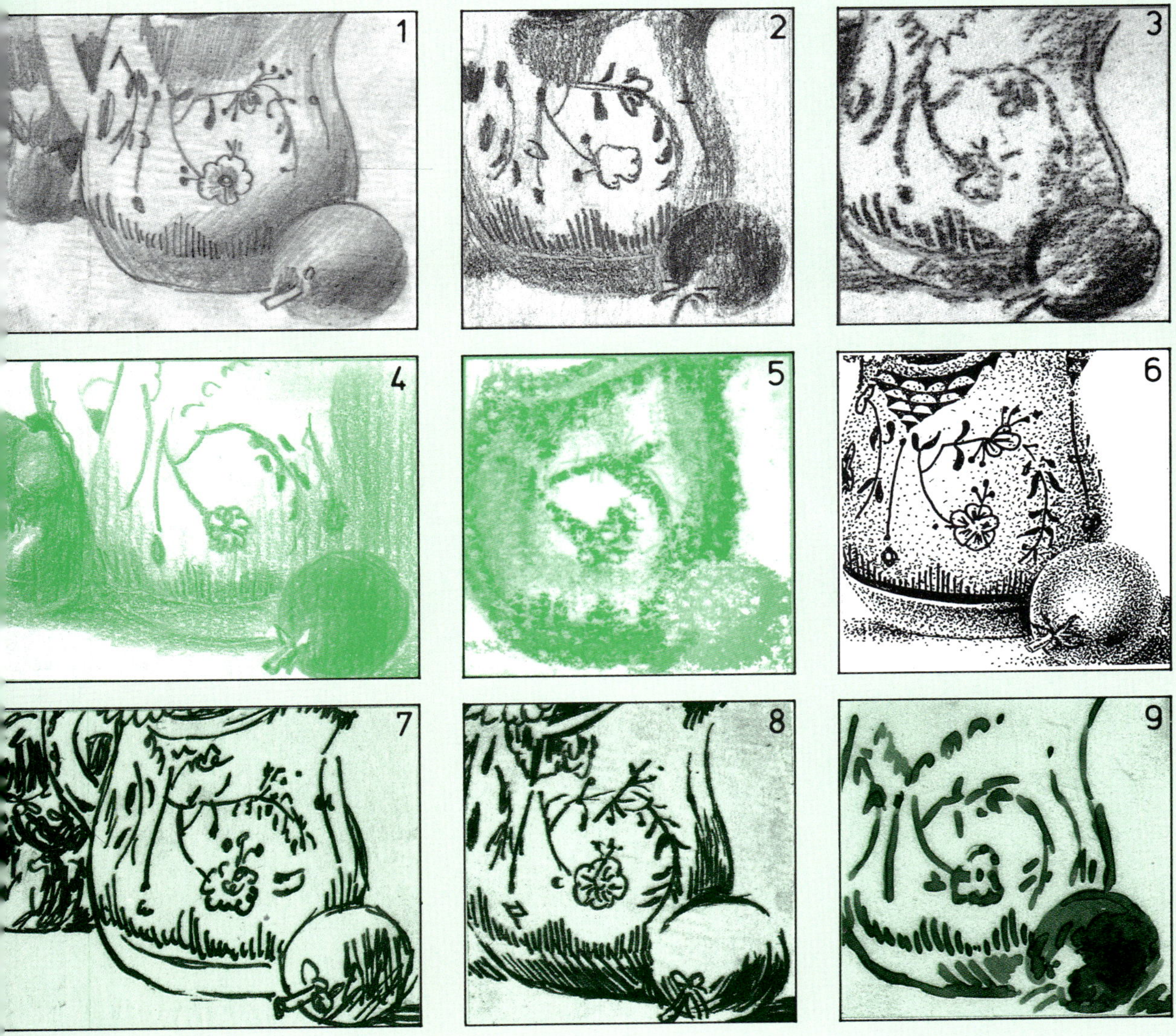

Part Three

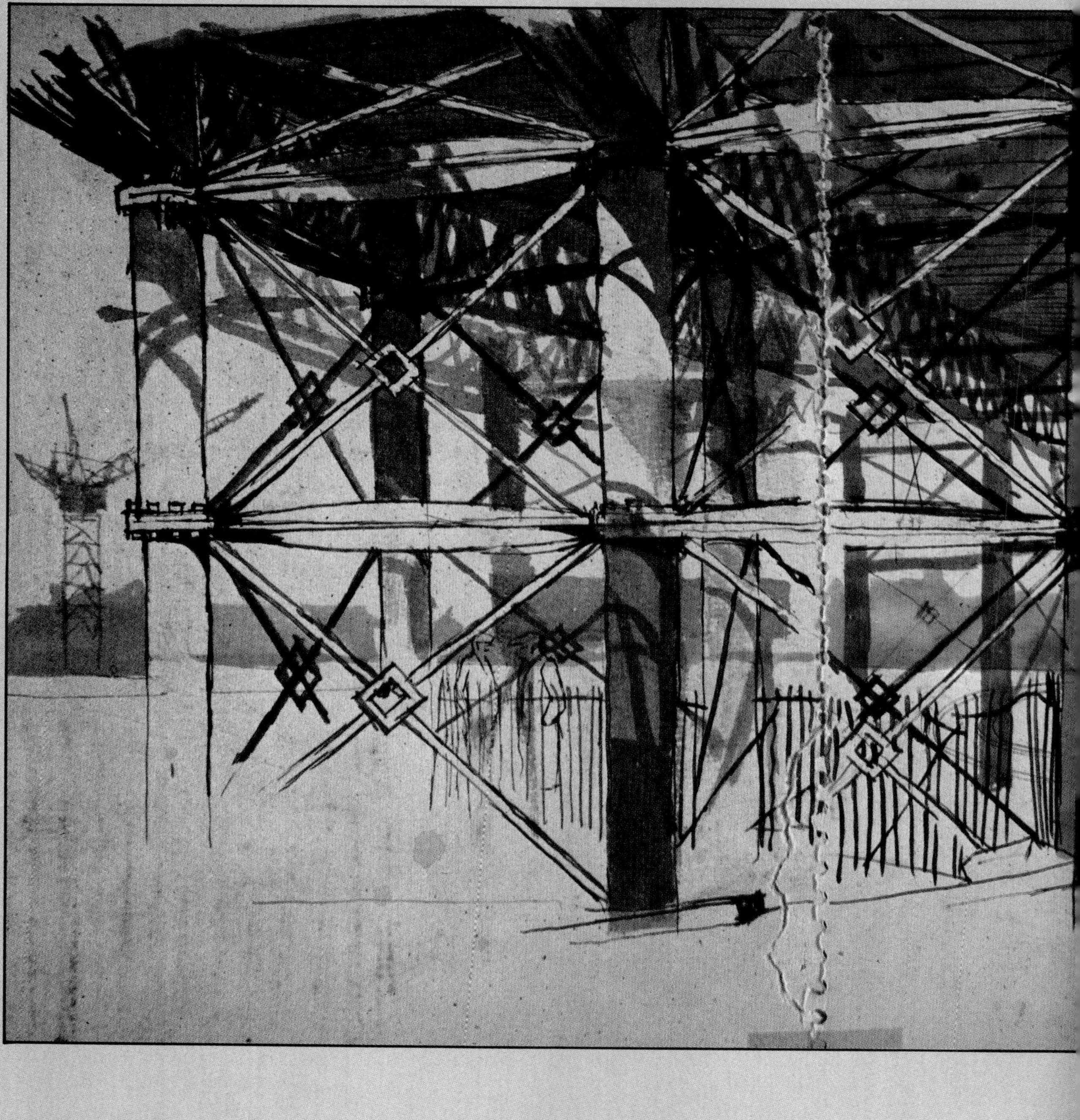

THE SUBJECT: PLACES

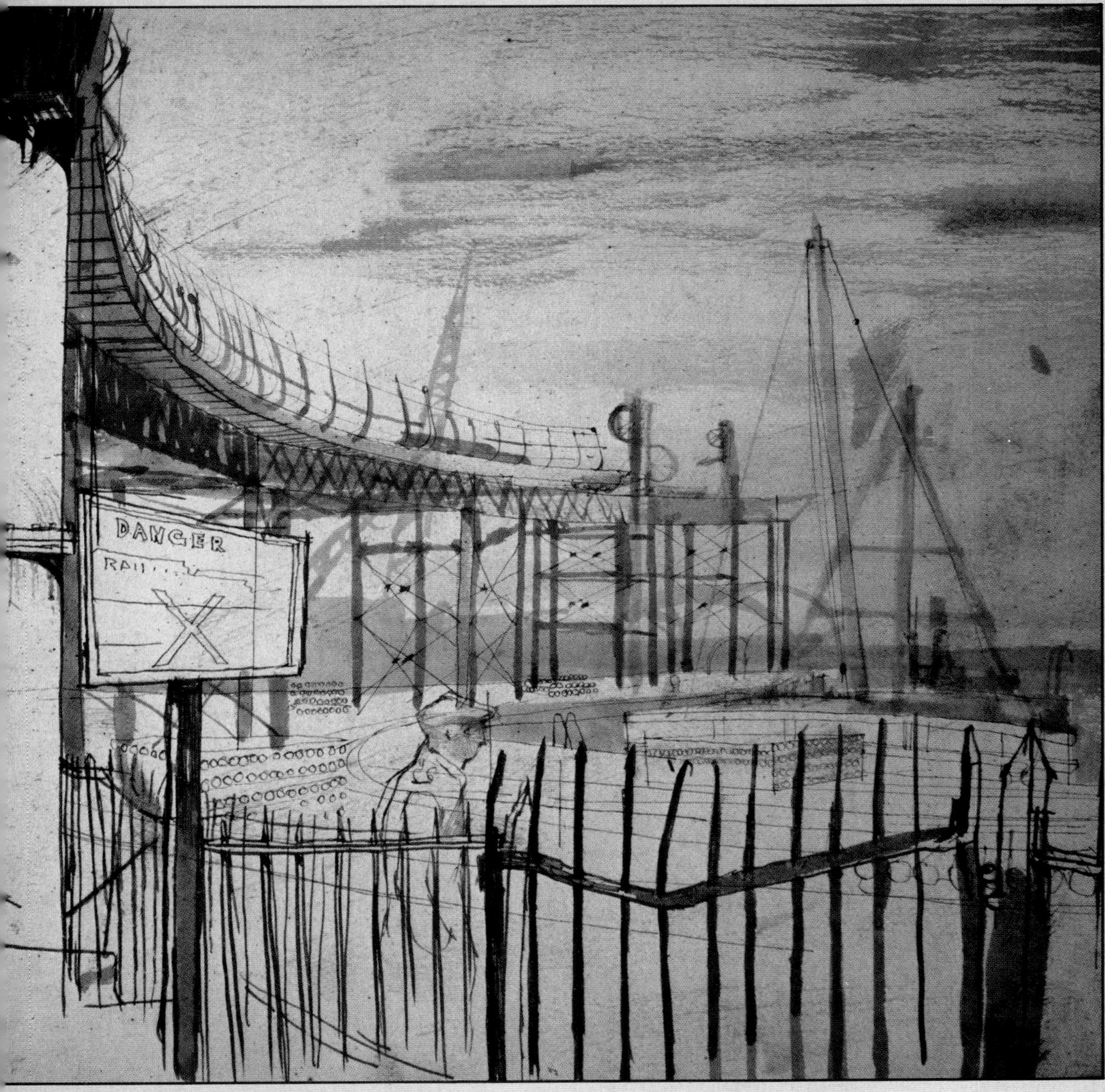

still life

Drawing objects or groups of objects is valuable experience because you can very largely control your subject. You need only look carefully at your object, and draw what you see accurately, for your drawing to be satisfactory. The next ten pages offer you advice on drawing individual objects, composing a group and creating an interesting drawing of your selected subject. After you have chosen the objects and your view of them, you need to study three aspects: first, the representation of the forms (that is the space they fill); second, the light and shade (that is the environment); and third, the textures and colours (that is their surface qualities).

Old doll
(Pencil drawing by Michael, aged 15)
As you can see (*below*), a good still life drawing is most often the result of a careful choice of objects. Look in cupboards, on shelves and among junk for objects whose nature offers the chance to explore interesting shapes.

Jug and fruit
(Brush drawing)
Objects with a variety of surface qualities make stimulating combinations. In the drawing (*right*), you can see a smooth surface next to a rough one, a reflective surface against a dull skin and dark against light.

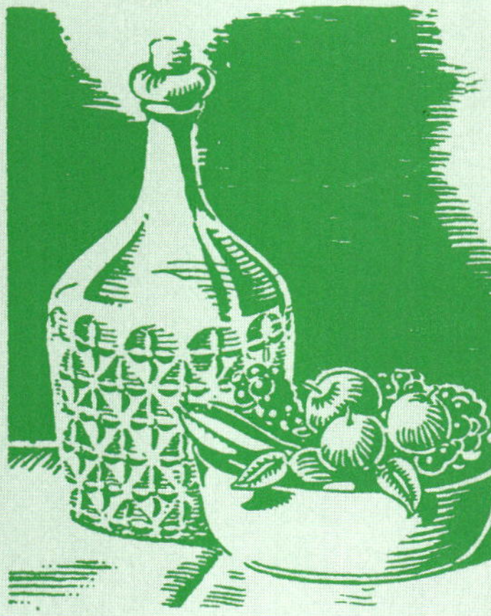

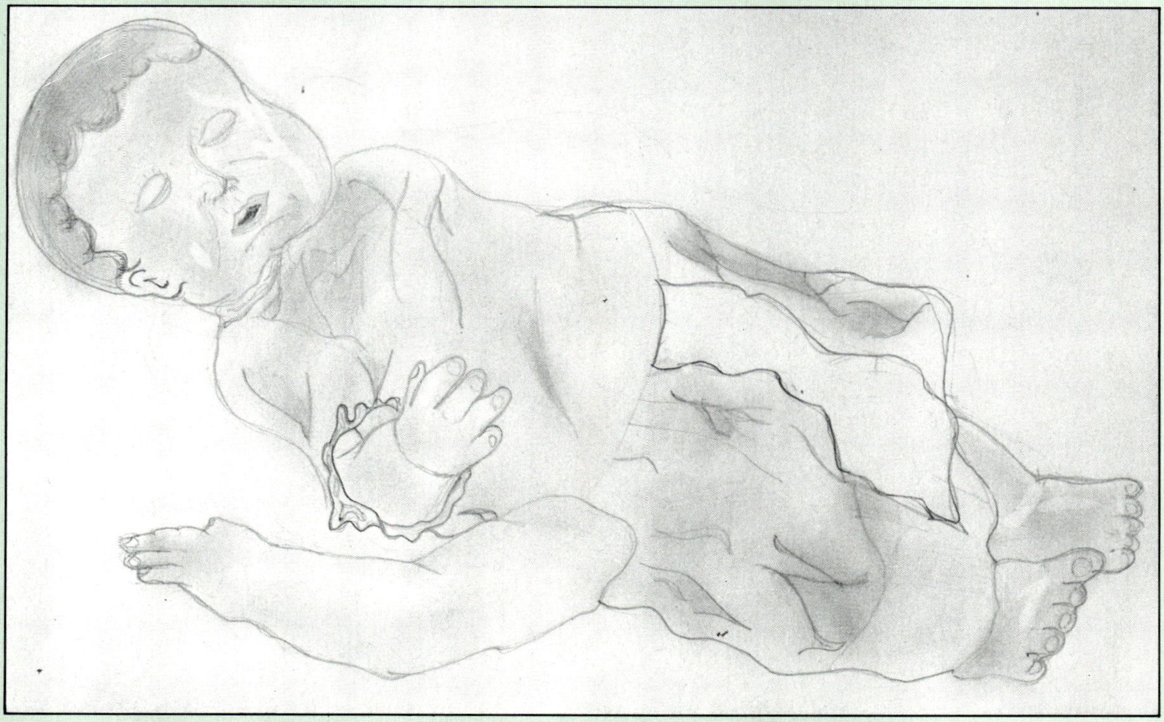

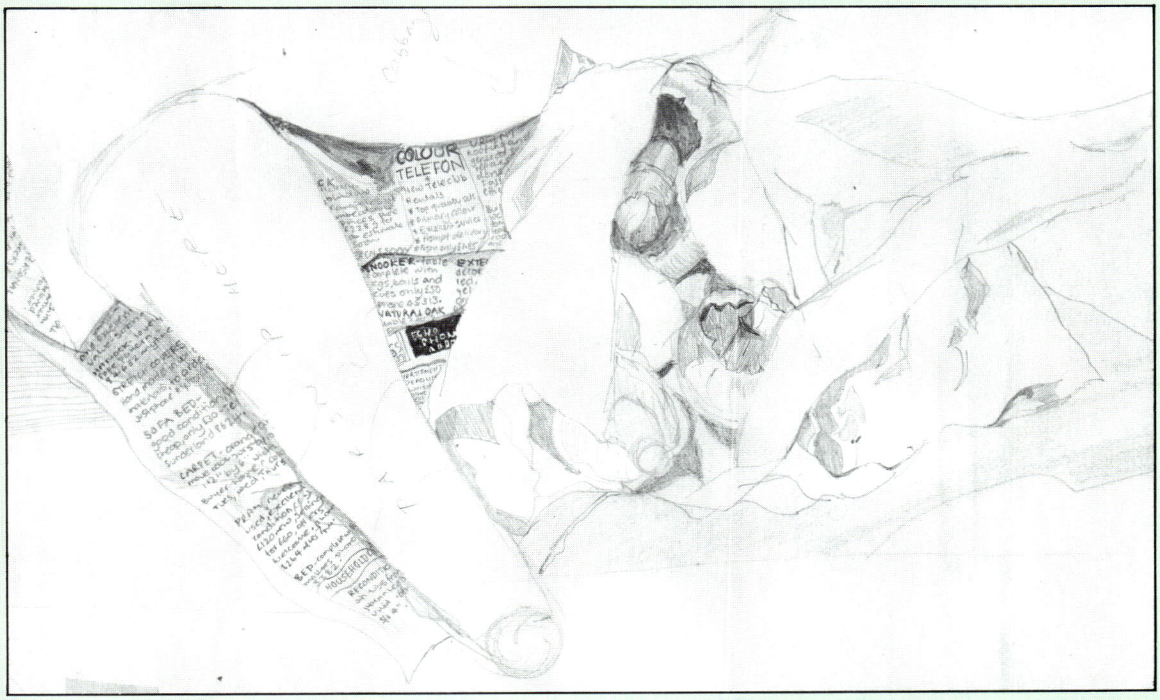

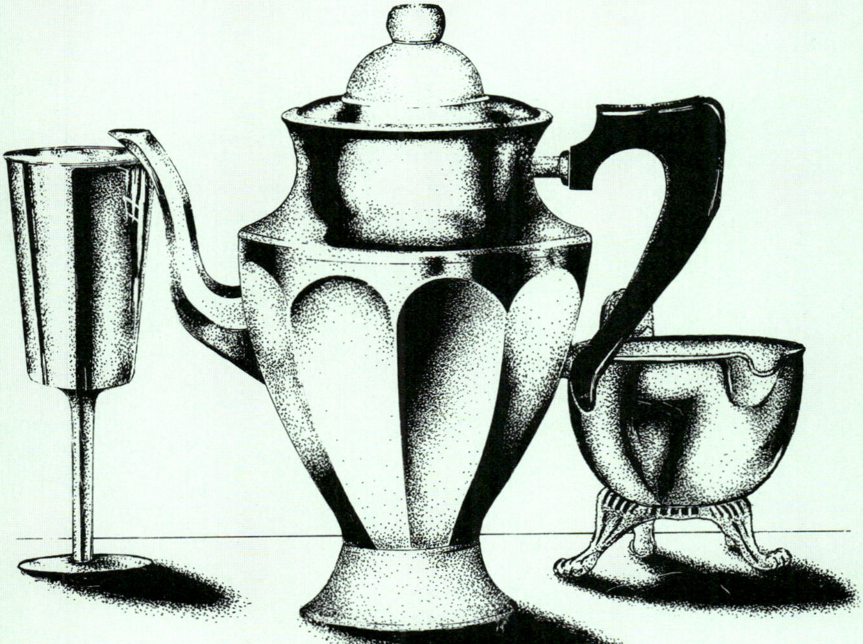

Mushrooms on newspaper
(Pencil drawing by Anne, aged 16)
Drawing complex groups, with spaces, shapes and textures mixed up (as *above*) creates problems of clarity. Initially draw carefully some areas only, labelling others by name, then study them separately. So that you can correct and revise, a pencil is the best tool.

Coffeepot and cups
(Pen and ink drawing, *left*)
Great care must be taken when drawing regular shapes, so that the symmetry and construction of the solids is shown correctly. The inaccuracy of a drawing of mushrooms on crumpled paper is less noticeable than an incorrectly drawn cup.

still life

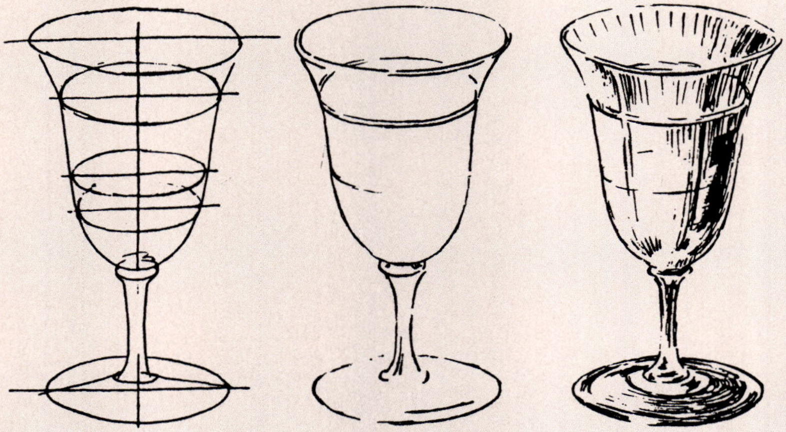

Drawing the form
Each object occupies space. Practise drawing articles whose volume you know, like glasses, so that you can imagine the amount of space they fill. Think through an object to its inner forms. First construct the basic elements, then add detail. It is easy to misjudge the relationship of volumes by emphasising smaller parts.

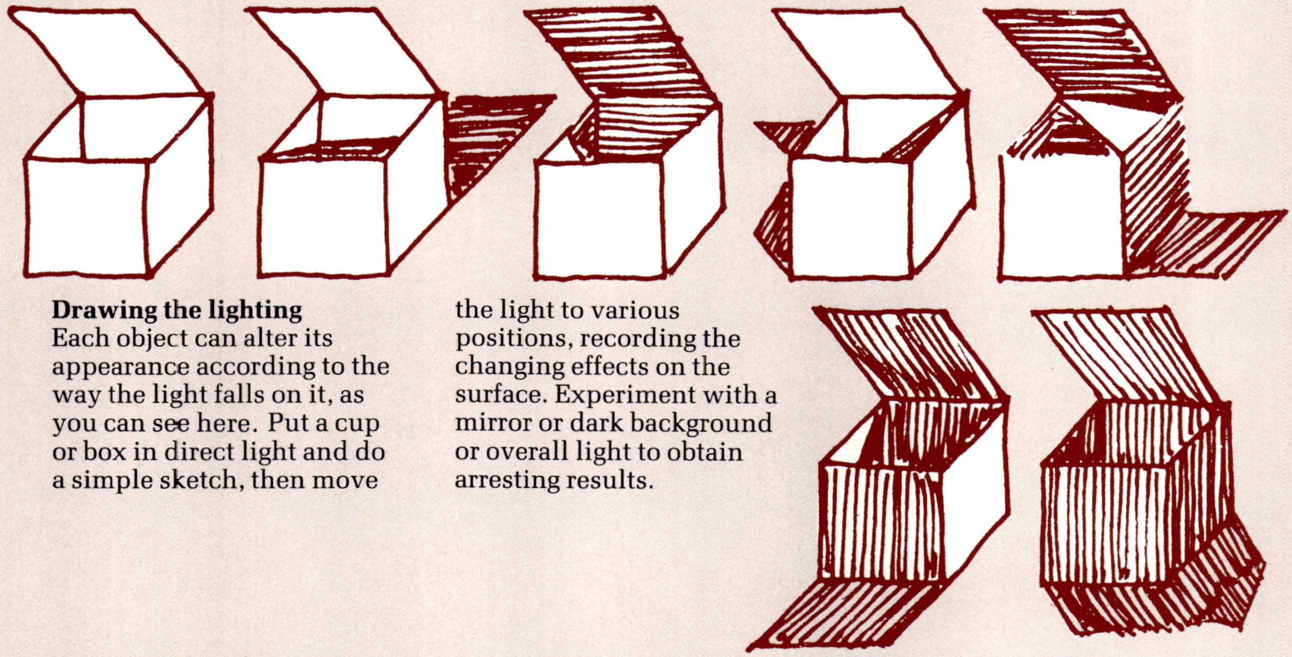

Drawing the lighting
Each object can alter its appearance according to the way the light falls on it, as you can see here. Put a cup or box in direct light and do a simple sketch, then move the light to various positions, recording the changing effects on the surface. Experiment with a mirror or dark background or overall light to obtain arresting results.

Drawing the surfaces
Each object has particular surface qualities. Try drawing a range of reflective surfaces. Spoons are particularly difficult to draw as their shape is hard to capture. Note the different qualities of the shadows on the spoon and on the tablecloth (*right*).

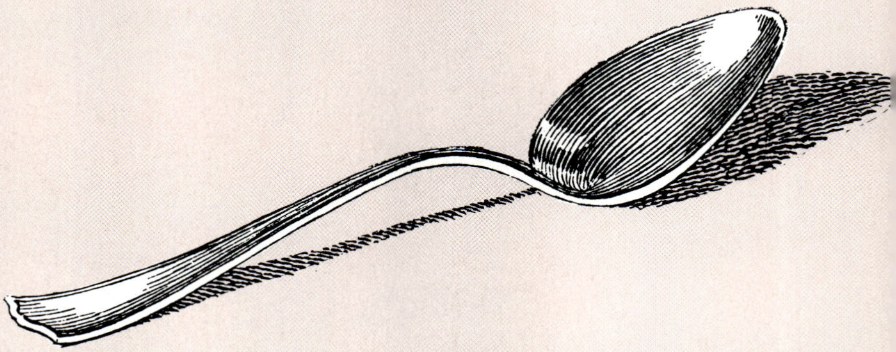

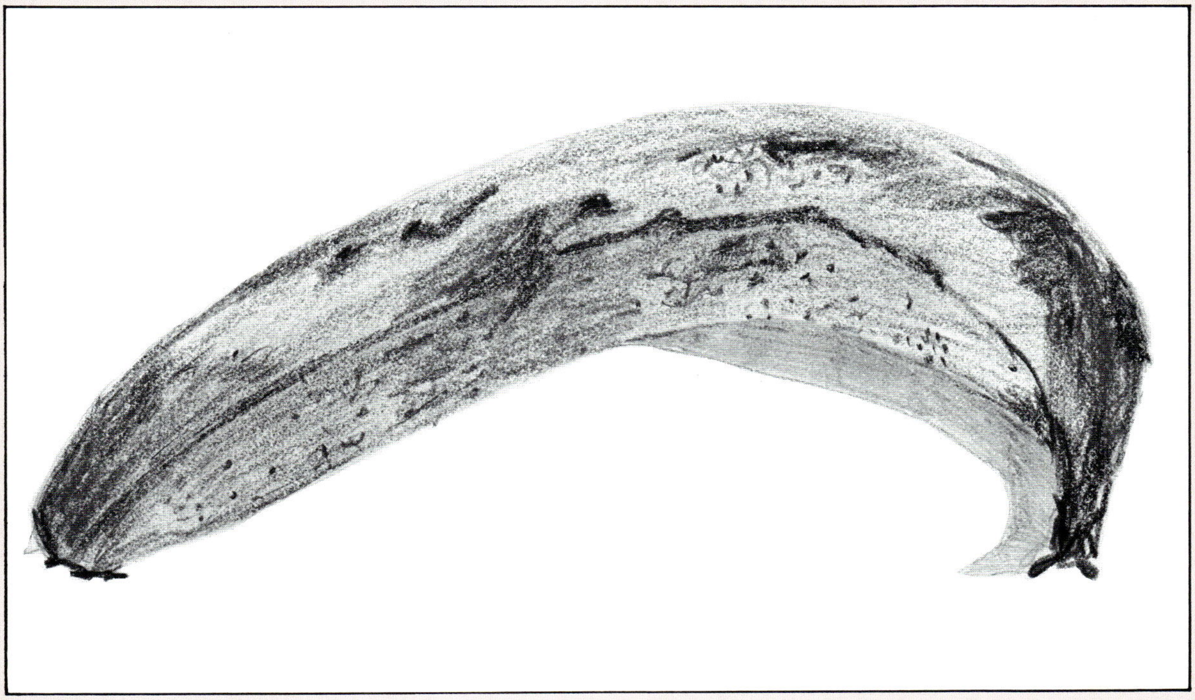

A banana
(Pencil drawing, originally in colours, by Anne, aged 17)
Great skill was needed to show the quality of softness and bruising (*above*).

Selection of craftsman's tools
(Professional artist's drawings *right* and *below*)
The quality of each tool is clear: worn, new; glossy, rough. The hammer has a soft rubber handle, shiny shaft and hard head.

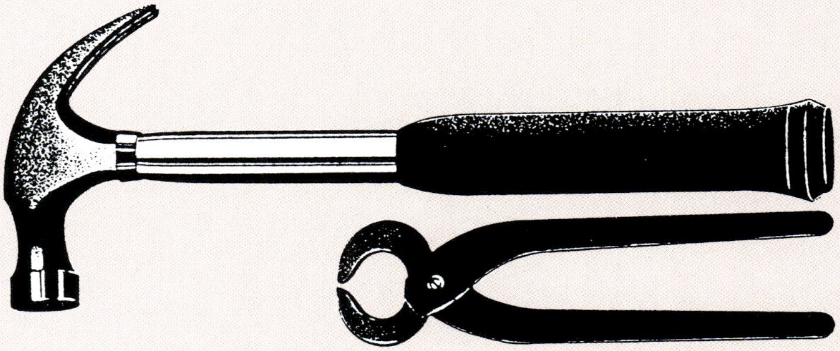

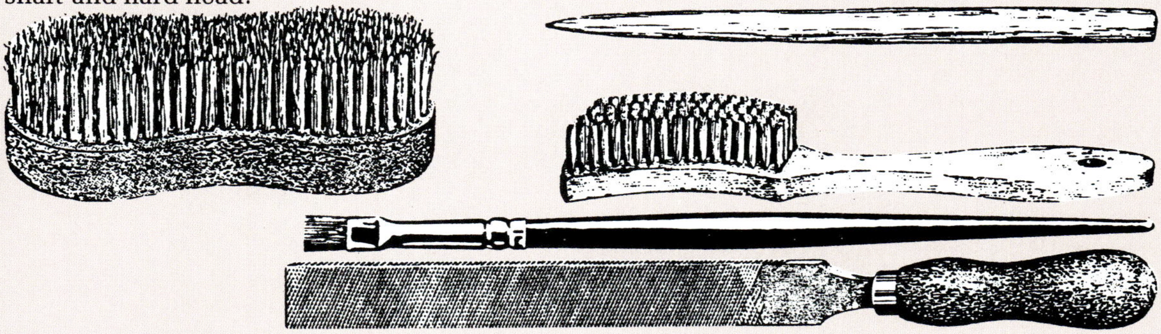

still life

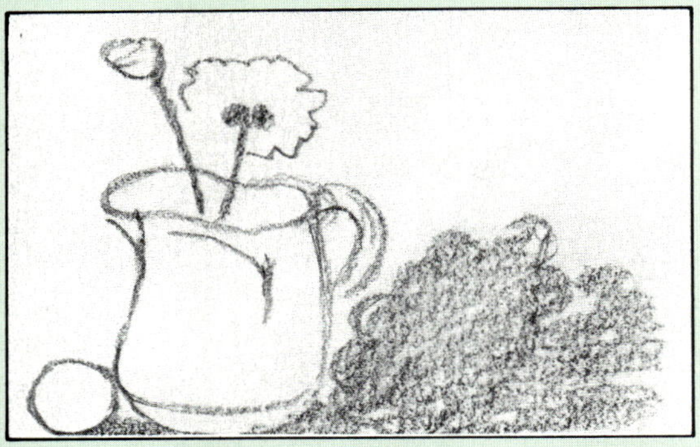

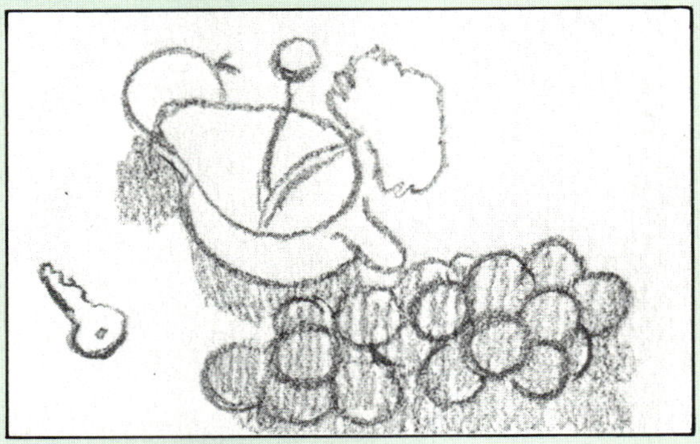

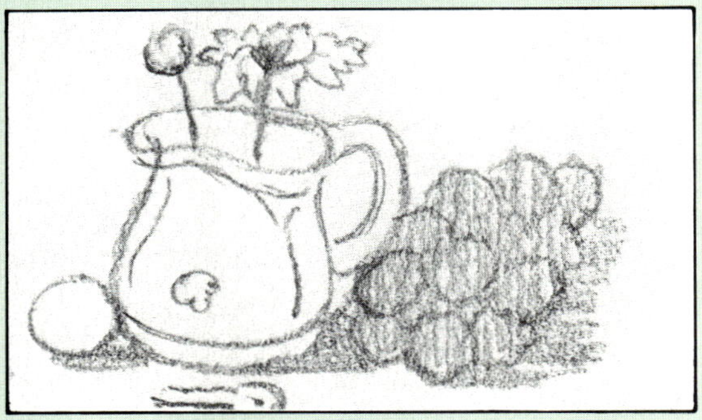

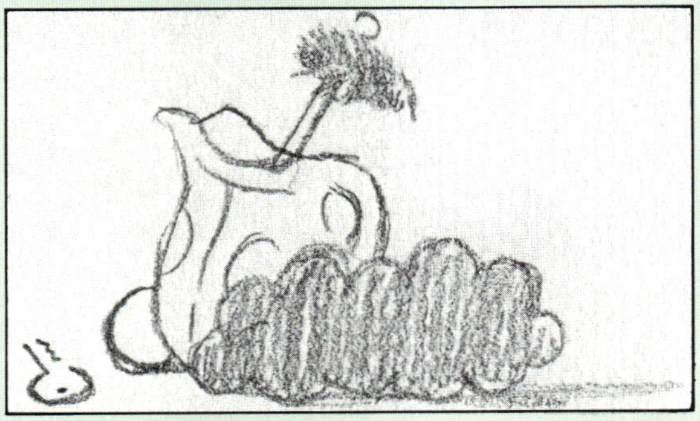

Your drawing of a group of objects depends upon four factors: first, the choice of objects; second, the view of those you choose; third, the composition you select within your picture area; and fourth, the lighting.

Choosing the objects
Try to select a group of naturally associated objects, for example different types of food, articles on a drawing desk or on a dressing table, or work tools. Or choose objects whose basic forms are contrasting, for instance rectangular books with spherical fruit or cylindrical cups.

Selecting a view
(Pencil drawings of a jug and fruit)
Arrange the objects on a board resting on an adjustable pile of books, and sketch quickly in pen or pencil. Then record the results of raising or lowering your viewpoint and of rearranging the group (see *above* and *right*). Select simple views.

Selecting a composition
(Pen drawings of a jug and fruit, *right*)
View the group close up and at a distance, then to one side, then the other. Sketch the results. To help choose their compositions many artists use a reducing glass. The images appear smaller and the composition simpler, with all the elements seen as a unit.

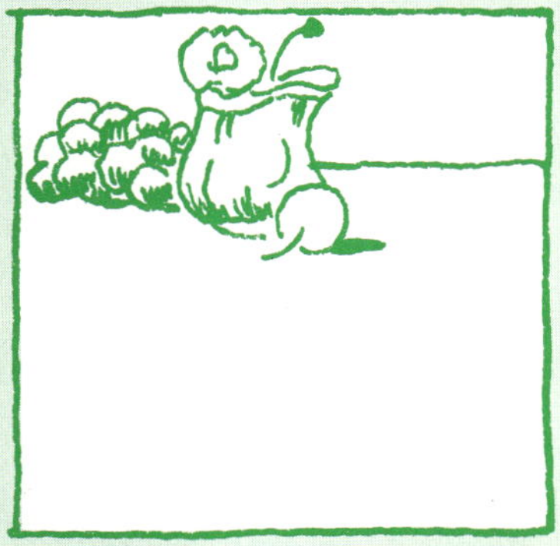

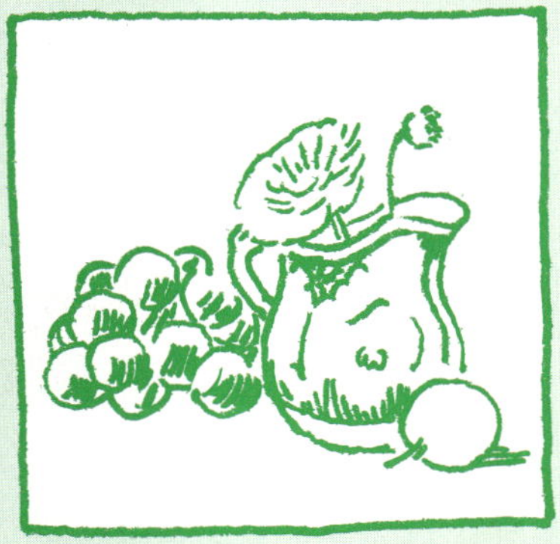

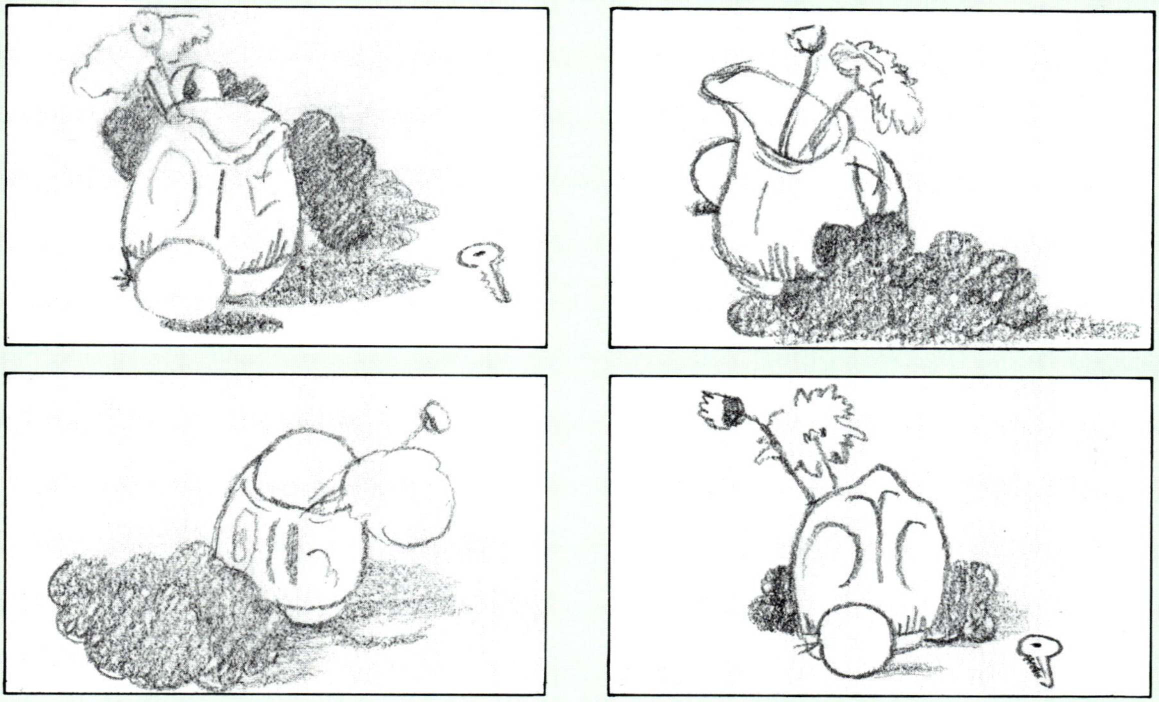

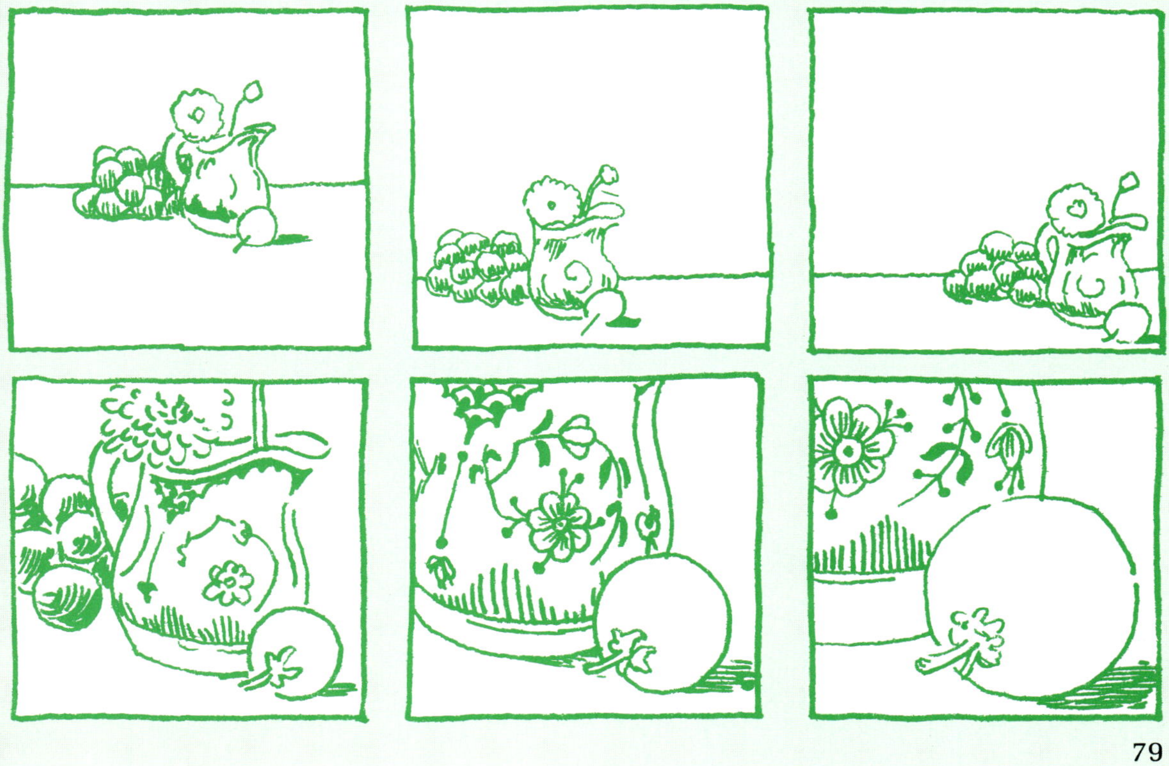

still life

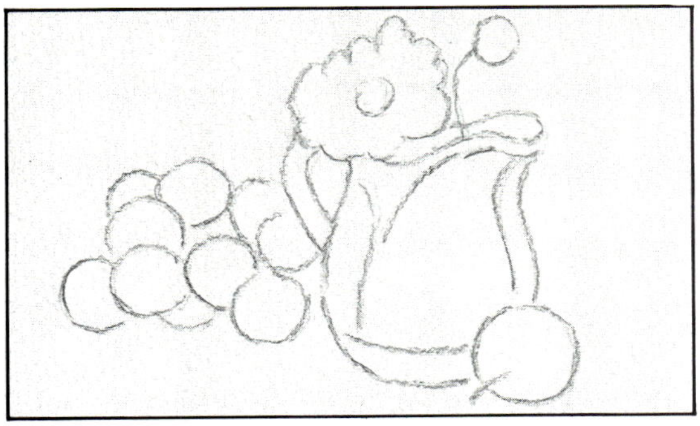

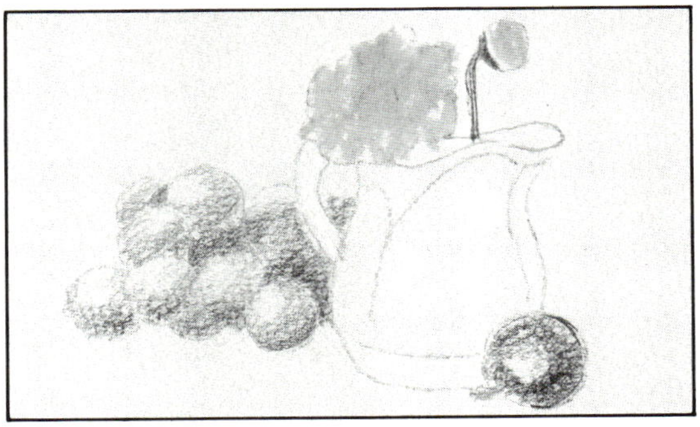

Jug and fruit
(Coloured pencil drawings)
Working with a soft pencil, begin by sketching lightly the main parts of your group. Most marks can be erased but this affects the paper and the quality of the lines. Next, fill in the main tonal areas, including the shadows, slowly darkening the tones. Avoid reflections or parts you may want to leave light Continue to work over the whole drawing, first ensuring that the tones and colours are correct before filling in details. Finally, observing the tiny, individual elements, pencil them in. The dark textures (*right*) result from using coarse paper, fine for pencil, charcoal, crayon, but not for pen and ink. Section, actual size, (*below*).

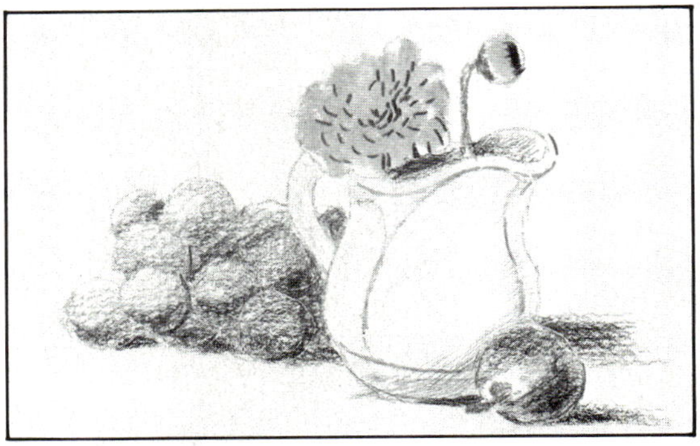

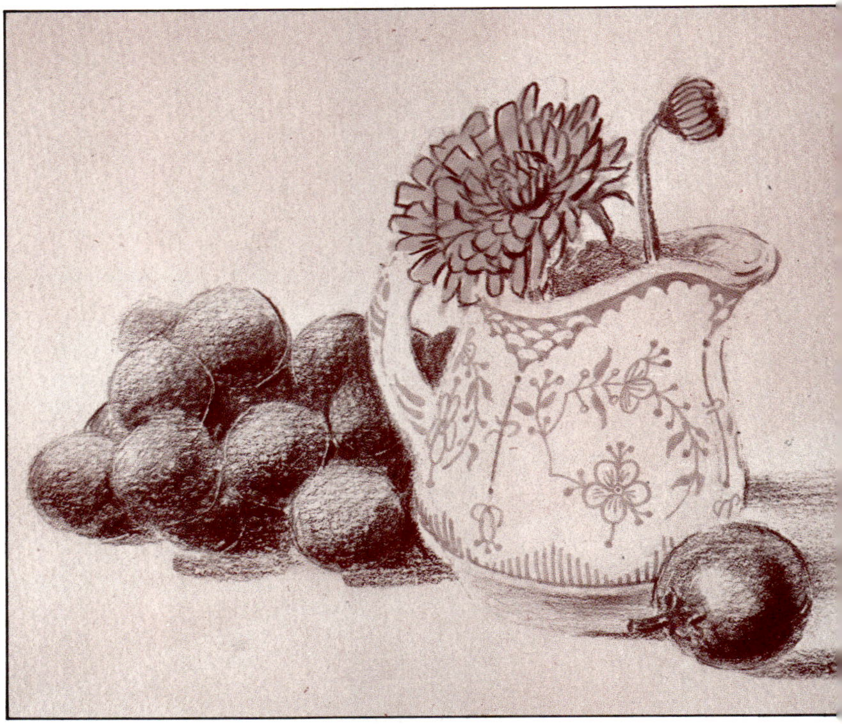

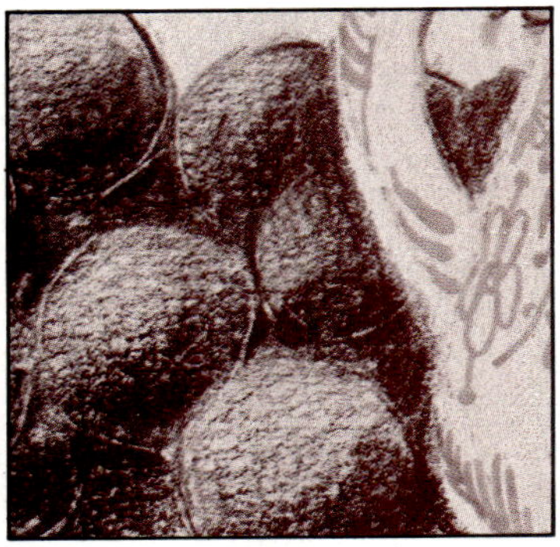

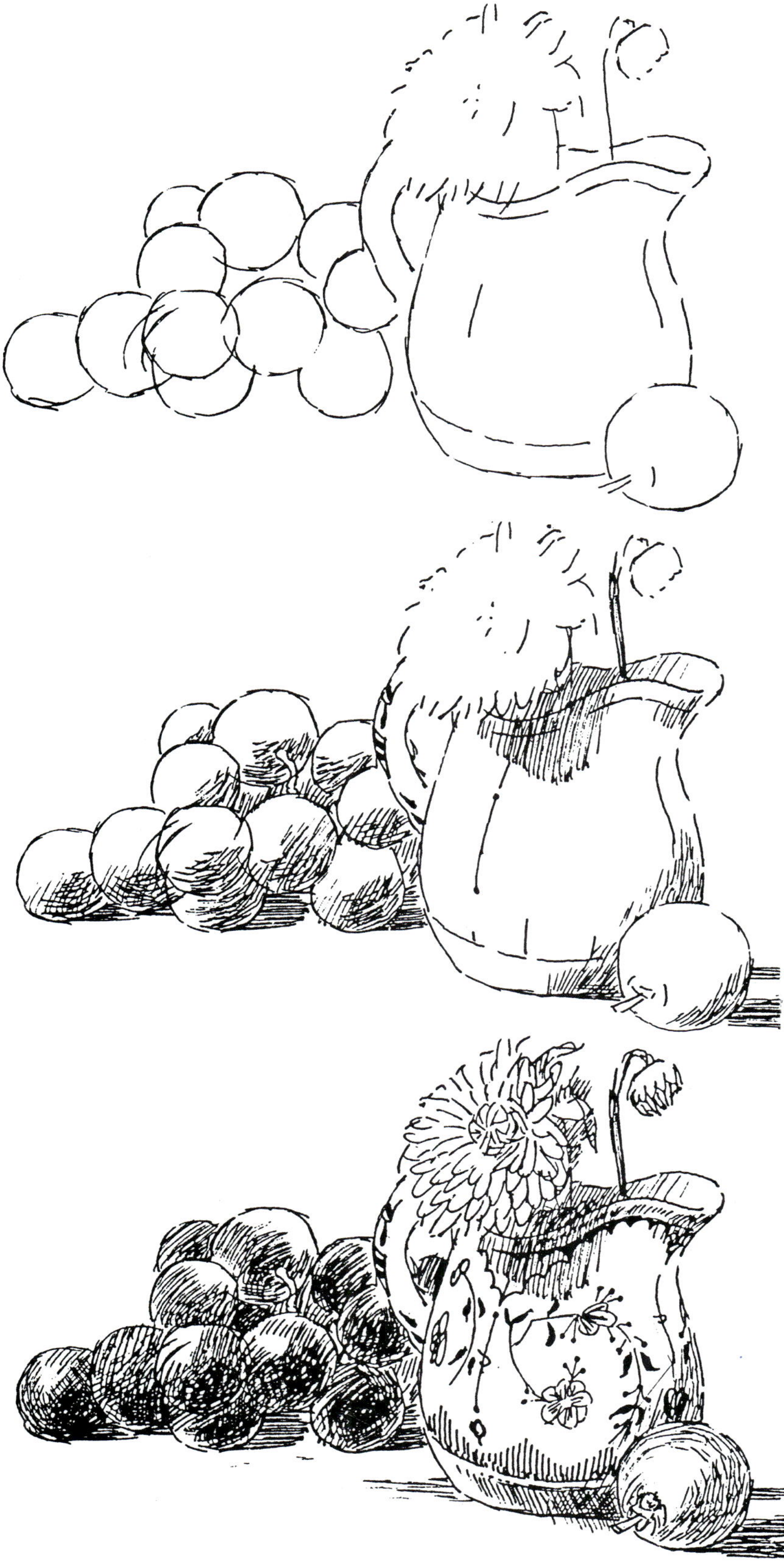

Jug and fruit
(Pen drawings)
As with pencil drawings, begin with an overall plotting of the forms. Your pen is only capable of producing lines, so build up tones by stroking the forms, and by cross-hatching, always following the direction of the form, as in the three stages (*left*). Detail, actual size, (*below*).

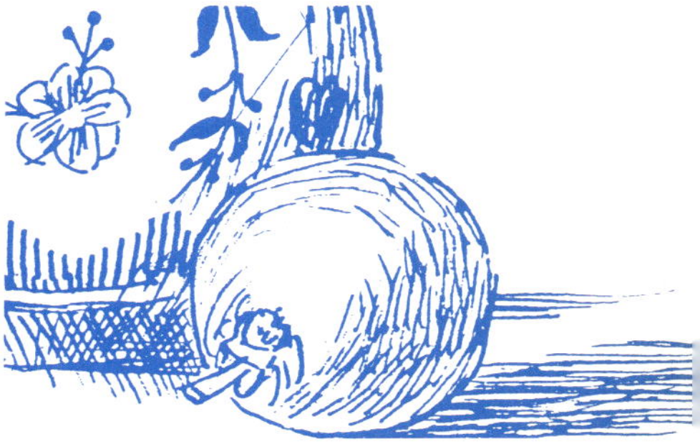

Jug and fruit
(Brush drawing)
Once your study is complete, it is easy to convert the areas of tone and colour to simple patterns, thereby creating very powerful and contrasting shapes (see *below*). This type of drawing is most suitable for reproducing your own greetings cards.

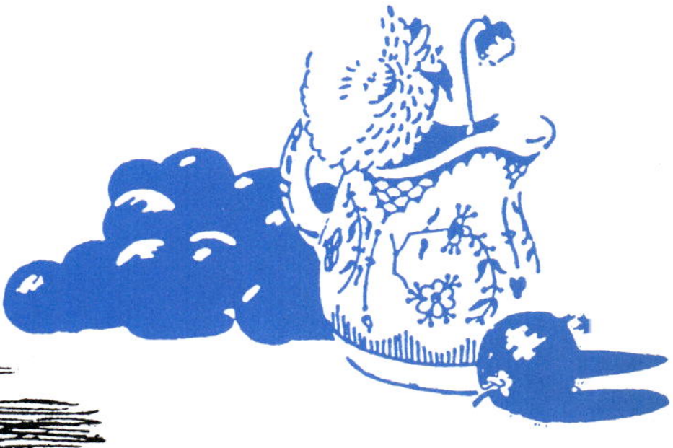

still life

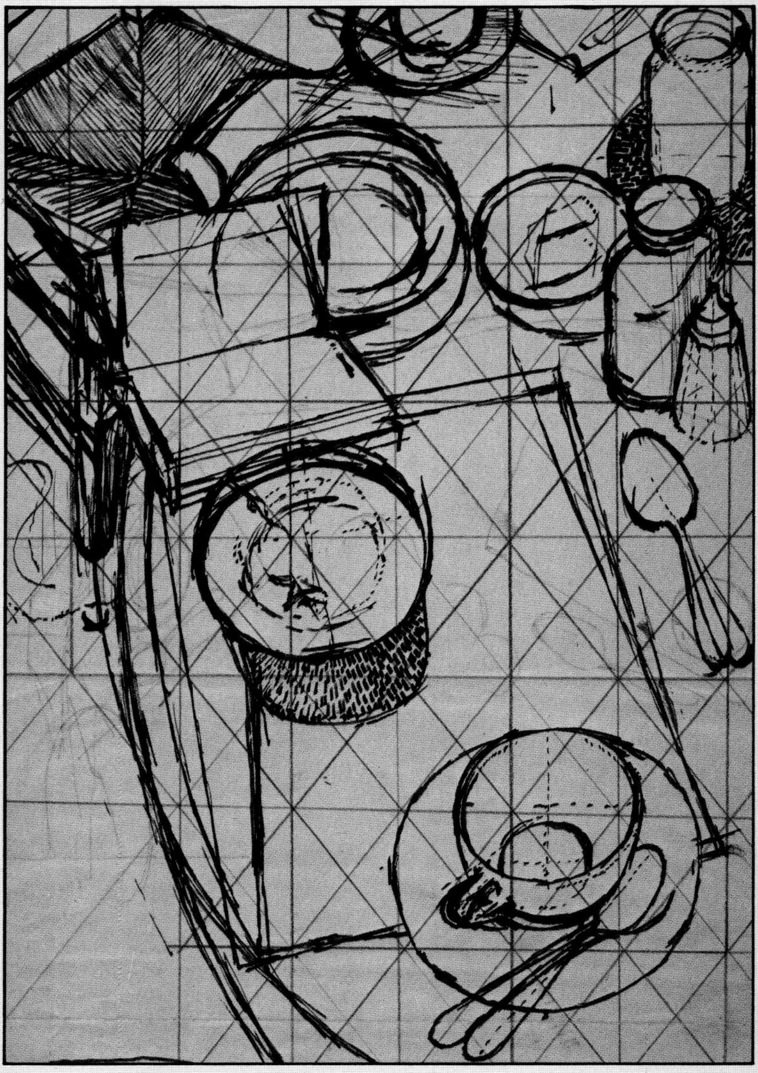

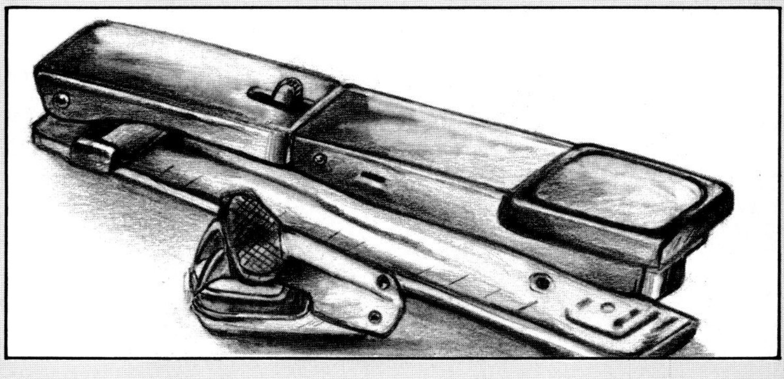

Almost all interesting still life compositions are the result of considering three factors: your view of the subject; the creation of realism; and the selection of objects.

Breakfast table
(Pen drawing)
By viewing objects from above, and by cutting off shapes at the edges of the picture, the drawing (*left*) is a very unusual composition of a group of objects in everyday use. The grid of triangles was added after completion so the artist could enlarge and transfer the drawing to canvas for painting.

Office notice board
(Pencil drawing)
The composition (*right*) is of very thin objects which present hardly any protrusions. The effect of realism is the result of careful attention to the lighting and to the different surface qualities of the objects.

Office equipment
(Pencil drawing)
Try to choose unfamiliar articles to draw, as Steve has done (*left*). Although simple objects, the stapler, the staples and the tool for removing metal staples make a memorable composition.

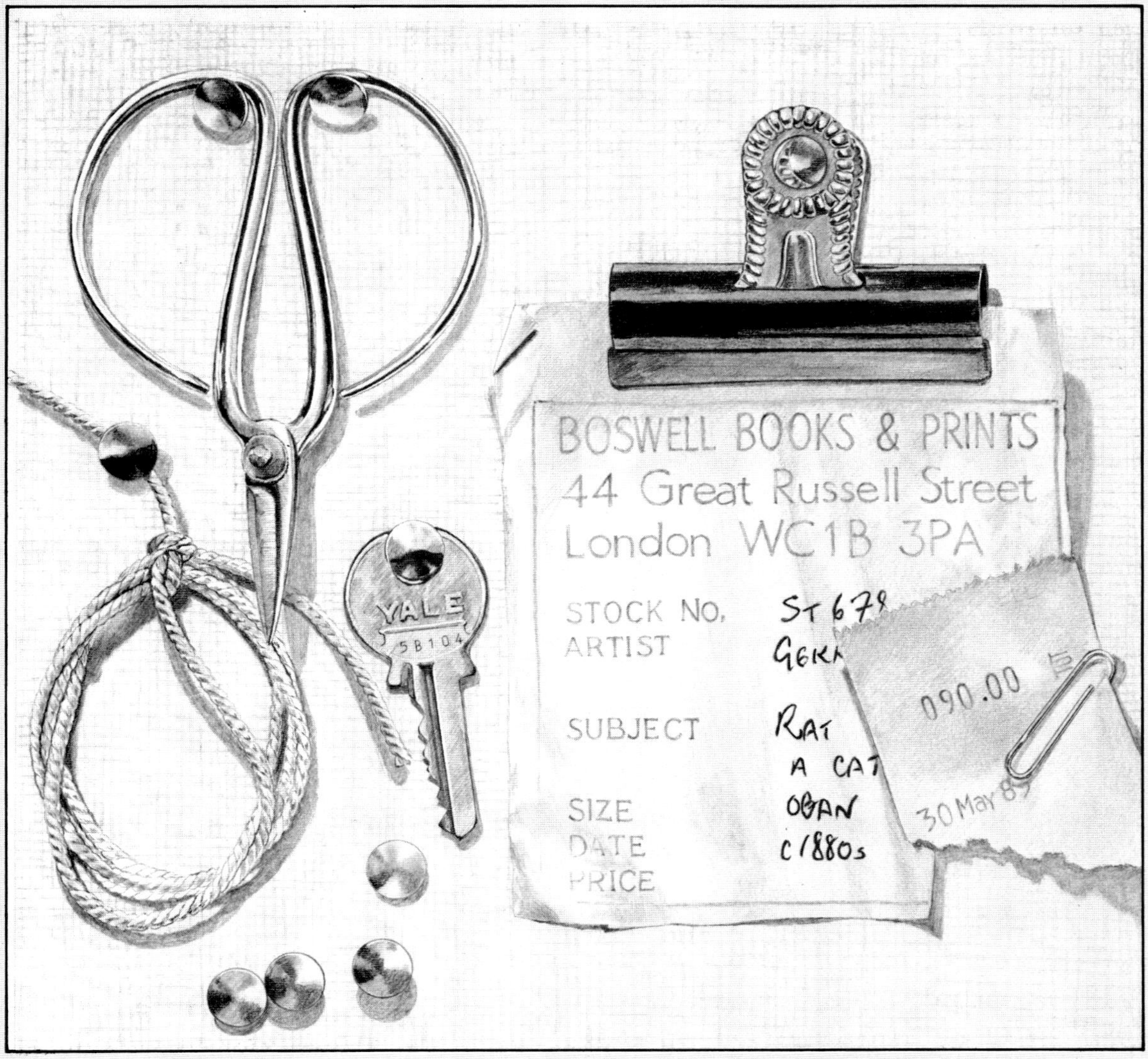

©DIAGRAM

Your personal checklist
After each drawing is finished try the following exercise:

1 Put the drawing aside for ten minutes. Go and make a cup of tea, or do something completely different.

2 Reapproach your drawing and squint through half-closed eyes at it and at the objects. Then ask yourself the following questions:

1 ARE THE LIGHT AND DARK TONES CORRECT?

2 DO ANY OF THEM JUMP OUT FROM MY DRAWING?

3 ARE THE EDGES OF THE OBJECTS CORRECTLY SHAPED?

4 ARE THE PROPORTIONS OF EACH OBJECT TO THE OTHERS CORRECT?

5 IS THE SPACE, DEPTH, TEXTURE ACCURATELY DRAWN?

6 DOES THE DRAWING "FEEL RIGHT?"

Item 6 is the age-old question every artist asks himself to make sense of what he feels is right. **Only you know the answer** to the quality of your drawings.

interiors

Drawing interiors consists almost entirely of solving the problem of representing flat receding spaces set into the picture frame. Watch for clues like floor patterns, chair legs and corners of rooms. Take great care to plot the points where objects touch the floor, or where planes meet. Because an interior is composed of a combination of the spaces and the special surface details on the objects in it, the portrayal of its particular atmosphere is a challenge. It is important to create the sense of space. Study the individual objects with great care, storing up information to be used later. Try to include figures in order to establish the scale.

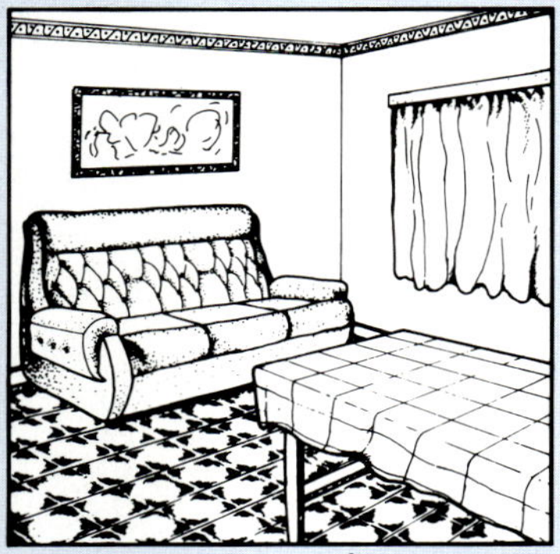

b

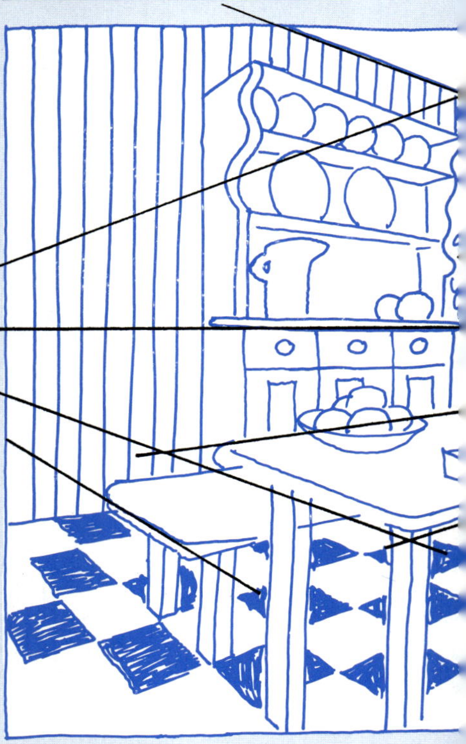

a

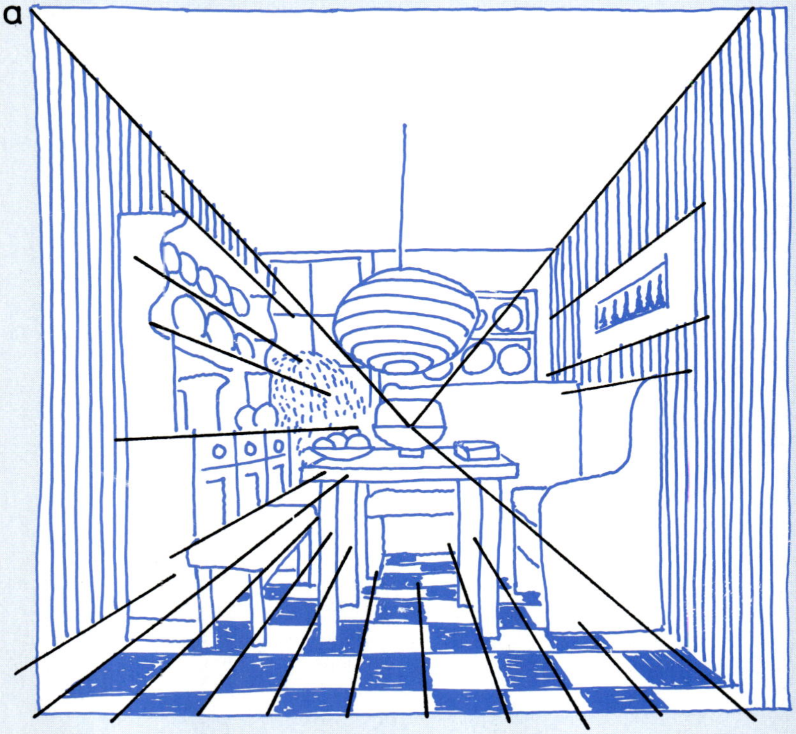

Constructing the interior
Depending on your position in the room, the walls will converge either on (**a**) a centre point (*left*), or on (**b**) two separate vanishing points (*above*). In both cases the method of constructing the main lines of the drawing is the same: hold up a pencil and judge, against the vertical, the

Room corner
(Pen drawing)
Room furniture is usually put parallel to walls so that its horizontal edges will recede, in your drawing, parallel to the lines indicating the walls of the room. Look closely at textures and patterns on all surfaces so that you can establish parallel alignment of the detailing (*left*).

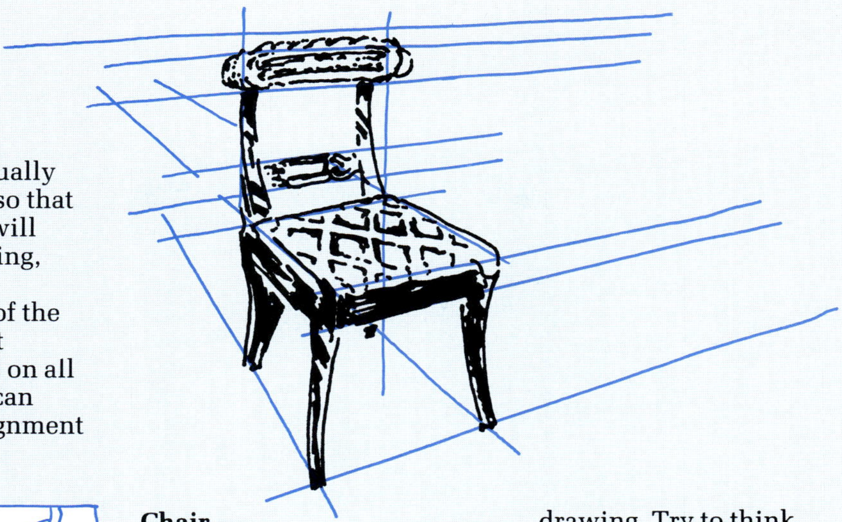

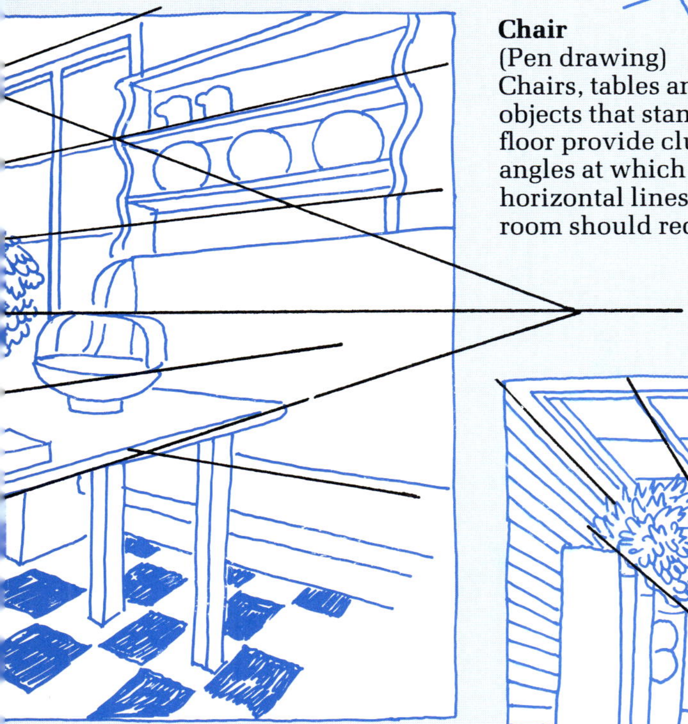

Chair
(Pen drawing)
Chairs, tables and other objects that stand on the floor provide clues about the angles at which the horizontal lines in your room should recede in your drawing. Try to think yourself into the space that the objects occupy, and plot carefully those lines and points that are in a common plane, as has been done for the chair (*above*).

angles at which the walls recede. Draw in the lines representing the edges of the walls. Then extend these lines until they reach a common point, or points. If you look up or down in a small enclosed space (as in (**c**) *right*), you may find the converging lines are the verticals.

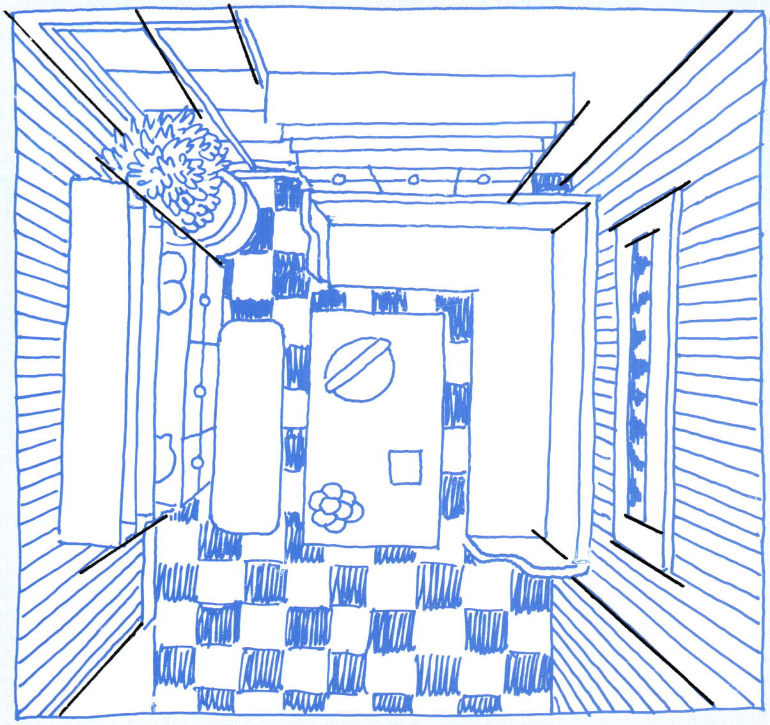
C

interiors

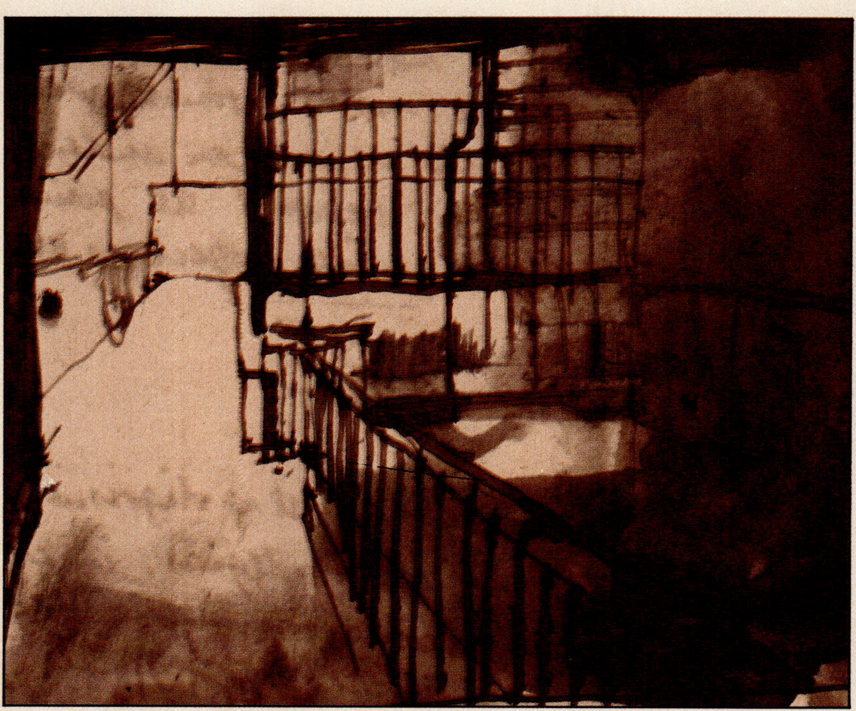

Anne's room
(Pen drawing)
It is possible to sit in a room and imagine the space all around you. Turn slowly in a full circle to help you create the illusion that you are looking down on the room from above. It is often easier to describe all the objects in such a view in outline only, as in Anne's room (*right*), without studying colour, texture, lighting or intricate forms.

19th-century apartment block, New York
(Pen and watercolour drawing)
When drawing interiors it is often helpful to select a view which contains strongly receding elements. The central handrail of the sketch (*above*) combined with the intensely dark area of tone, helps to convey a feeling of depth.

Public bar, Dublin
(Pencil sketches, *right*)
Drawing with soft pencils and using your finger to smudge in tone helps establish an atmosphere of smoke and bar-room haze. Don't be afraid to draw people on top of the background. It is better to capture the feel of the interior than to insist that the exact forms of each shape fit together correctly.

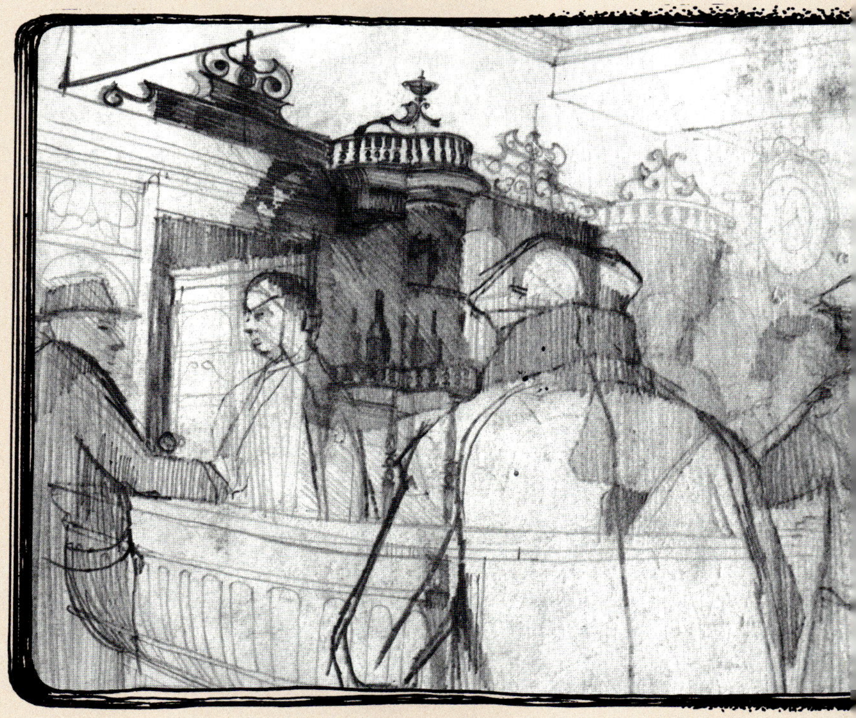

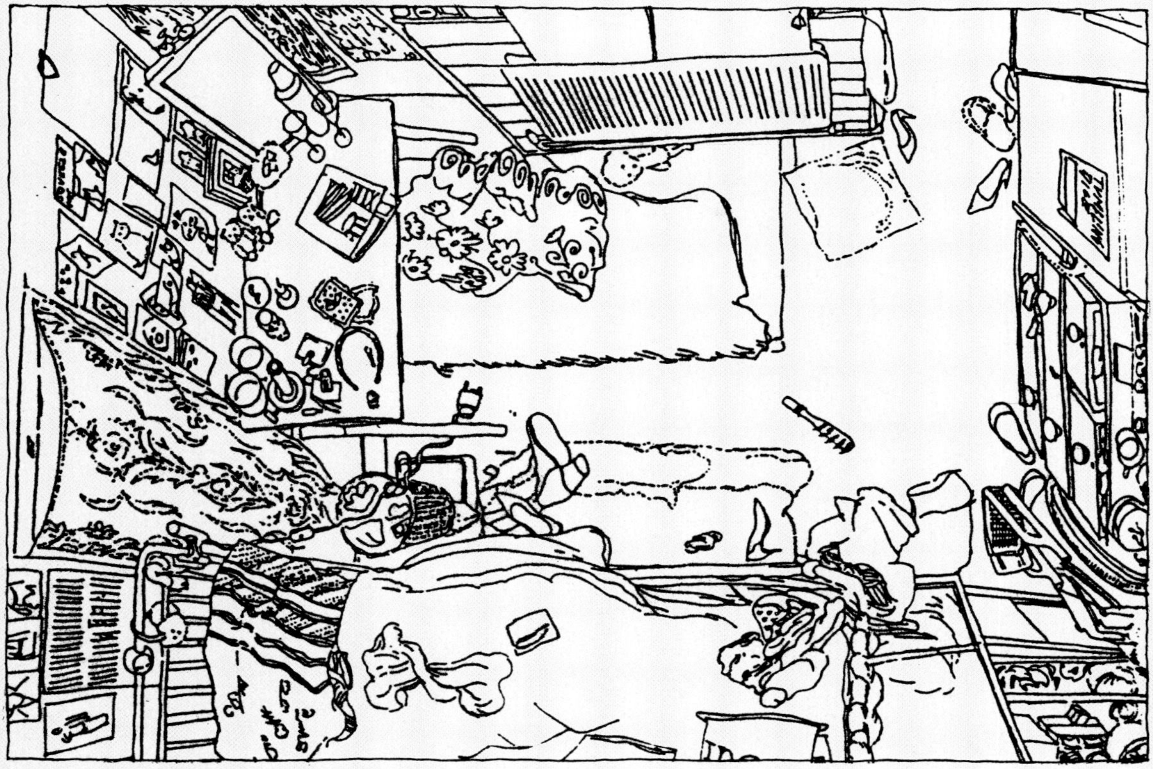

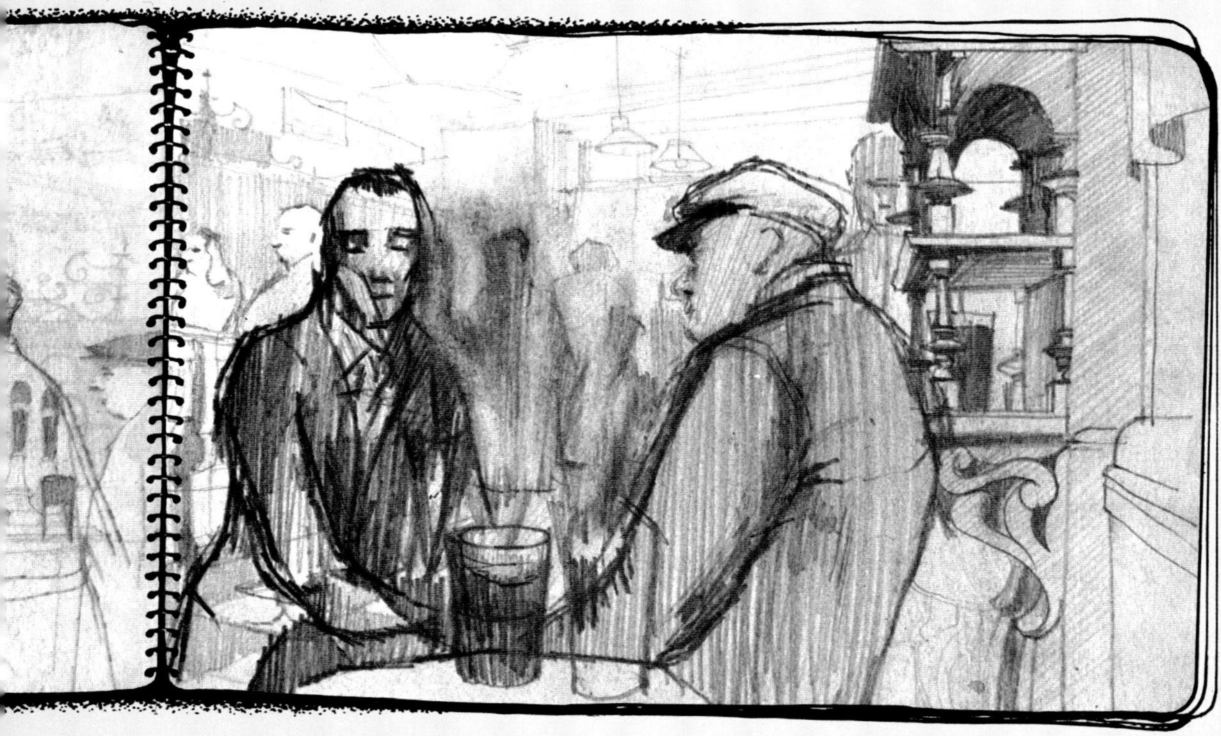

interiors

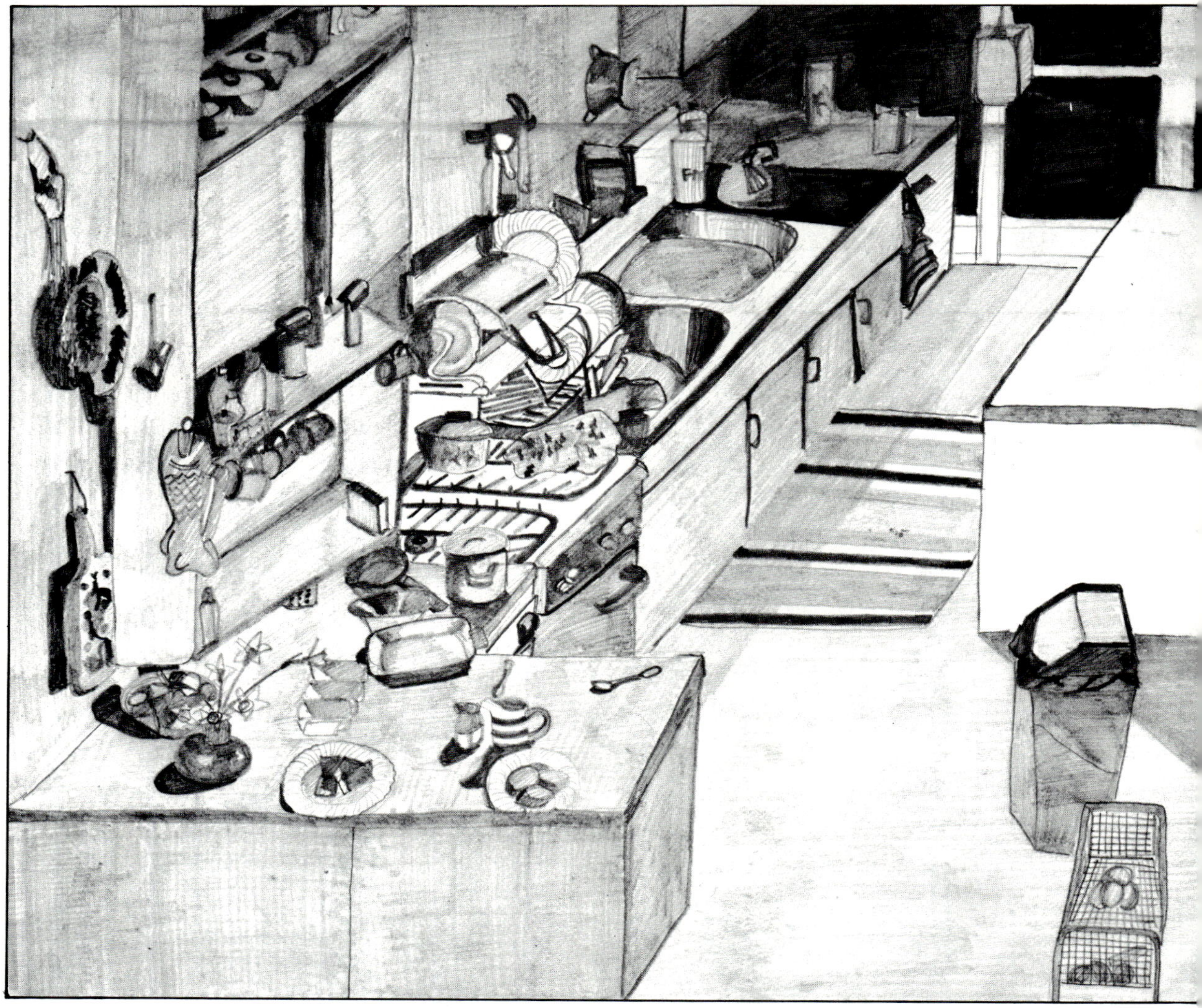

The kitchen
(Pencil drawing by Jane, aged 15)
Pencil provides the means to build up tones and convey colours. Jane's drawing (*above*), although unsure of perspective and spatial construction, shows real care for detail. The brass fish moulds, zinc sinks and the blue and white jugs are beautifully described.

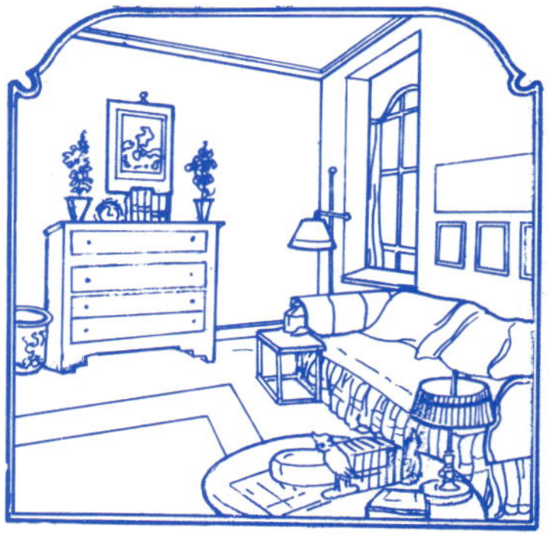

Sitting room
(Pen and ink drawing)
Interiors (as *left*), are ideal for drawing decoratively. The regular shapes of pictures, windows and furniture provide easy subjects with which to represent receding planes.

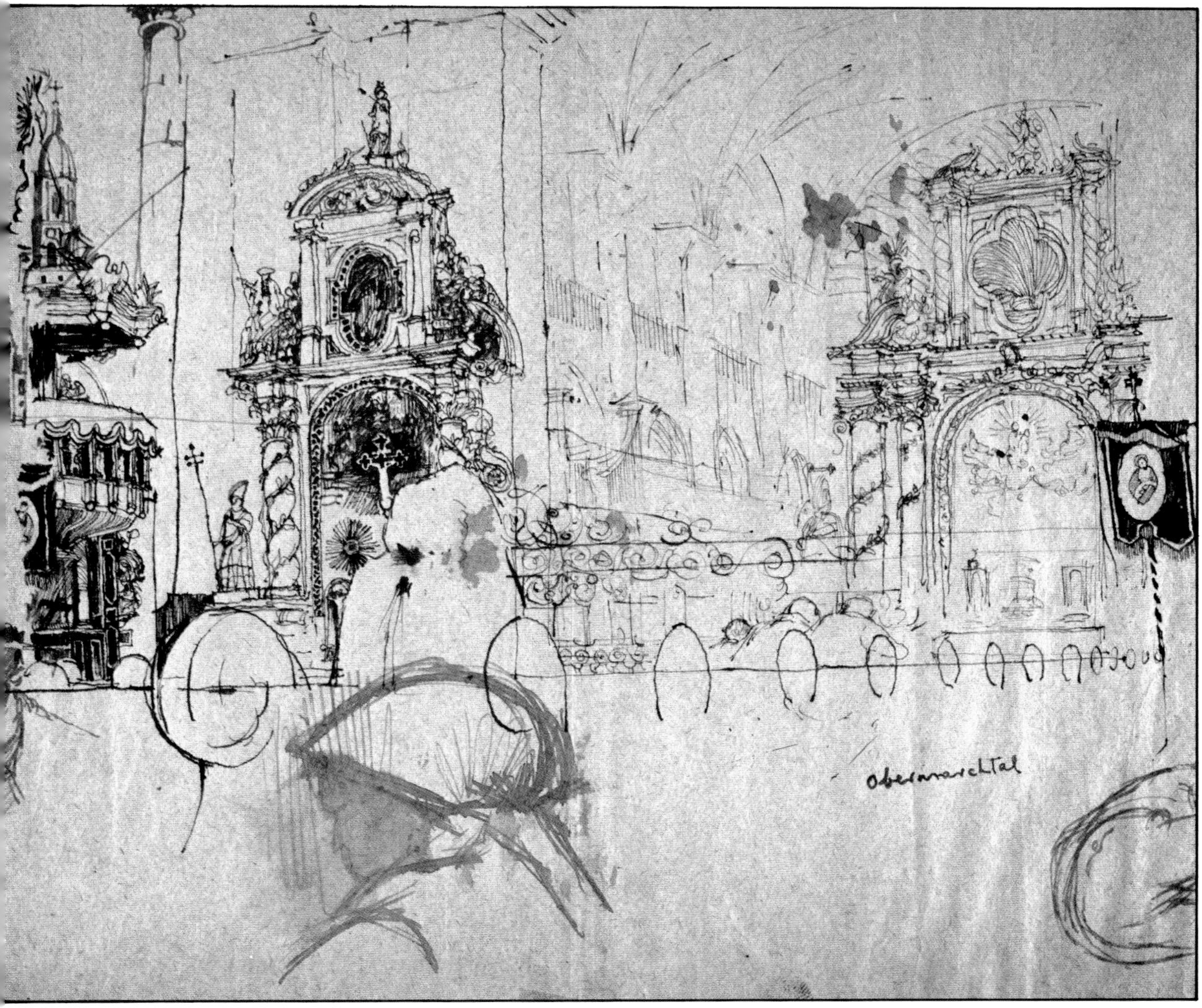

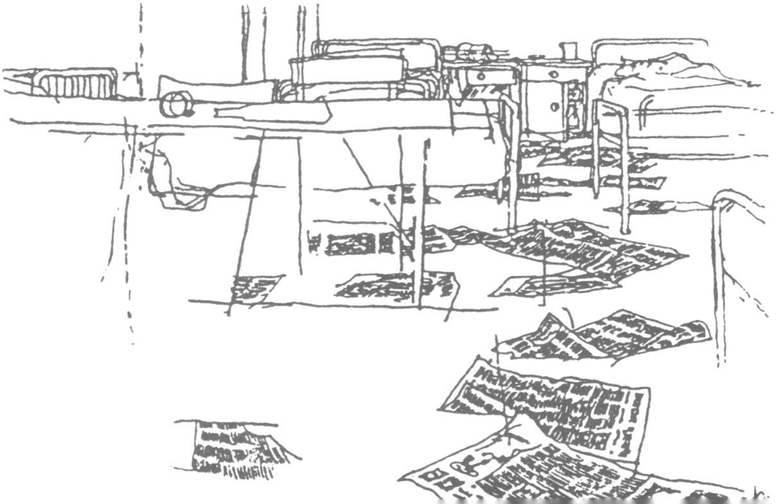

Church interior, Bavaria
(Pen and ink drawing)
You can sit quietly in a church and study the intricate decoration. Don't draw in everything; the aim (*above*) was to record information for later.

Army barrack room floor
(Pen and ink drawing)
Discarded papers, chair and bed legs... each gives a key to the receding space in this room (*right*).

buildings

Buildings are rectangular boxes with flat surfaces punctuated with hollows and humps which are revealed by the light. The next six pages propose ideas for examining buildings. Keep a sketch book and do lots of outdoor studies. Don't try to draw complex groups. Drawings of buildings are valuable records of your observations of detail and character. Work up from basics to fill in the small distinctive features.

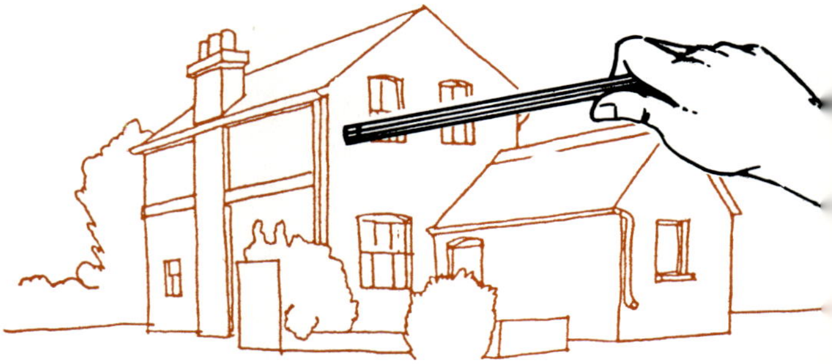

Constructing your drawing
Check that the horizontals in your drawing recede to a common vanishing point by holding up a pencil against the horizontal lines of the building and then against the lines on your drawing.

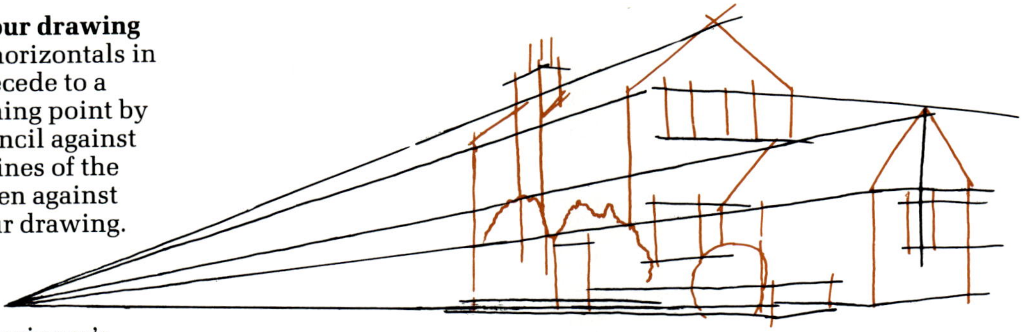

Buildings in a beginner's sketch very often appear odd. They **don't look right** because inaccuracy in the receding lines is conspicuous, whereas inaccuracies of proportion and detail are hard to detect; no one examines the drawing minutely against the real building.

a

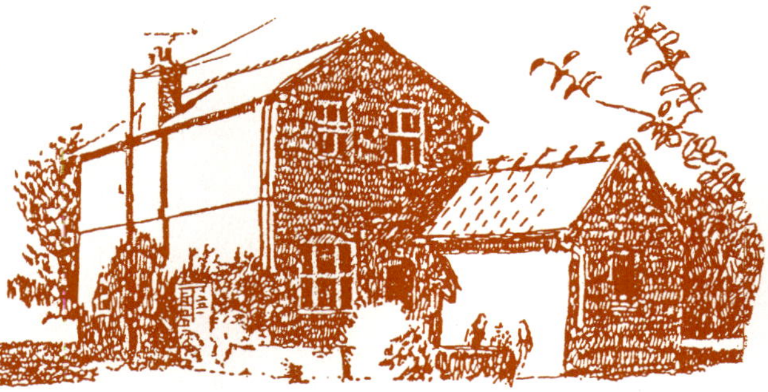

When drawing a building, consider whether you want to show the effects of the light (shadows, dark tones and light : **a**) or the colour of each part (paintwork, slates, bricks, foliage: **b**) or both combined. Whichever you choose, remember that the building must conform to the principles of perspective. **Verticals are all parallel... horizontals converge into a common vanishing point.**

b

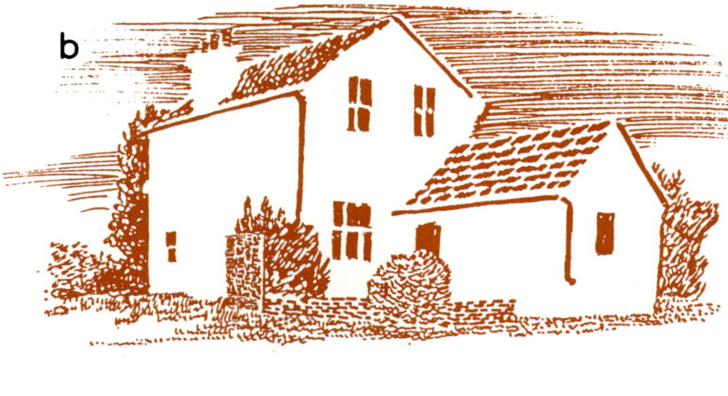

a

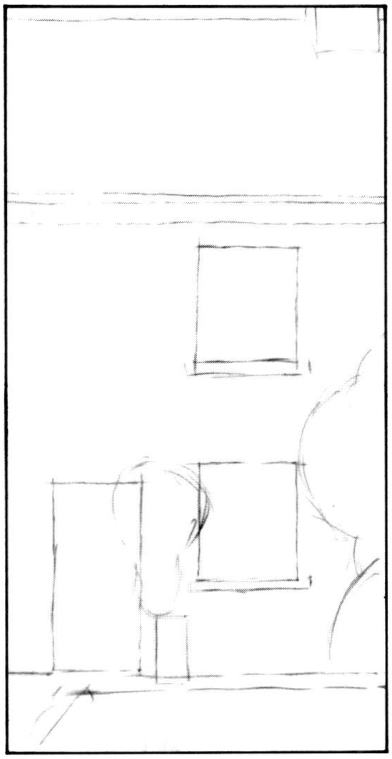

b

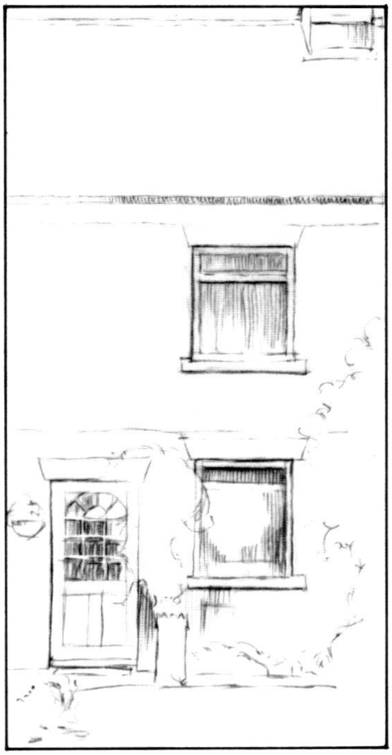

c

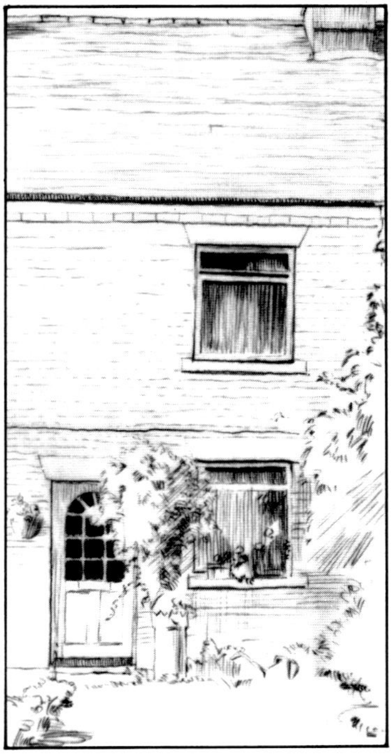

d

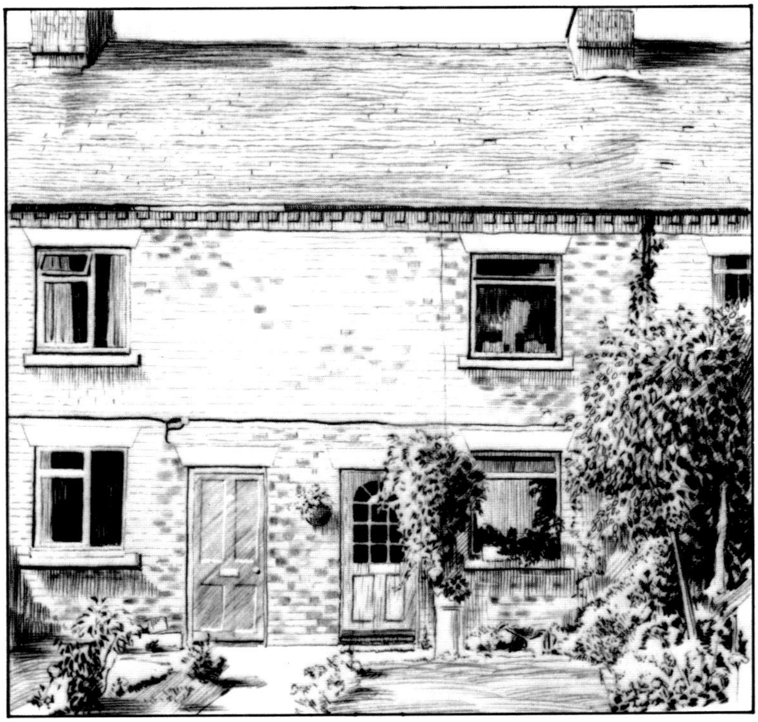

Graham's home
(Pencil drawings)
First plan the basic elements, sketching out an overall net of structure so that the larger proportions are correct (**a**). Then begin to fill in the drawing, covering it wih basic values and tones (**b**). Move on to add the more individual items, the small distinctive features (**c**). Finally, work over the whole drawing to achieve an even quality of texture and tone (**d**).
When drawing always try to create an image with a clear personal individuality, so that what you draw expresses both your view of the building and the building's own unique qualities.

buildings

Carefully choose your building in order to study its character; or an odd or complex grouping; or the effects of light on different faces; or the surface textures – brickwork, window-frames; and examine in detail the quality of your final drawing. Work with pencil, pen, brush – whichever is easy and quick. Always remember to keep verticals upright.

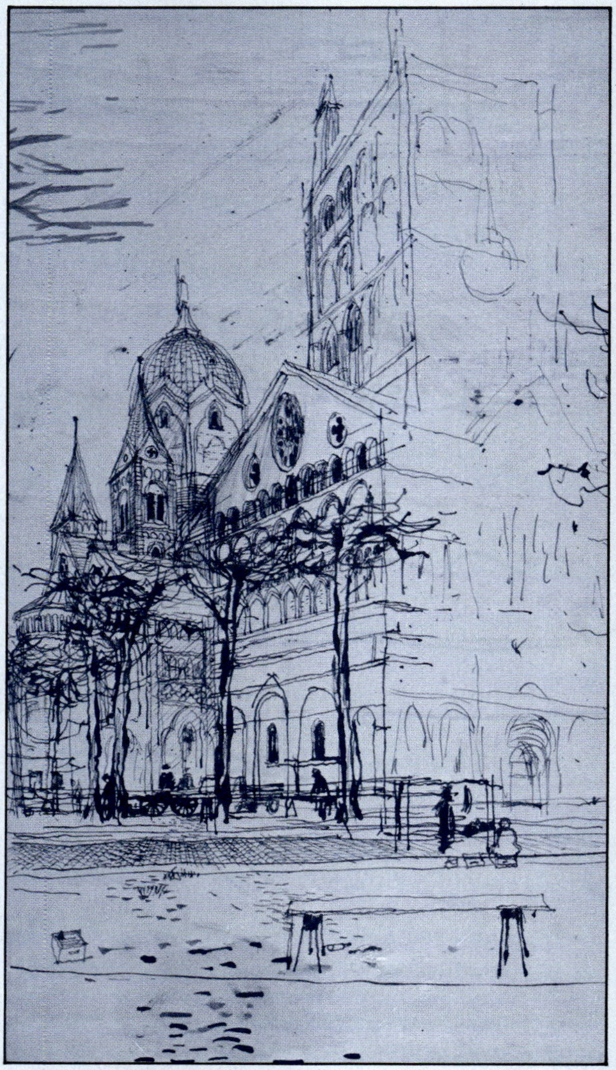

Romanesque Cathedral, Nuess
(Pen drawing)
Stand well back, as in the view (*right*), so that you can capture the overall construction. Remember the rules of perspective, and add decoration on to your basic forms.

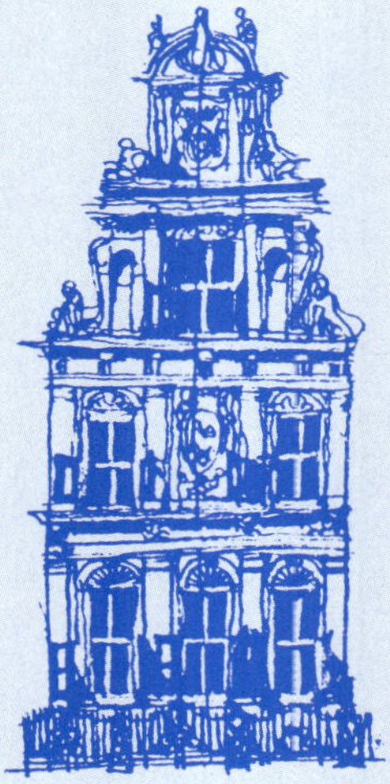

House façade, Antwerp
(Pen drawing)
Often when out sketching you will find an exciting façade ornament; record it (as *left*) for future use. Remember, flat views, seen head on, are easier than oblique facades.

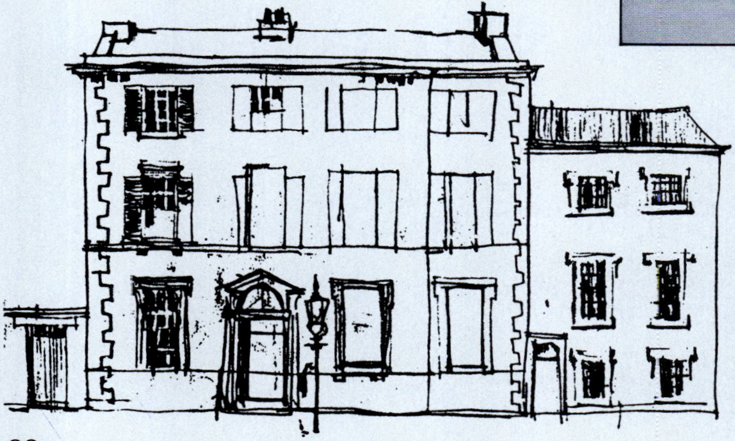

Georgian houses, York,
(Pencil drawing, *left*)
You need not document all the details in your sketch if they are repetitive; only one window shutter need be drawn which will enable you to do a more finished drawing later.

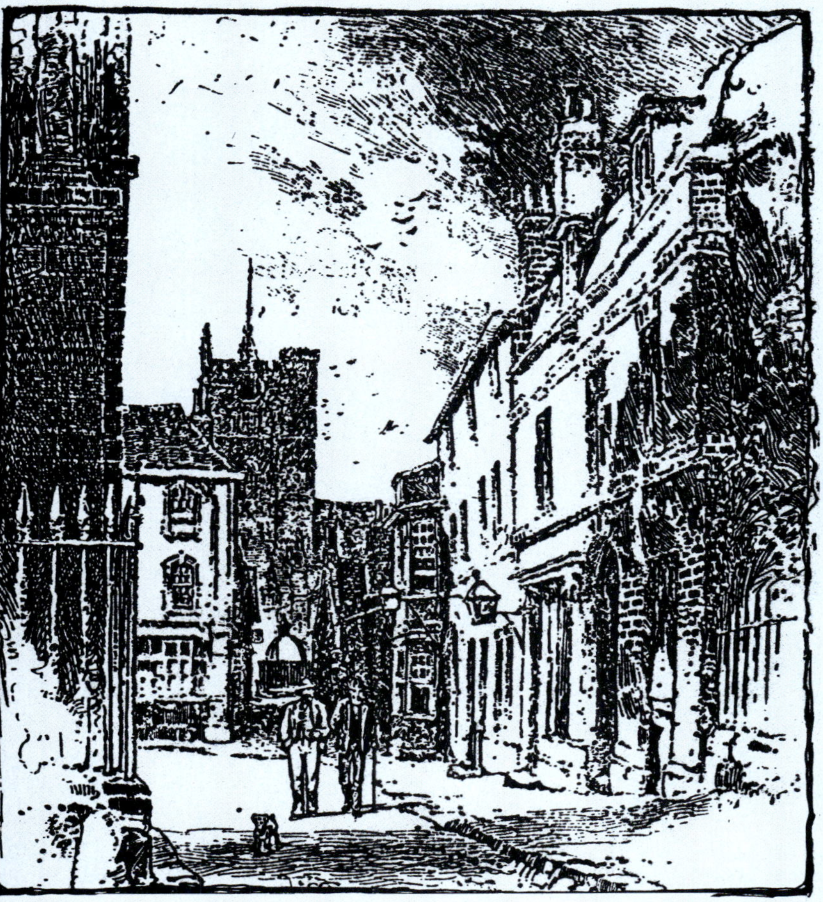

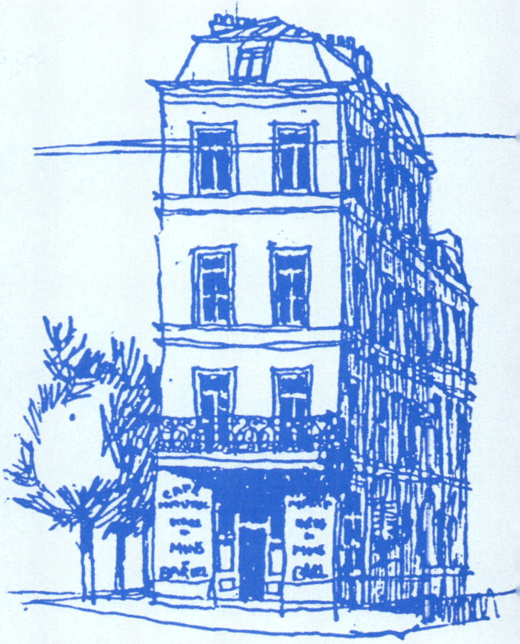

Street corner, Paris
(Pen drawing)
The quick, irregular line of the drawing (*above*) is in keeping with the old, crumbling paint of the building. Sharp, straight lines would not capture the neglected appearance of this façade. Be alert for the odd, unusual qualities that make some buildings striking.

English village square
(Pen drawing, *above left*)
The shadows on the stone, the darkened sky, the worn curb and road, combine to convey age and tranquillity.

Durham City, England
(Pencil drawing, much reduced)
The firm lines on the drawing (*left*) describe the confusion and arbitrary groups of the old Durham buildings.

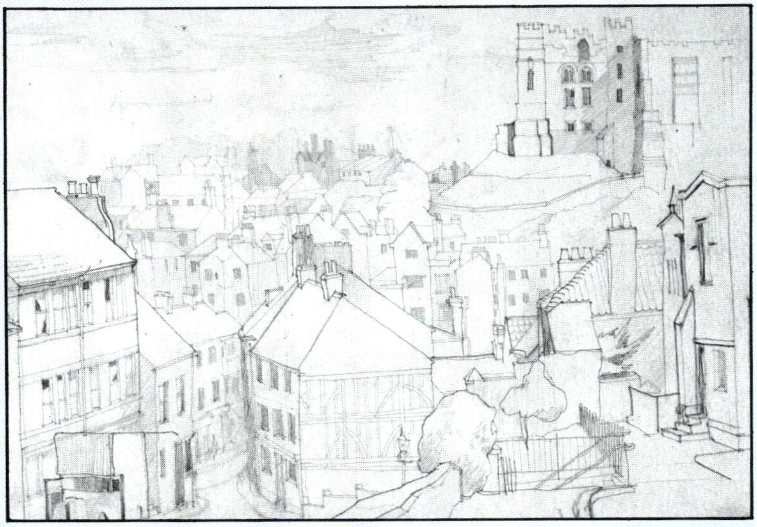

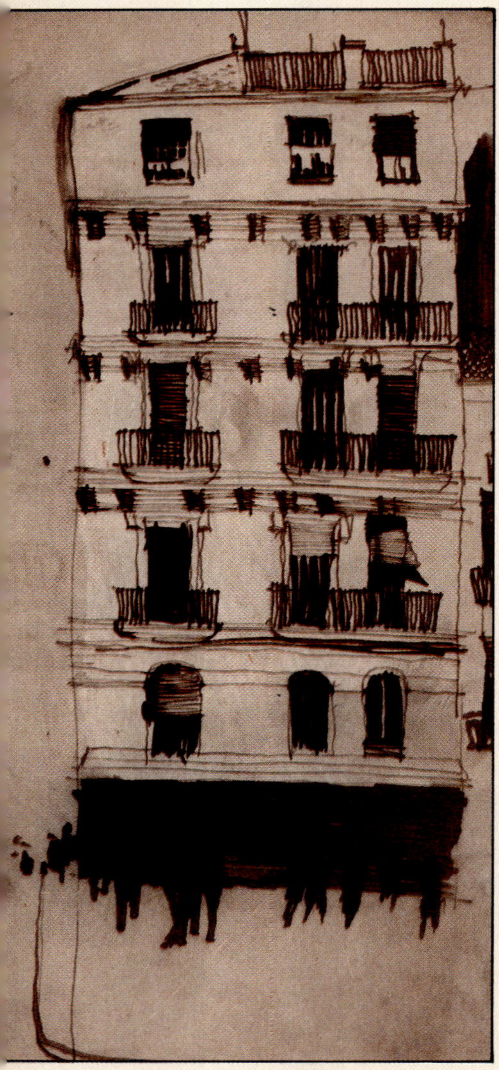

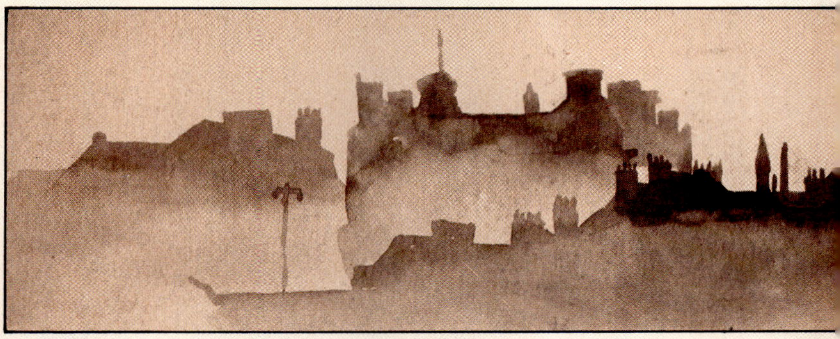

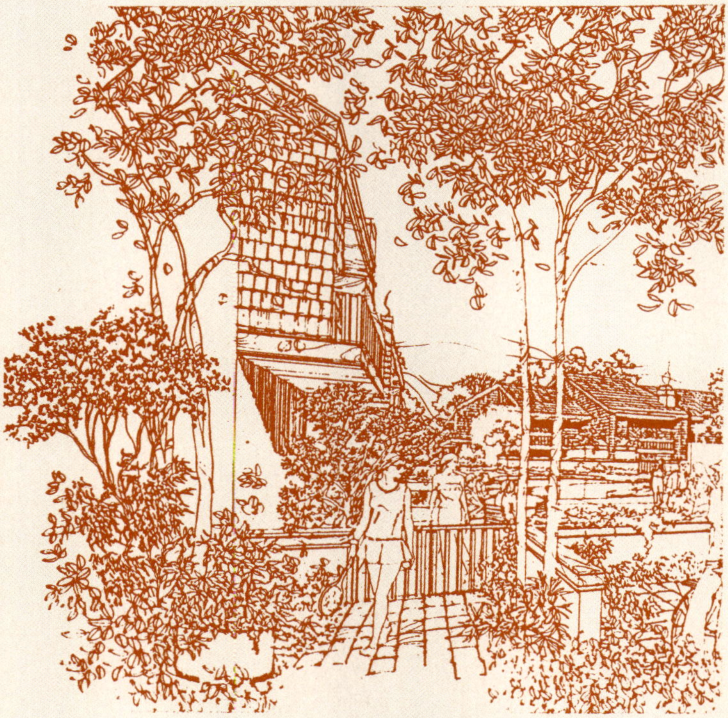

Boulevard corner, Paris
(Pen and ink drawing)
In the scene (*above*) strong sunlight at noon creates deep shadows and greater contrasts in the shallow detail. Try to achieve a sense of the time of day and convey the nature of the light striking the building.

Condominium buildings, New York State
(Pen drawing)
The drawing (*above*) depicts buildings not yet constructed. The artist has added people, trees and foliage to enliven the architect's plans for a new housing development. By adding figures and trees you can soften the effect of box-like structures.

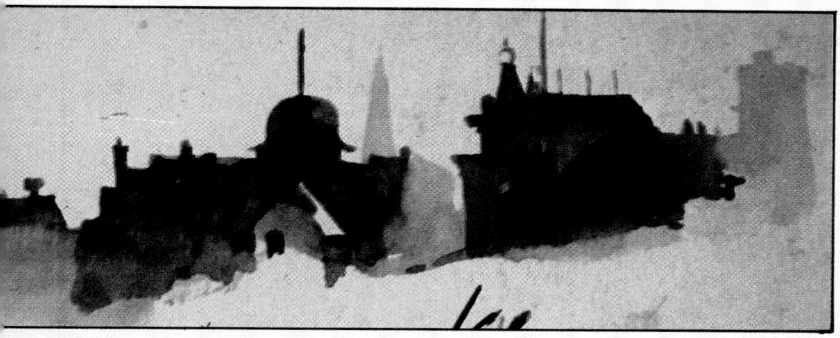

Industrial city skyline, Newcastle
(Brush and ink drawing)
Catching the edges of buildings in evening or morning sunlight (*left*) helps bring out individual features and creates atmosphere. As the buildings are in shadow, colour, texture and surface details are not visible, so the drawing can concentrate on the edges.

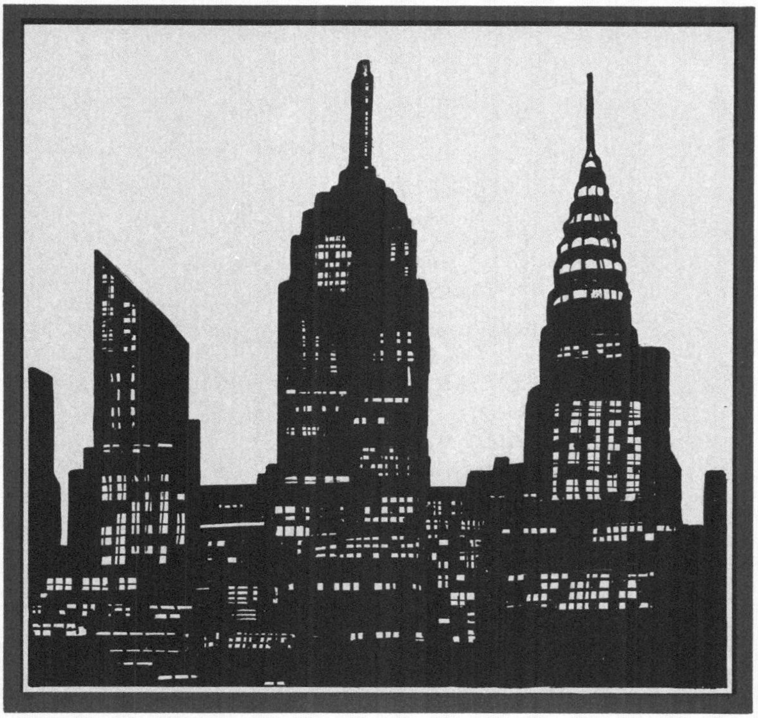

Manhattan, New York
(Brush drawing)
The three main New York buildings (*above*) are at least a mile from each other and could never be seen together as they are here. The artist has moved the skyscrapers together to form a symbol of the Manhattan skyline. Drawings like this use the individual structures of buildings as decoration.

The Cathedral of Learning, Pittsburg
(Pen drawing)
This drawing (*right*) emphasises the Cathedral of Learning's verticality. With the ascending forms drawn in this dynamic way the building is seen as rising into the sky. Presumably this was the architect's aim so he created strong verticals without horizontal shadows.

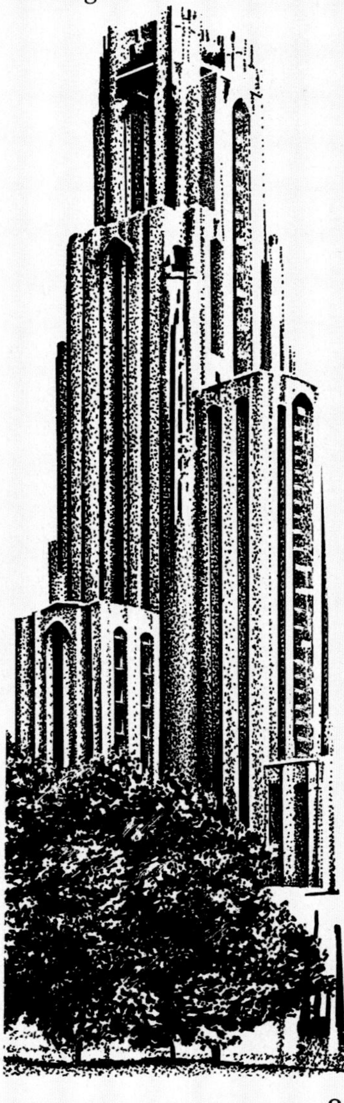

plants

Plants have a charm and beauty which, if captured, can offer you excellent results. They are one of the best subjects to study because of their innate variety of forms, your opportunity to study them very closely indeed, their decorative qualities and the wide variety of colours, textures, shapes and forms available.

Try working with a variety of tools, and maybe use coloured paper and pastels, maybe inks, maybe brush and ink. The same plant can be used for your experiments with unfamiliar tools. If successful, your drawings will make excellent pictures to frame, or send as greetings cards.

Plants all conform to regular structures; the leaves of each plant are all similar and only appear different because of their position in relation to your view of them. Plants are basically circular in plan, growing out from a central core. Try always to think of the space the plant occupies and draw the shapes in relation to one another within this space. Draw always the particular not the general.

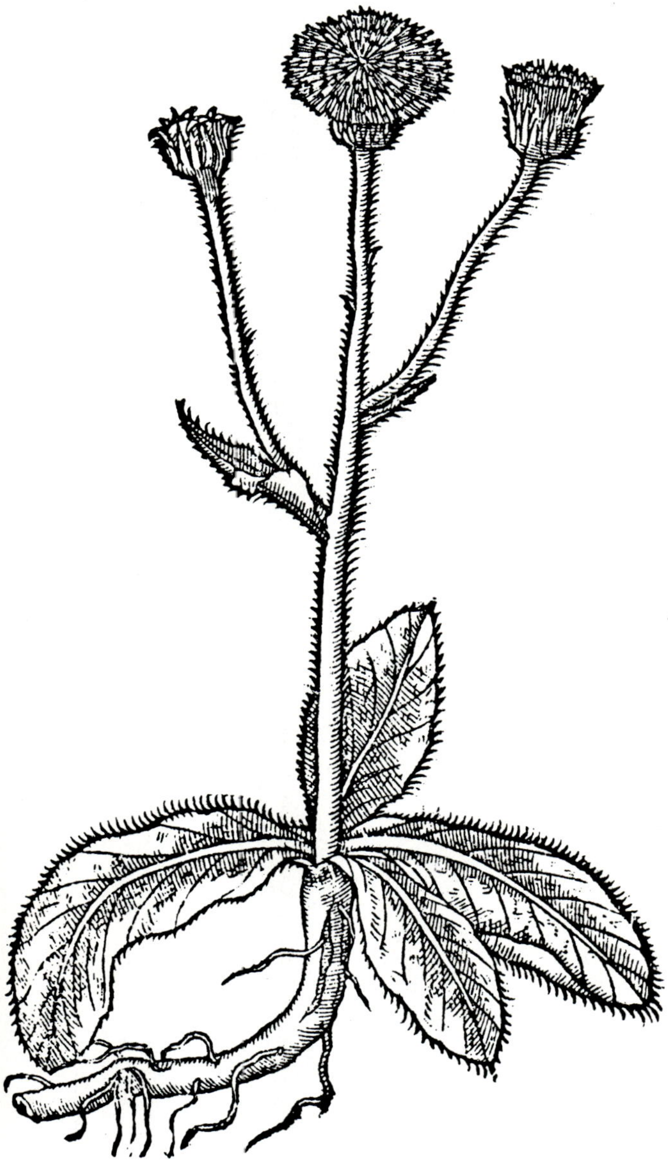

Hawkweed
(17th century woodcut)
Early herbalists exaggerated the details so that the plant could more easily be recognised. The drawing (*left*) clearly shows the hairy stems, broad leaves and tubular roots. The artist included side and top views of the flower for clarity. The drawing is a sort of police identity kit of detail, not an accurate drawing of a particular example.

Various plant drawings
(Pencil, felt pen and pen drawings)
The infinite variety of shapes (*right*) – some spiky, some bunched, some thin, some stocky. All have a central main stem from which thinner branches grow, but how frequently, and in what order, is variable.

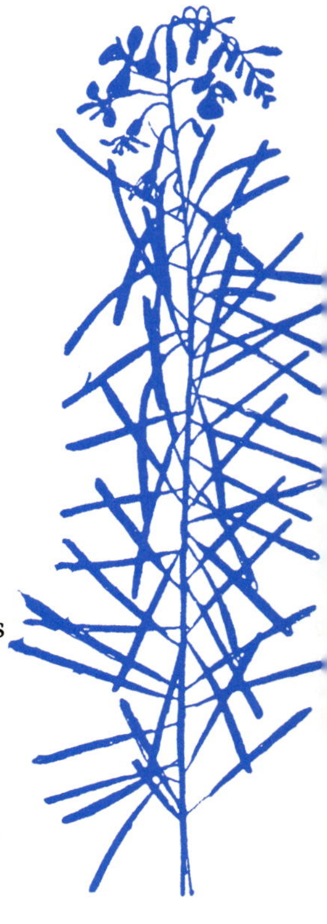

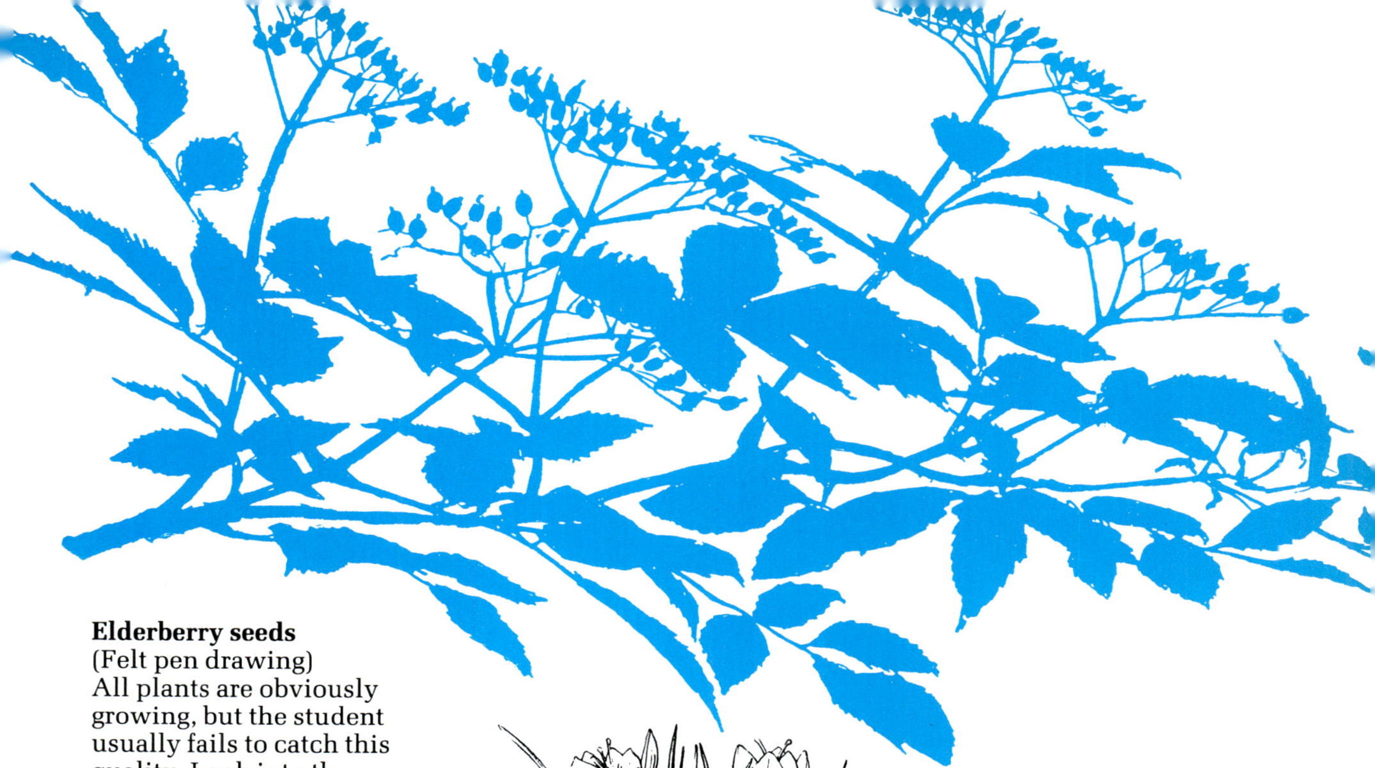

Elderberry seeds
(Felt pen drawing)
All plants are obviously growing, but the student usually fails to catch this quality. Look into the elements to find the springy, tense lines of the growth process (*above*).

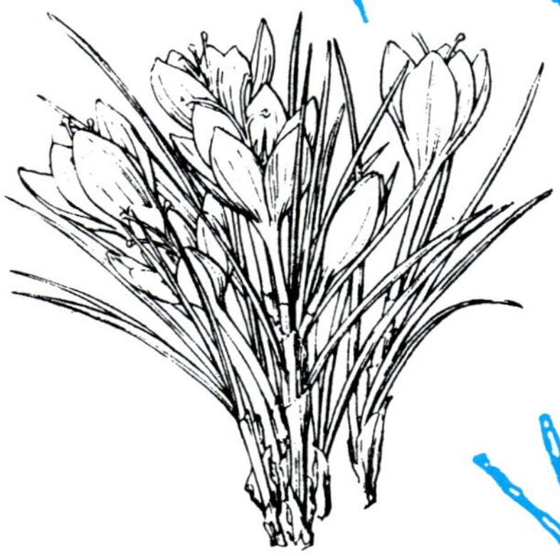

Spring crocuses
(Pen drawing)
The fresh, fragile quality of the fine leaves and heavy blossoms is beautifully captured in the study (*right*). Each bulb and blade-like leaf is an individual within the cluster.

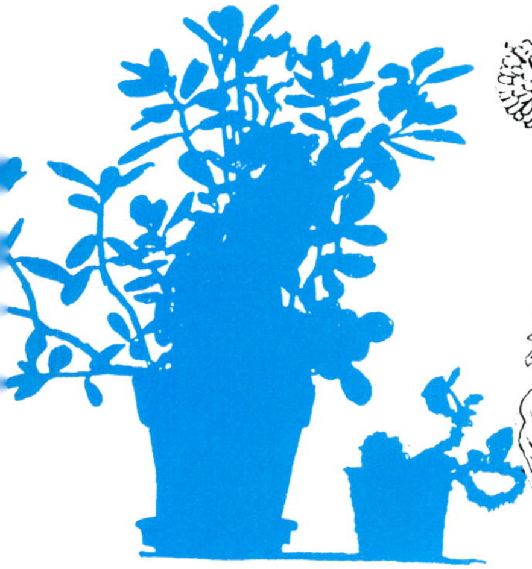

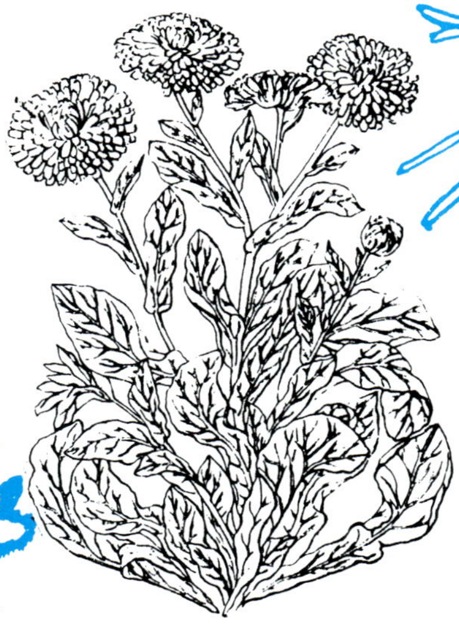

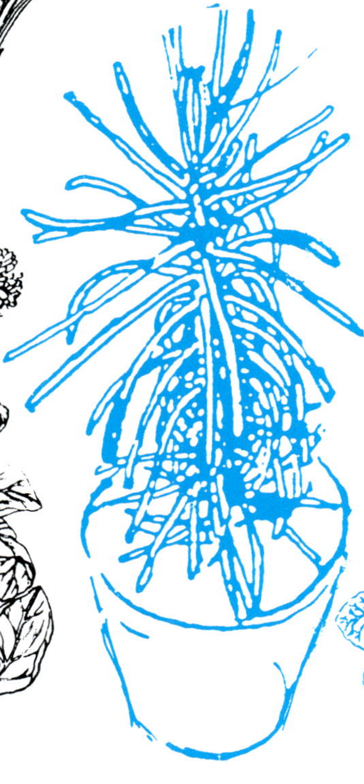

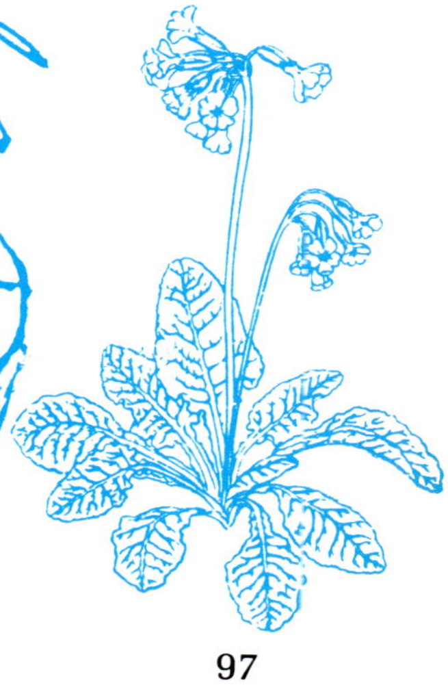

plants

Flower garden
(Pen drawing)
Being able to sketch different types of plants easily and with confidence can be great fun. The drawing (*right*) was very much larger than reproduced here. This is an imaginary garden. Once you feel confident enough to depict different types of plants, you can have fun planning your next year's colour scheme. Drawings like these are a sort of calligraphy. It is not necessary to construct each blossom. They are just sketched in as textures, differing clusters, drawn as flicks of the pen. Note the lupins in the distant corner, simple towers of dotted lines, or the climbing rose or clematis on the back wall.

Broad-leafed house plant
(Pencil drawing by student)
The first drawing (*right*), from a side view, fails to observe the basic principle of plant forms, namely that they radiate from a central core. Asking the student to draw a plan view of the same plant, then to label matching leaves, reveals the discrepancies.

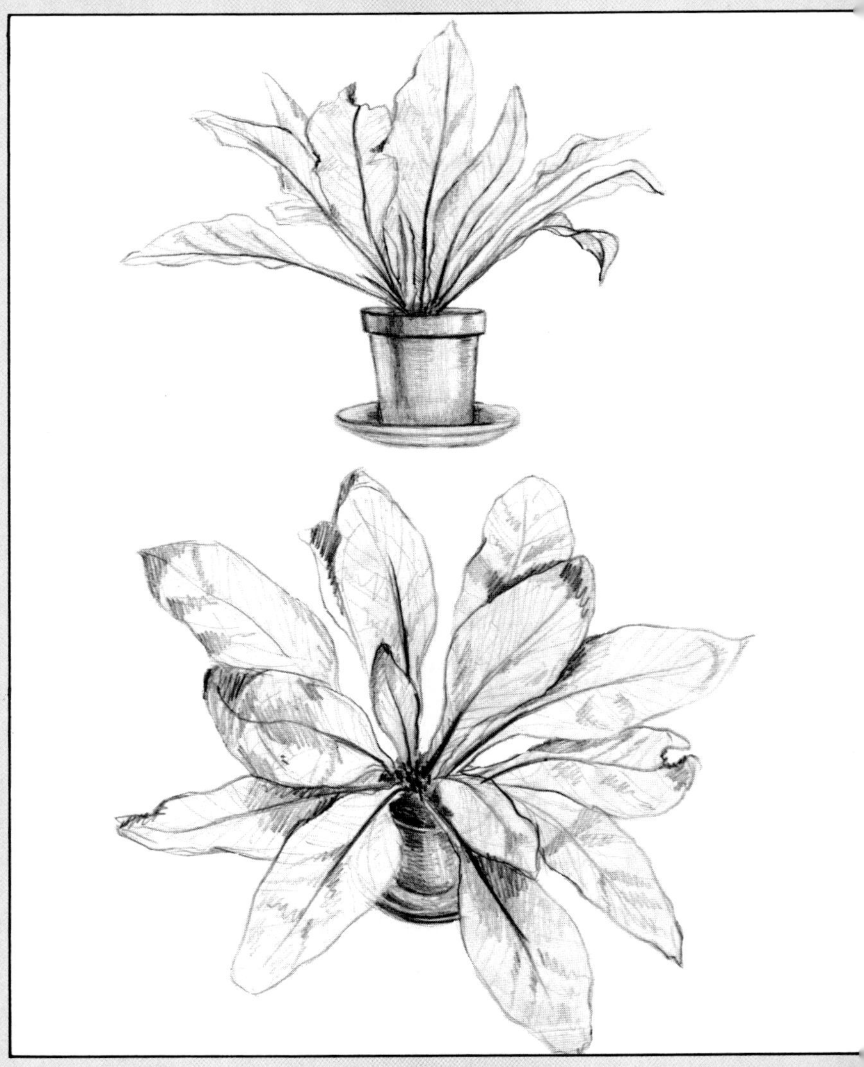

Drawing exercise
Try to draw a plant, imagining it to occupy a wire cage (similar to a lamp shade *below*). Plot the points of the leaves within this framework, trying to describe accurately these spatial relationships.

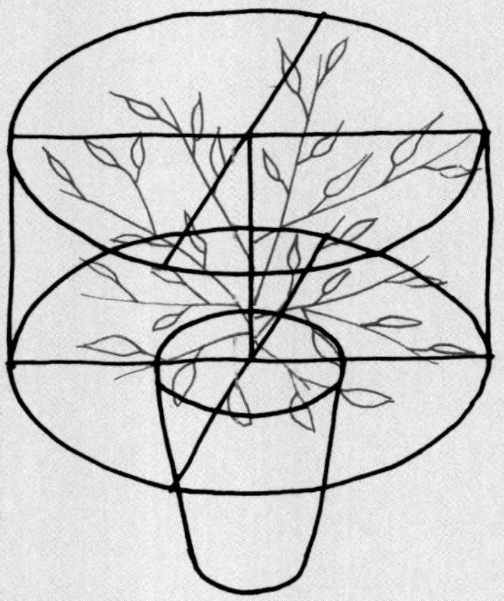

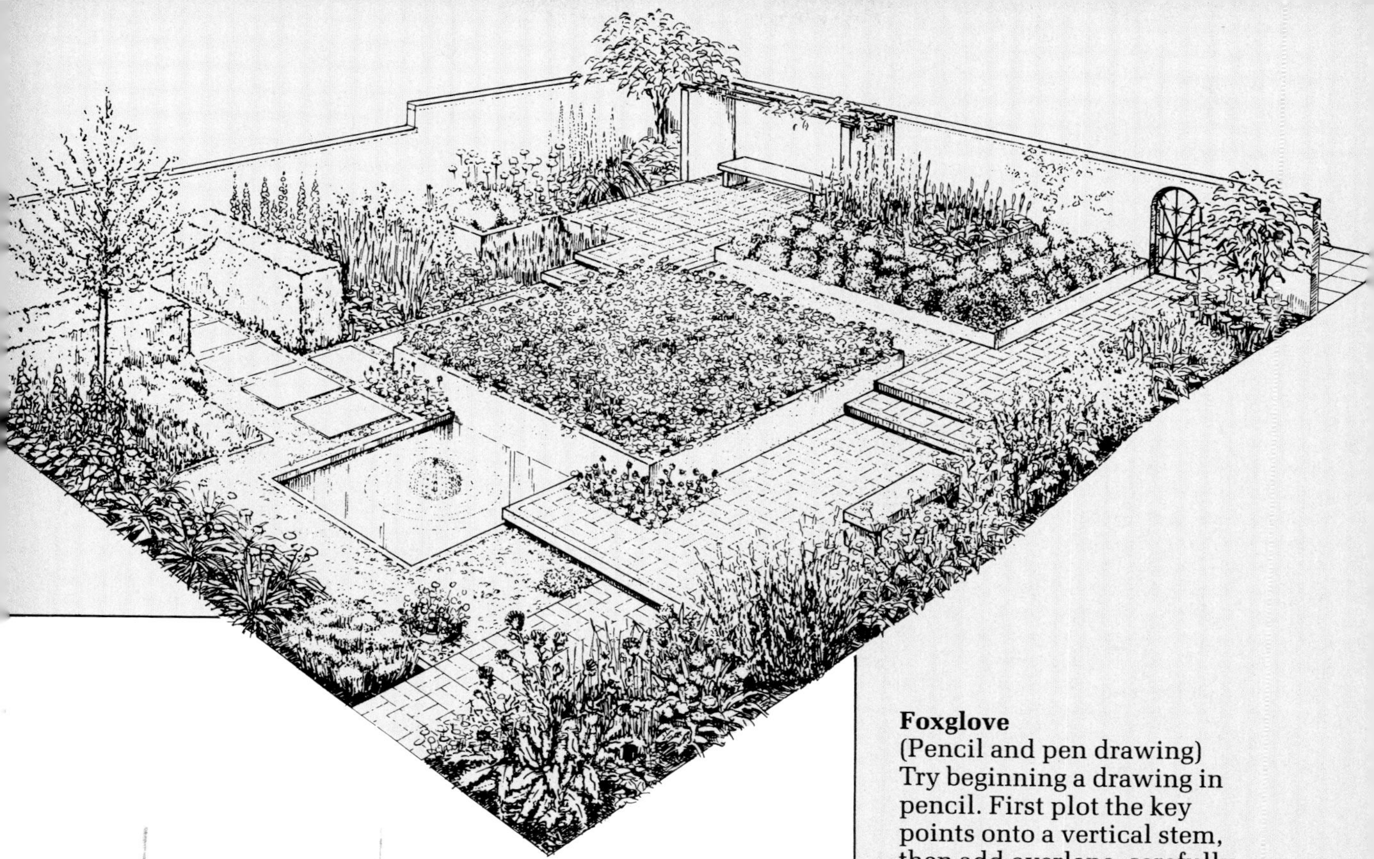

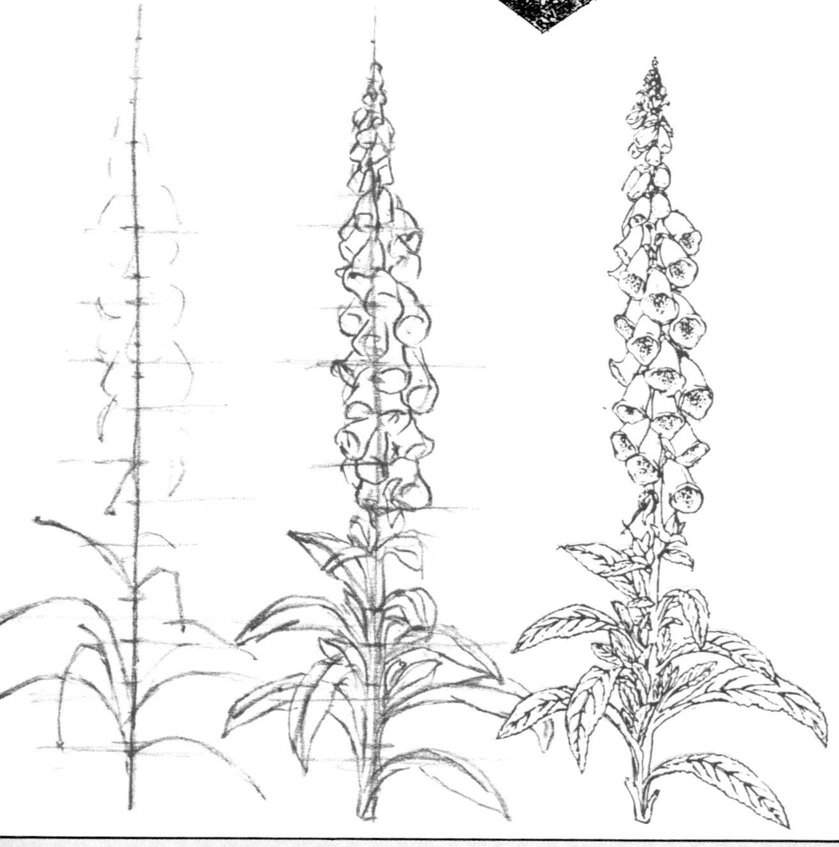

Foxglove
(Pencil and pen drawing)
Try beginning a drawing in pencil. First plot the key points onto a vertical stem, then add overlaps, carefully constructing the leaves that turn towards you. Finally, overdraw the detail (*left*) in ink, ultimately rubbing out your pencil work.

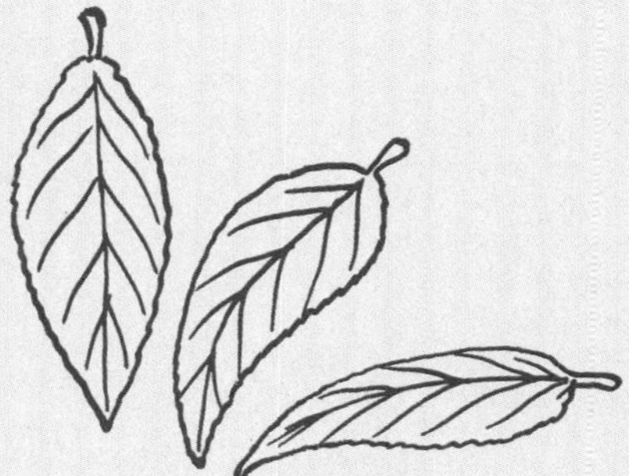

Drawing exercise
Try drawing the same leaf from different views.

trees

Trees provide valuable models for study: they are accessible, stationary and very varied. If examined and drawn with care, they can greatly enhance your skill at drawing space. And you must know something about tree structures to be able to tackle landscapes. All trees are three-dimensional. A frequent mistake is to see them in silhouette, or at a distance, and the beginner tends to draw them as if flat. Look for clues to their form and direction in light and shade, in bark texture, tones, overlaps and curves. Investigate the overall textures of different species by sketching leaf features *en masse*. **Draw particulars from observation.**
Study groups, understand distant shapes, capture the "space cage" of branches, try unusual views. Make up your own compositions and landscapes. Apply them as decorative motifs. Above all try to catch the quality of nature.

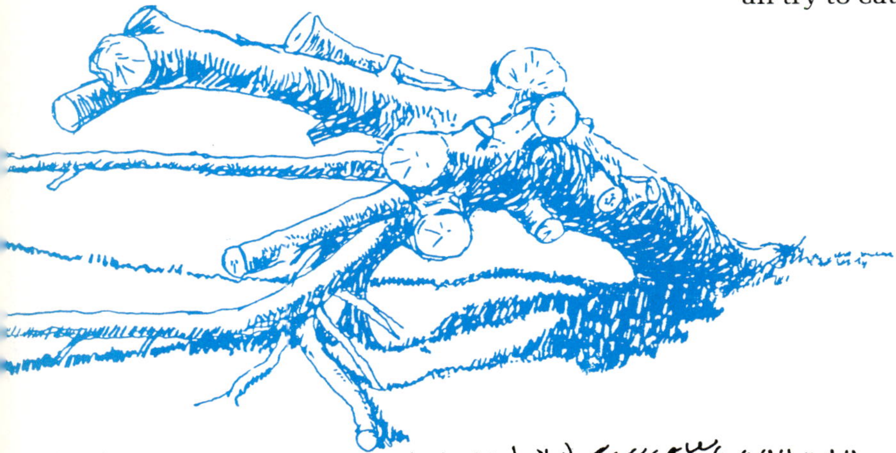

Fallen tree
(Ball pen drawing)
Tree branches grow out in all directions (see *left*). Although distant trees look flat, it is vital you understand the space a tree occupies. Train yourself to think *round* a tree, feeling its full volume. Practise studying trees from unfamiliar angles or, best of all, a tree which is lying on the ground.

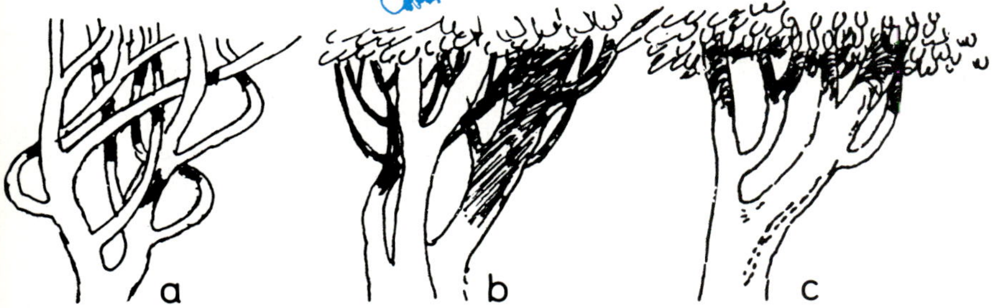

Branch studies
(Pen drawings)
Look for evidence of the direction of branches (*left*): shadows on a branch cast by others in front (**a**), shadows of branches in the background (**b**) and shadows from foliage (**c**).

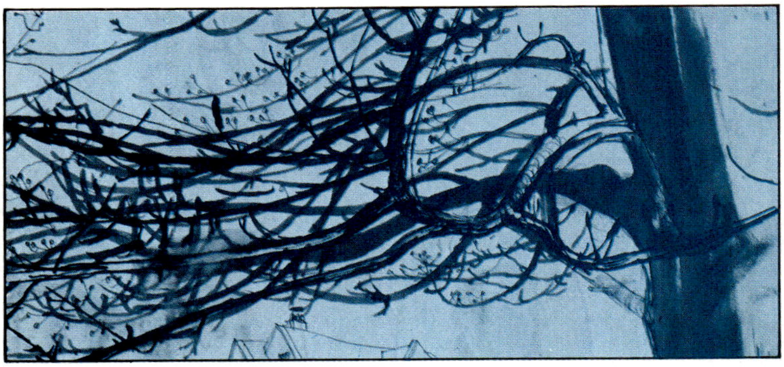

Winter branches
(Pen and wash sketch)
Curves, overlaps and shadows help to indicate the position of branches. Texture and tone, carefully observed and drawn onto a branch (*left*) show whether the limb is growing towards you or away. Look closely at bark texture which also helps in establishing directions.

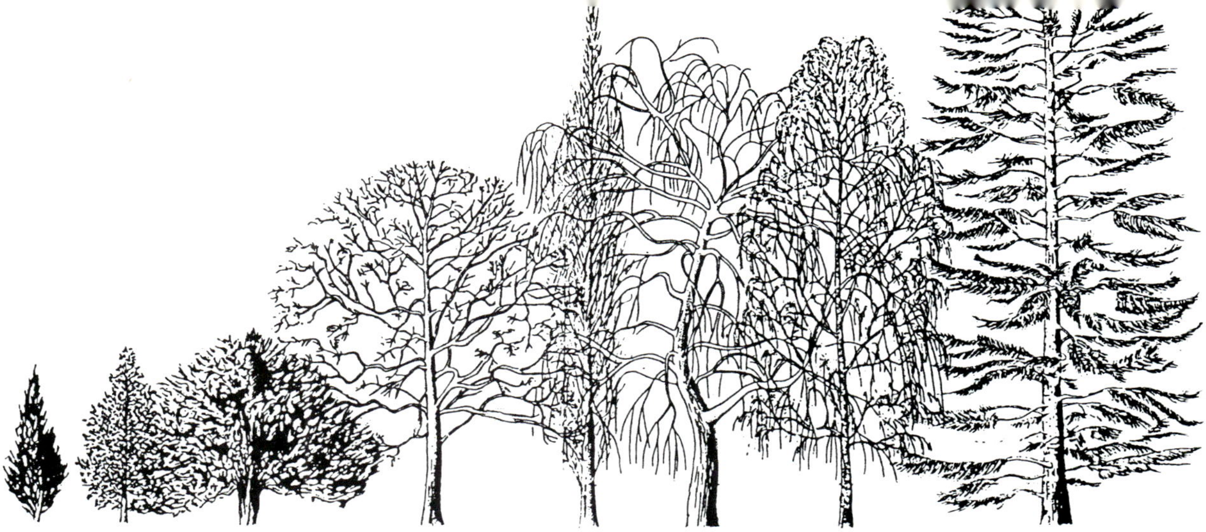

Selection of types of trees
(Pen drawing)
Each tree species has its own shape, thickness, transparency or opaqueness. Some species are tall and narrow, some short and fat. Winter is often the best time to appreciate these features. Try to draw your trees so that a gardener could recognise them (*above*).

Leaf types
(Chinese brush drawings)
Just as character is revealed by a person's handwriting, so leaf shapes (*right*) help to identify trees. Make a collection of tree foliage in your sketch book, even if you don't know the names; these studies will aid you when you draw trees from memory.

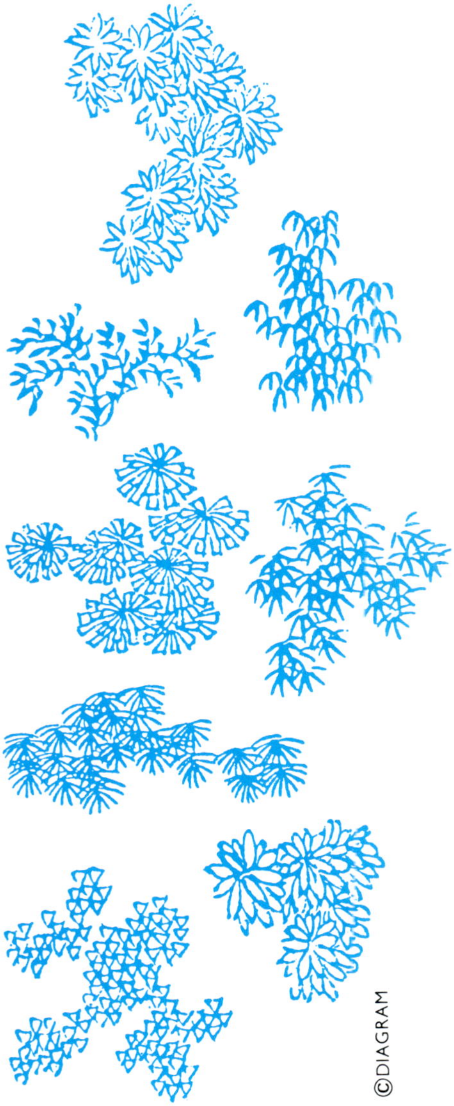

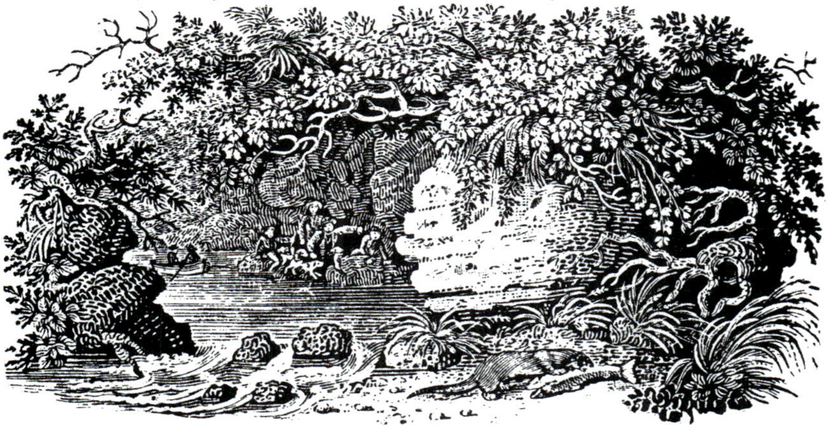

Riverside trees
(Thomas Bewick wood engraving)
Bewick spent hours in the forest sketching. His book illustrations (as *above*) reveal an expert knowledge of tree colouring, shapes and textures. This enlarged detail of leaves (*right*) clearly shows several different tree types.

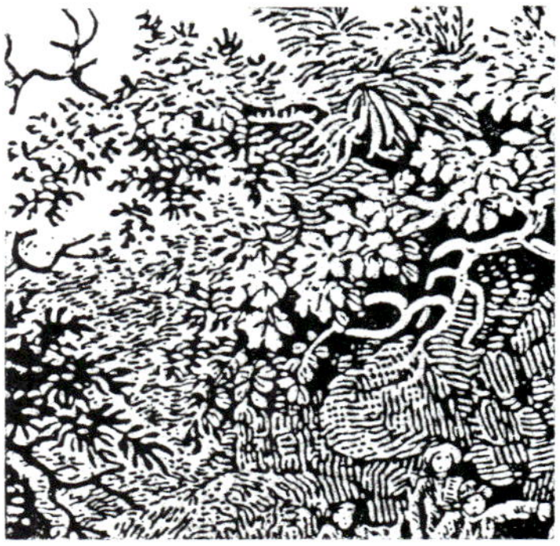

trees

Trees on Hampstead Heath
(Pen drawings, *right*)
Look for trees in groups and practise examining the combination of separate individuals by drawing the same group from different viewpoints. With the light behind them, trees provide good experience in drawing their particular shapes and studying their characters.

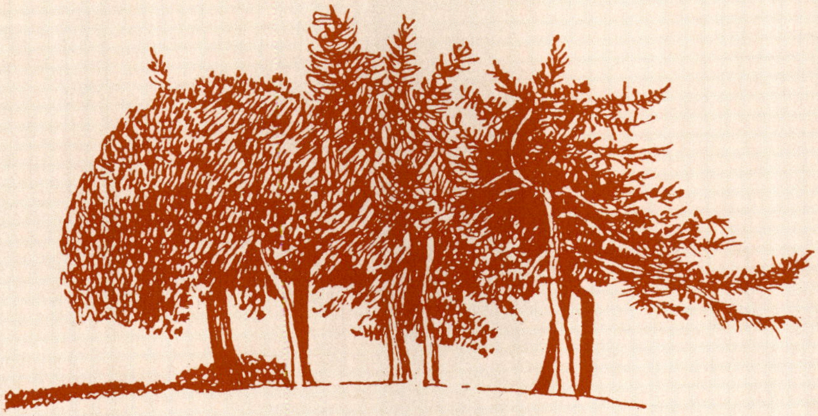

Simplifying groups
(Pen drawing, *right*)
Clumps of trees seen close up give a stippled effect which can be described by drawing the texture (**a**), or the shaded areas only (**b**). Distant groups appear flat (**c**). Far away, tone and colour are identified by light against dark (**d**) or dark against light (**e**). Finally, they become simple flat shapes (**f**).

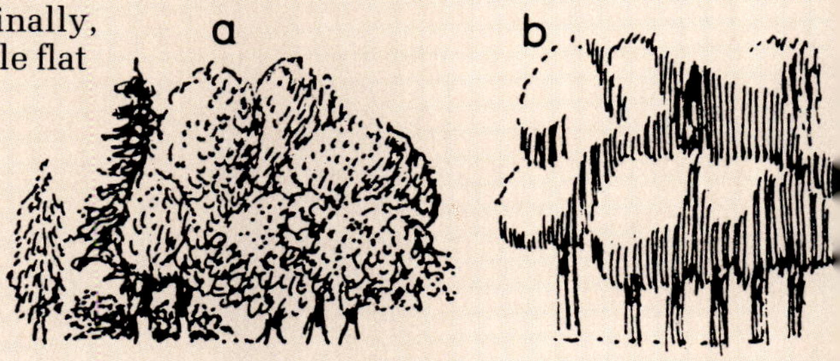

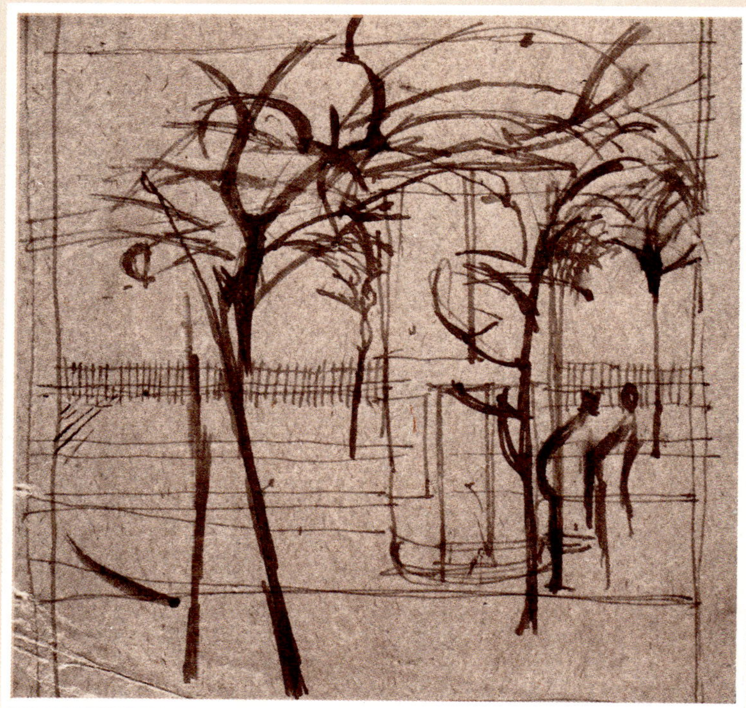

Bus stop, Dusseldorf
(Pen drawing)
Whenever the occasion arises, such as while you wait for a bus, sketch clumps of trees, trying to concentrate on the space enclosed by the branches, as in the drawing (*left*).

Pine woods, Ravenna
(Brush drawing)
You can sit beneath the branches of a group of trees and draw the outstretched limbs from below. As the drawing (*right*) shows, the choice of an unfamiliar angle to look into a collection of trees is often the way to accomplish an attractive drawing.

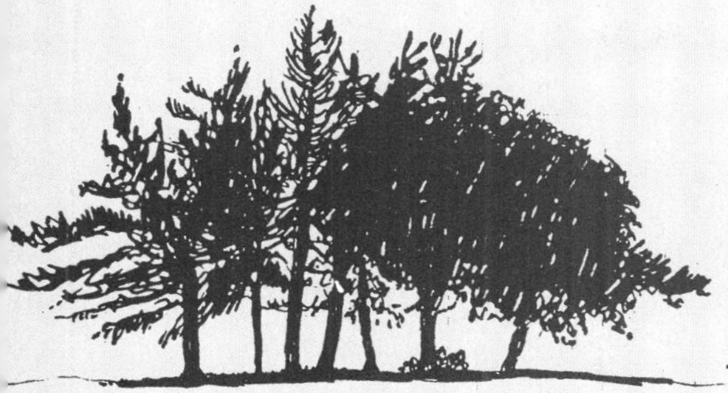

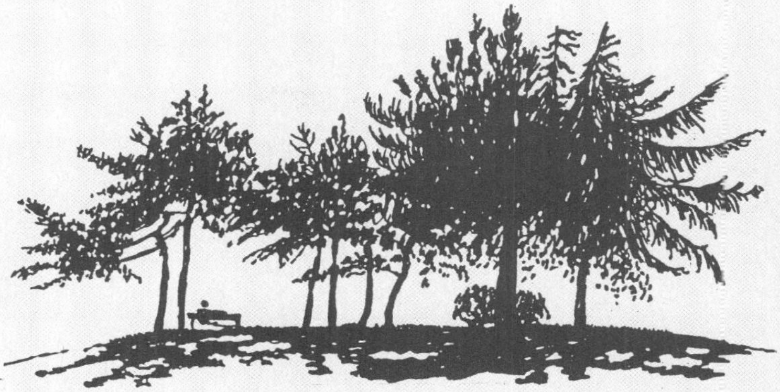

c

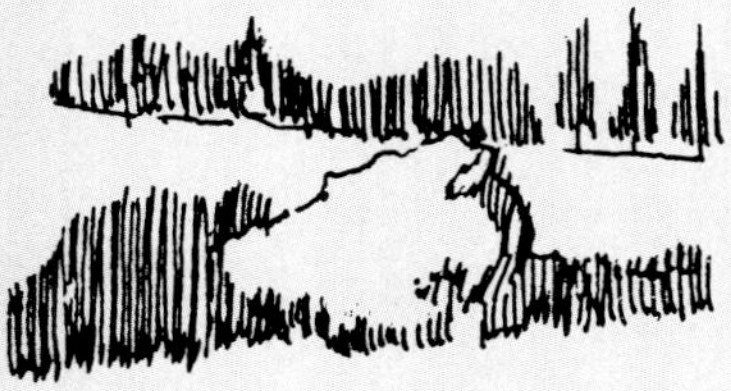

d

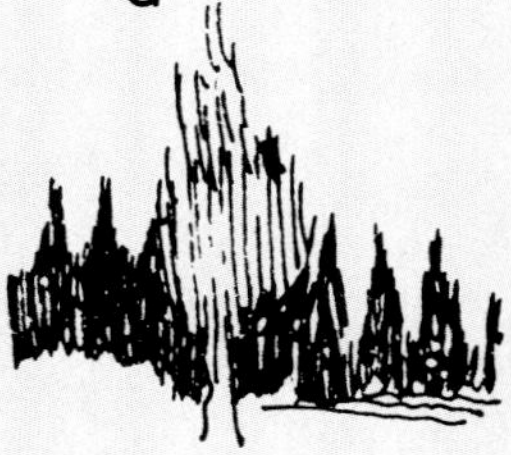

e

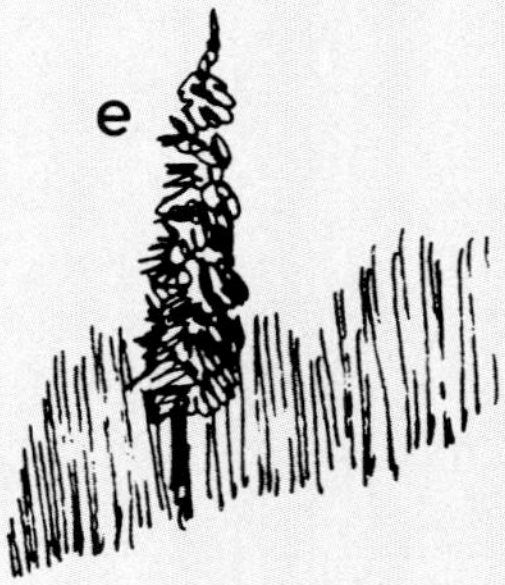

f

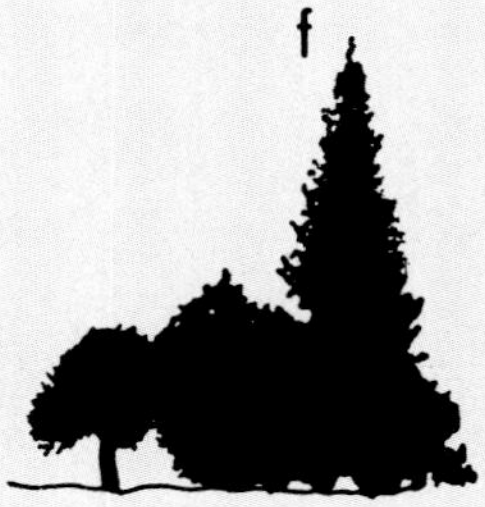

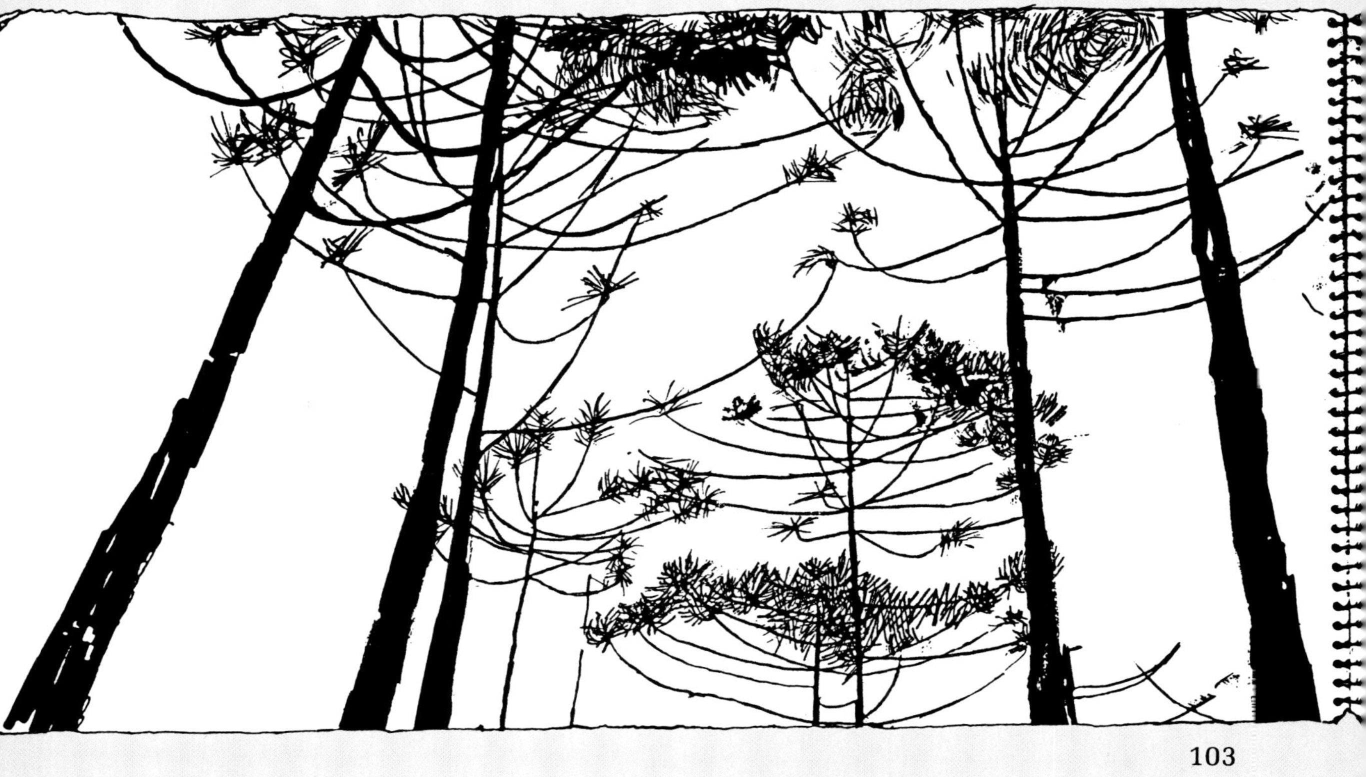

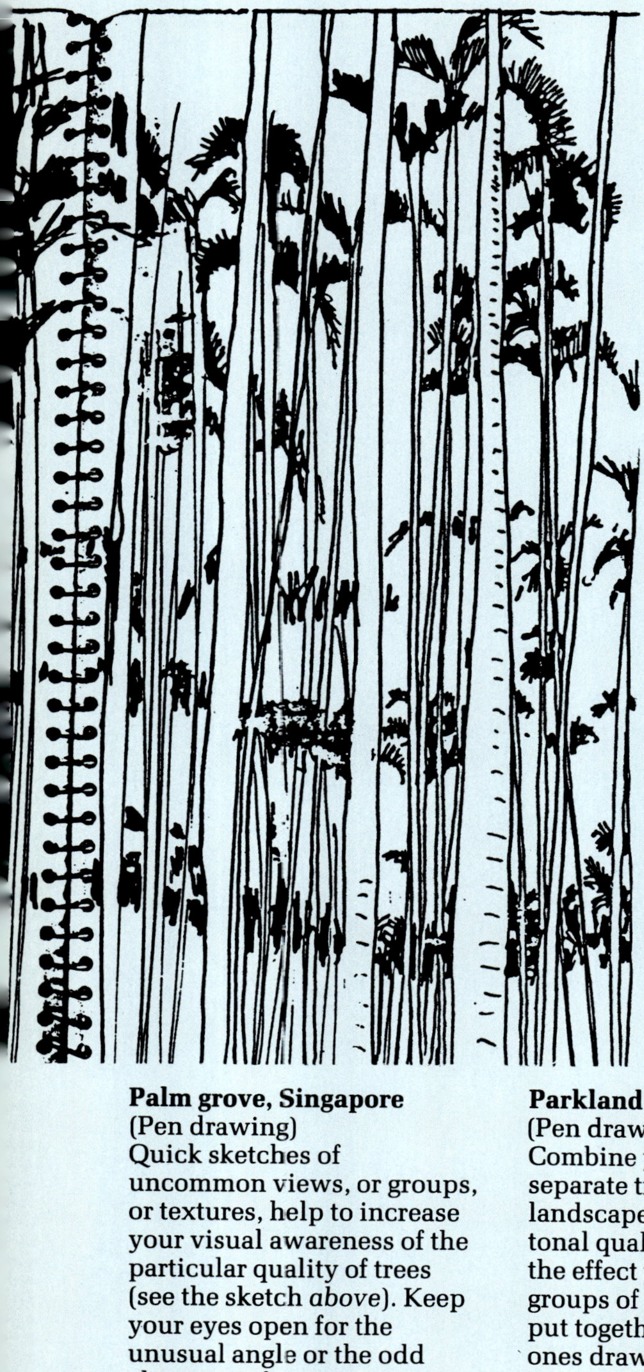

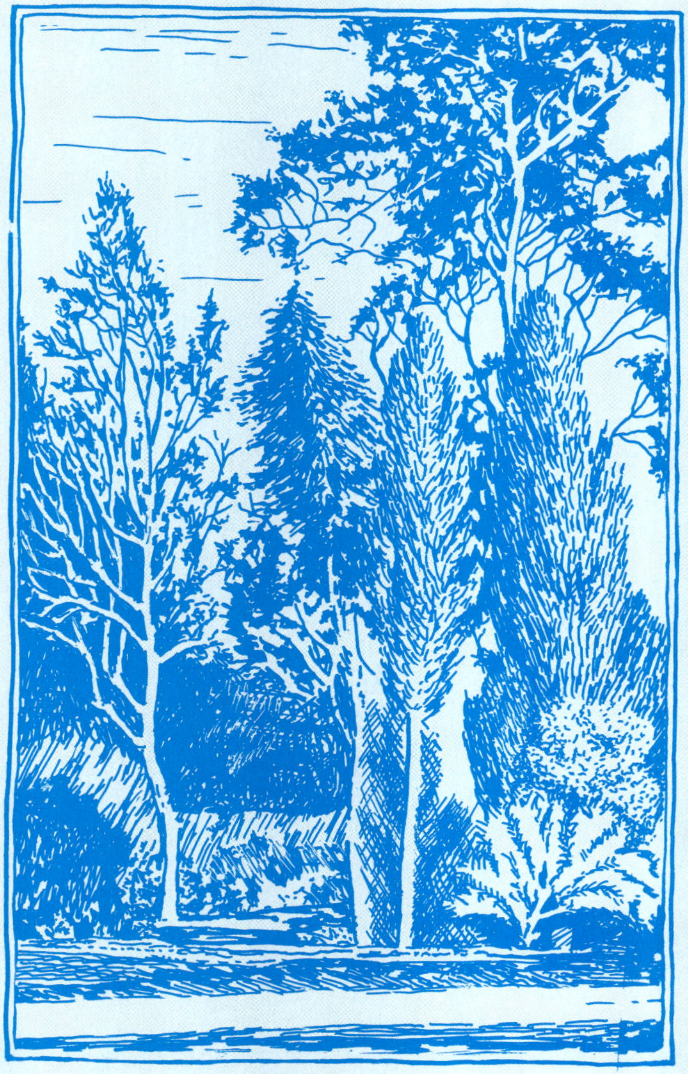

Palm grove, Singapore
(Pen drawing)
Quick sketches of uncommon views, or groups, or textures, help to increase your visual awareness of the particular quality of trees (see the sketch *above*). Keep your eyes open for the unusual angle or the odd character of some trees.

Parkland woods
(Pen drawing)
Combine your sketches of separate trees to create a new landscape. Work on the tonal qualities until you find the effect you want. The groups of trees (*above*) were put together from separate ones drawn all over the park.

Roots
(Pen drawing)
Through drawing trees you can express some special feeling about nature: wildness, or the coarse-textured effect of winter on trees; or (*right*) the strange, satanic quality of forest roots.

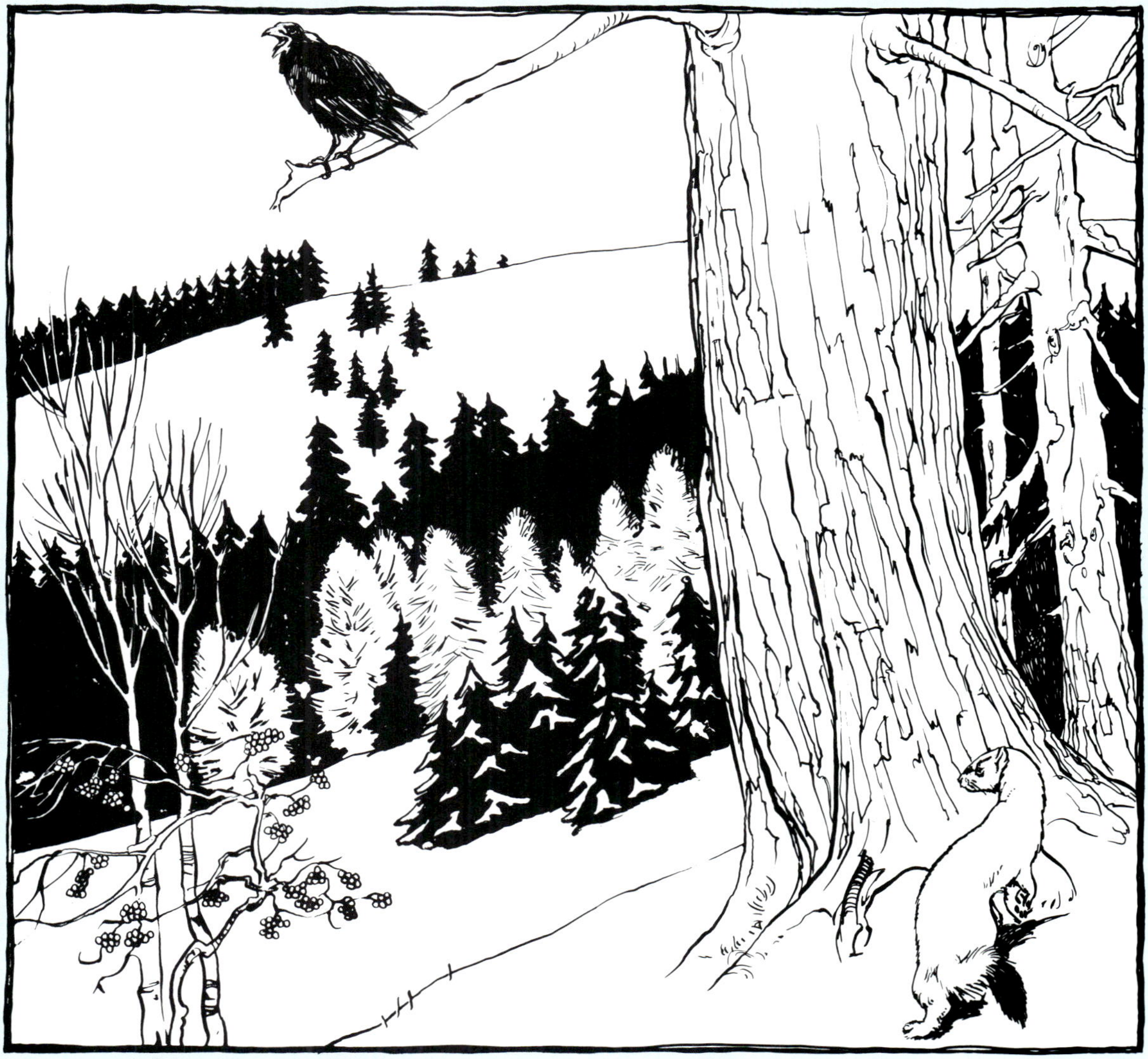

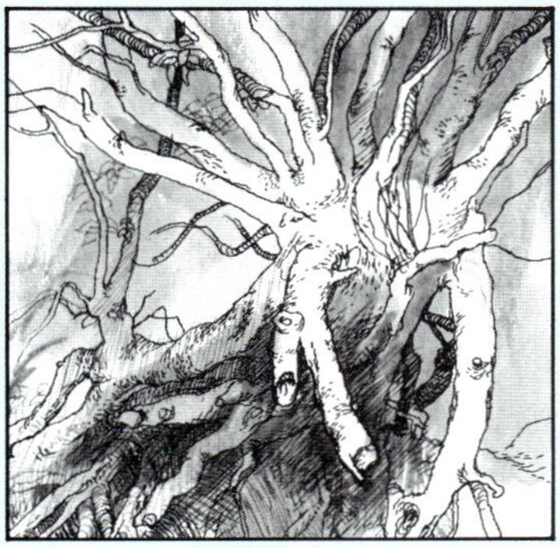

Woodland group
(Brush, pen and ink drawing)
A range of textures and tones offers material for decorations (*above*). First draw the design in pencil; then paint in the main areas before adding detail with a pen or with white.

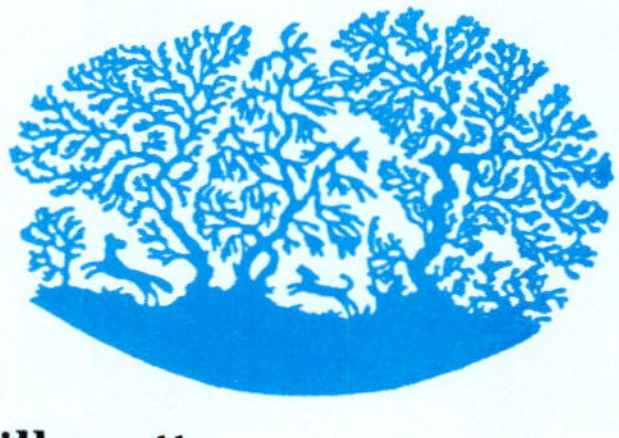

Silhouettes
(Paper cut)
Motifs of trees are ideal for decorating gift cards, book plates and stationery.

landscape

Landscape is the perfect subject for the beginner. It offers the chance to sit quietly outside and observe the world. The scene all around is interesting; every place can stimulate you to create arresting pictures. To convey a feeling of space, all landscape drawing involves perspective, which is easily reproduced if you record carefully all receding lines, spaces and features and the overlap of objects. Make a conscious effort to compose the picture and choose a particular view that captures the character and atmosphere of the whole scene. Try sketching quickly the actual composition before starting the larger drawing; this helps you recognise basics. **Frame your view of the world,** setting the edges of the composition against the edges of your picture frame. Remember that by turning slightly to the right or left you move the overall landscape area selected.

Suffolk fields, England
(Pencil drawing)
The simple landscape (*right*), with its horizontal areas of tone, is an ideal subject. The sense of space is achieved by the diminishing scale of the telegraph poles.

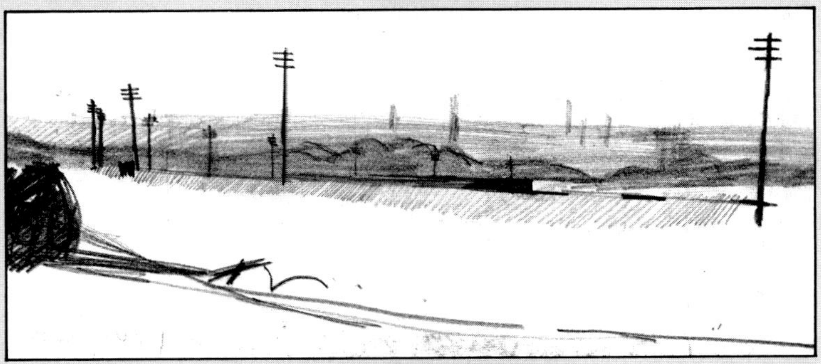

Rhine Embankment, Düsseldorf
(Pen drawing)
Complex receding objects are hard to establish in a scene. In the townscape (*right*), the feeling of space is created by the overlap of regular shapes and by the increasing congestion in the distance.

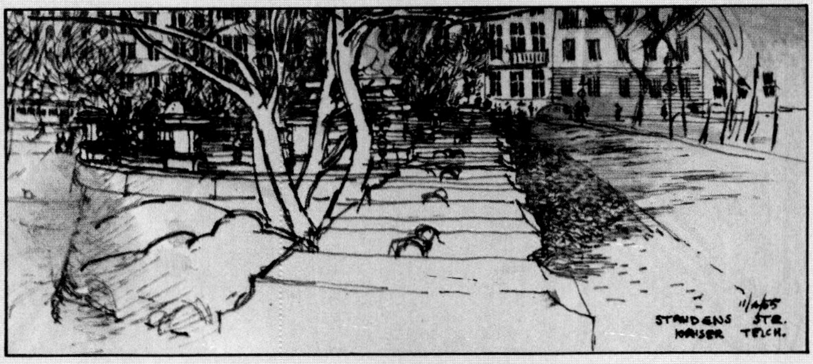

Selecting your composition
When out sketching try to see the landscape through a frame. Carry a small card with a rectangular hole cut in it (*right*) or make a box with your fingers, or hold up your sketchpad to block off each side of the landscape in turn. Compose your view. Never let the shape of your sketchbook, or the place where you began drawing, determine your composition. Think all over the view. This is editing your vision of the world to create the effect you think the subject requires.

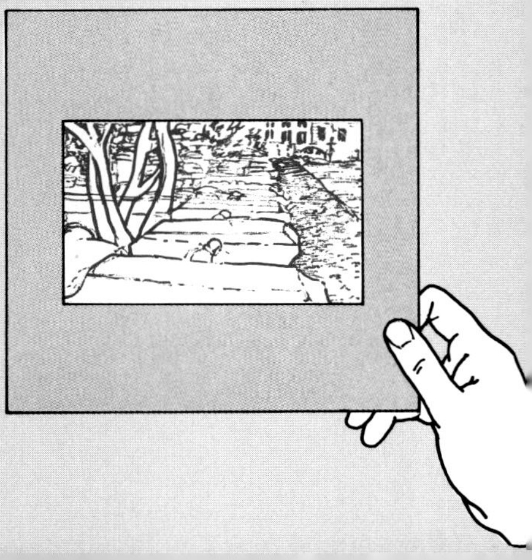

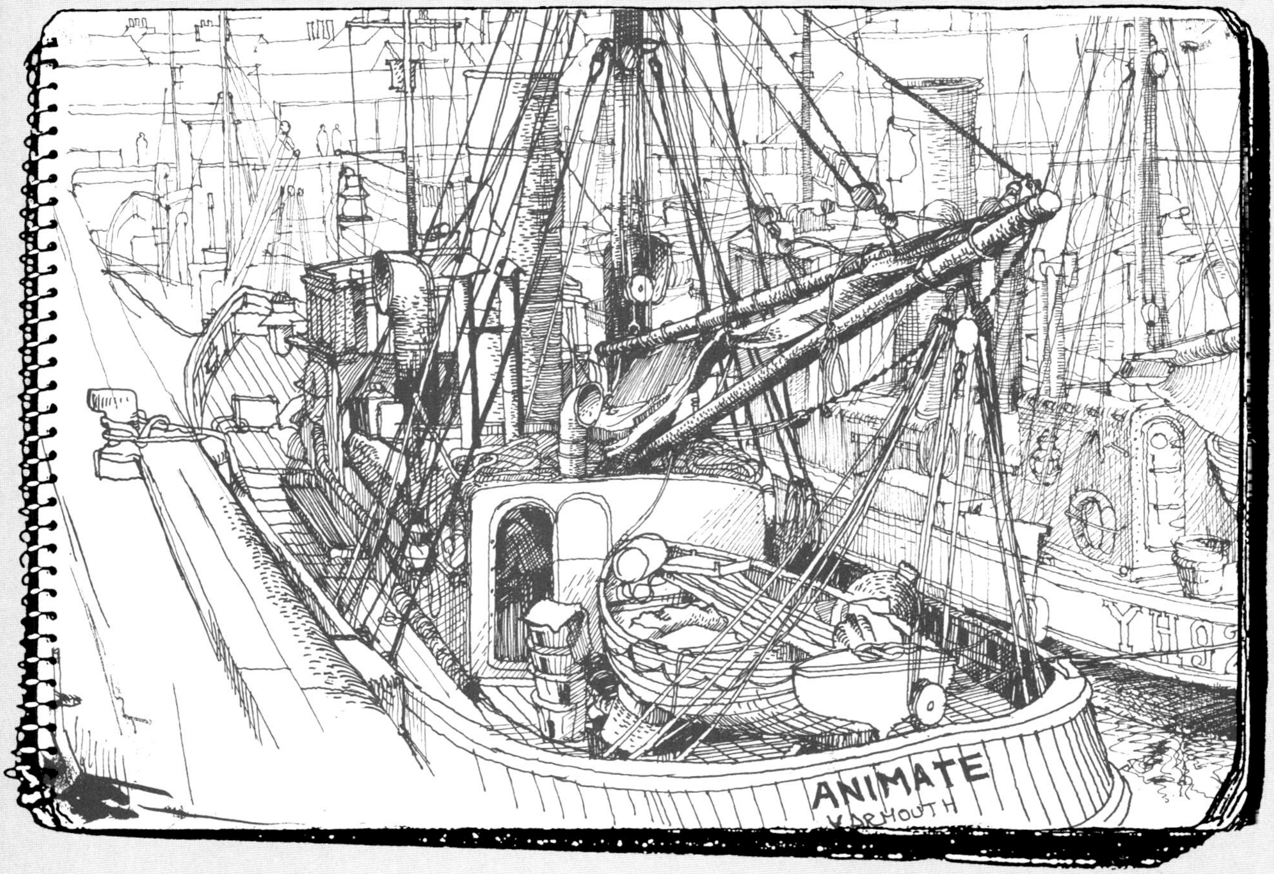

Fishing boats, Aberdeen
(Pen and ink drawing)
If you select a complex subject with intricate, small elements, like the boats (*above*) be sure to plan the basic structures first. The outline of cabin and mast were drawn in pencil before adding all the detail. See detailed study (*right*) to help you understand the objects.

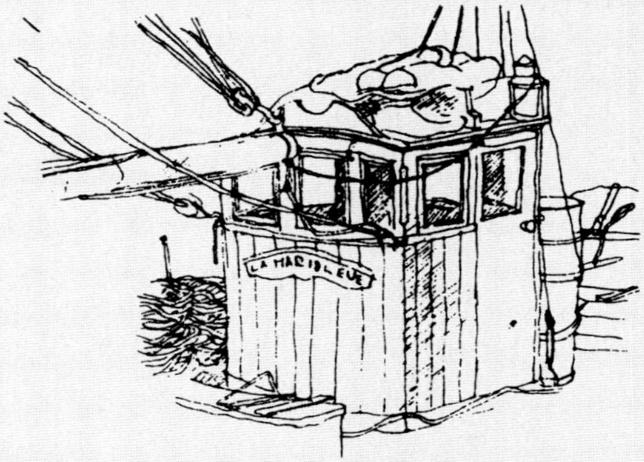

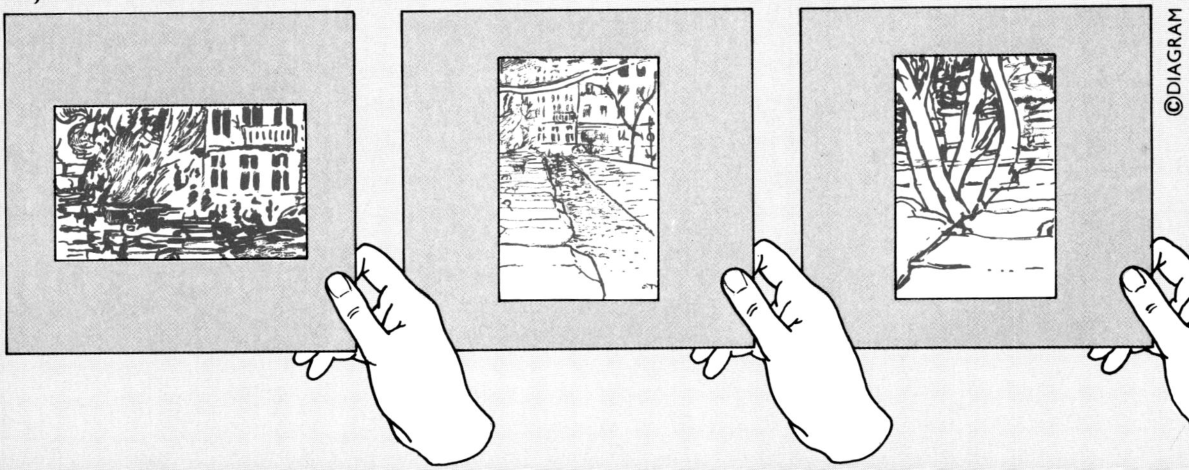

landscape

Drawing landscapes provides an opportunity to create a sense of distance on your piece of paper – like looking out of a window at a world which is receding away from your viewpoint. There are a number of techniques that will help you convey space and distance. You can choose a view that has receding features; include objects that reduce in size as they are placed deeper and deeper in the composition; alter the thickness of your lines; or choose objects that overlap.

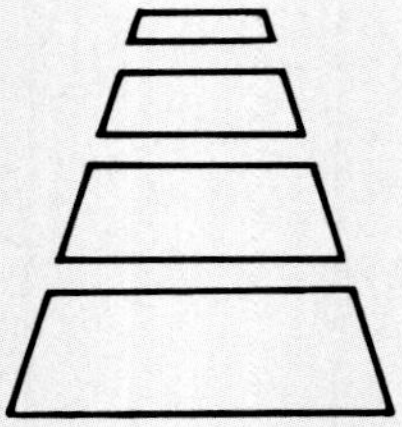

Quayside market, Antwerp
(Pen drawing)
The simplest way to compose a landscape is to choose a view with lines that converge on the vanishing point. The many parallel features in this drawing help to create a space that is receding from the viewer.

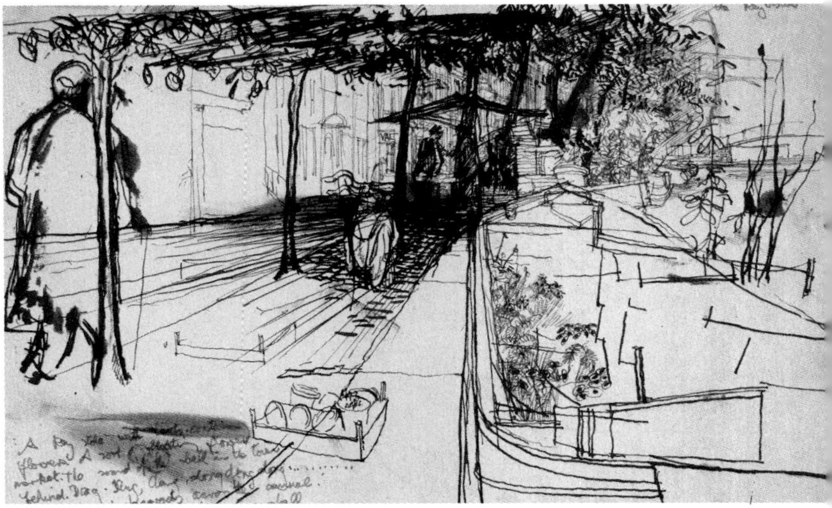

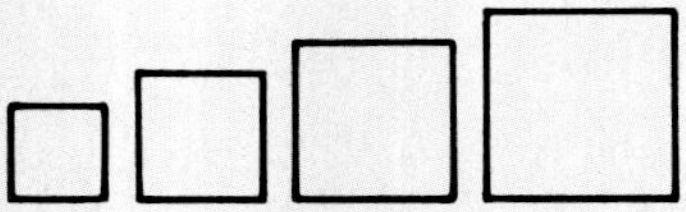

Docks in Newcastle
(Pencil drawing)
Here objects that are the same size in reality reduce in size as they are placed deeper and deeper in the composition. The telegraph poles are really all the same size but are drawn in decreasing scale as they recede into the picture.

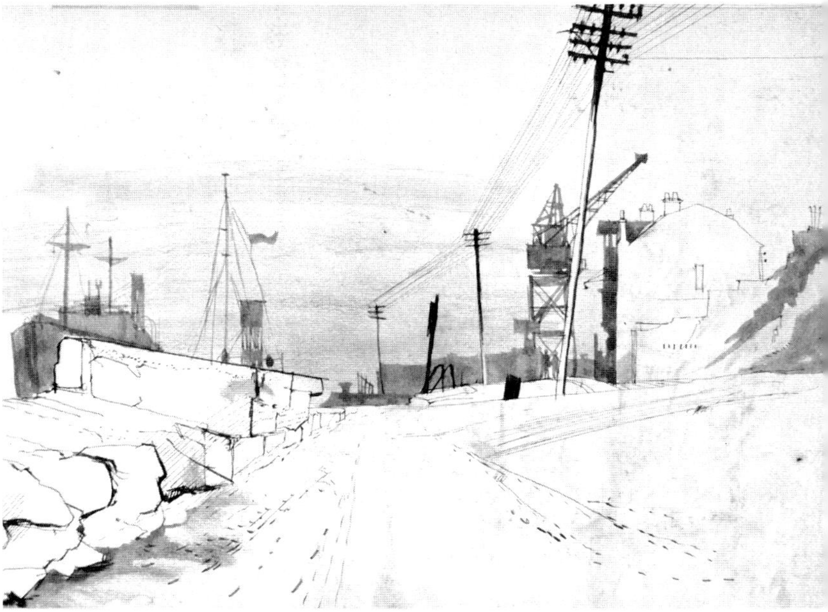

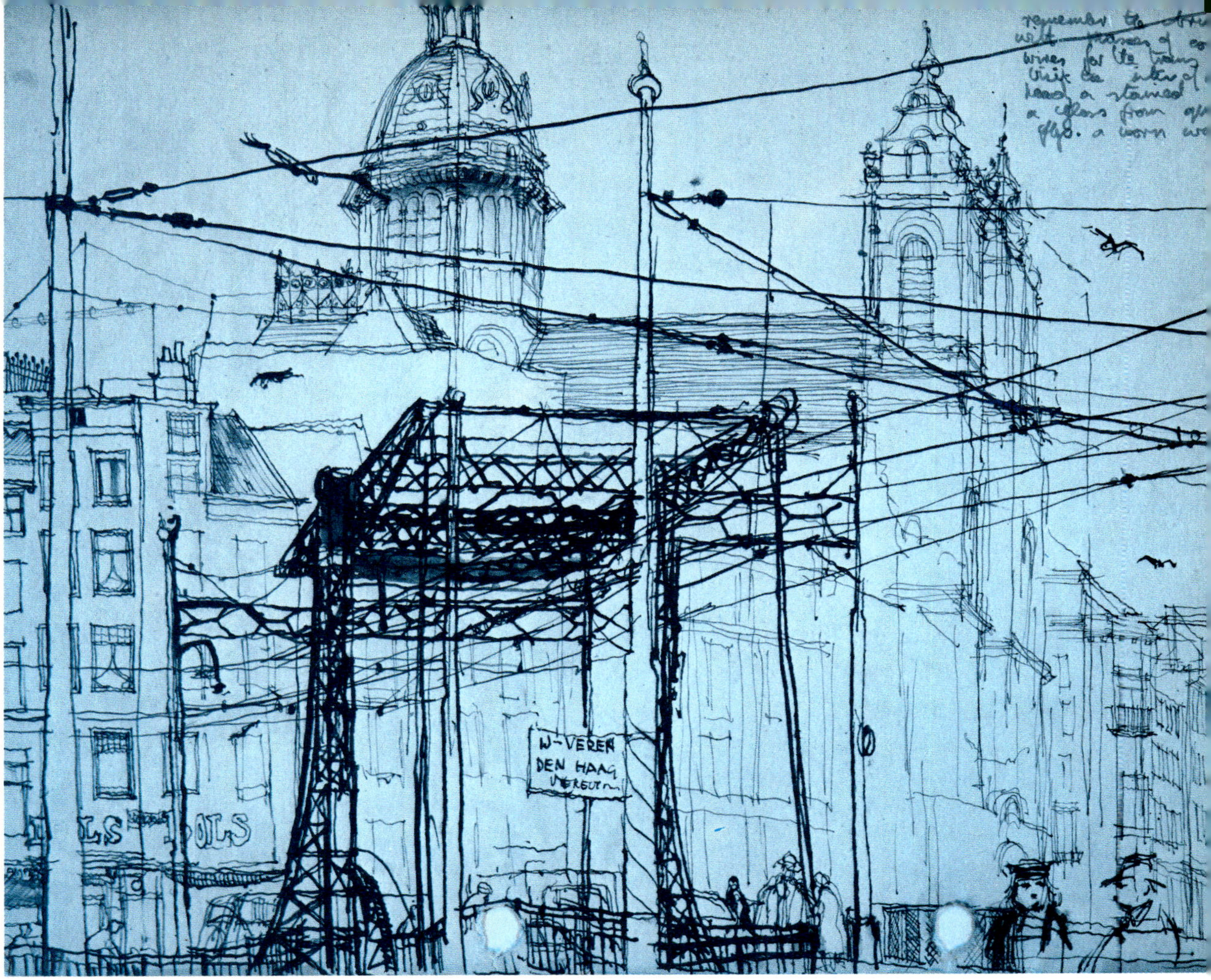

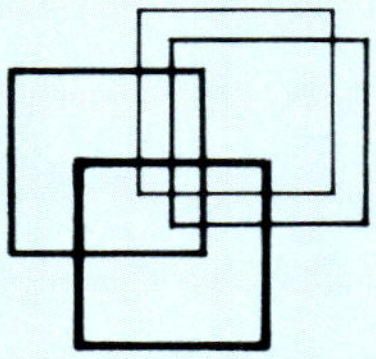

St Michael's Cathedral, Amsterdam
(Pen drawing)
Here a sense of space and distance is achieved by drawing objects in the foreground in a thicker line than those that are further away (*above*).

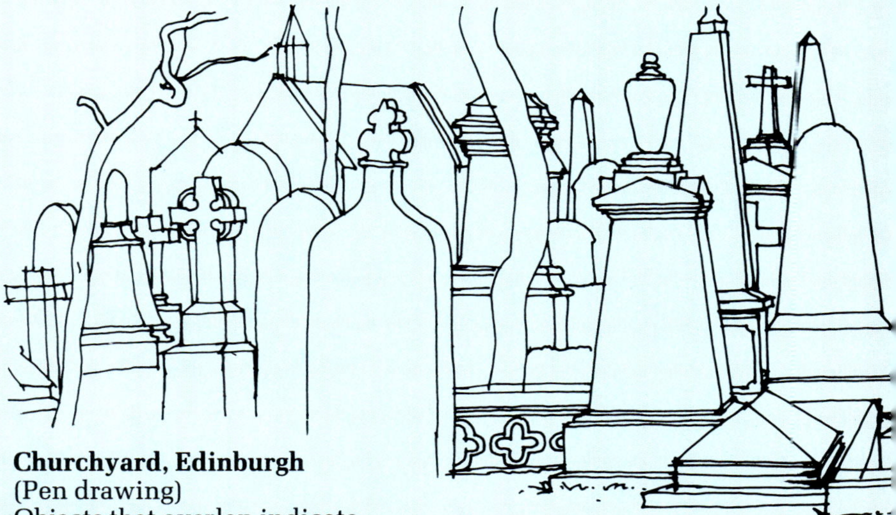

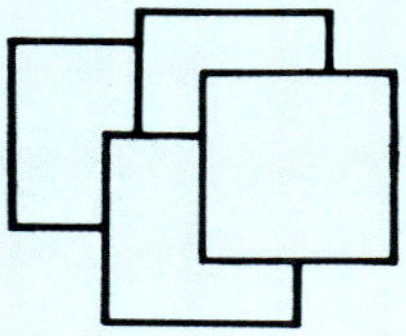

Churchyard, Edinburgh
(Pen drawing)
Objects that overlap indicate their position in the composition as being close to or far from the viewer.

landscape

Understanding receding space
In a composition objects occupy three areas: foreground, middle distance, background. When starting a landscape, place objects within a frame and also in the picture on a 'floorplan'.

Coal gatherers, industrial beach, Northern England
(Pen and ink drawing)
Look at the drawing (*bottom*) and the diagrams (*below*). The large blocks are in the foreground (**A**); the seated people and wooden wall in the middle distance (**B**); the town and distant figures in the background (**C**). Space is indicated by overlap (**1**) to show recession, lines of direction (**2**) to show convergence, and reducing scale (**3**). You should think into the composition and check on the spatial relationships of the objects.

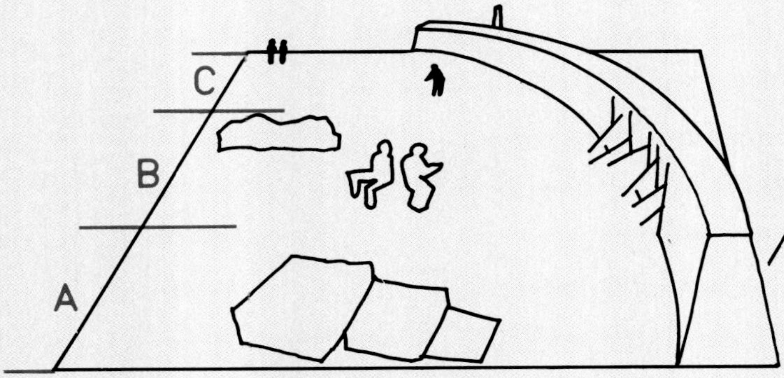

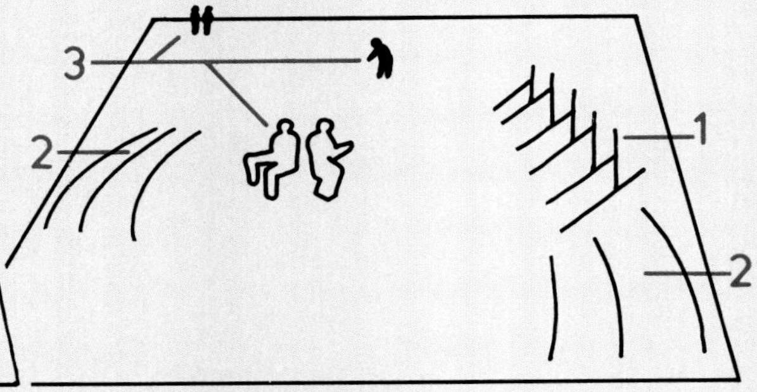

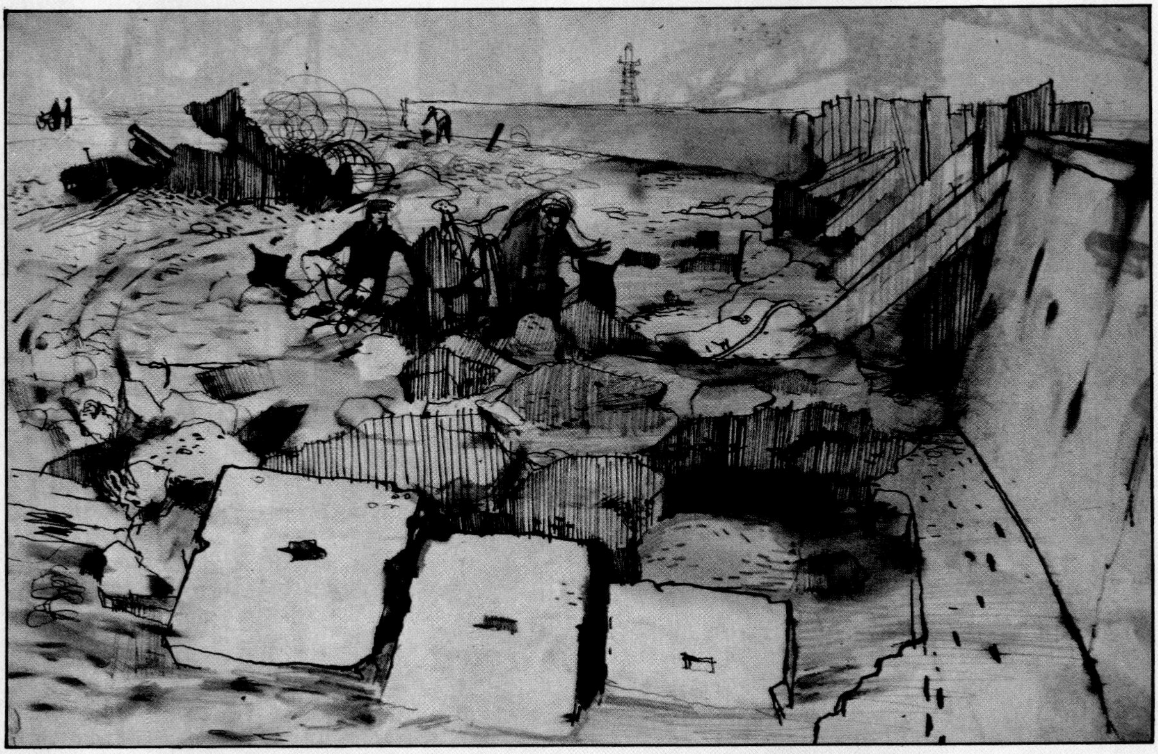

Constructing a composition
Within the rectangle of your frame, first establish some major elements of the scene and place them off centre, or in positions where their relationships with each other balance the interest in the composition (*below*).

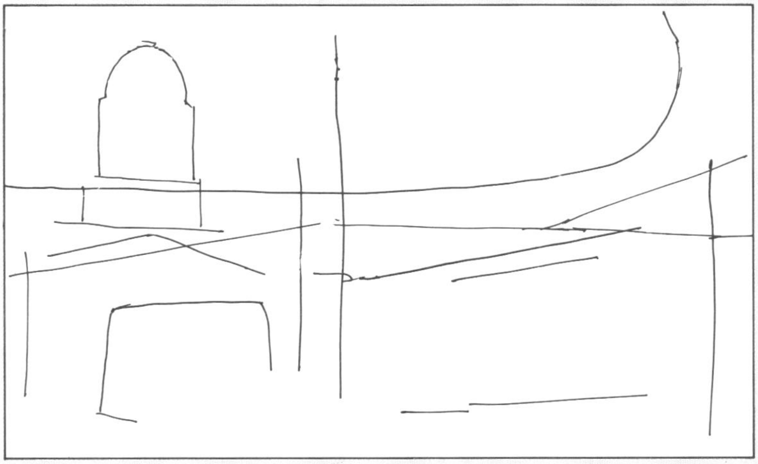

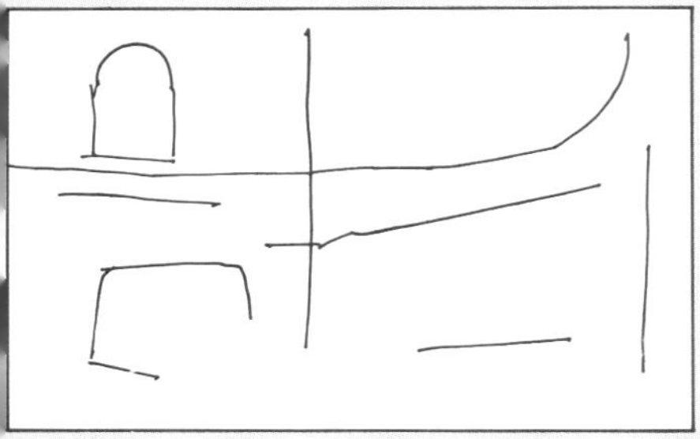

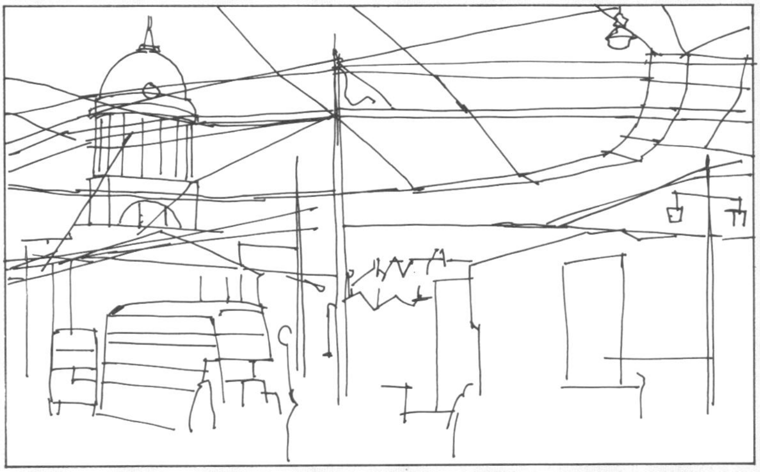

Building up the picture
First sketch the key parts. In the picture (*top right*), these are the lamp post, the dome, the sweep of the overhead wires and the line of the distant buildings. Then add interconnecting elements, such as the wires, other verticals, the main shape of the bus and the structure of the dome. Finally, add small details such as the lamp, people, windows, columns and chimneys (*right*).

Nottingham city square
(Pencil drawing)
In addition to the compositional features, try to instil in your drawing a sense of the place. This drawing was done on an autumn evening with fog closing in and people hurrying home (*right*).

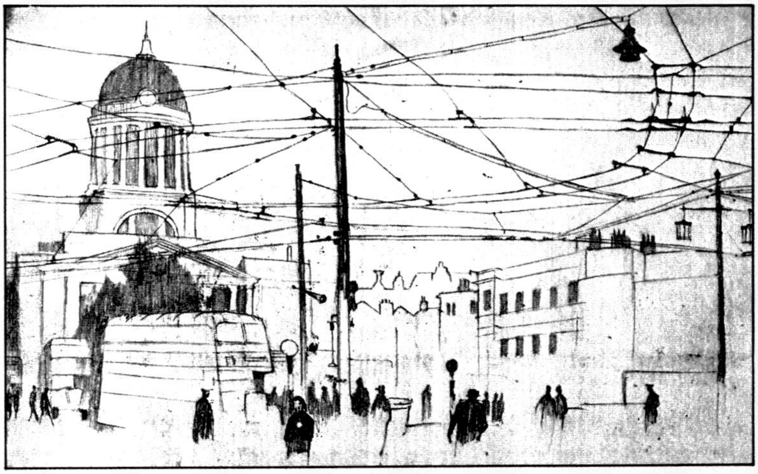

landscape

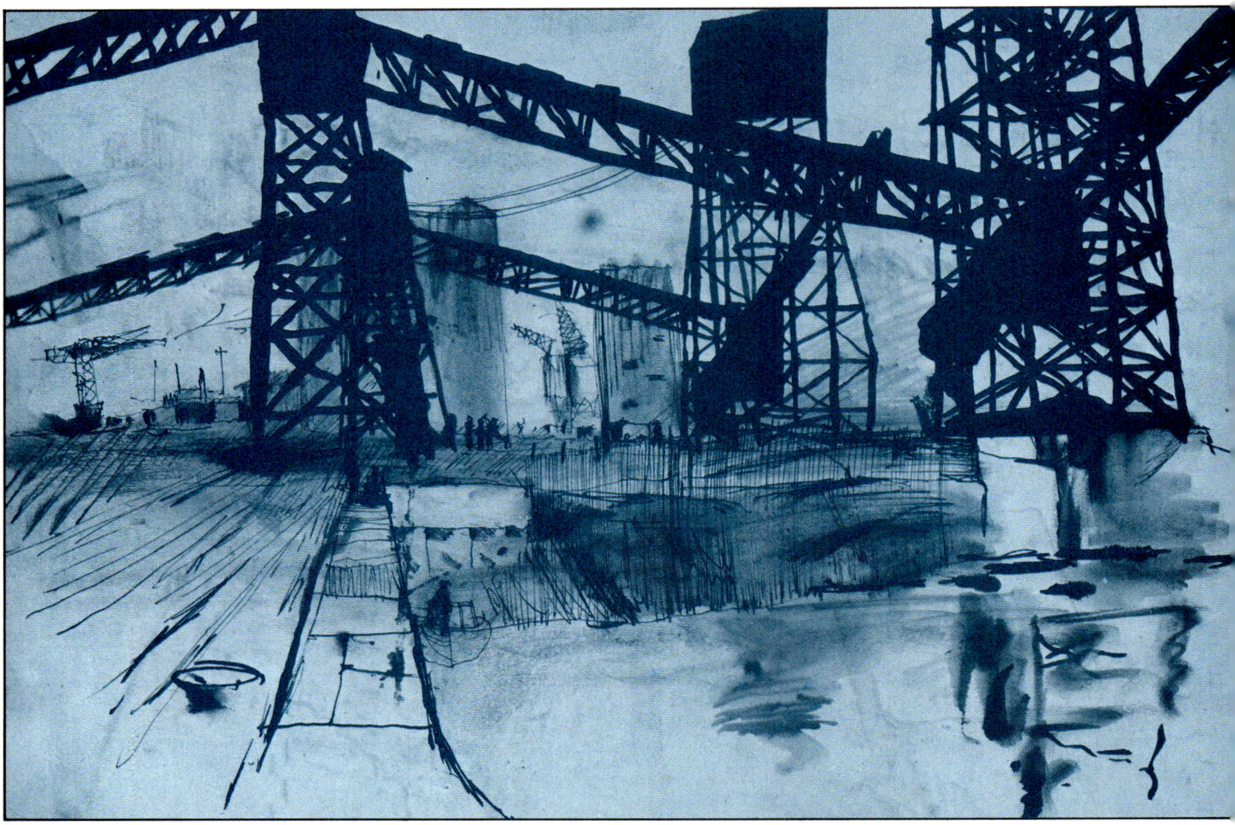

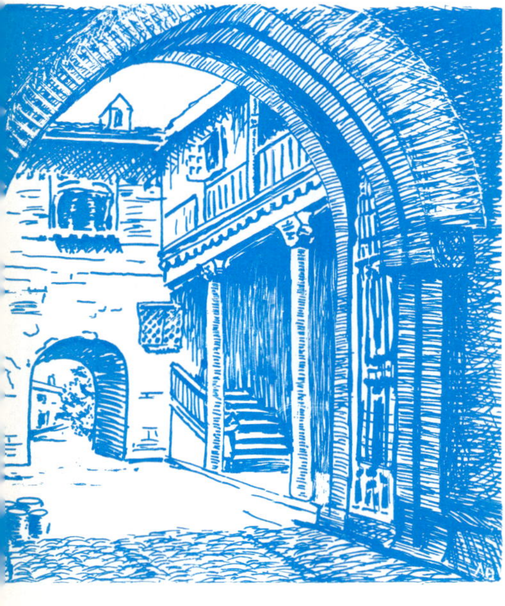

Medieval courtyard, Gubbio, Italy
(Pen drawing)
The archway provides an attractive, simple frame to the composition of the courtyard (*left*), and the contrast between the darkness and light draws the viewer into the picture. The strokes of the pen, directed inwards, help to establish that the space is receding.

Working outside often means using only a pen or pencil, but if you can carry a jar of water, brushes and a small mixing palate, your opportunities for portraying fine scenes expand.

Dockland loading cranes, Hamburg
(Pen, brush and ink drawing)
Although at first appearing to be unsuitable for drawing, heavy industrial locations can provide valuable subjects for study. The stark, black structures and the dirty gravel ground in the dockland (*above*) combine with the reflections in the river water to instil a strong sense of place. The character of a landscape is often its most striking quality.

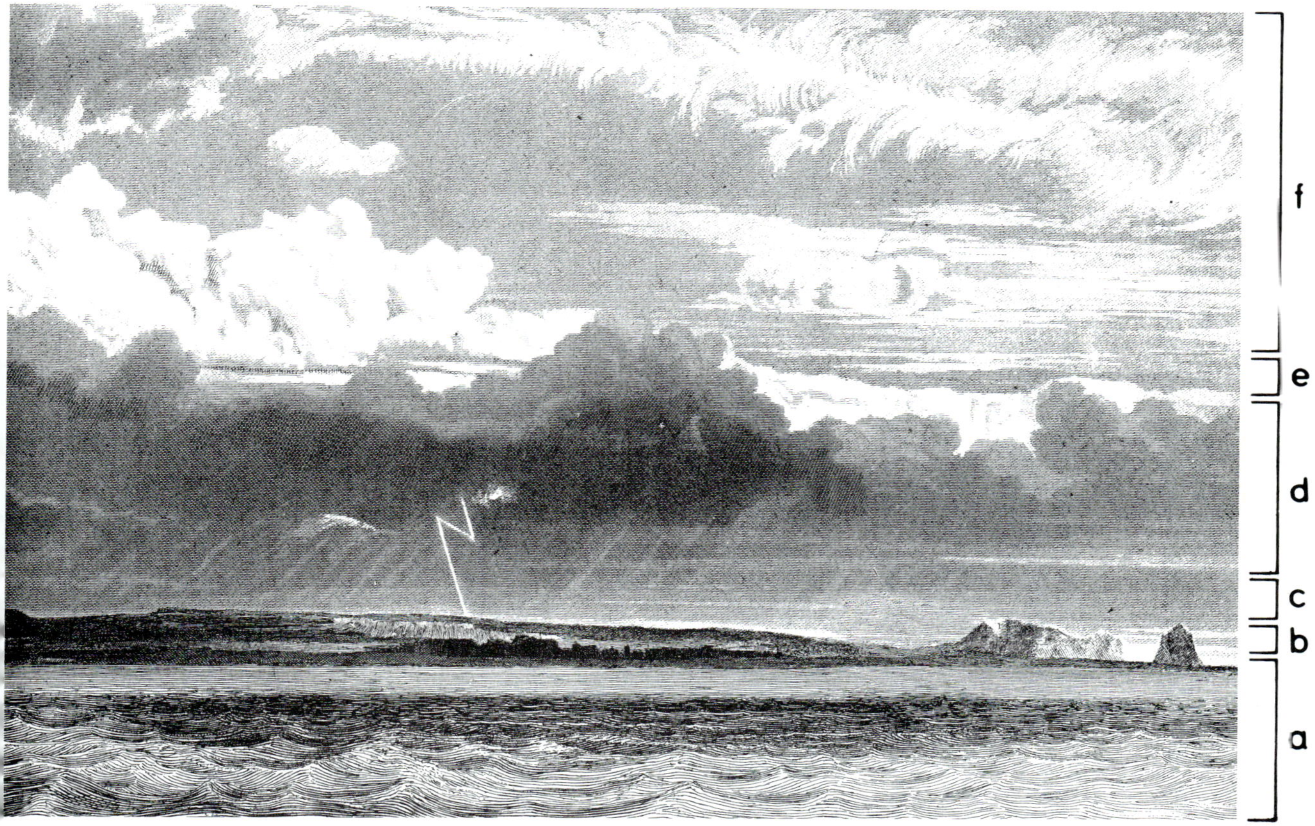

Winter sea, Scottish Islands
(Etching)
The striking atmosphere (*above*) is conveyed by: turbulent waves (**a**) darkened with cloud shadows; a dramatically lighted distance (**b**) also subjected to rain (**c**); heavy, dark clouds (**d**); paler clouds lit from the side (**e**), and wild, speeding clouds (**f**).

French chateau
(Pen drawing)
Almost all the drawing (*right*) is of water reflections, signalling a quiet afternoon.

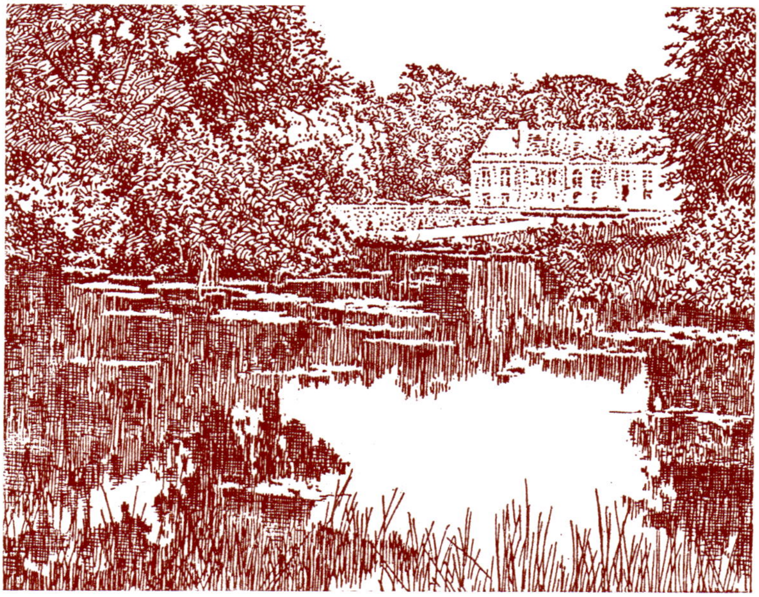

Part Four

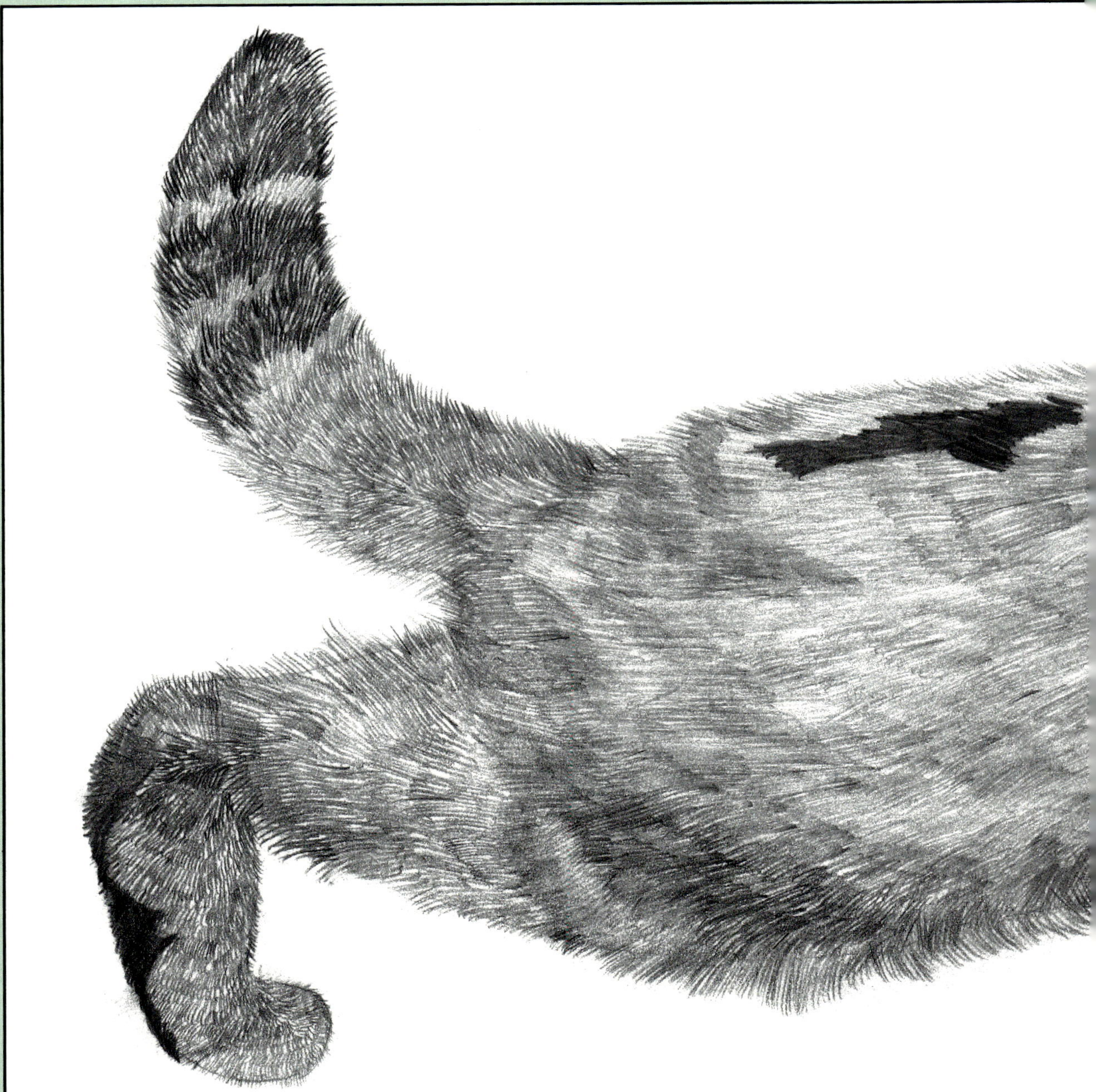

THE SUBJECT: PEOPLE AND ANIMALS

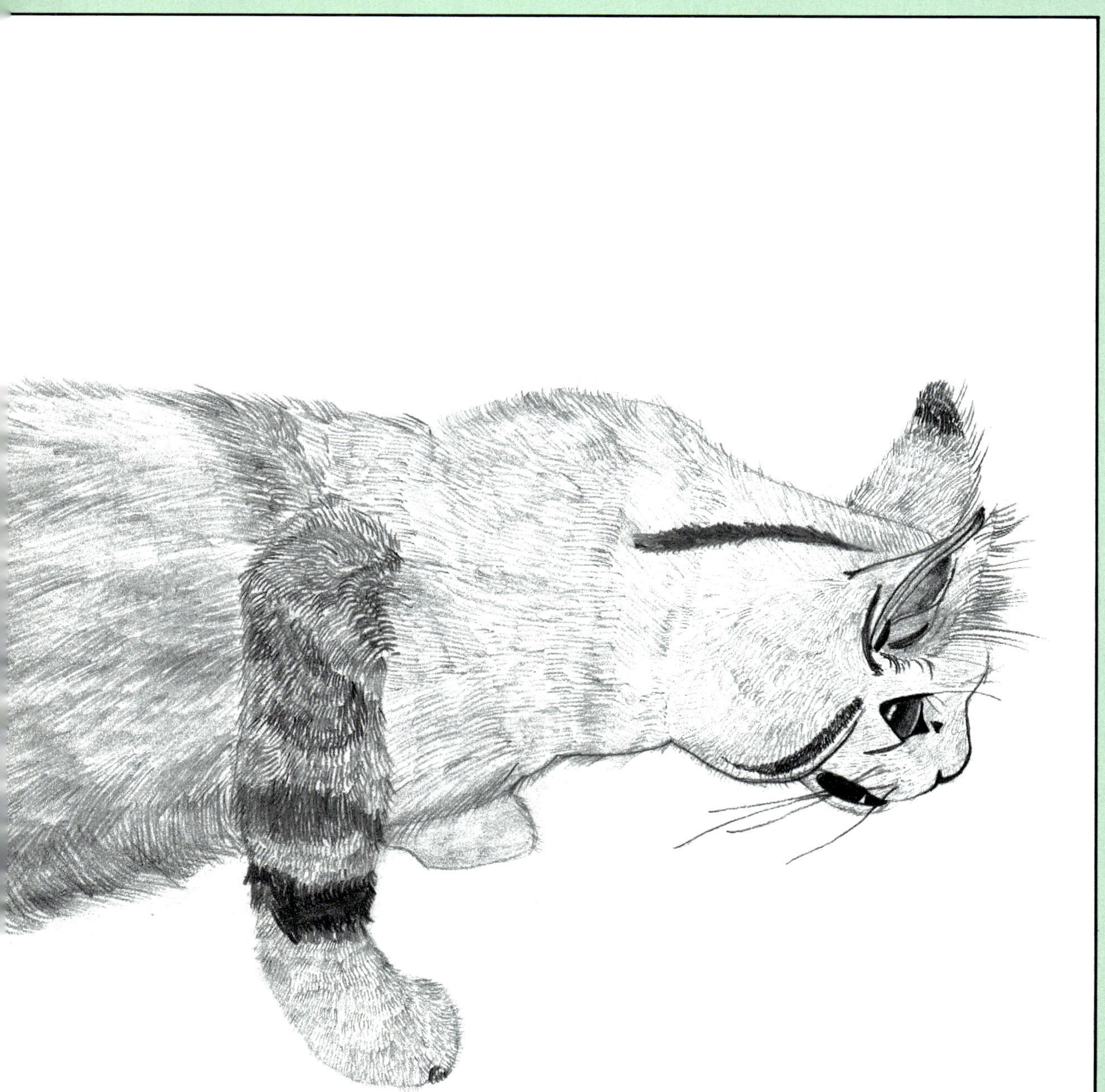

the human form

Everyone knows what people look like; and we all have preconceptions of the characters of others. So you have a knowledgeable audience. "It doesn't look like her" seems a damning criticism, but don't be put off. Drawing people is the most challenging and rewarding of all kinds of drawing. You may draw to collect information, to form impressions or to capture the character of a person or a mood.

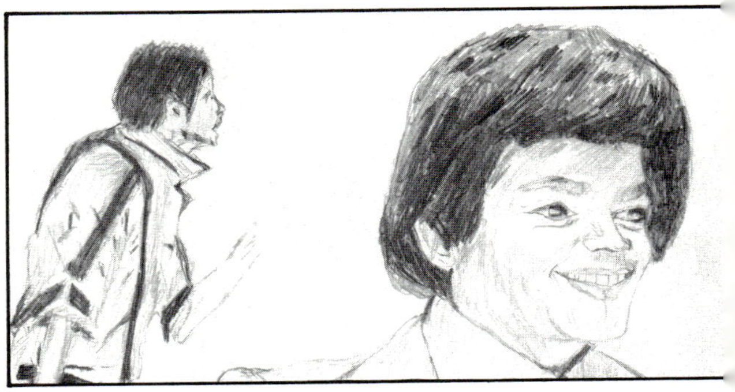

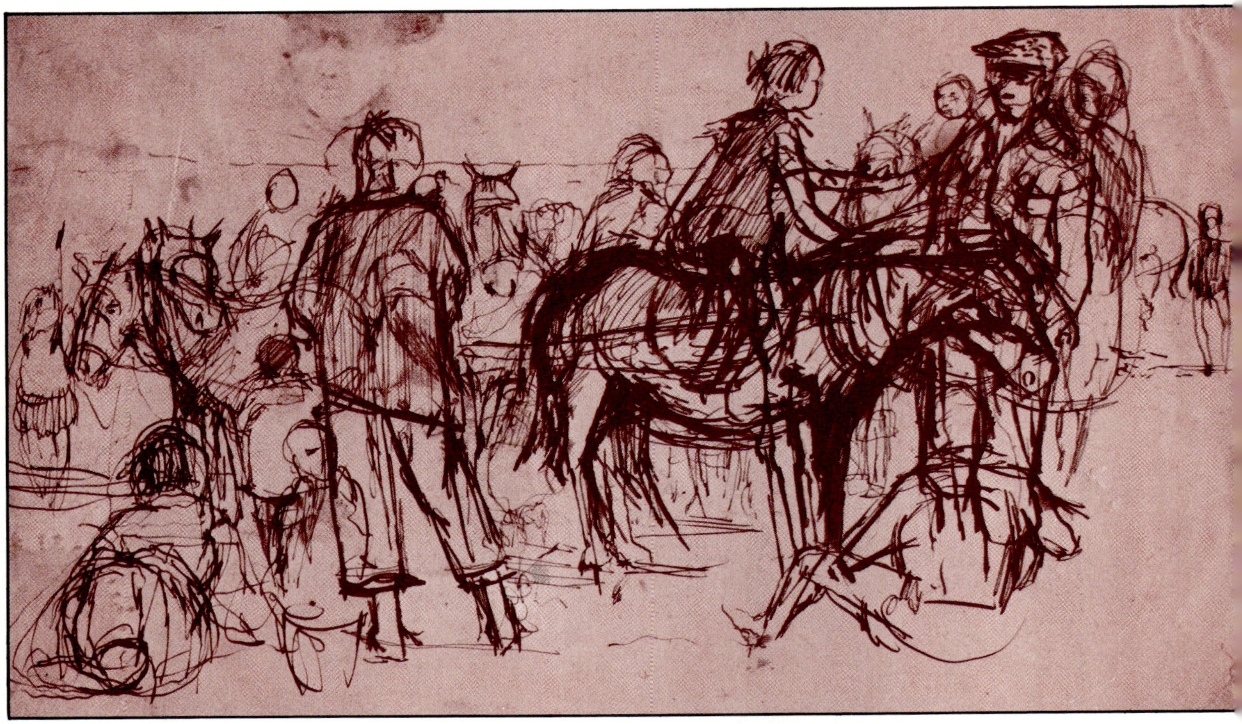

Crowd on a beach
(Pen and ink drawing)
When drawing movement and people in action, recognise and keep in your mind an after-image of the main shapes. The drawing (*above*) looks rather a scribble but don't be afraid of missing the detail. Search for the most characteristic elements of the scene.

Male figure
(Pencil drawing by Dürer)
When the chance occurs, study figures and record with great care all the measurements and their relationships. Dürer has imposed his own theories of proportion onto a figure, and ignored real elements which do not fit his ideas (*right*).

Michael Jackson
(Pencil drawings by Steve, aged 16)
The drawings (*left*) show the most convenient way to produce a likeness – work from a photograph. The even tones can be copied carefully and you can achieve a higher standard than by drawing from a model.

Some simple points:

- **Keep a sketch book**
- **Collect photos of figures in action**
- **Practise drawing careful studies**
- **Copy artists' drawings and draw statues**
- **Try to complete each study**
- **Practise difficult areas: hands, face, feet. Never discard a "failed" drawing**

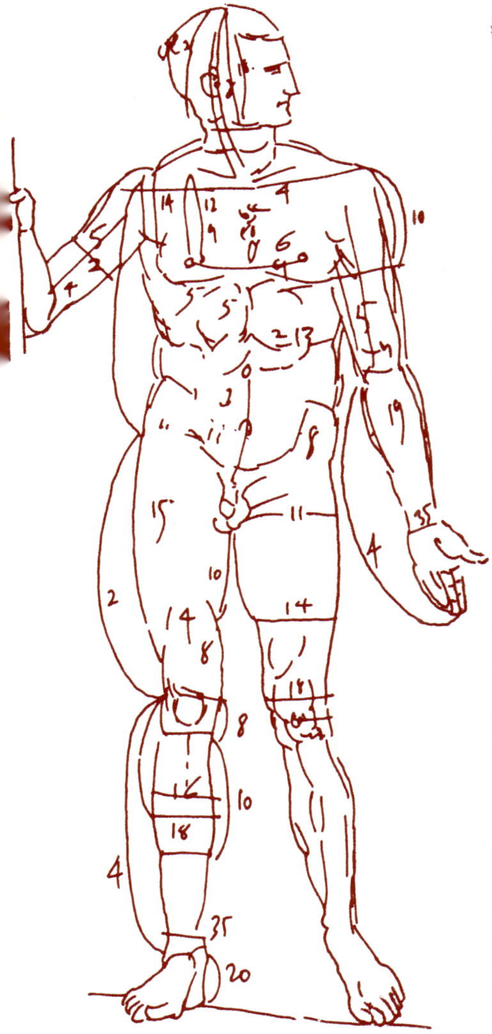

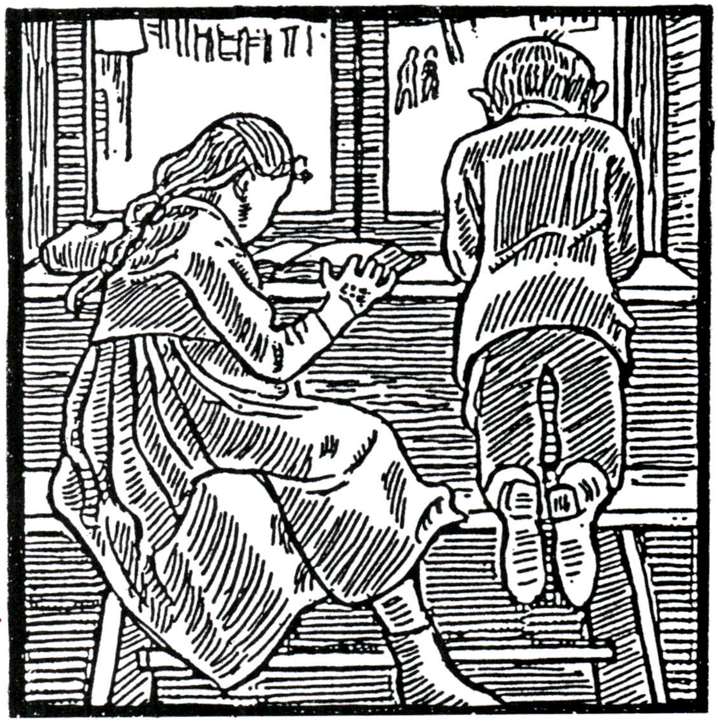

Children at a window
(Woodcut by Hans Thoma)
It is easiest to draw people in poses they can hold: reading a book or looking out of the window (*above*).

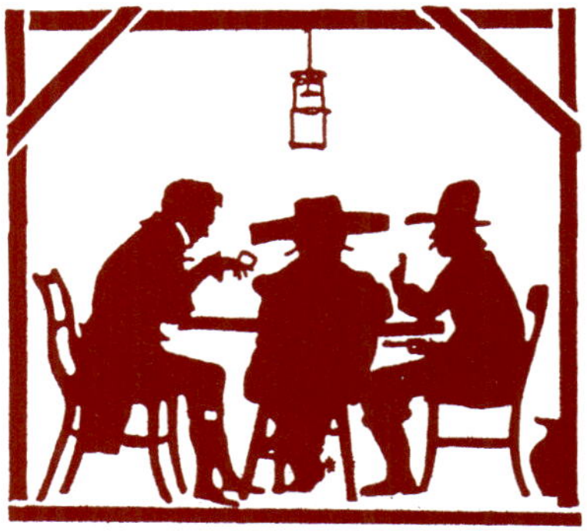

Card game
(Pen and ink drawing)
The silhouettes (*left*) explore different attitudes in an imaginary scene.

the human form

We normally see the human figure clothed. Drawing the nude can usually only be done in art school or from sculptures or photographs. Nevertheless an understanding of the basic forms of the body helps enormously when drawing clothed figures. Most people are afraid of drawing the human body because the result can too often reveal mistakes or misunderstandings. After all, everyone knows what a human being looks like. So when you start, establish the chief elements and don't be confused by distortions which are the result of your own particular viewpoint.
Try to see the basic proportions under the clothes. Always attempt the hard forms – hands, feet, face. It is by mastering the difficult elements of the human figure that we gain confidence.
See all the figure, all the time. Don't just draw bits.

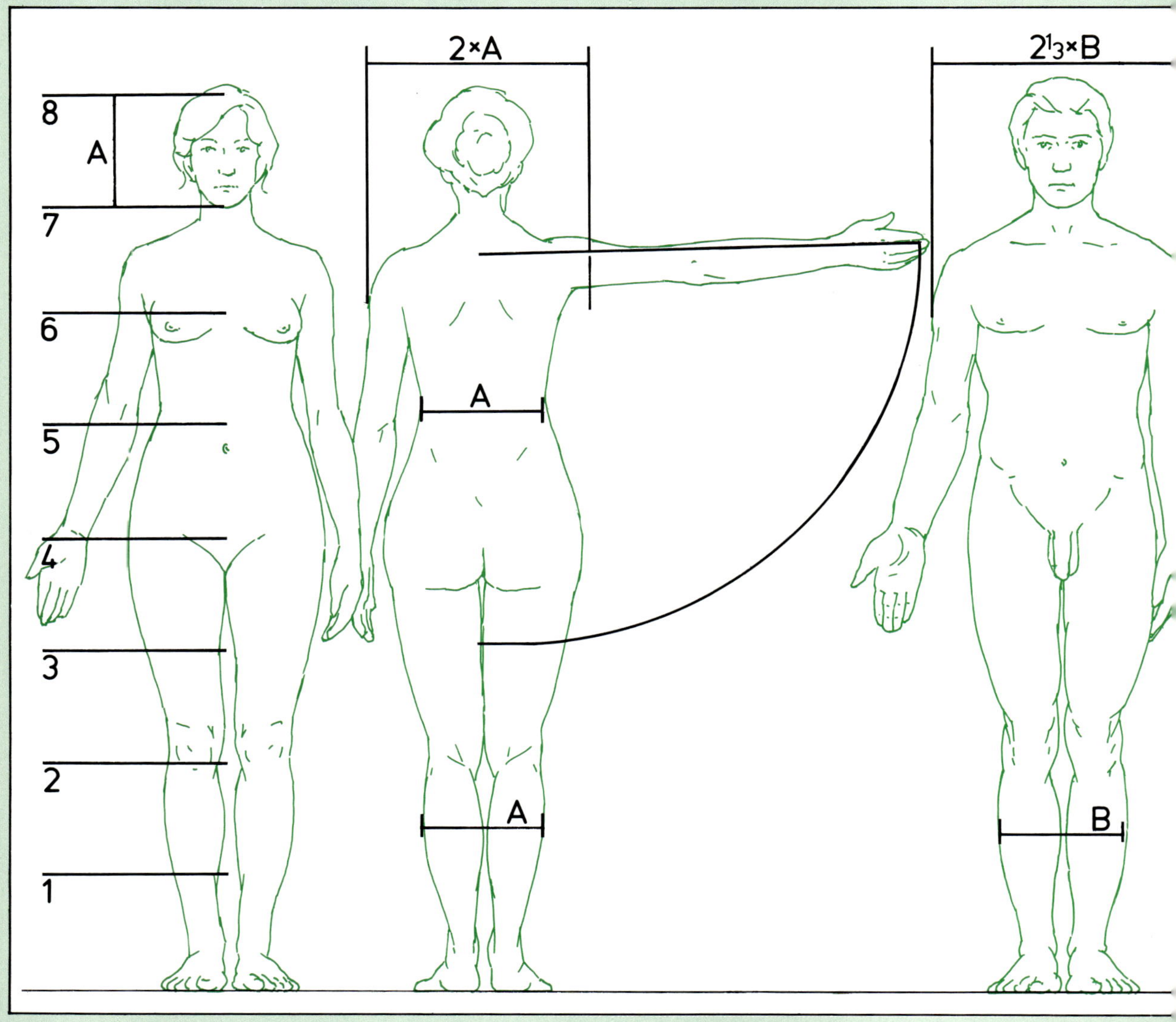

Basic human proportions
Every body conforms to certain basic interrelated proportions; for example, shoulder width to length of head (see *below*). Shapes vary – fat, thin, tall, short – but recognising major relationships helps you to draw well.

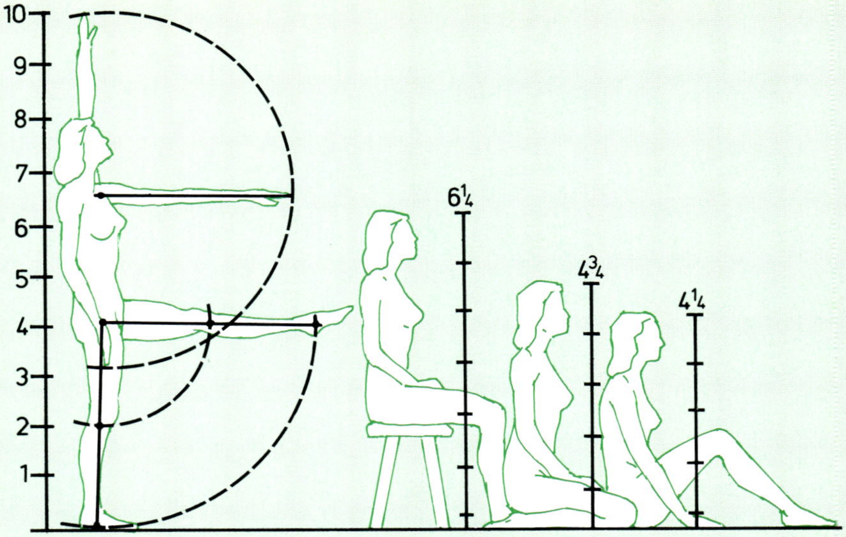

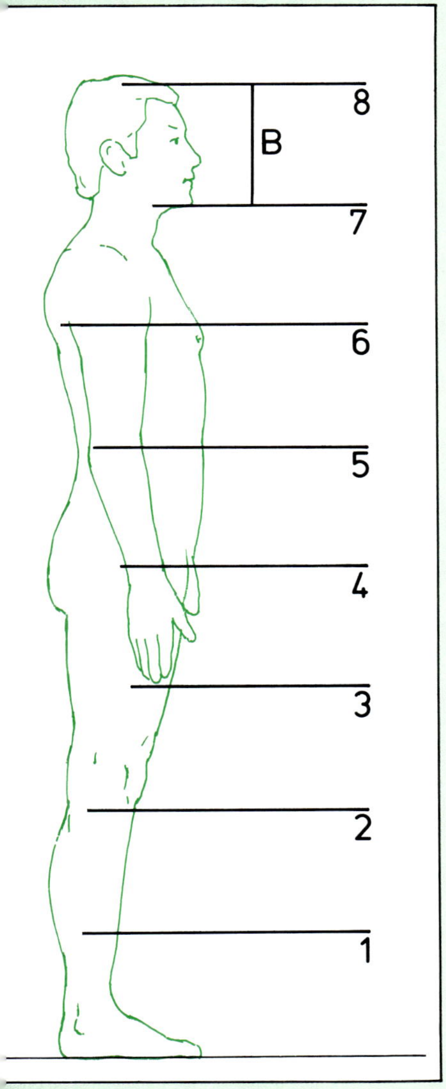

Moving figures
The basic proportions remain whatever position the body and limbs occupy (*above*).

Changing proportions
With body growth the relationships between parts alters. In small children the head is a quarter of the total height; in an adult it is one eighth. When drawing figures check constantly to make sure you use these proportions whatever your view and however confusing clothes may be (*below*).

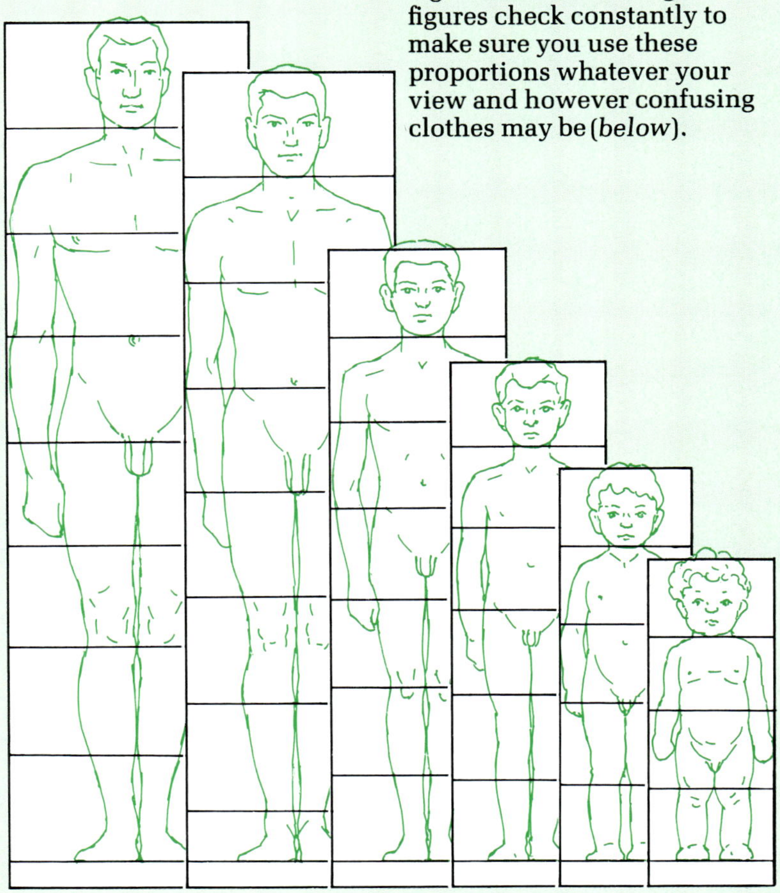

the human form

The human body is basically symmetrical, and if a vertical line is drawn through the centre of an upright figure, the two sides should be balanced, except perhaps for the limbs; if one leg is thrust forward, the other will be put back. You should always be aware of this balance in your drawings.

Constructing a figure (*right*)
1 When planning the form, first construct a rectangle: choose the height, and divide it into 8 equal sections; the width will be $2\frac{1}{3}$ times $\frac{1}{8}$ of the height. Draw diagonals within this rectangle. You now have most key points for completing the detail.
2 The grid intersections on your figure will remain, whatever your viewpoint, although if the figure is drawn turning away, remember that the horizontals will converge in the distance. Set into your framework a two-dimensional, flat plan of the figure.
3 Finally, build up the smaller forms, using the grid and keeping the proportions correct.

Changing the viewpoint (*right*)
If you want to draw a receding, reclining figure, or one seen from an unusual angle, the same method of construction applies:
1 First construct a four-sided frame, remembering to taper the lines to the distance.
2 Draw in the diagonals, then divide the frame into 8 equal, transverse sections.
3 Set your figure in the grid.

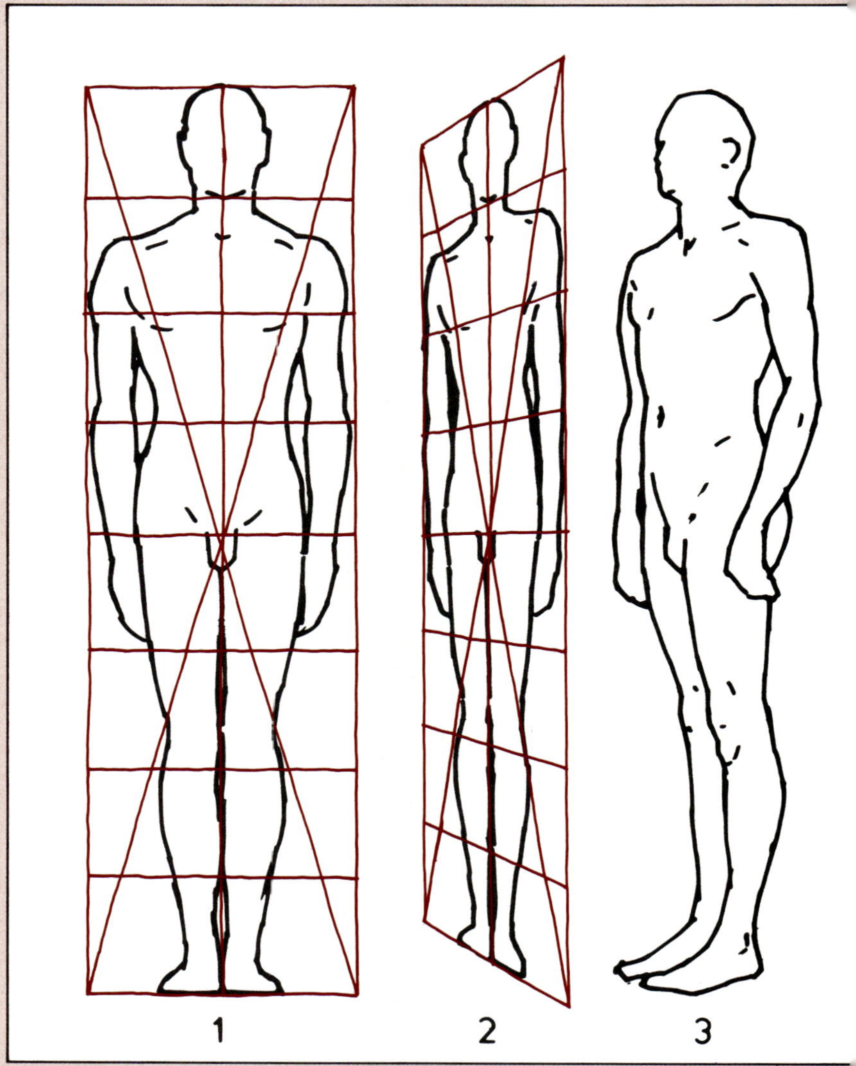

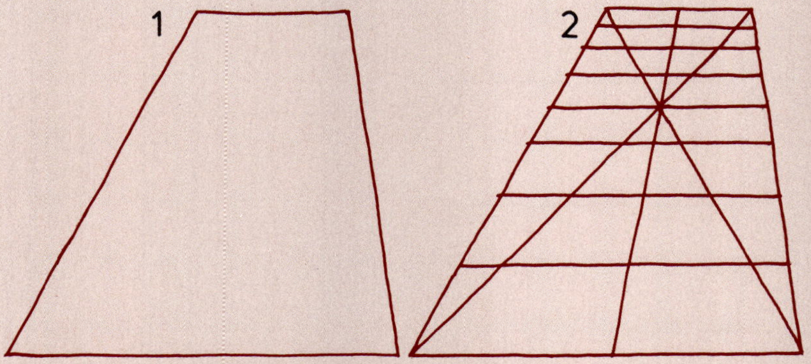

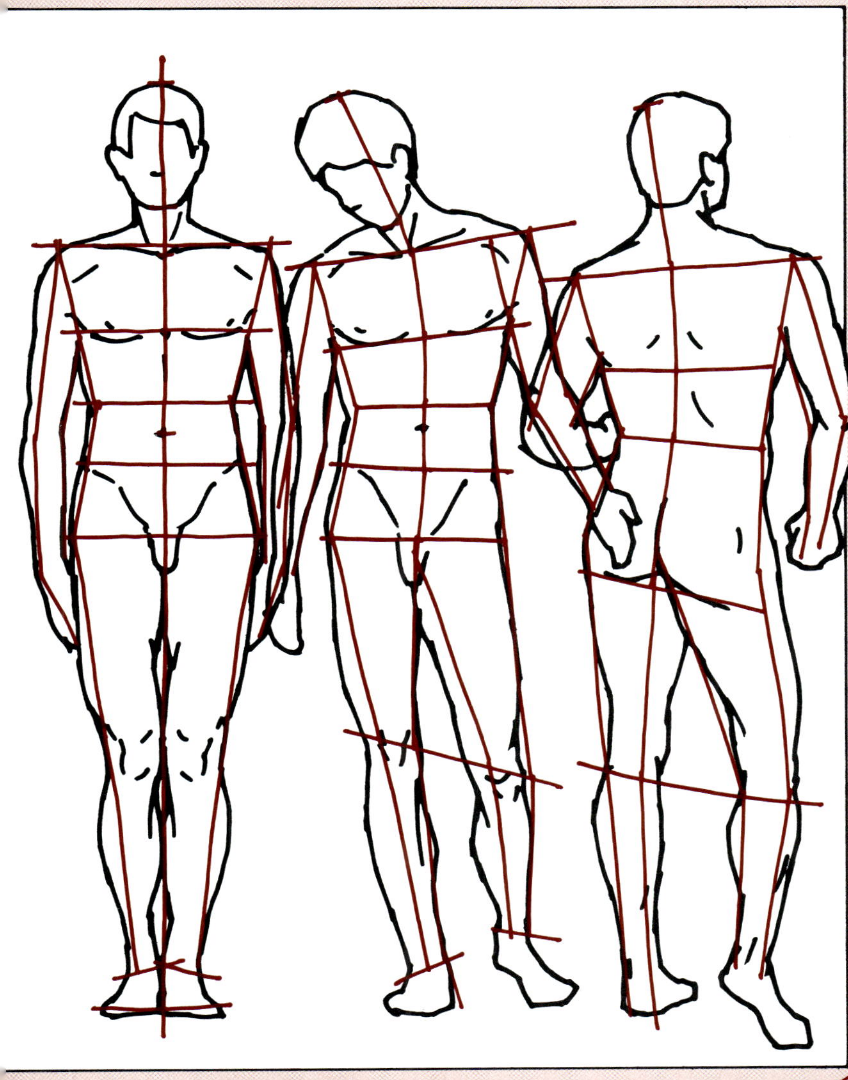

The moving figure (*left*)
Balance and tensions influence the positions of the limbs. Remember all the horizontal relationships and check each side of your vertical central line.

Space man (*below*)
The human figure fills space, and its torso and limbs are rounded. Imagine the body as a space-suit made up of bands.

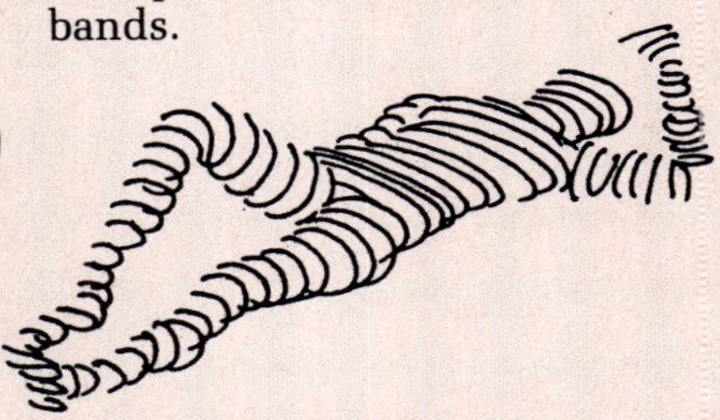

The figure's volume
To create volume, and draw asymmetrical limbs, imagine a cage in which the forms fit. This gives you several major points of reference for arms, legs and body.
Try always to see the figure in the round. The torso is like a tree trunk and its limbs like branches.

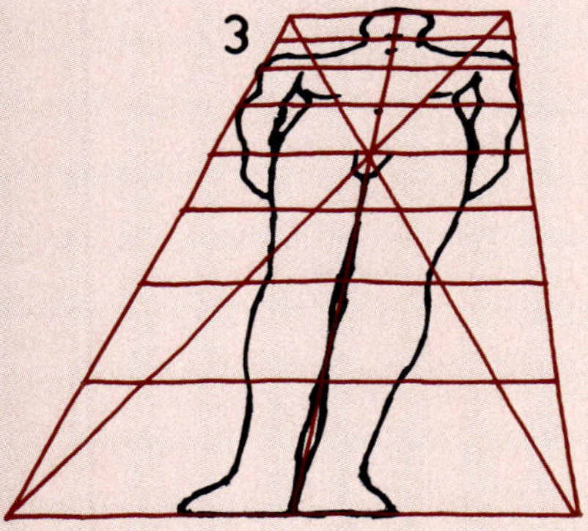

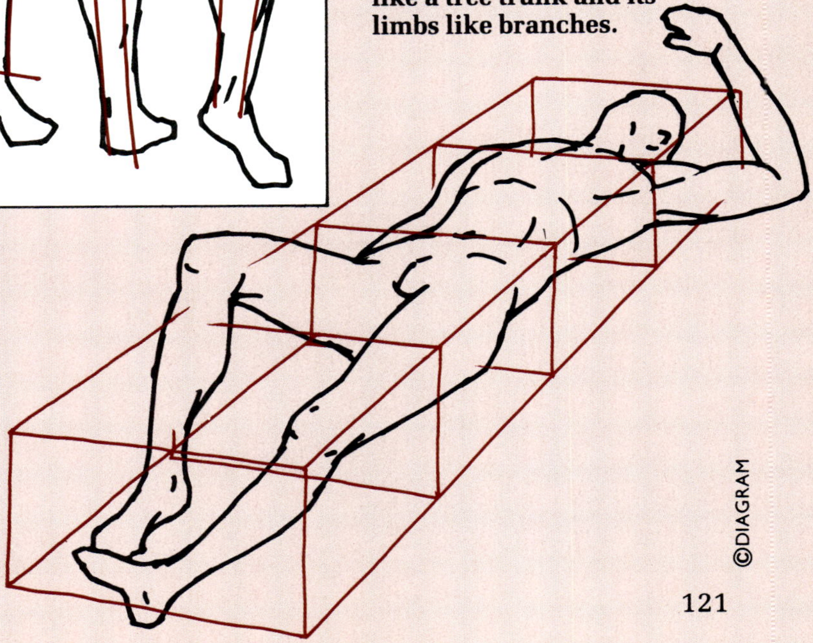

the human form

When drawing a friend certain conditions will make the job easier for both of you. Find a pose which is easy to hold – lying or sitting comfortably, or standing with weight evenly distributed on both feet – and which can be taken up again without difficulty. Thirdly, position your model so that you can examine a specific quality – the arrangement of forms, character or atmosphere, for example.
Every drawing of a model increases your awareness of the human form, and no study is a waste of time.

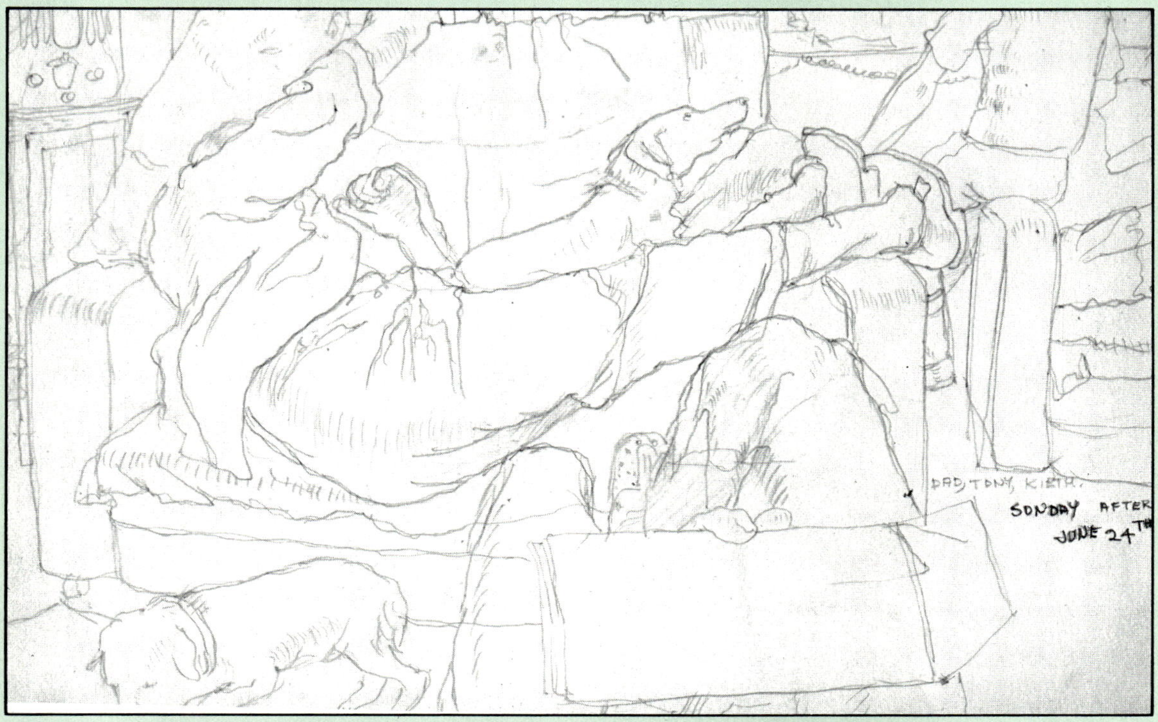

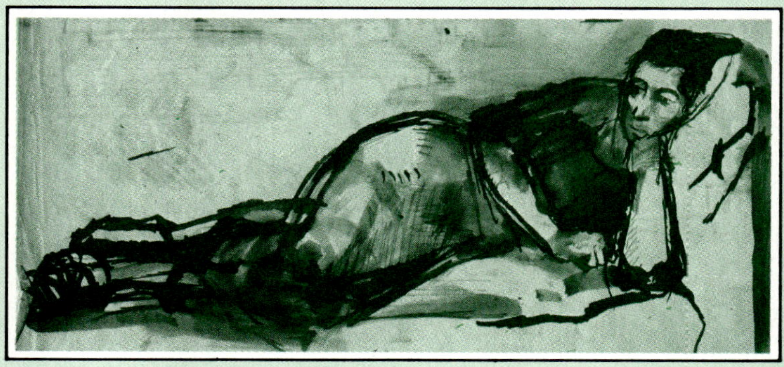

Sunday afternoon
(Pencil drawing)
In the study (*above*), the man on the sofa is asleep, the boy is absorbed looking out of the window, and the dog obviously moved during the drawing.
Resting figure
(Pen and ink drawing, *left*)
Lying on cushions, the figure held a pose for a long time.

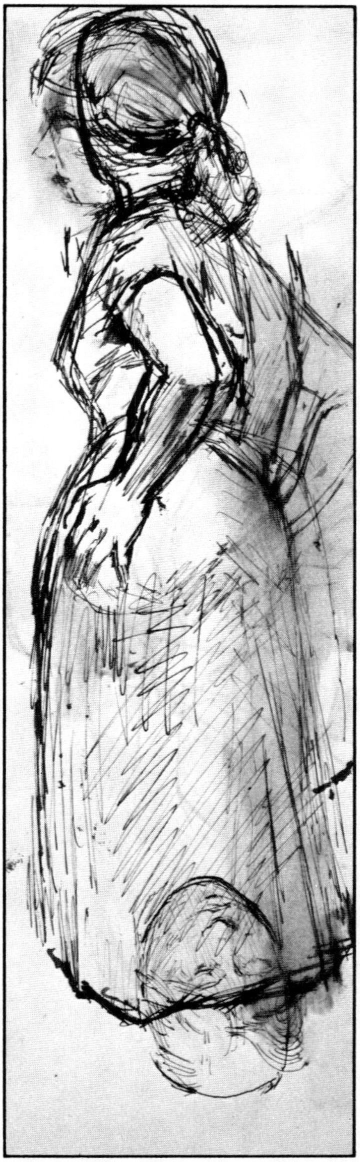

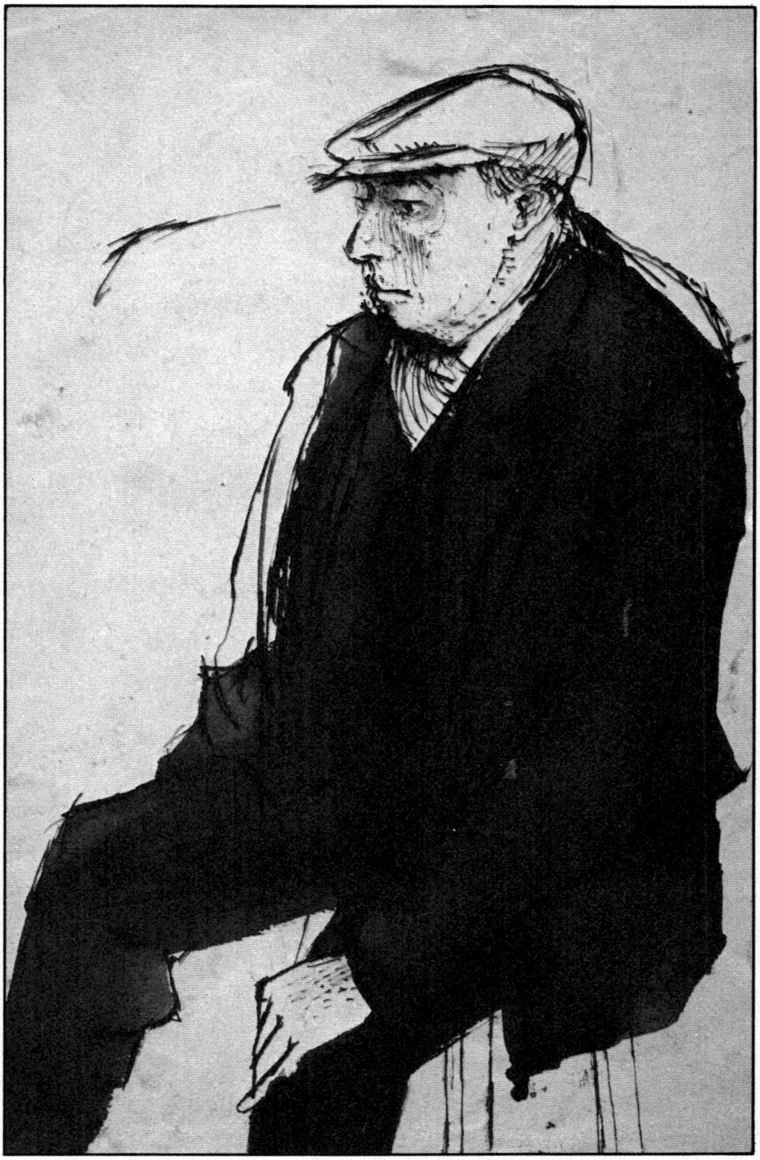

Standing figure
(Pen drawing)
The stance of the heavy model (*above*), weight carried by both feet and arms akimbo, could be held still for some time while the artist searches for ways of catching the basic mass and bulk of the figure.

Seated coal miner
(Pen and brush drawing)
Study the difficult features – hands and faces especially – and just block in the body very simply (*above*).

Seated youth
(Pen drawings)
In the study (*right*), the artist has sketched the body and concentrated on the shape and quality of the head.

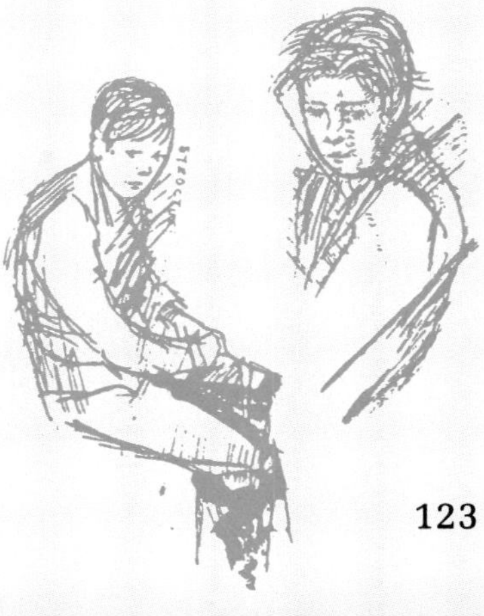

the human form

Varied and interesting results come from changing the direction of the light falling on a model and on the surroundings. Take time to consider the particular effects of the light source, and study the consequences of moving first the sitter and then the light. Experiment by drawing with a light-coloured chalk or white paint on dark paper, working from the highlights into the dark areas.

Profile studies
(Felt pen drawings)
Light falling on the side facing you permits you to select detail; but changes in form are not so easily identified where the lighting comes from behind (*below*).

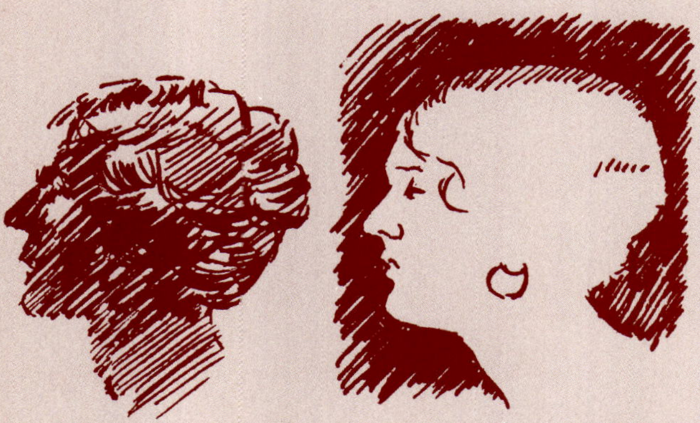

Exploring the lighting
(Felt pen drawings)
The head was the same in all the studies (*right*); but some sources of light described forms better than others.
a Light from above is common so forms are quickly detected.
b Side light may produce dark areas which obscure detail.
c Light from below is good only for theatrical effects.

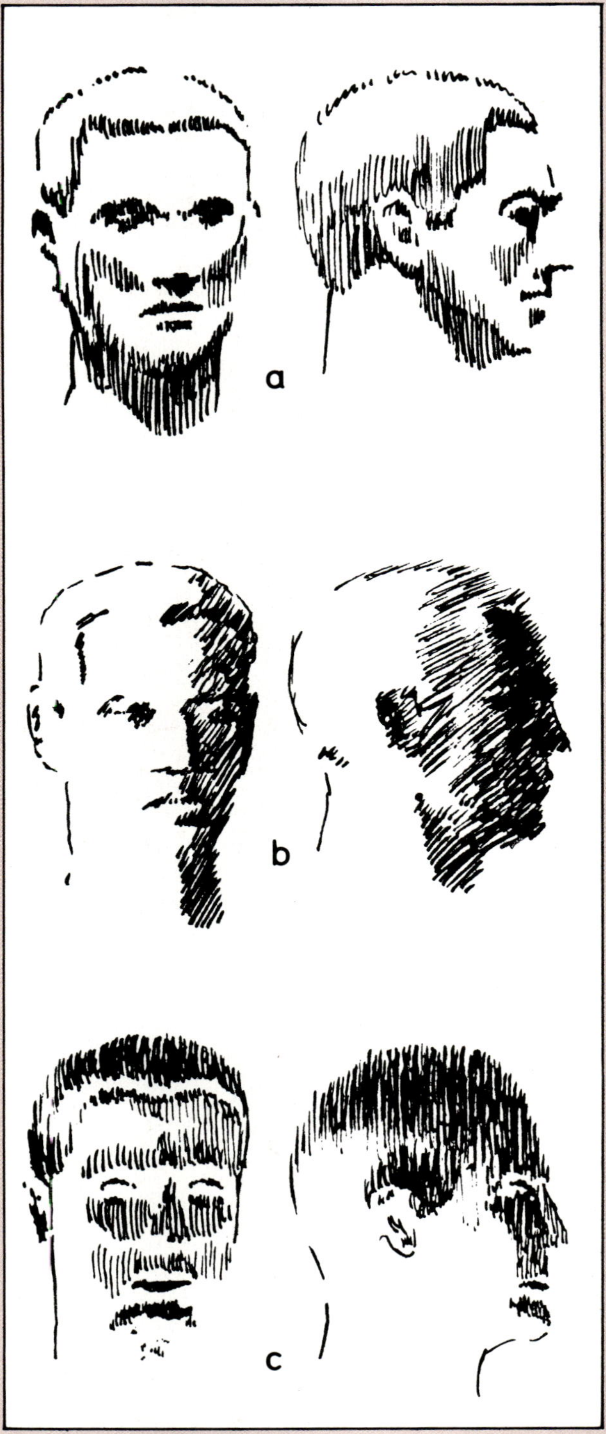

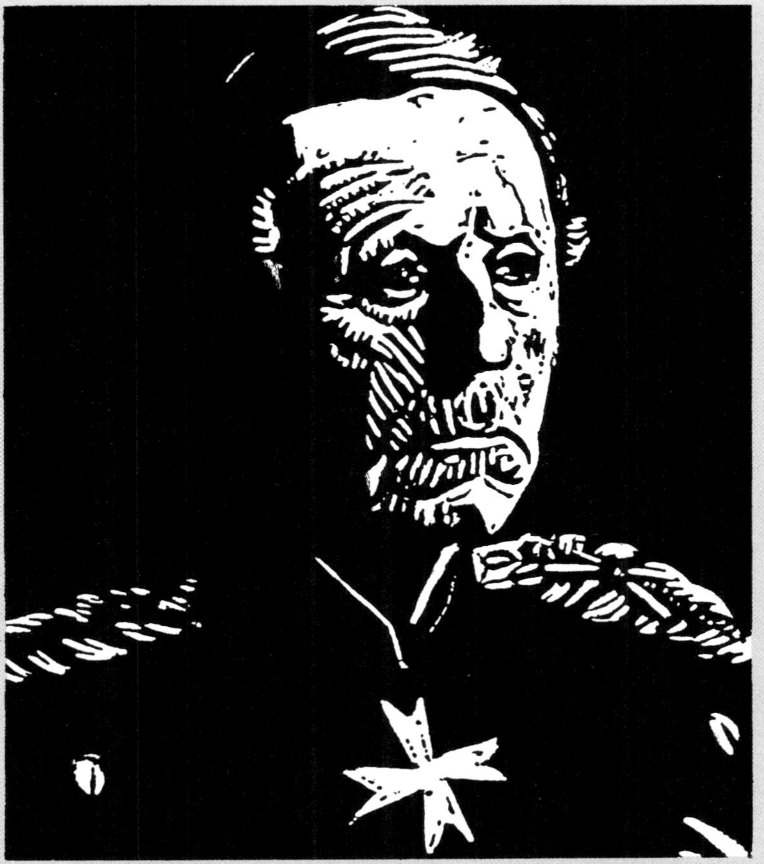

German officer
(Woodcut by
E. Wurtenberger)
The woodcut (*left*) was done by moving from light to dark. Darker areas sink into the background and large parts can only be interpreted through minimum light forms. Reverse the subject (*below*), and the resulting information is not as easy to understand.

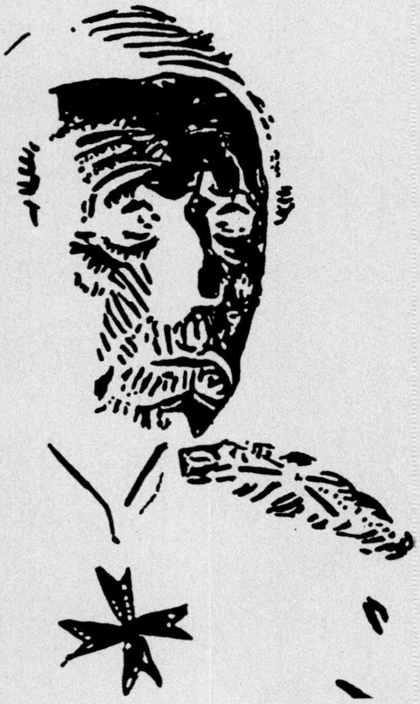

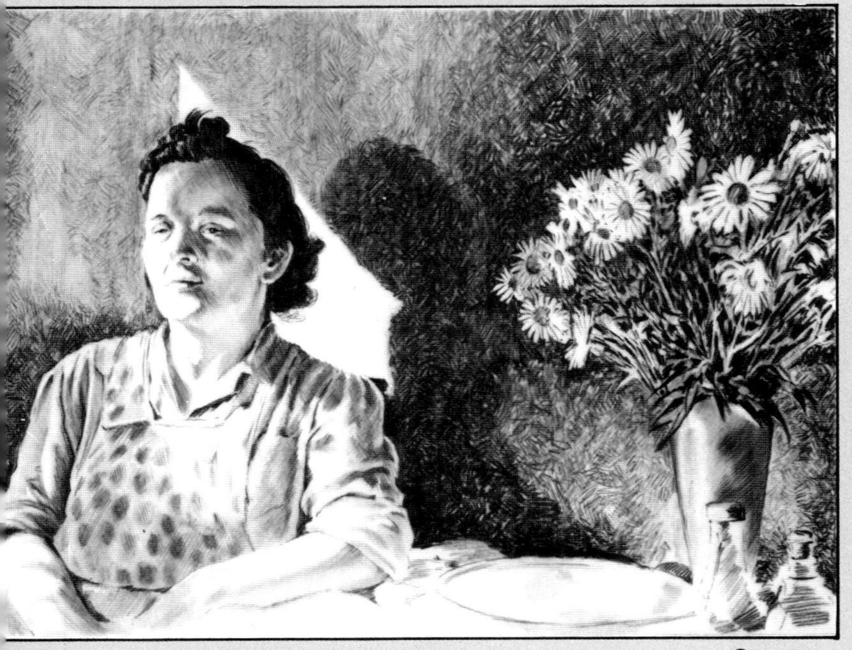

Figure with flowers
(Pencil drawing)
The presence of the light shining in darkness (*left*) sharpens the forms and helps establish mood and character.
To consider the effects of light, half close your eyes and view your subject in a blur before beginning to draw.

heads

Drawing heads is notoriously difficult. If you use yourself as a subject, you can get plenty of practice on a constant model that can be re-examined whenever you choose. Think of your self portraits as explorations in drawing, and forget about other people's opinions of them as likenesses.
Whether you draw yourself or someone else, you will need to observe all the details of the head very closely, as well as understanding its basic construction. Pay special attention to the relationship between the different parts of the head, as it is the careful measuring of these points that makes for an accurate drawing.

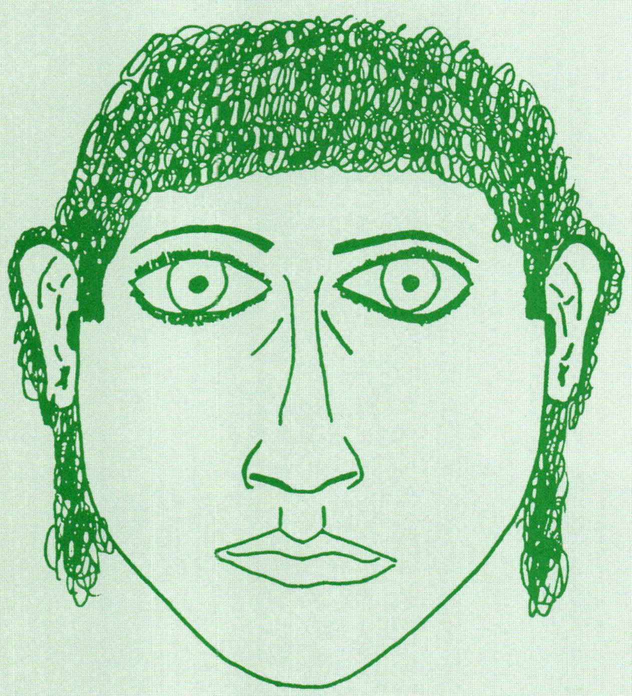

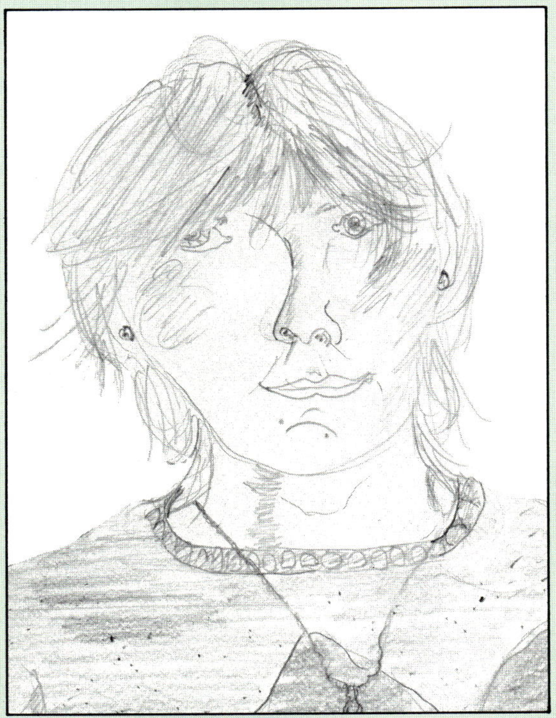

Steve, aged 17
(Felt pen drawing, *above*)
This beginner's self portrait shows a lack of knowledge of the structure and proportions of the head. Nevertheless, his awareness of the eyes and hair means that he has achieved a likeness, as can be seen from his photograph (*right*).

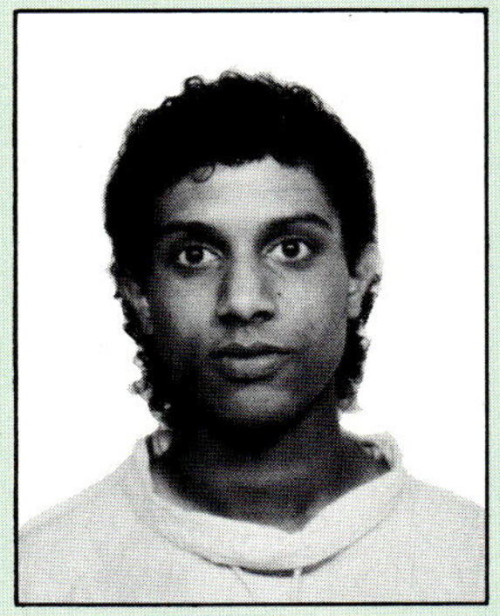

Anne, aged 17
(Pencil drawing, *above*)
In this self portrait Anne has not concerned herself with the construction of the head, but has tried to capture her own character.

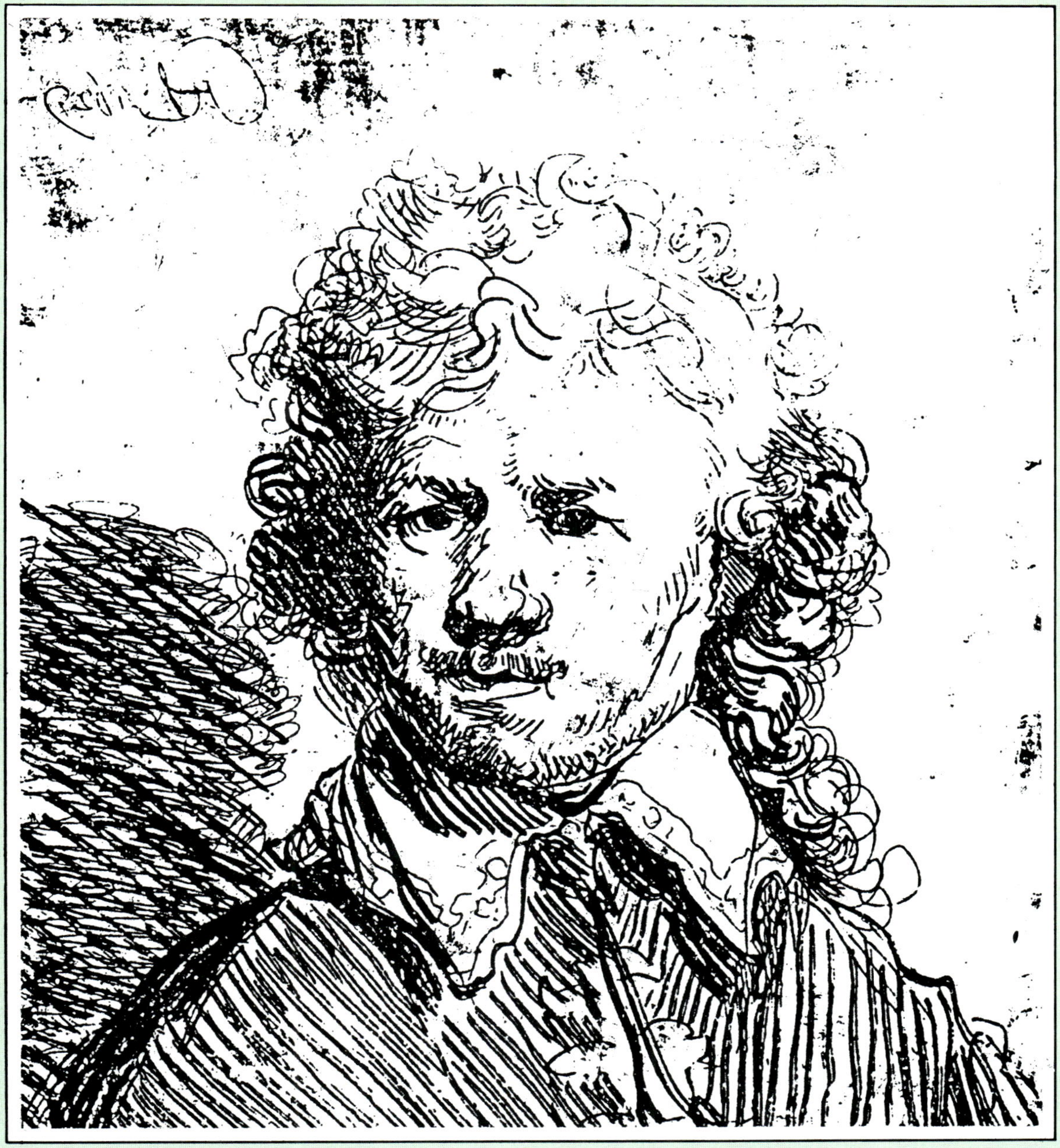

Rembrandt self portraits
(Engravings, reproduced actual size)
These self portraits show Rembrandt at 27 (*above*) and at 45 (*right*). His drawing shows a consistency in observation over the space of 18 years. He used his self portraits as a testing ground for his ideas, exploring expressions and lighting by using his own head as a model.

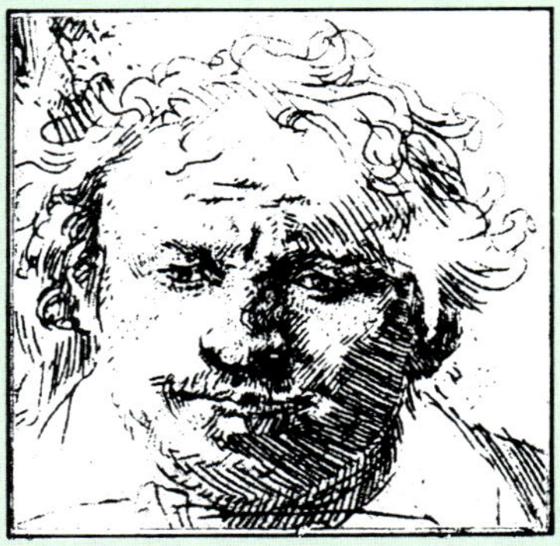

heads

Whatever we look like, our features – eyes, ears, nose, and so on – are in the same proportional relationship. A thin face and a fat face both have underlying skulls that determine these proportions. In order to draw heads well, you need to understand this underlying structure and the relationships between the features. You need to draw what is really there, not what you think is there: careful observation and checking is what counts when you are drawing a head. However, it is important that you do not let your understanding of the framework interfere with the feeling and quality of your drawing.

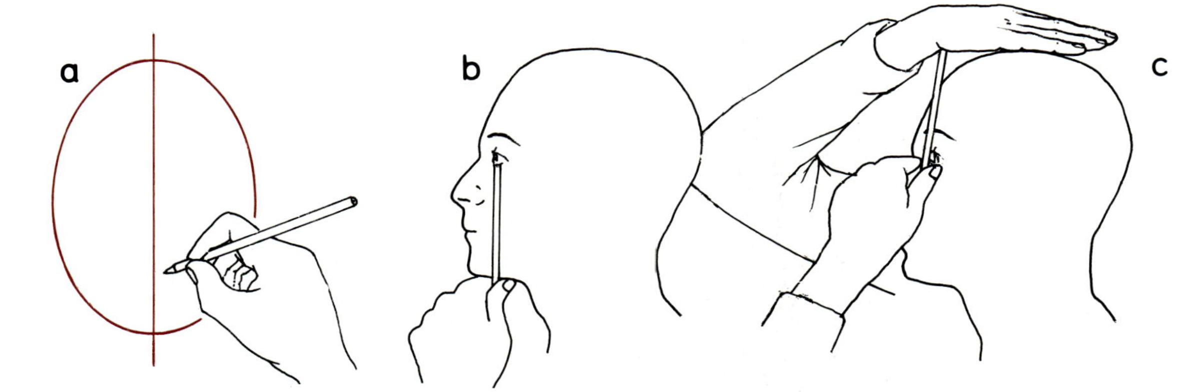

Face proportions
This exercise will help you to discover the proportions of your face. First draw an oval to represent your face, and divide it in half with a vertical line (**a**). Use a pencil to measure the distance from the base of your chin to your eye (**b**). Place a hand on the top of your head to establish the top of your skull, and measure the distance from your hand to your eye (**c**). If you plot these distances to scale on your oval, you will find that you have drawn your eye halfway up the centre line (**d**). If you continue to work out the relationships between your features, you will find the following:
measuring up from your chin, your nose is $\frac{1}{4}$ of the way up the centre line (**e**);
measuring down from your nose, your mouth is at about $\frac{1}{3}$ of the distance between your nose and chin (**f**);
the width of your eye is equal to the distance that your eyes are apart (**g**);
the tops of your ears align with your eyes and the bottoms of your ears align with the space between your nose and your top lip (**h**).

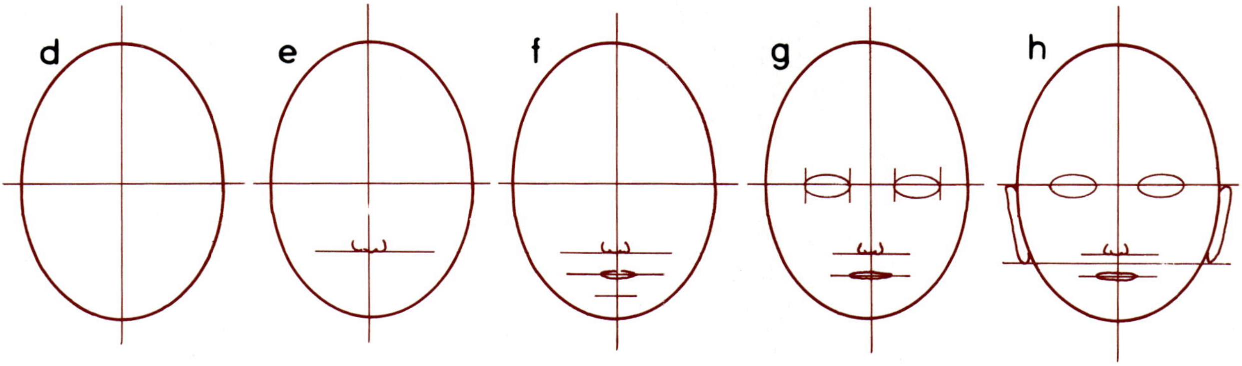

Parallel lines
The horizontal lines obtained by plotting the positions of the eyes, nose, and mouth are parallel. They remain parallel to each other whichever way the head turns. This banding of the features is one of the most common structures of the face, and the one that is most often forgotten.

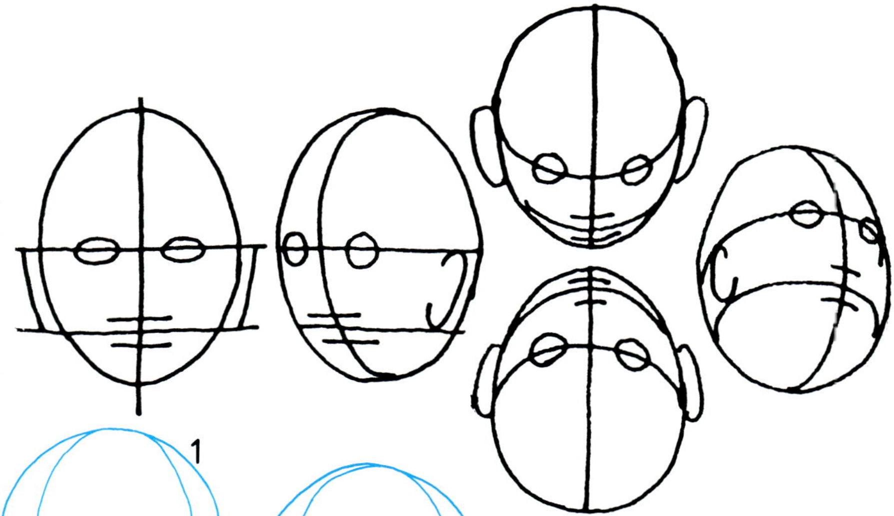

Constructing a head
It is often easier to understand the head's structure by thinking of it as interlocking geometrical forms. As a simple exercise, try this ball and bucket construction.
1 Draw a ball. Draw three lines around the ball, as shown.
2 Add a bucket to the bottom of the ball and extend two of the lines from the ball onto the bucket, as shown.
3 Draw a circle on the side of the ball at a point where the lines on the ball cross.
4 Remove the circular side segments. You now have a basic construction for a head.
5 Use the central vertical line to plot the positions of the features.
6 Add the features and complete the head.
7, 8, 9 The geometrical construction remains the same whatever the angle of the head.

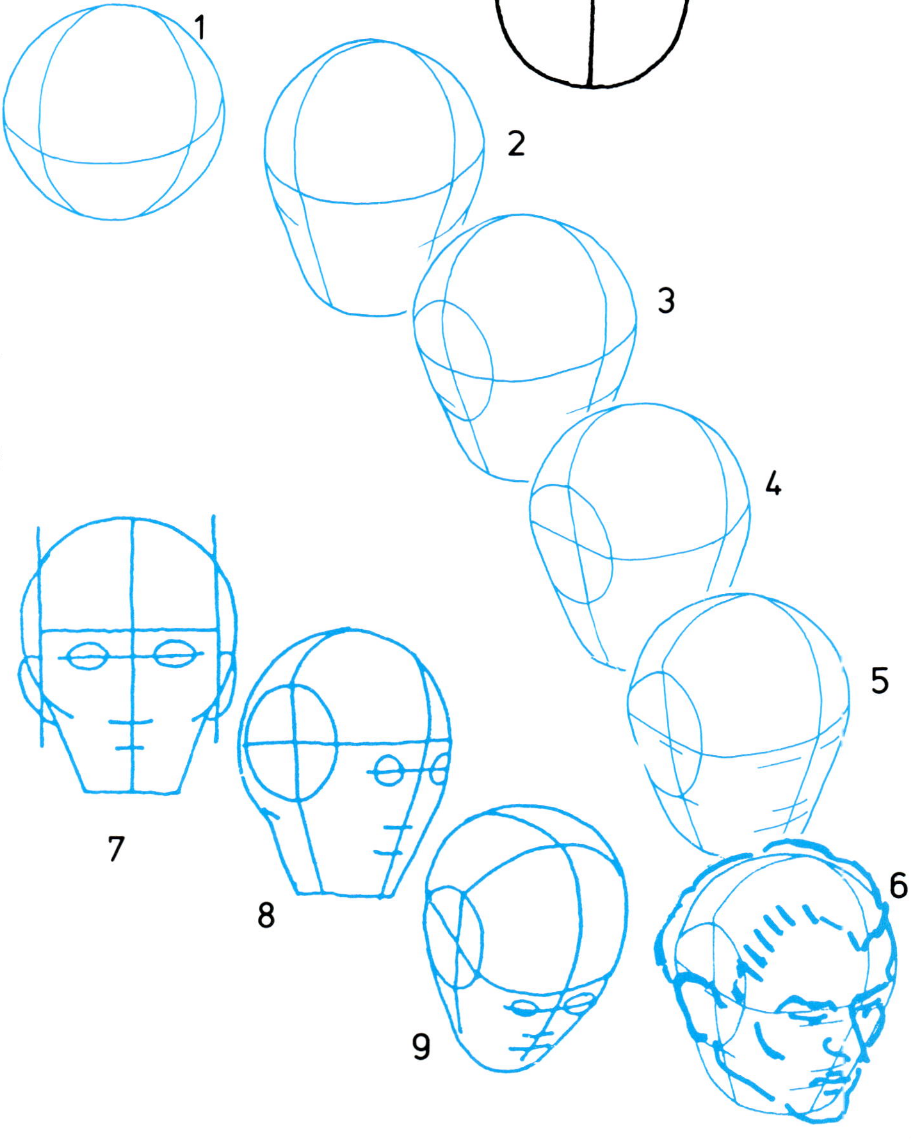

heads

The same rules about checking details and underlying structure apply whether you are drawing yourself or someone else. Remember that good drawings are the result of good observation. When you are planning the head, try to ignore the deceptive line of the hair and instead see the basic construction of the skull. Place all the features correctly, using basic principles and simple measuring devices. At the same time, try to show the characteristics that give that person's face its own individual quality.

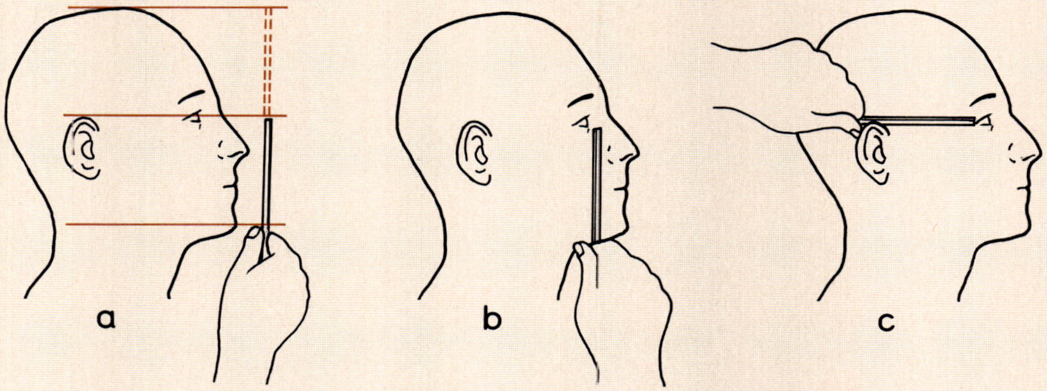

Placing the ear
You can use the relative proportions of the features to help you place the ear correctly when you are drawing a head from the side. First check the proportions on your own head. Your eyes occur halfway up your head and the top of your ear is on the same level as the centre of your eye (**a**). Measure the distance from your eye to your chin (**b**) and compare it with the distance from your eye to your ear (**c**). You will find that the distances are the same. You can then use this principle – that the distance from chin to eye equals the distance from eye to ear – to draw your subject's ear in the correct place. Study your subject carefully and sketch in the profile. Measure the distance from eye to chin on your drawing (**d**), then plot the same distance back into the head (**e**). You will then have established the position of the ear. The triangle formed by joining the ear, eye, and chin is very helpful in establishing the central areas of a side view (**f**).

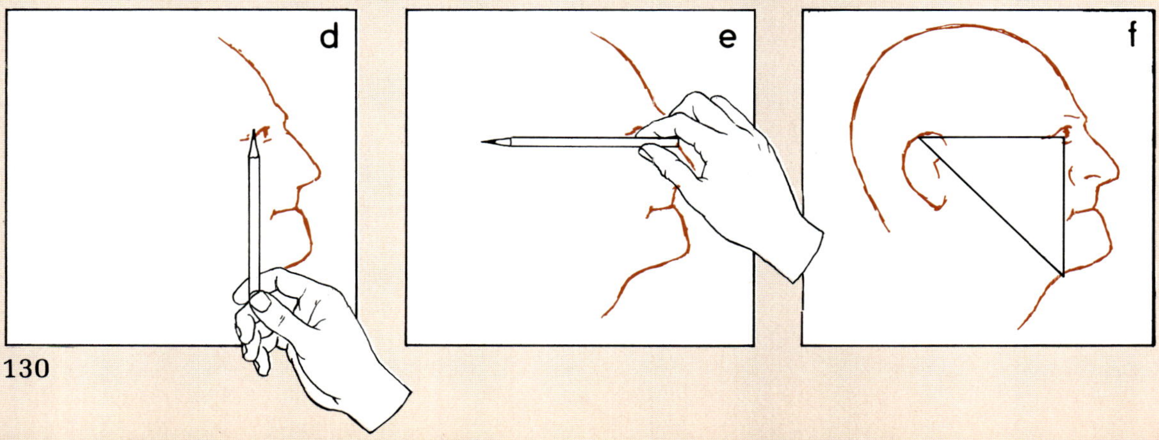

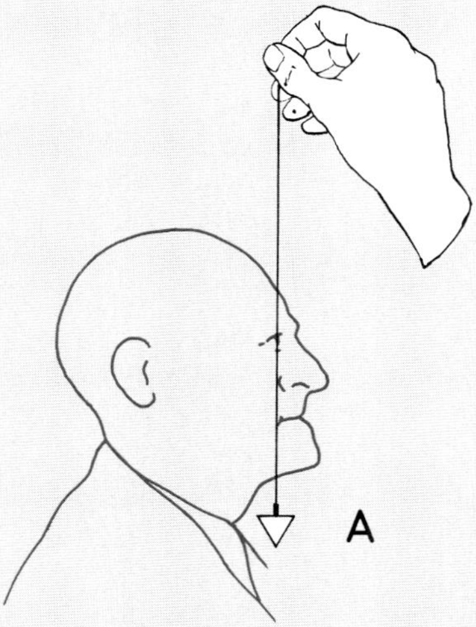

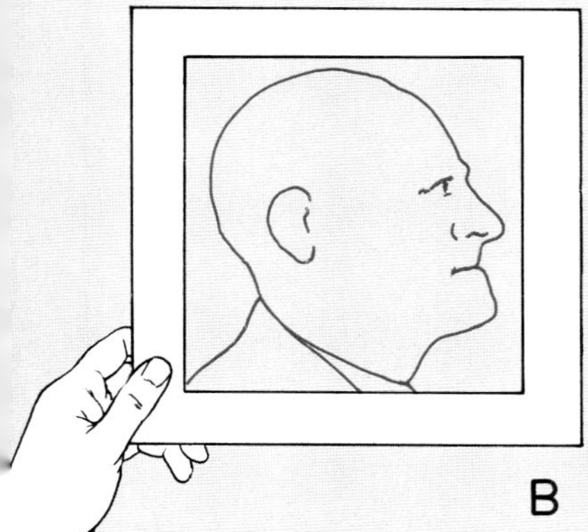

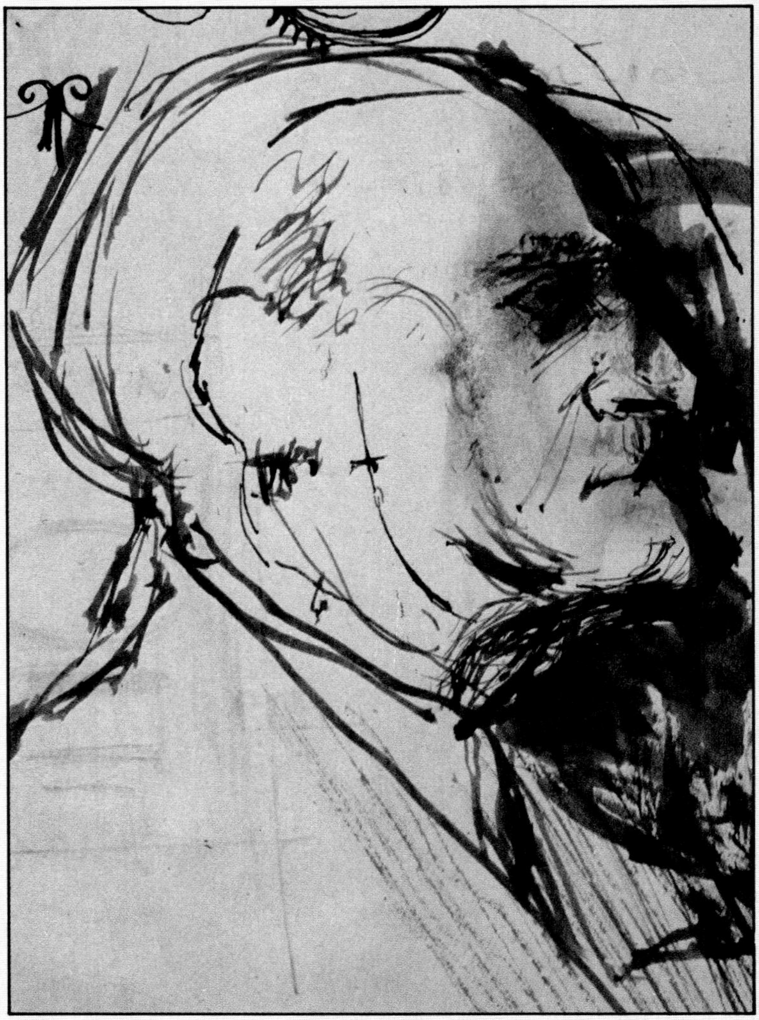

©DIAGRAM

Old man
(Pen and ink drawing, *right*) The strong characteristics of this head were carefully checked for vertical alignment. This can be done either with a plumb line (**A**) – a thin cord with a weight attached – or by viewing the head through a cardboard frame (**B**).

Squared photographs
Dividing a photograph into squares and then transferring the details in each square into a similar square on your drawing is a useful way to learn more about the relationships between the features, as all the horizontal and vertical alignments are clearly shown.

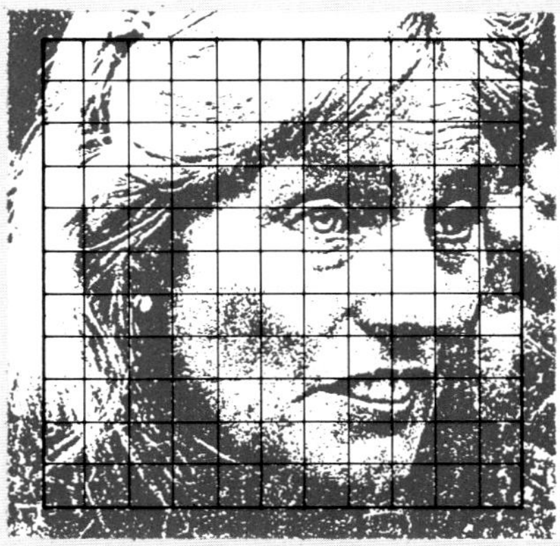

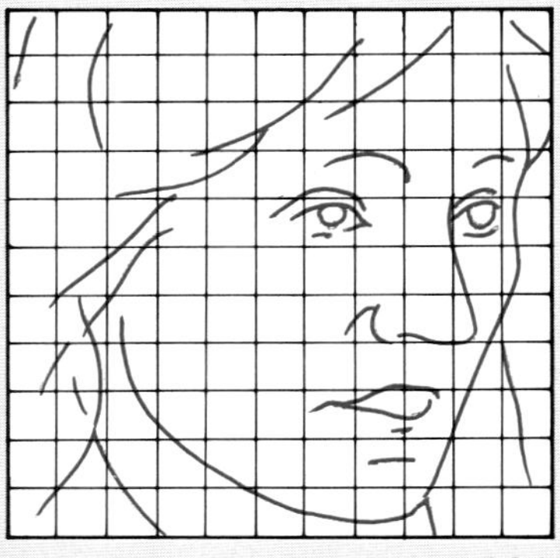

heads

Once you have some basic knowledge of the construction of the head, you can apply the principles when drawing heads from unusual viewpoints. The head is usually the part of a drawing that requires the greatest accuracy, so get as much practice as you can.

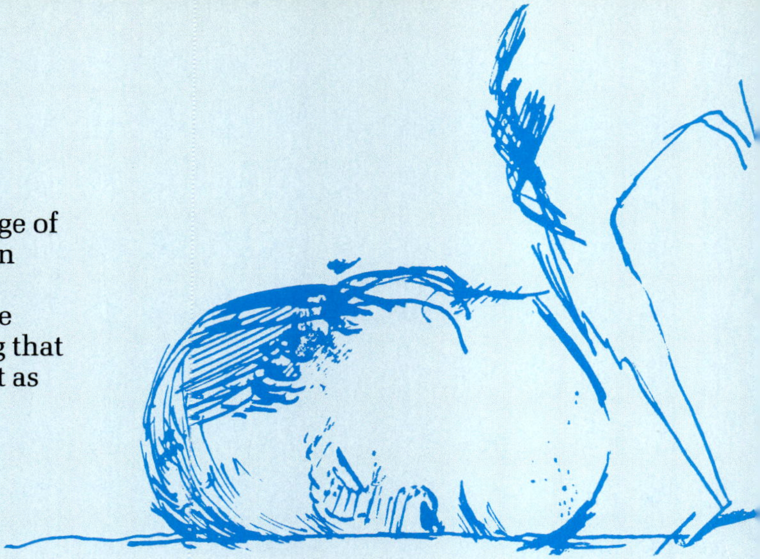

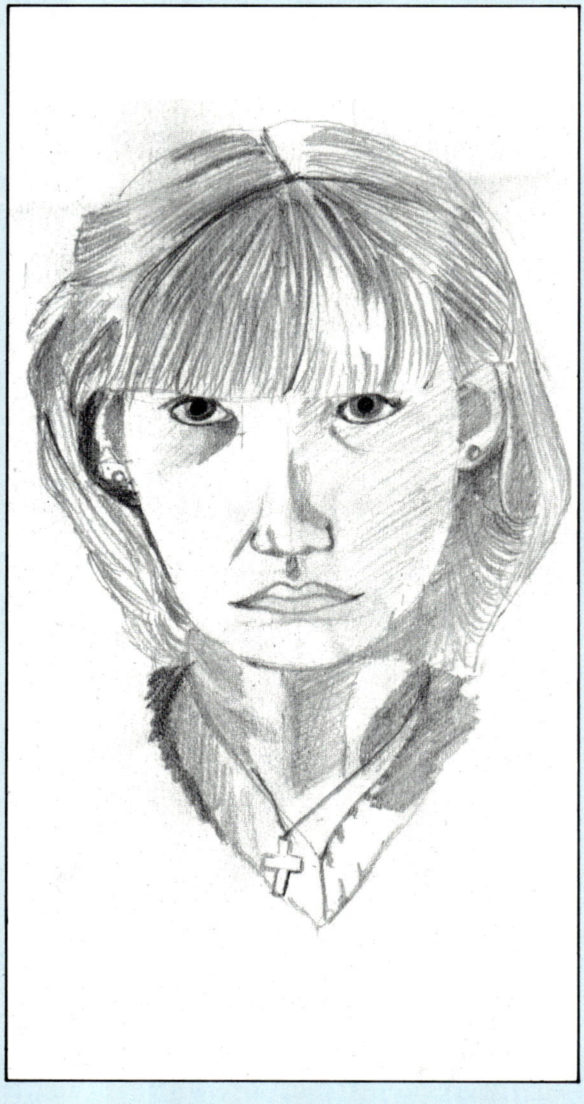

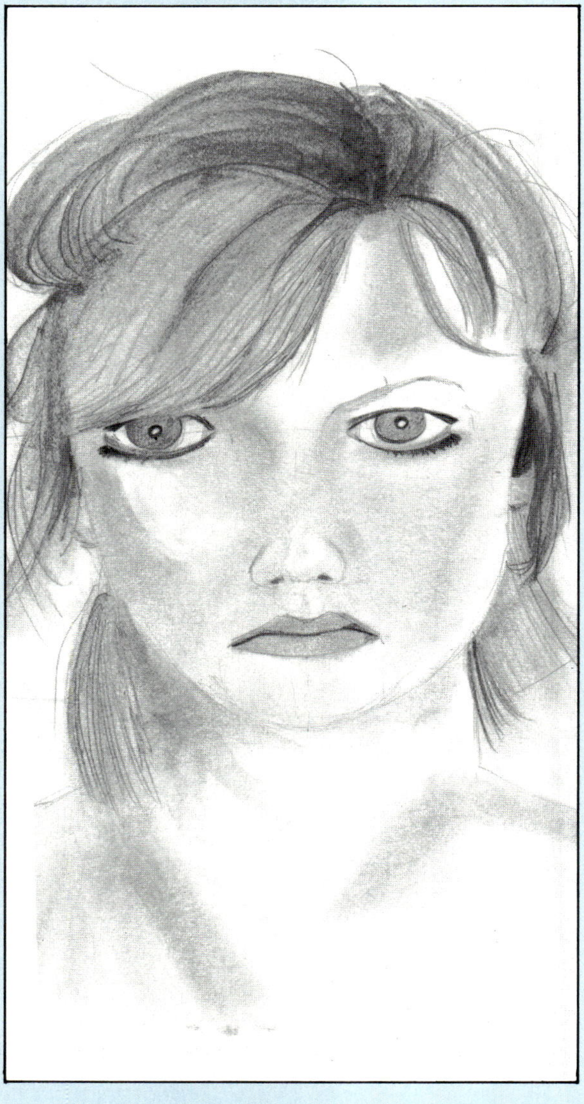

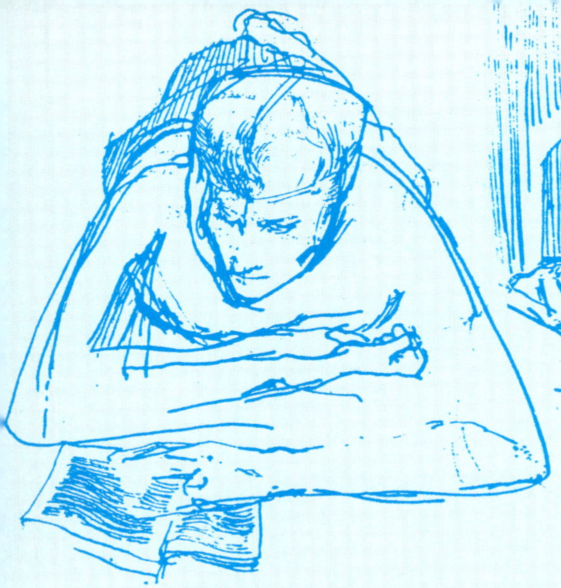

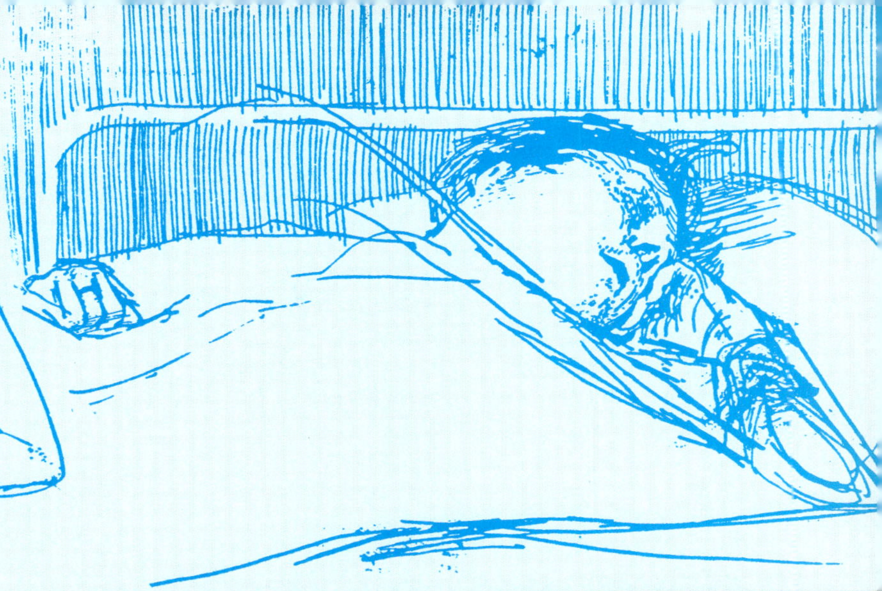

Resting figures
(Pen and ink sketches)
Each of the drawings (*above*) is a study of a head from an unusual viewpoint. Sleeping figures give you the chance to study heads from angles which would not be possible if the subject was awake. The direction and thickness of the pen lines help to convey the volume and curvature of the head.

Jane's self portraits
(Pencil drawings)
These self portraits of Jane at 16 (*far left*) and 20 (*left*) both show an excellent ability to observe particular details: strands of hair, eyelids, the curves of the lips. Always try to draw the particular and only sketch in the general.

Bruce, aged 18
(Pen and ink sketch)
When you are using yourself as a model to explore form and construction, don't be afraid to draw lines that reinforce your enquiries. As can be seen in this self portrait, the checking and overchecking produce duplications of lines, but the total impression is one of a solid figure (*right*).

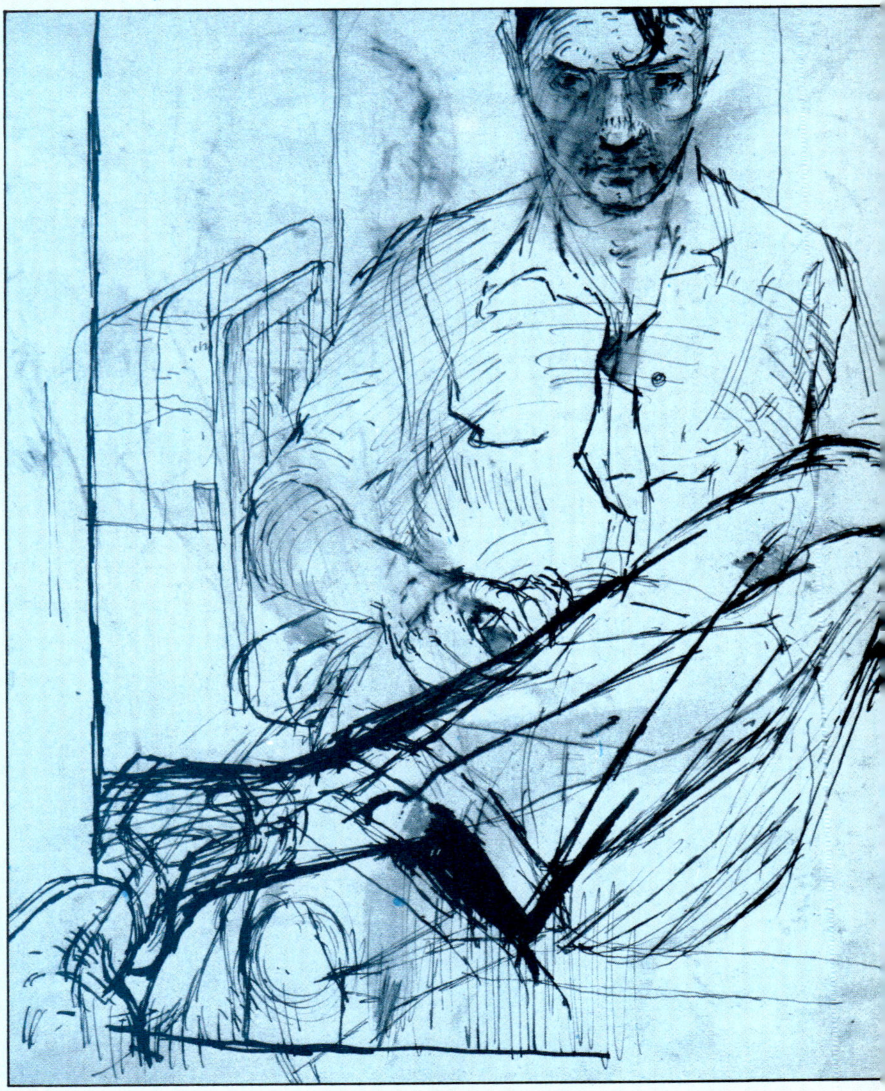

heads

Character studies must not be confused with caricature. The former attempts to capture some strong element of the person, his individual qualities; the latter exaggerates and distorts, usually to ridicule. Your drawing will be more realistic if you can search out the inner character in your subject by close observation of detail or expression.

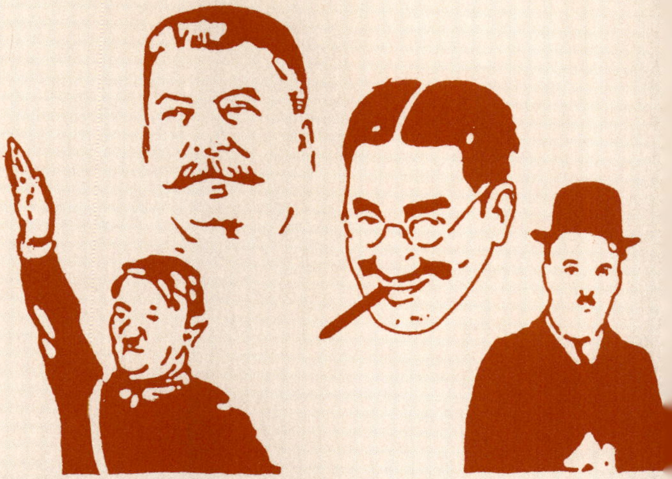

Four men with moustaches
(Brush drawings)
Although Hitler, Stalin, Groucho Marx and Chaplin (*above*) all grew moustaches, the different styles gave a clue to their individual personalities.

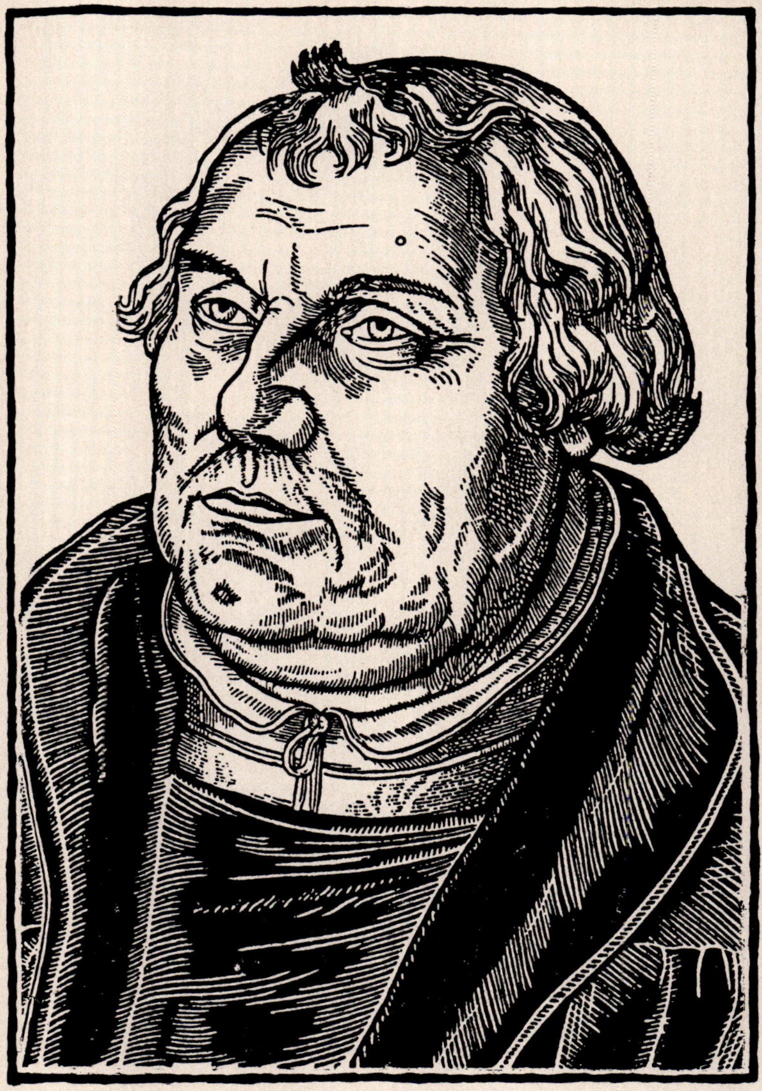

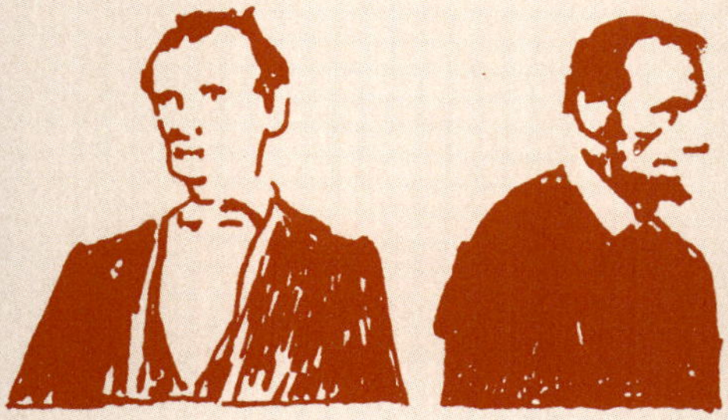

Abraham Lincoln
(Two brush drawings)
The American President (*above*) only grew a beard at the age of 52. Stamps, coins, films and monuments have created in our minds a face with a small chin beard, his appearance for only four years before his death.

Martin Luther
(16th century woodcut by Cranach)
This artist's ability to observe the qualities of his subject is excellently revealed (*left*). Note the mole on Luther's forehead.

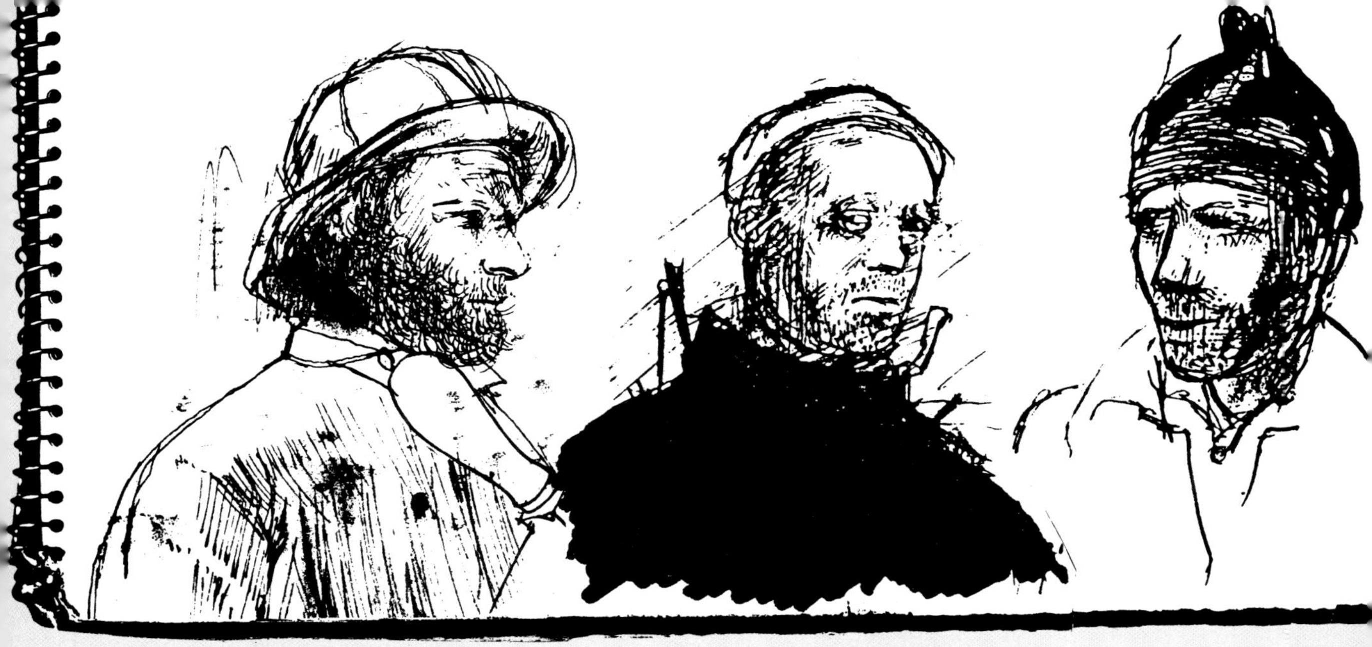

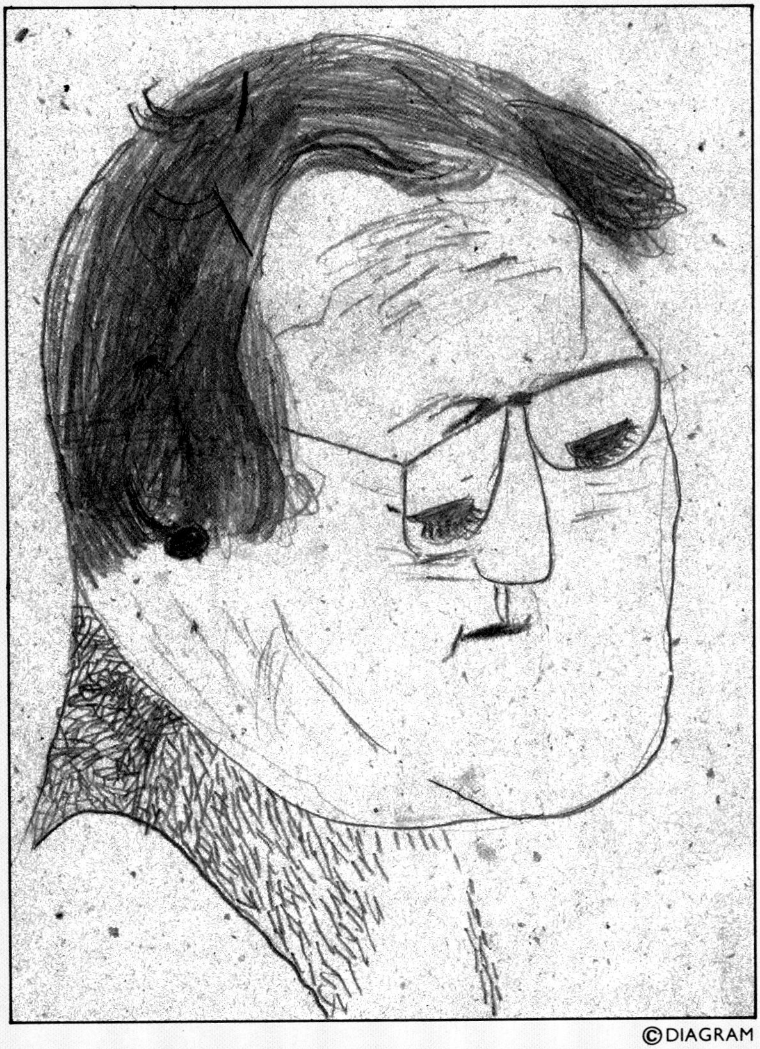

Fishermen
(Pen drawings)
Three crew members (*above*), each with a different quality of face. The weather-worn texture of the skin, and the heavy eyes due to short periods of sleep are observed in the individuals' facial expressions.

Anne's granny
(Pencil drawing by Anne, aged 9)
The distortion of the anatomical details (*left*) helps considerably to capture the qualities of Anne's granny. Young artists are often very good at noticing the particular: older artists smooth out, generalise details.

Anne's mother
(Pencil drawing by Anne, aged 10)
The figures (*below*) are reduced to a Russian doll. Nevertheless the domesticity of the figure is well captured.

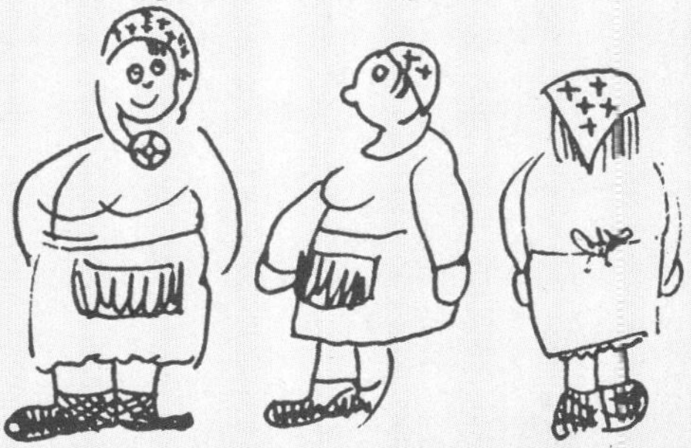

hands

Hands are notoriously difficult to draw but practice is the answer – always complete the hands in your figure studies. Imagine the flexibility of the individual fingers and remember their basic flat shapes when you look at them from different or unusual viewpoints, or when the fingers are curled up and the underlying relationships are hidden.

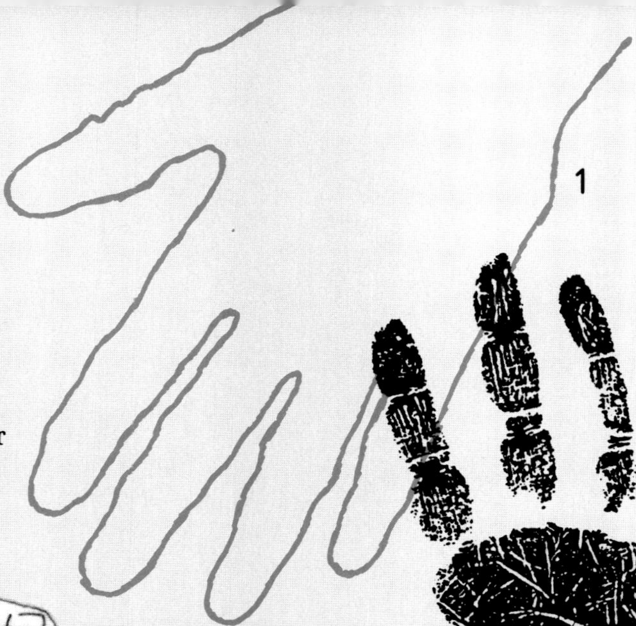

1

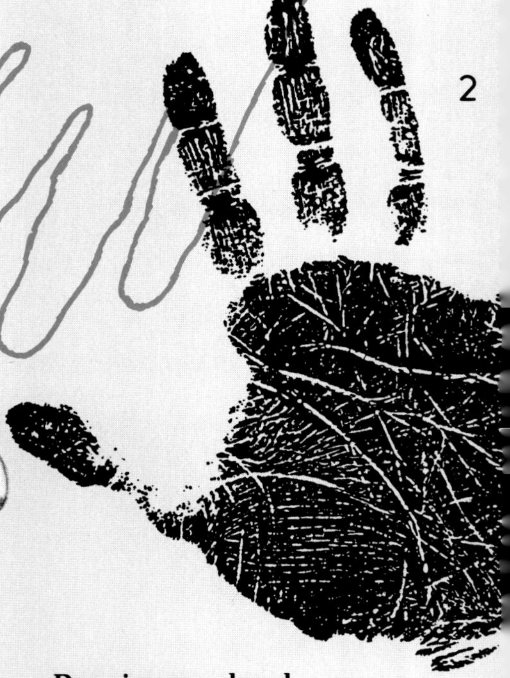

2

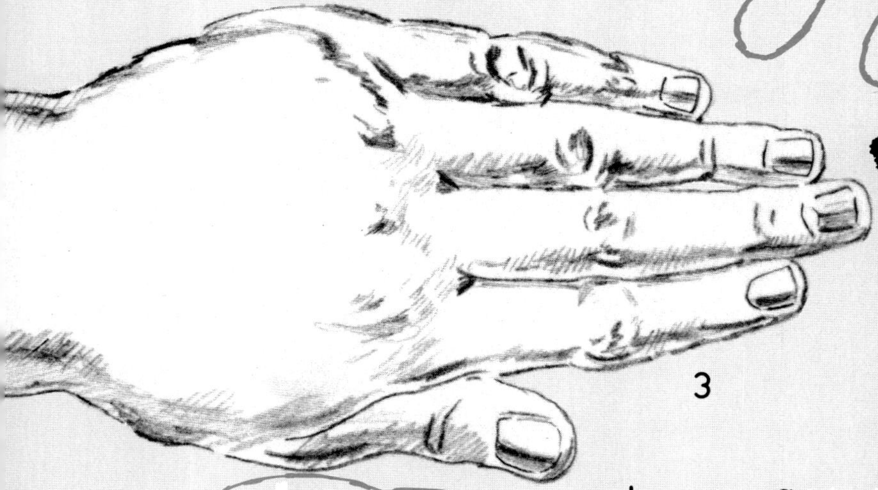

3

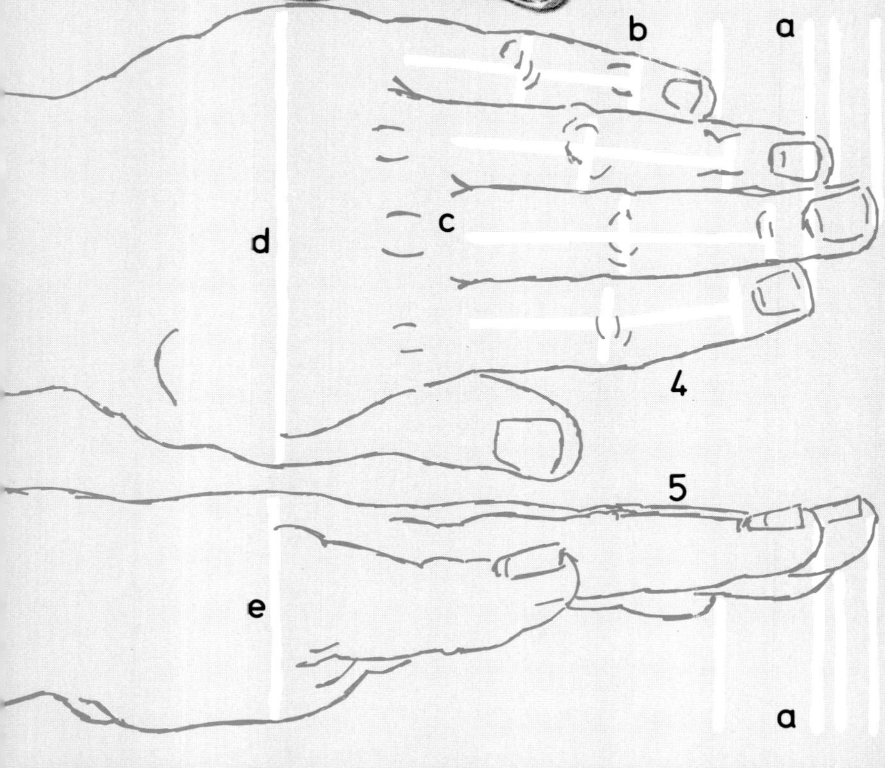

Drawing your hand
(Pencil drawings and an ink print, *above* and *left*)
1 Draw round your hand to produce an outline which shows the variable finger lengths.
2 Make a print by pressing your hand on an inky pad and then transferring the impression to paper. This reveals the basic parts of the fingers and the shape of the palm.
3 Rest your hand palm down and draw it, measuring the separate parts.
4 and **5** Points to notice:
a Variable length of fingers
b Variable position of joints
c Directions of fingers
d The broadest parts
e The thickest part
Try to remember this basic structure when drawing hands in different positions.

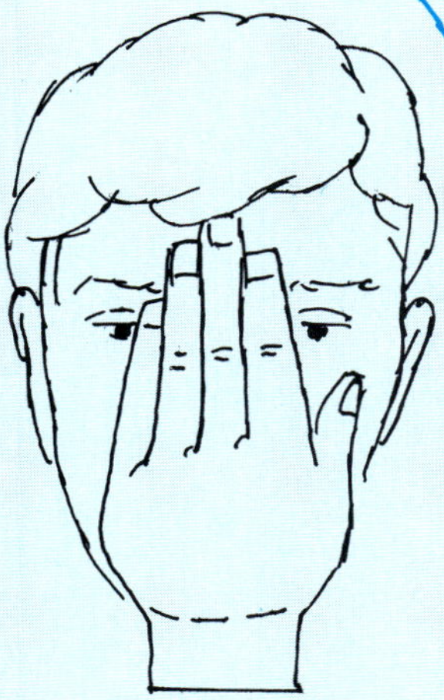

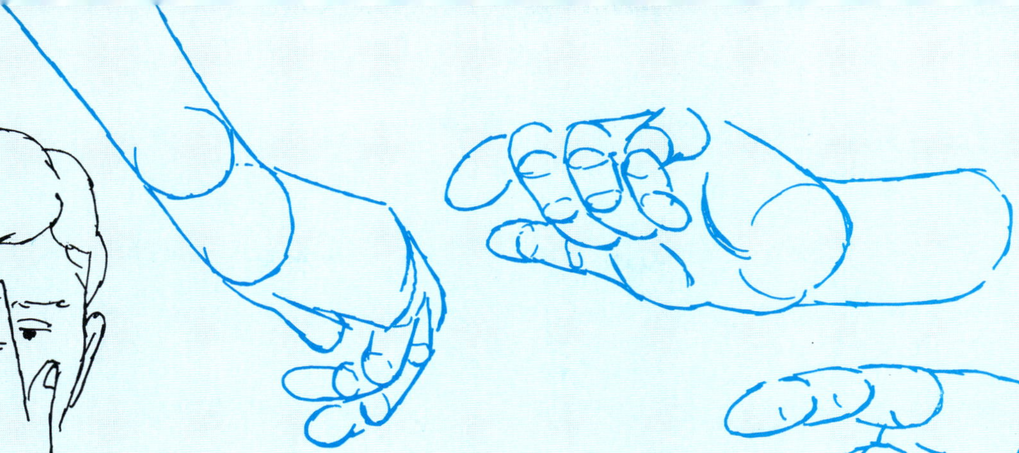

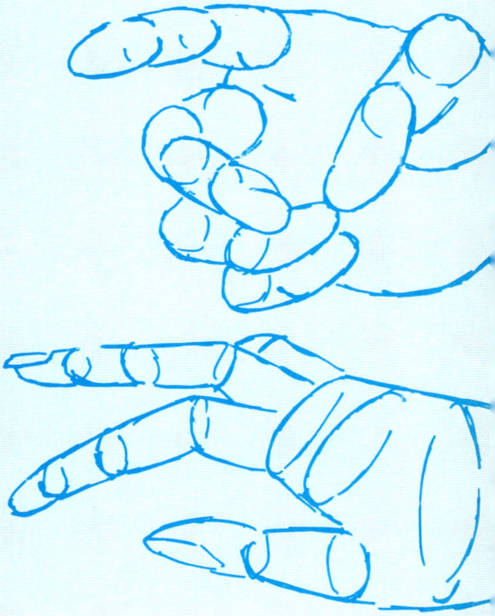

Hand size
The hand is usually as long as the distance from the chin to the hair line. Try this test on your own hand (*above*).

Volume of hands
(Pencil studies)
Think of hands as a collection of interlocking tubes (*above* and *right*), each finger being able to move independently and slightly out of alignment with the next. This simple way of drawing hands in a variety of positions clearly reveals their flexibility.

Studies of hands
(Pen and ink drawings)
Fill pages of your sketch book with studies of hands. Draw from photographs, copy hands from other artists' work, and sketch your free hand in the mirror doing a range of tasks. With experience, you will be able to draw imaginary hands doing whatever you require of them (*right*).

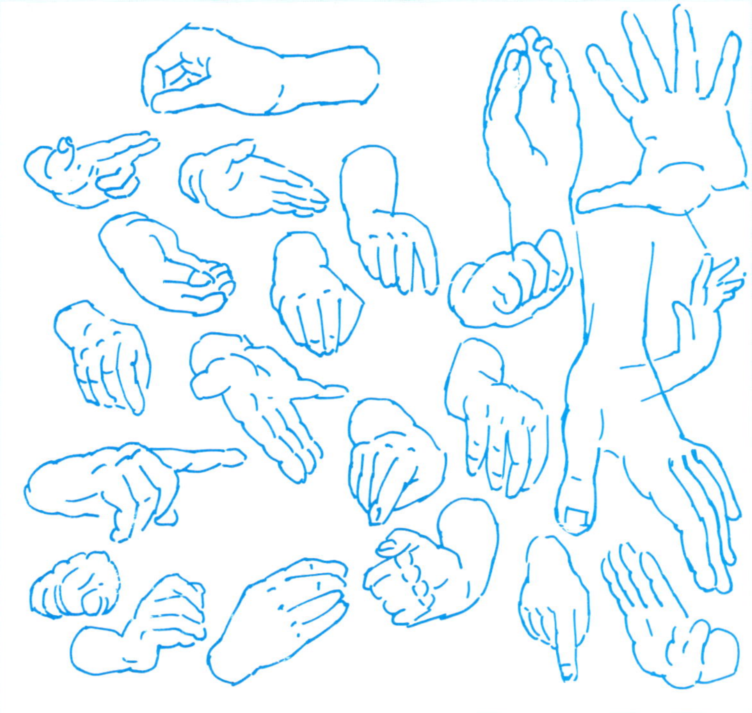

legs and feet

A person's legs are normally identical but may appear dissimilar because of the different amounts of weight carried by each limb, so notice the dissimilarities and recognise the reasons for them. Bare feet are seen infrequently but a knowledge of their characteristics will help you put your figures firmly on the ground or floor and establish their bases. Try studying and sketching legs and feet from photographs, statues, and drawings and paintings by artists.

Drawing the form
(Pen and ink drawings, *right*)
Look where the muscles curve round to the other side of the leg (**a**). In your drawing curves help to indicate the roundness of a limb. Notice the firm patches where bones are just under the skin (**b**), at knees and ankles; these are useful checking points.
Studies of feet (*below*).

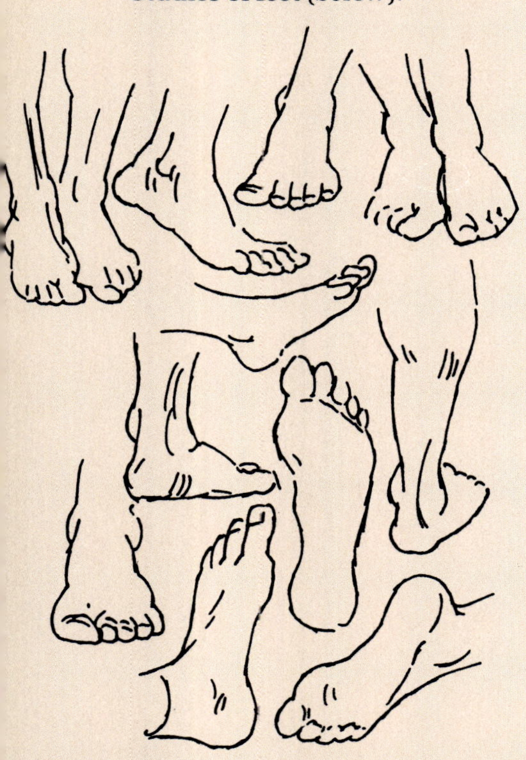

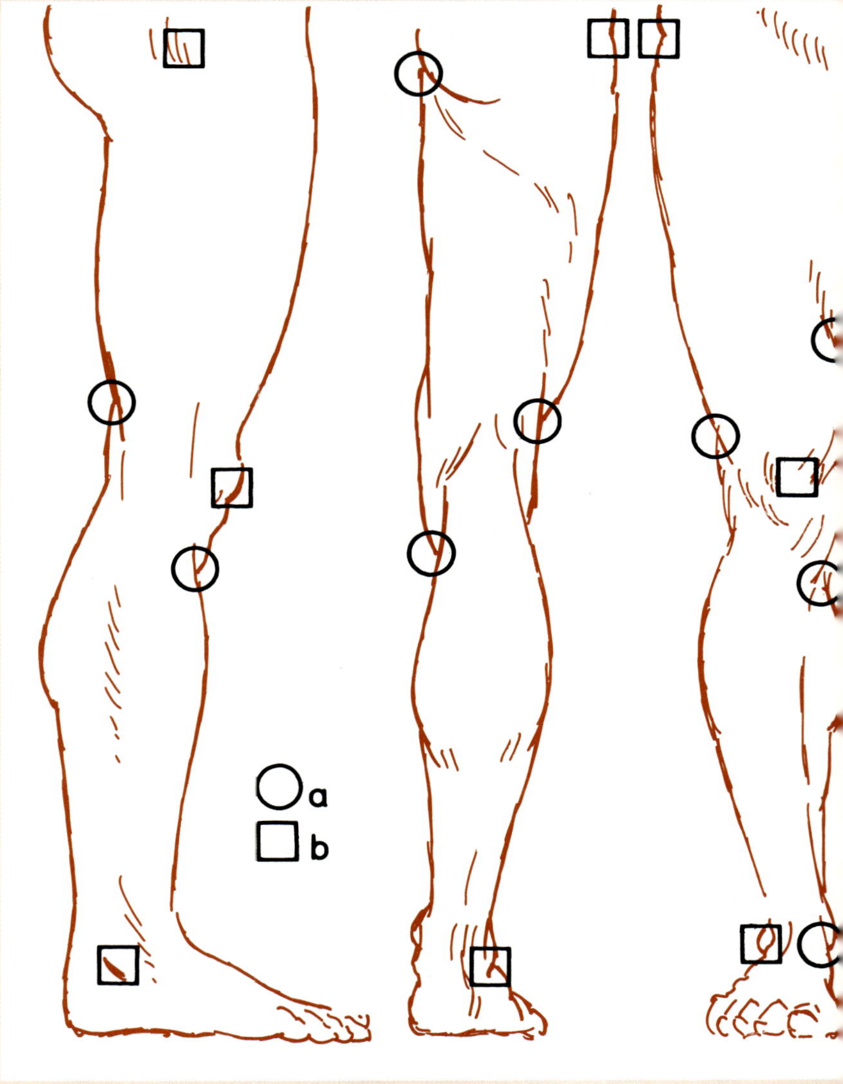

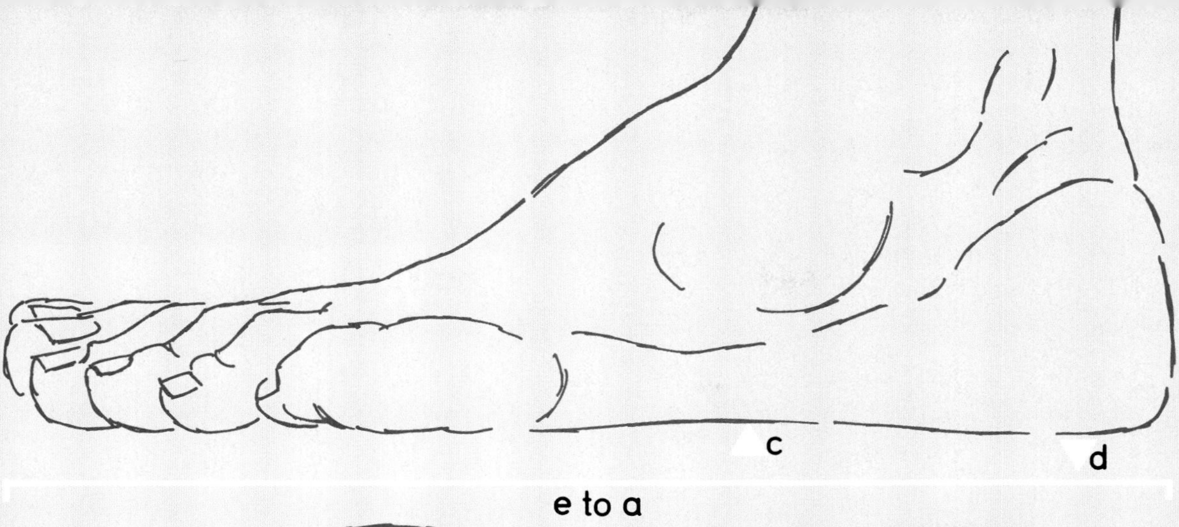

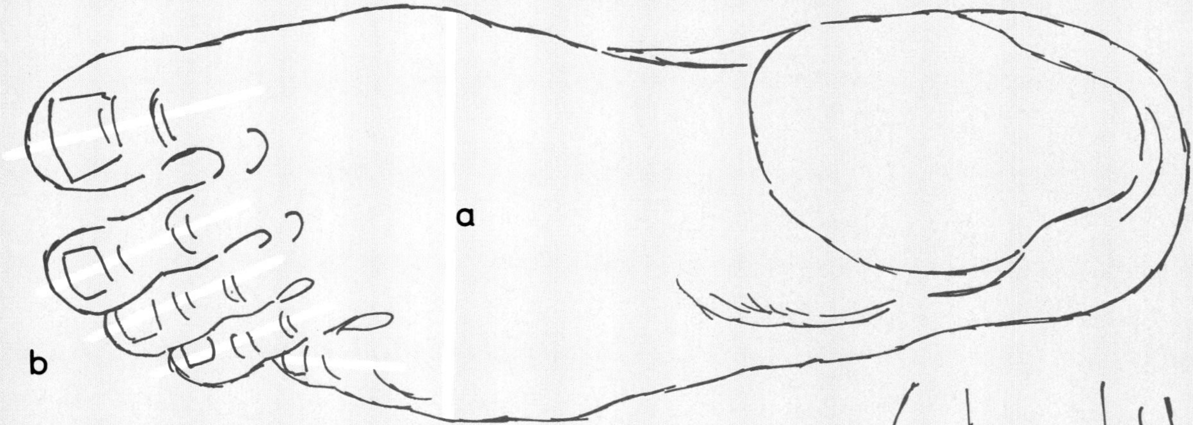

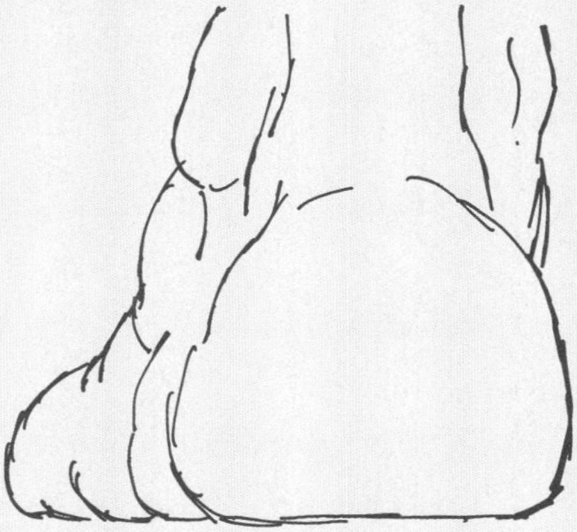

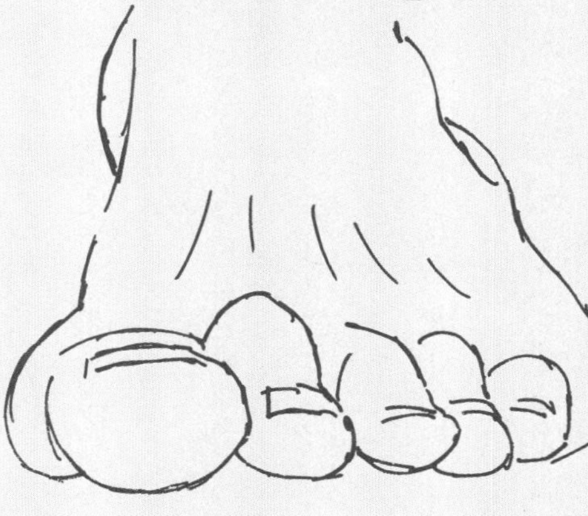

The human foot
(Pen studies)
The studies (*above* and *right*) are based on measured drawings by the 16th-century German artist, Albrecht Dürer.
Points to notice:
a The widest point
b Directions of toes
c Hollowness under the centre
d The weight-bearing point
e The proportion of width to length
The foot lacks the flexibility of the hand so if you remember the underlying structure you are more likely to draw feet correctly. The appearance of the feet will probably alter with a change in viewpoint rather than because of a new position.

people

You can compile a memoir of your observations of people and how they move, sit and occupy space by using your sketch book to draw groups of figures and their gestures. Sketch gatherings in theatres, churches, pubs, cafes, libraries, lawcourts, at home and in buses and bus stations. The seated figure is an ideal subject for examination.

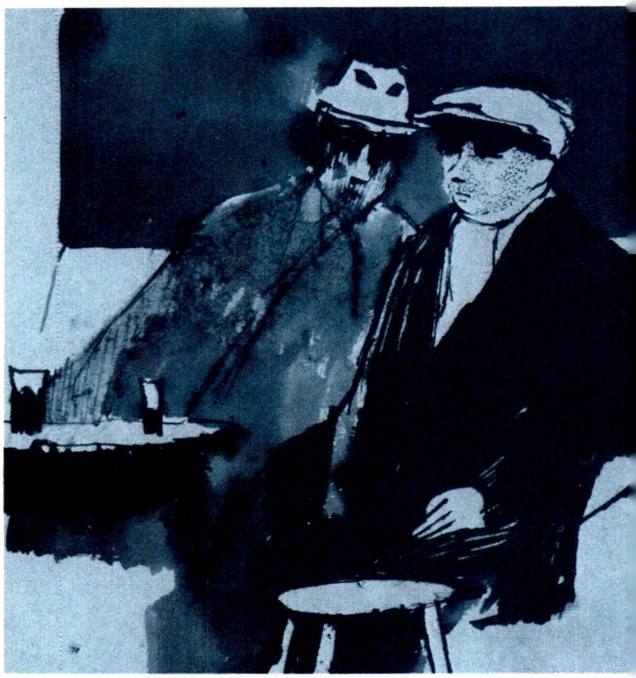

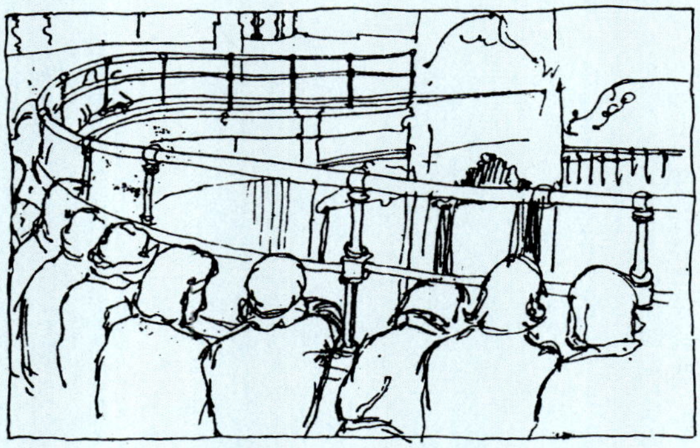

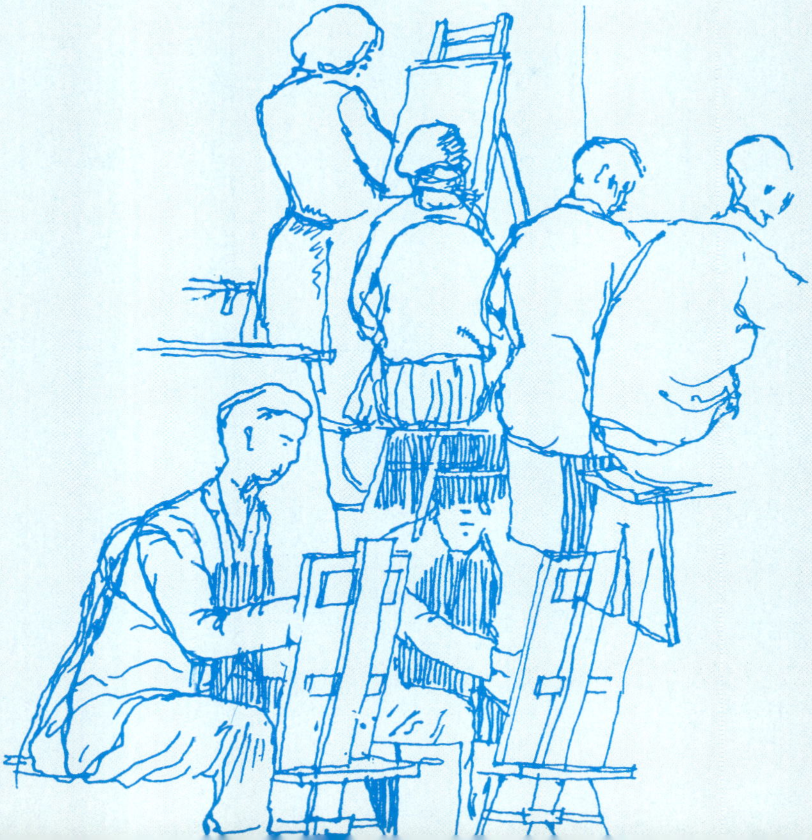

Bar conversation, Dublin
(Pen, brush and ink drawing)
Unselfconscious subjects in repose can be found in a bar (see *above*). Study fat and thin people and their own particular way of moving

Theatre interval, Paris
(Pencil drawing)
The interval in a play provided relaxed groups of figures for a study (*above left*).

Life-class pupils
(Pencil drawing)
For a break in your life class, observe your fellow students. The unusual combination of shapes and the distinctive characteristics of each group make for a striking study (*left*).

Public library, Sunderland
(Pencil drawing by a 15-year-old)
A public library supplies peace, quietness and excellent models for sketching. Outline their positions and complete their faces as far as possible afterwards. The artist of the scene (*right*) was able to spend more time on the details of the walls, floor and furniture than on the passing figures.

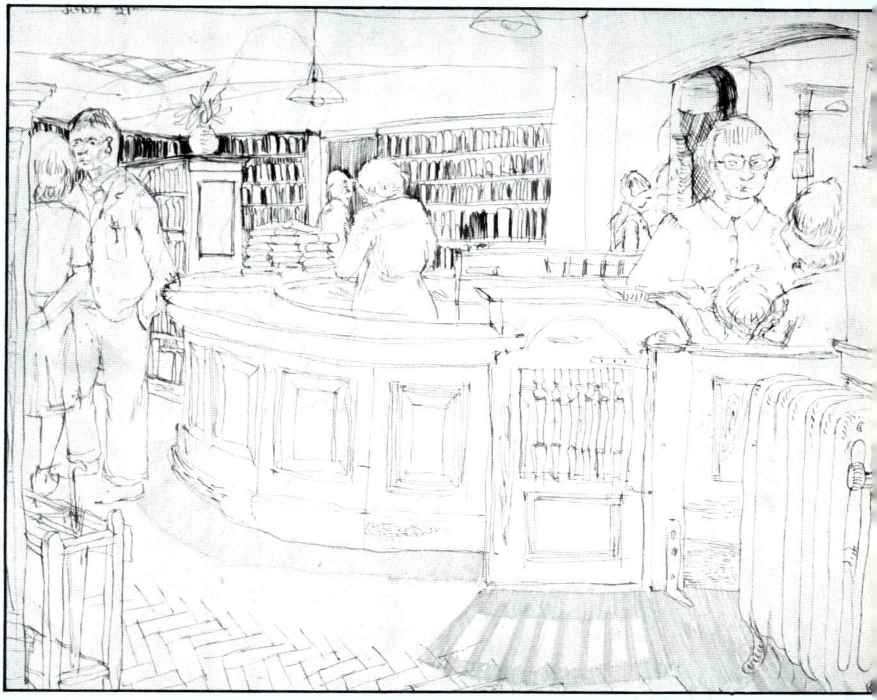

Library readers
(Pen and ink drawing)
A person reading is likely to remain still long enough for you to study detail. Facial features are carried on a rounded form occupying space – always try to capture the sense of volume, as in the drawing (*below*).

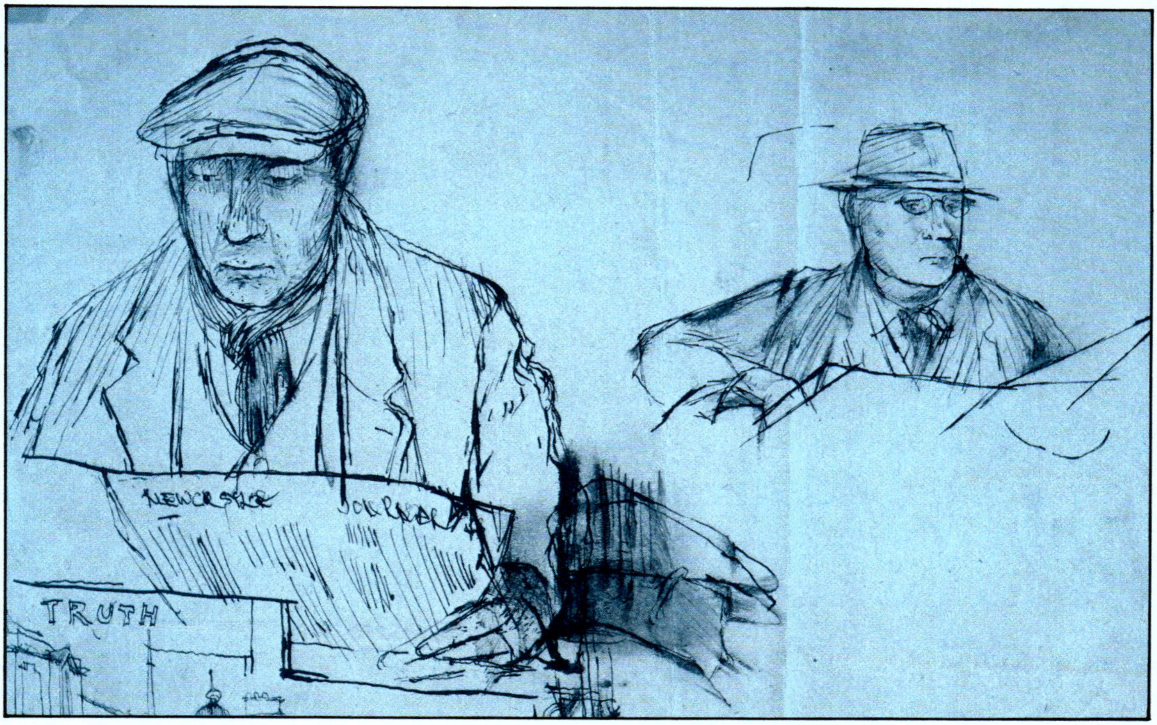

people

Sketching outside is absorbing and valuable, so always carry your sketch book with you. You will be searching for information – the unique, the odd, the particular – completing a bank of sketches to make you fluent in depicting how the human figure moves and relates to its surroundings and other people.

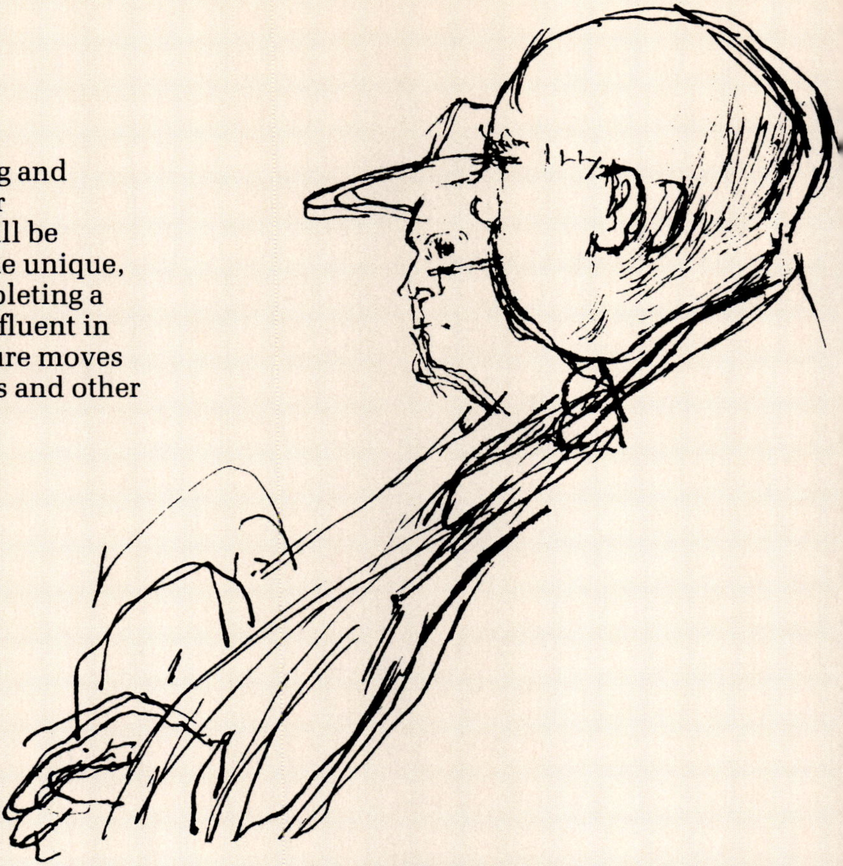

Old men on a bench
(Pen drawing)
Closely observing heads enables you to compare forms, as shown (*right*), in which the larger, more spherical head is contrasted with the thinner, angular profile.

Summer afternoon, Central Park, New York
(Pen drawing)
When drawing activity, sketch rapidly (see *right*), adding detail as people reform positions similar to earlier shapes.

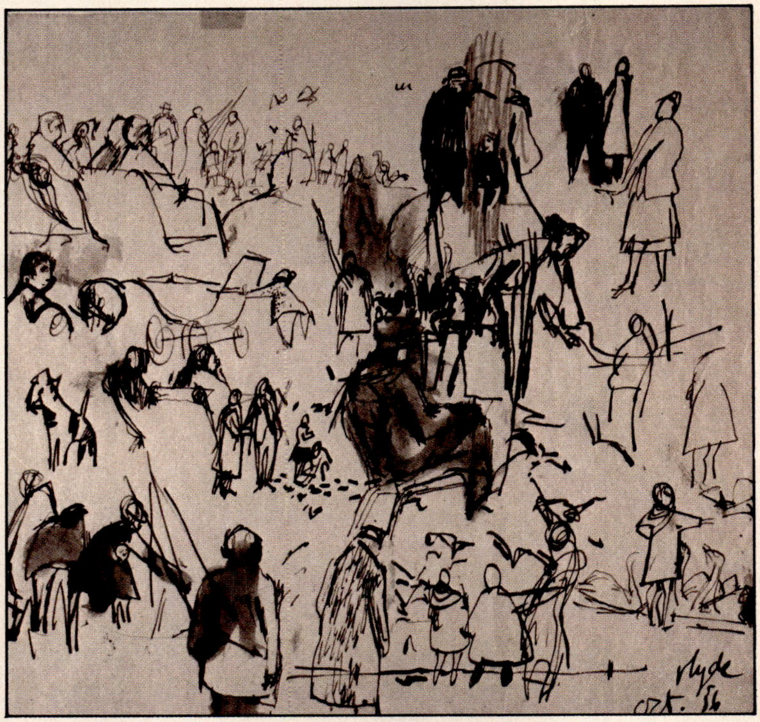

Old ladies on a bench, Paris
(Pen drawing, *below*)
Convey impression by odd detail – a hat, bushy hair, drooping shoulders.

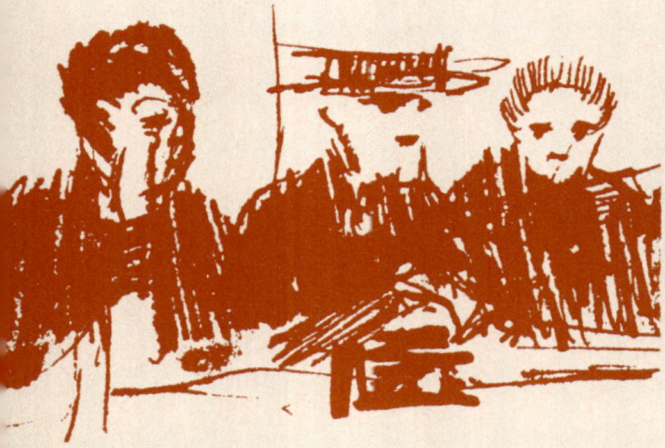

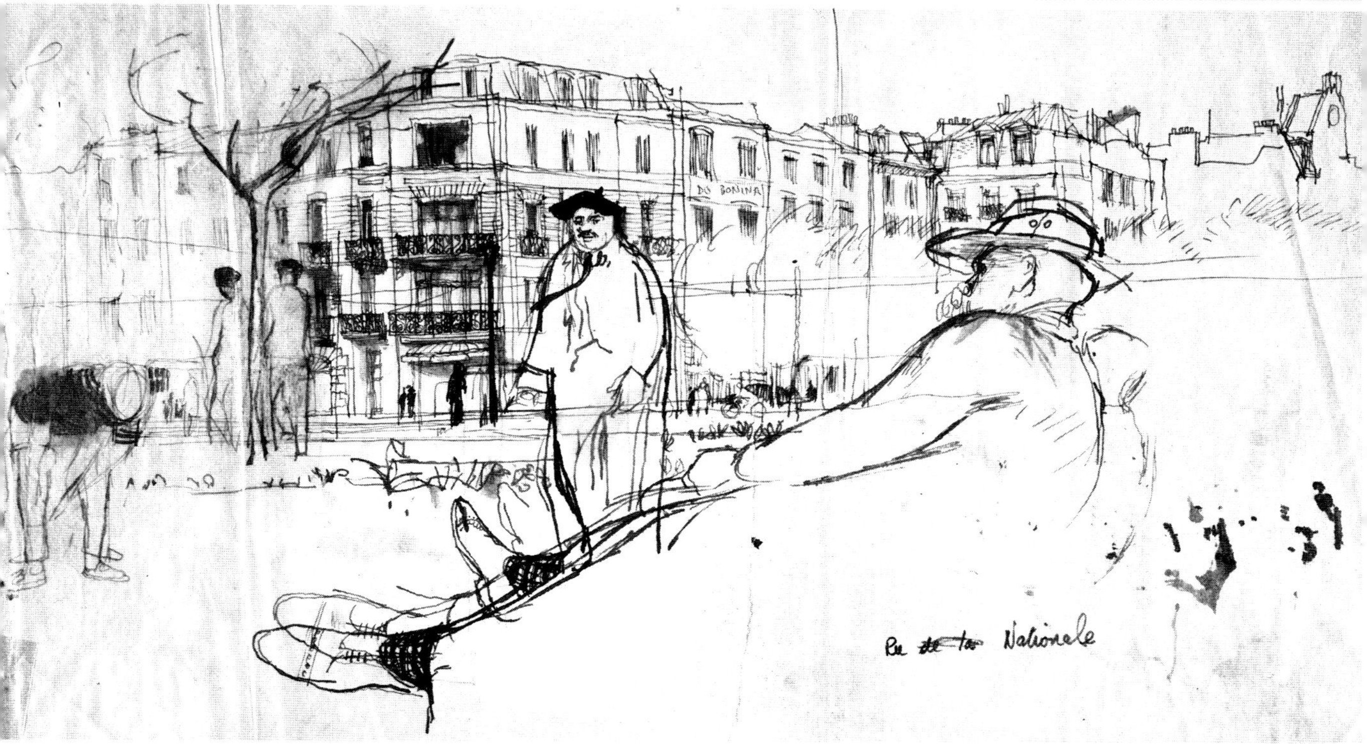

Rue Nationale, Lille, France
(Pen drawing)
If you have time, use it to draw in a street background with care; then as people pass, set them into the composition. The French scene (*above*) shows how to examine the different ways people sit and walk.

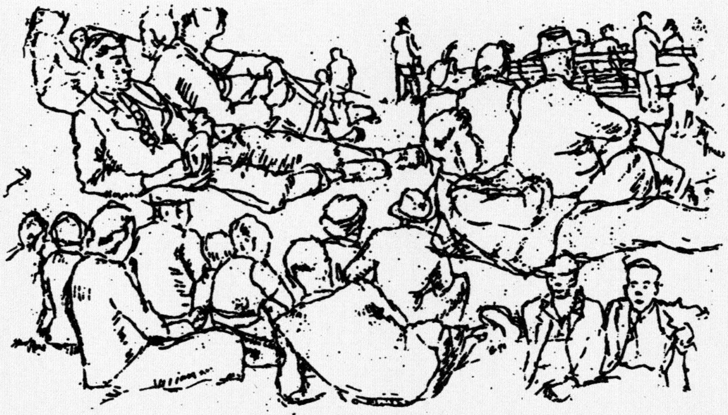

Listening to the band, Torquay
(Pencil drawing)
Reclining figures stay still long enough for you to study their shapes properly (*right*).

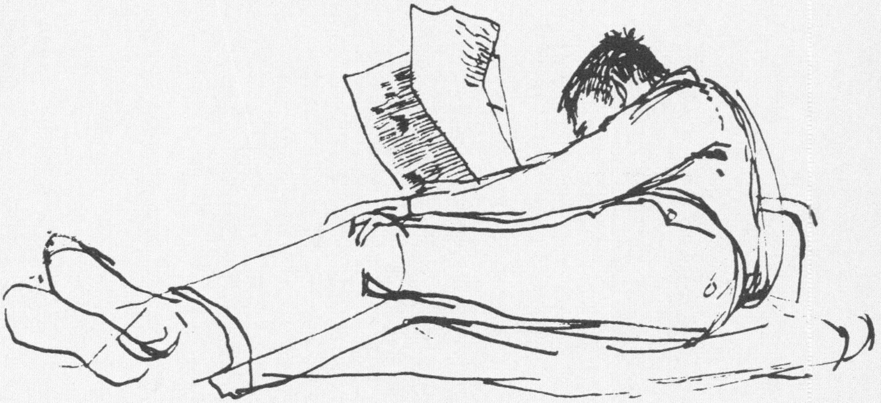

Soldier reading in a park, London
(Pen drawing)
When you see someone lying down, walk round them until you find an unusual angle (*right*).

people

The changing positions of moving figures mean you must sketch quickly, retain an after-image of each figure, its shape, stance and gesture, and memorise an overview. Often you can keep several drawings going simultaneously. Observe and draw people all the time; and try to capture their basic shapes and balance, and draw the whole figure, not the detail.

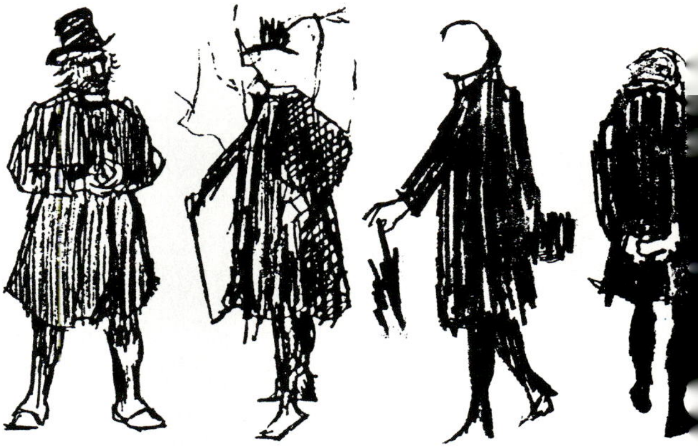

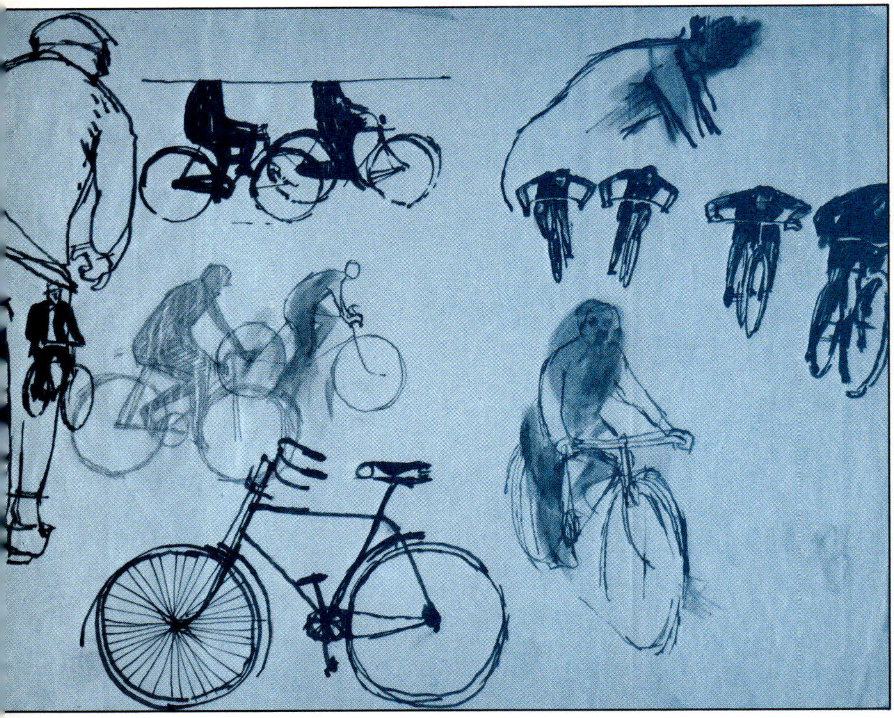

Bishop walking in a garden
(Pencil drawing, *above*)
As the bishop walked around the garden, four drawings were gradually emerging.

Bicycle traffic, Arnhem
(Pen drawings, *left*)
The cyclists passed by so quickly that the artist had to hold an after-image of their shapes while drawing.

Saturday market, Coventry
(Pen drawing)
The drawings (*below*) were made from numerous photographs of people talking, walking and shopping. They are not copies of photographs; they are interpretations of the figures.

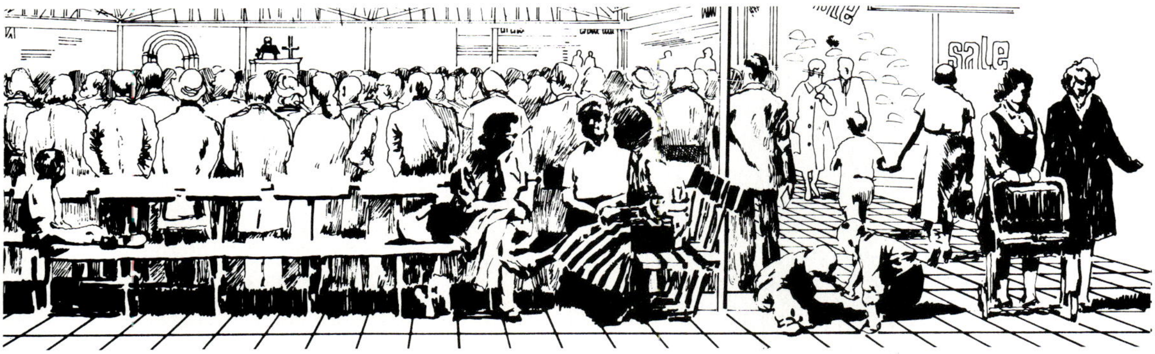

Going home, Canton, China
(Felt pen drawing)
In the short time available, the drawing (*above*) has caught the forward-leaning stance of the hurrying figures. Detail consists only of particular features that could be memorised.

Market in fog, Nottingham
(Pencil drawing)
Detail was hard to make out in the drawing (*right*) as it was a foggy day and the figures were cloaked in a grey mist. Only the basic shapes were visible.

Tennis technique
(Pen drawing)
The professional illustrator used many different photographs to draw the sequence (*below*) showing how to hit a backhand. Drawing such action figures needs very good reference material and considerable experience.

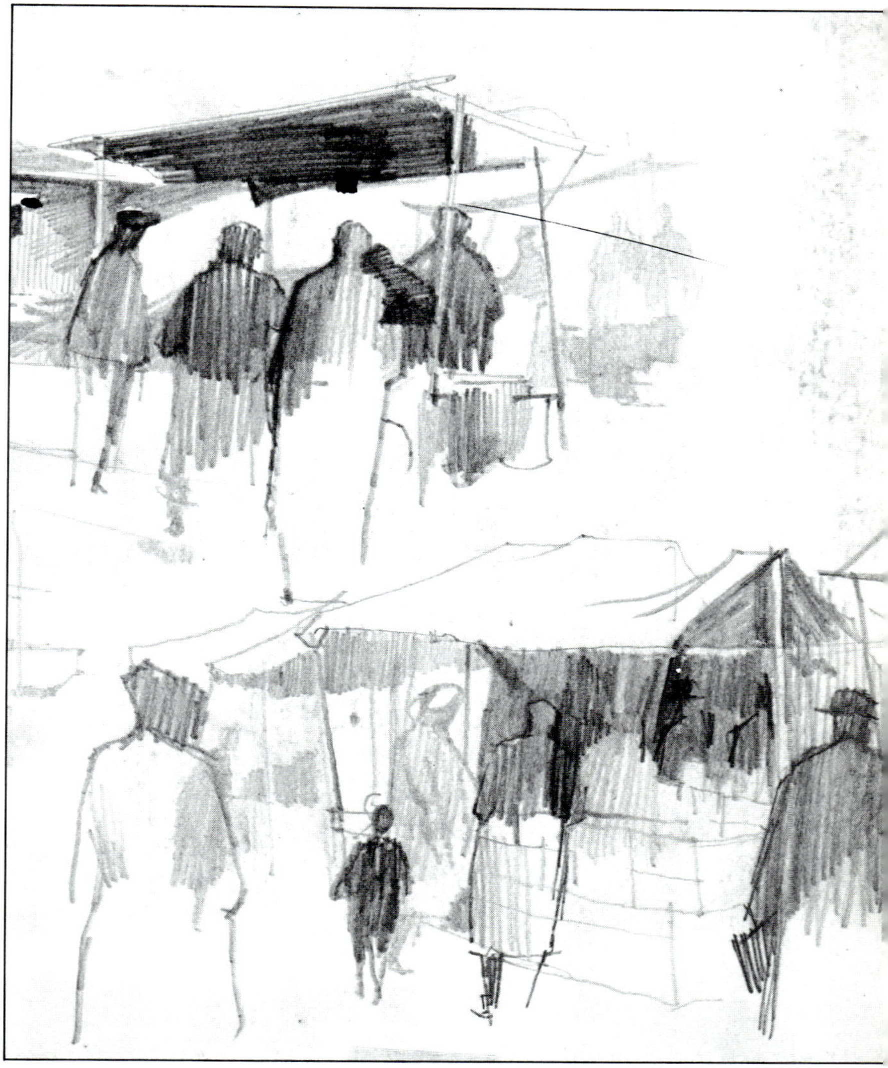

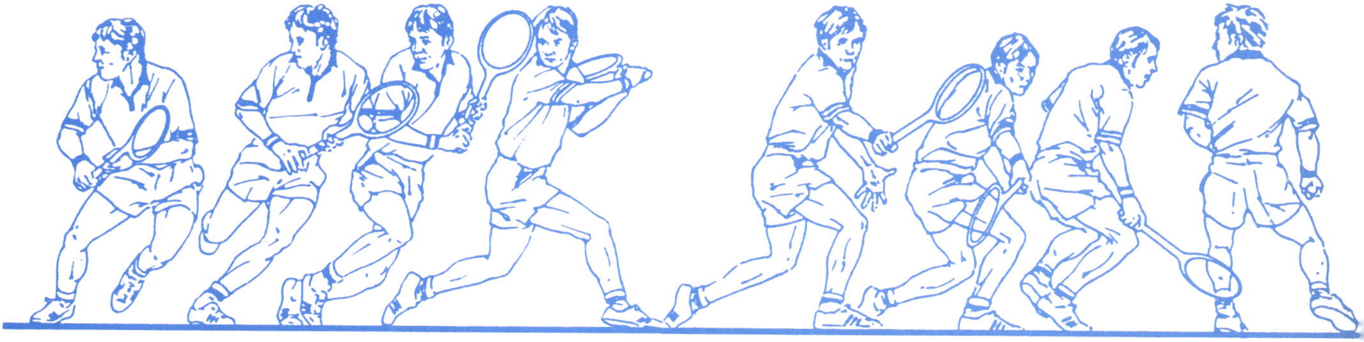

children

The proportions of the parts of a child's head are not the same as for an adult: young children have larger foreheads; and although the width of the head is slightly less than the height, the depth is the same as the height.

A child's head
(Pencil studies)
If you have the chance, draw a sleeping child and check the proportions to ensure that your head conforms to the following (*left*):
a top half is occupied by forehead;
b next quarter down is the nose;
c bottom quarter is taken up with the mouth and chin.

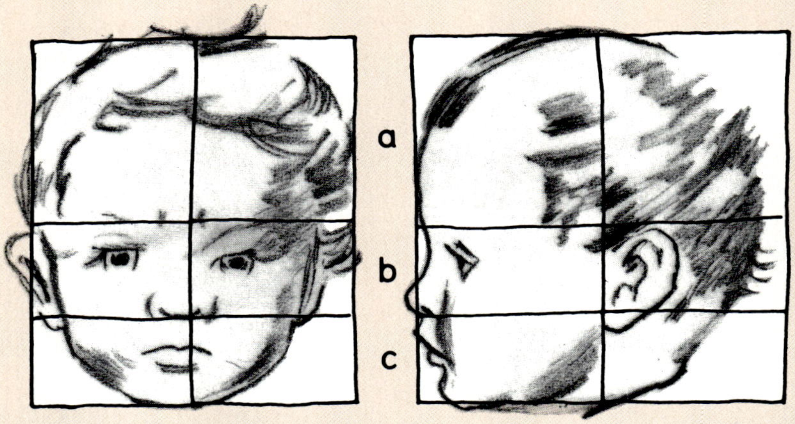

Boys in the park
(Pencil drawing)
All the sketches (*below*) are of the same boy. He kindly adopted lots of poses so that these detailed studies could be made – difficult to do from children playing in a park.

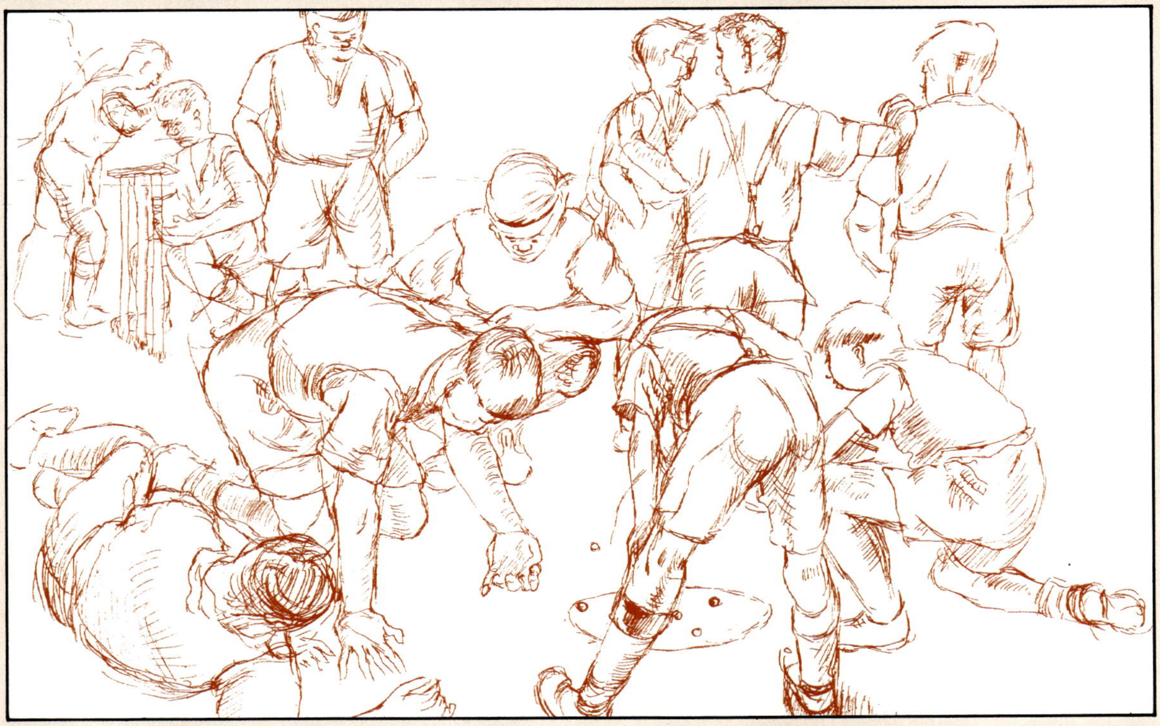

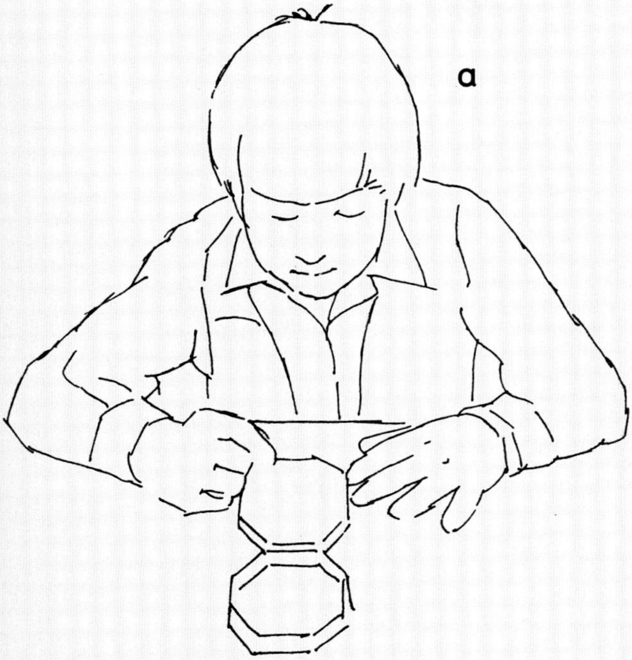

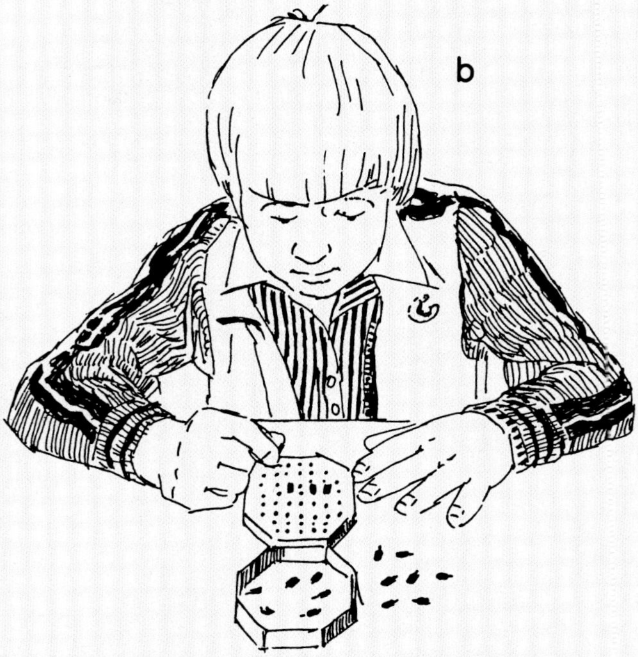

Child playing a board game
(Pen and ink drawing)
The best time to draw children is when their attention is absorbed in reading, playing a board game (as *above*), or doing homework. Then the body can more easily hold its pose and you have time to study detail closely. Begin with an overall sketch of the basic shapes (**a**), then build up to an examination of the tiny features (**b**).

Party games (*below*)
(Brush and ink drawing)
Working from quick sketches made at the time, or photographs, or memory, or all three, you can draw very attractive silhouette pictures suitable for greetings cards.

animals

Drawing animals is probably an artist's most difficult but most rewarding task. The frequent movements, the variety of poses, the unfamiliar anatomy, and the deceptive presence of fur all combine to make animal studies very demanding. They are an excellent way to improve your fluency and discipline as you pay attention to giving a true impression of the animal. Try sketching pets or zoo animals, or exhibits in natural history museums, or copy photographs from books and magazines. Draw details as well as whole animals, so that you build up a memory bank of information and extend your knowledge of different types of creature.

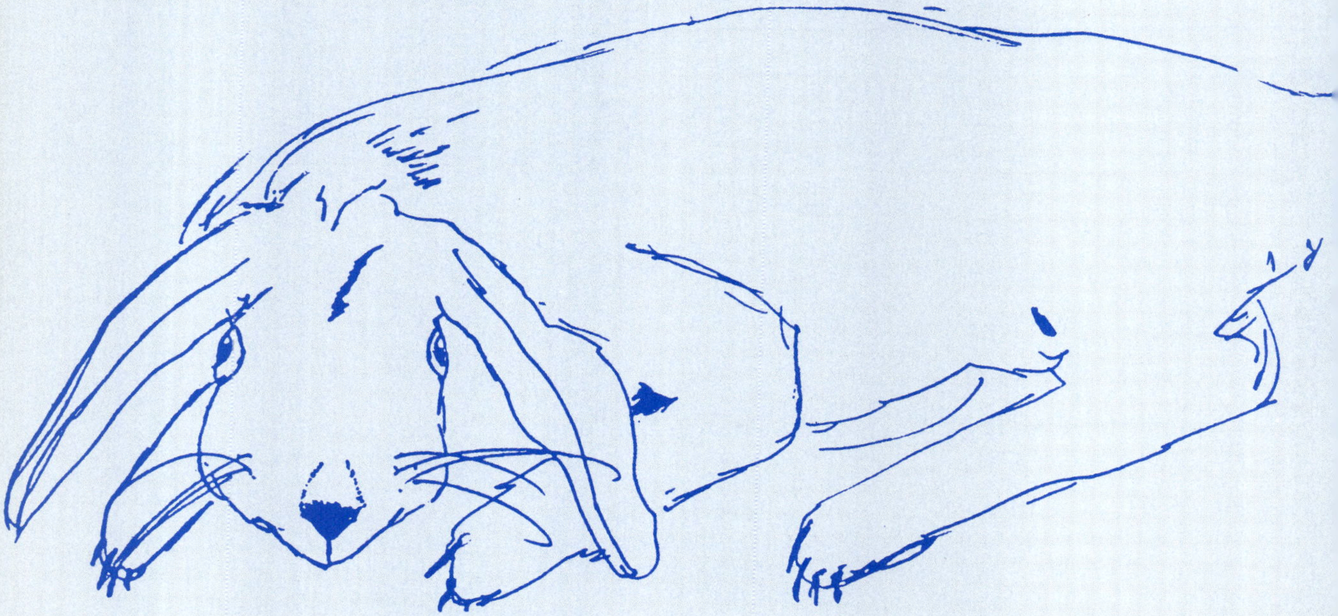

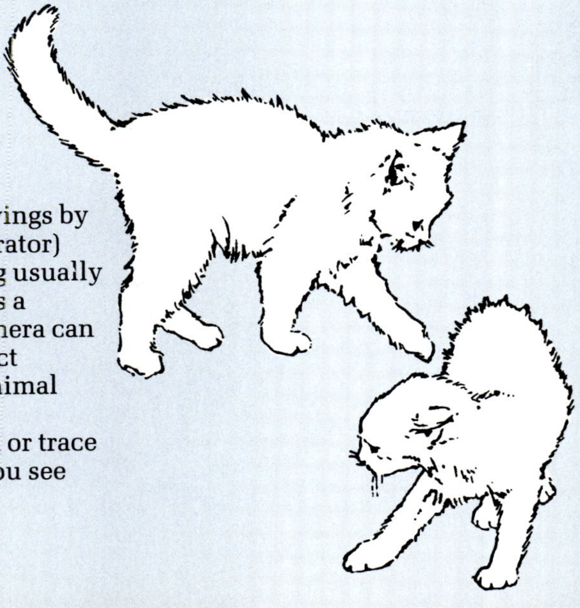

Honeybunny
(Pencil drawing by Jane, aged 11)
This resting, lop-eared, rabbit made an ideal subject for a study in an animal's expression. The construction of the body is not as important as the doleful look on the rabbit's face (*above*).

Frisky kitten
(Brush and ink drawings by a professional illustrator)
This type of drawing usually uses a photograph as a reference, as the camera can best capture the exact moment when an animal moves. Try copying photographs by eye, or trace over them to help you see the shapes.

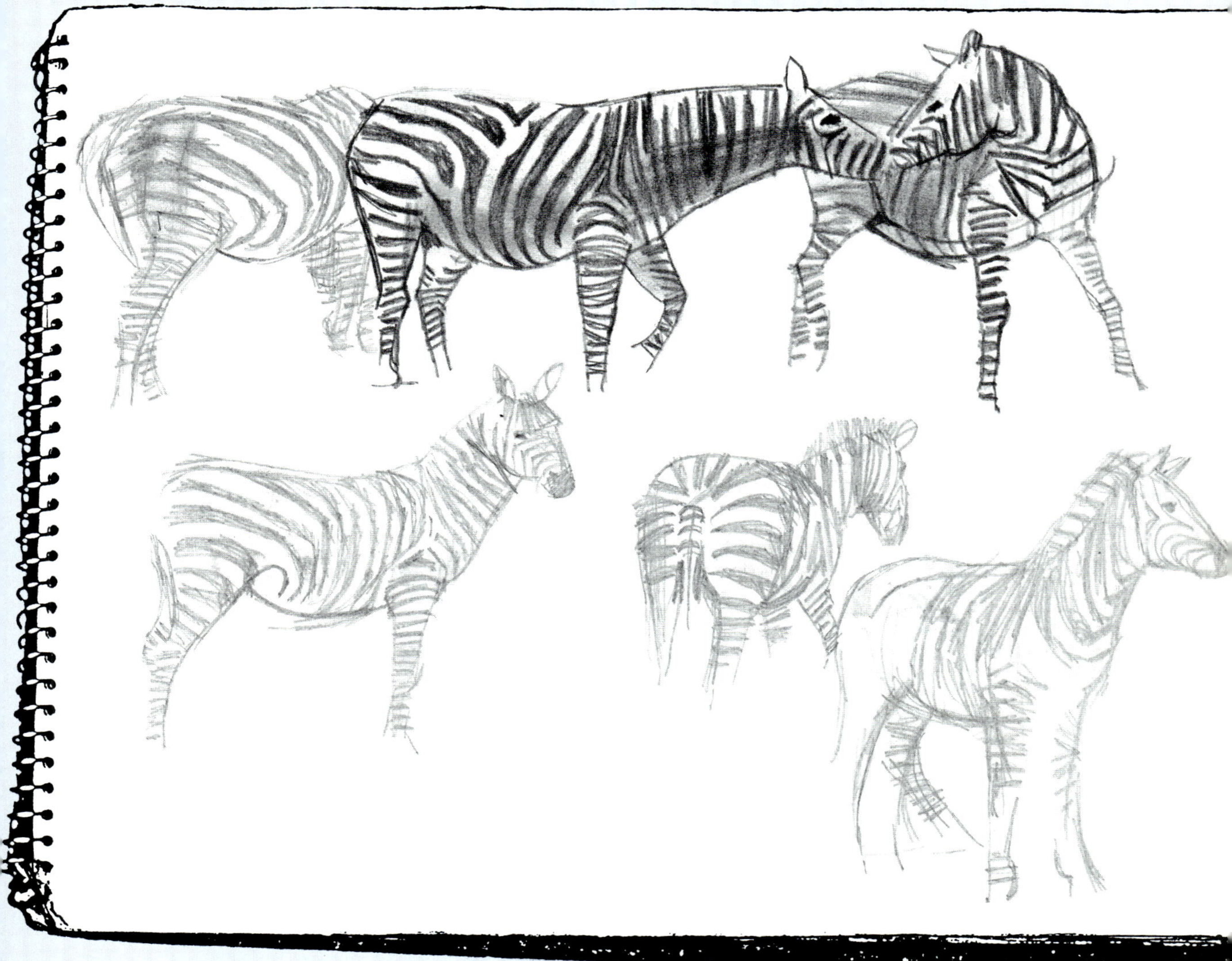

Zebra at the zoo
(Soft pencil, *above*)
These studies are all of one zebra. Because the animal was moving around its enclosure it was necessary to keep a number of sketches going at the same time.

Dog's paws
(Ballpoint drawings by a 16-year-old, *below*)
Take advantage of an animal's stillness in sleep to draw complex parts in detail.

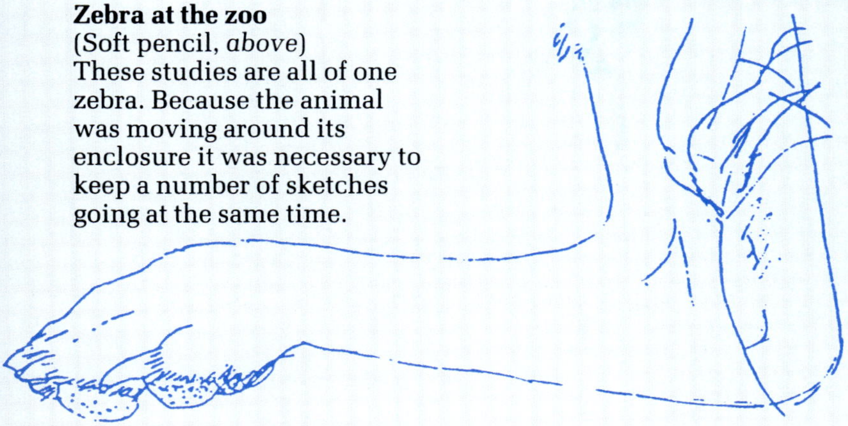

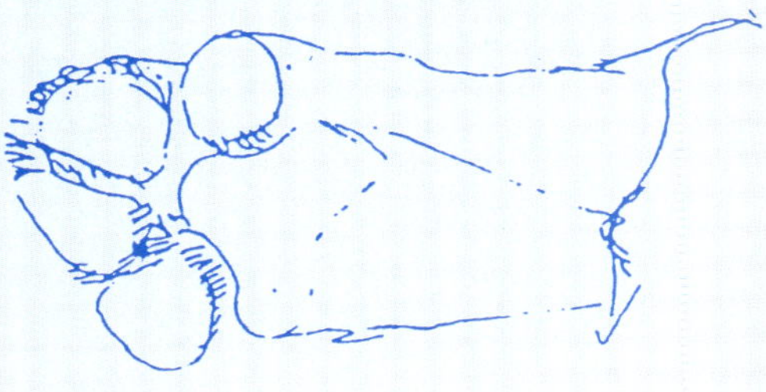

animals

Understanding the skeletal construction of animals greatly improves your ability to record their outer forms. Knowledge creates confidence which enables you to draw smooth, clear lines. Studying anatomy and form enables you to see the way the shapes formed in movement are the consequence of the inner structure. Try to draw stuffed animals in which the rigid assembly of forms is clear, and you have time to complete your studies. Memorize the overall structure by producing lots of sketches from life. Try to find skulls and other parts of skeletons to examine. And, most important of all, think into the forms of the particular animal.

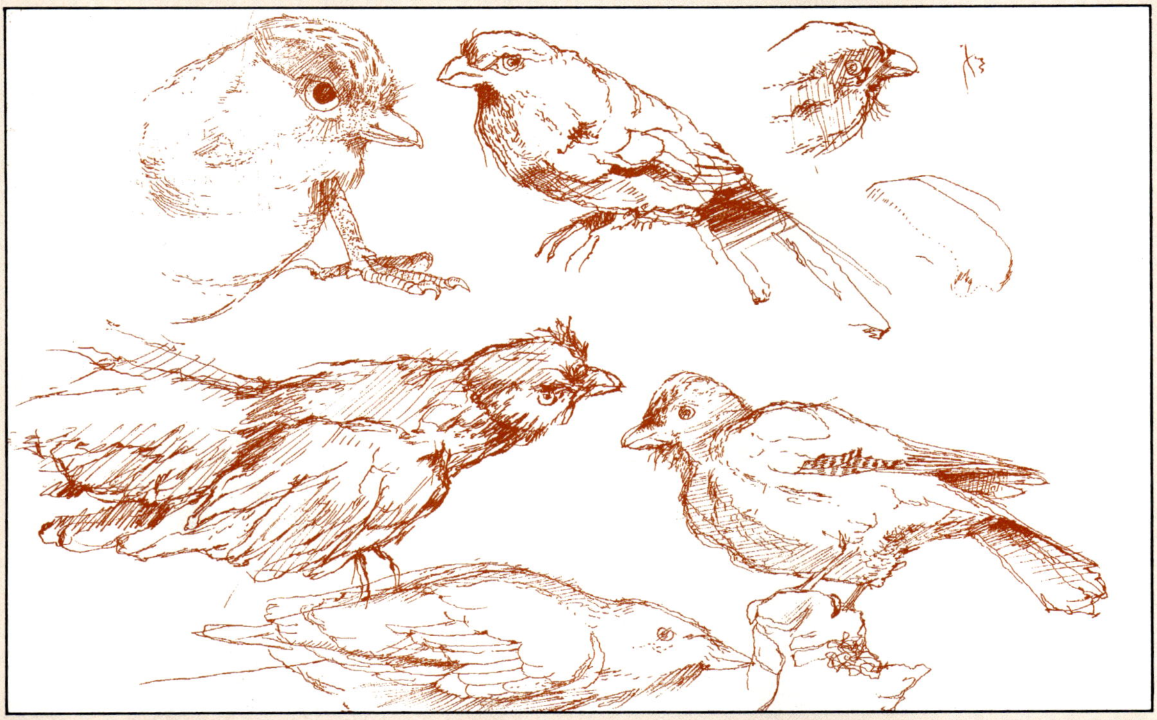

Bird studies
(Pen and ink drawings)
The birds (*above*) were drawn from display reconstructions. Life studies require close observation and practice.

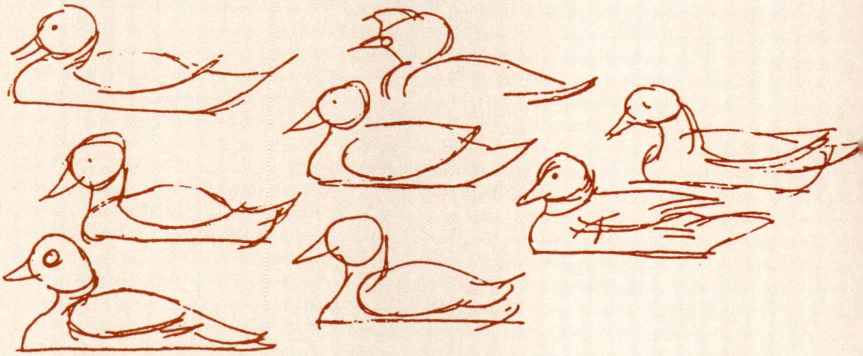

Ducks on a pond
(Pen and ink studies)
Many ducks (*right*) with the same form and structure. As they swim by, record their basic features.

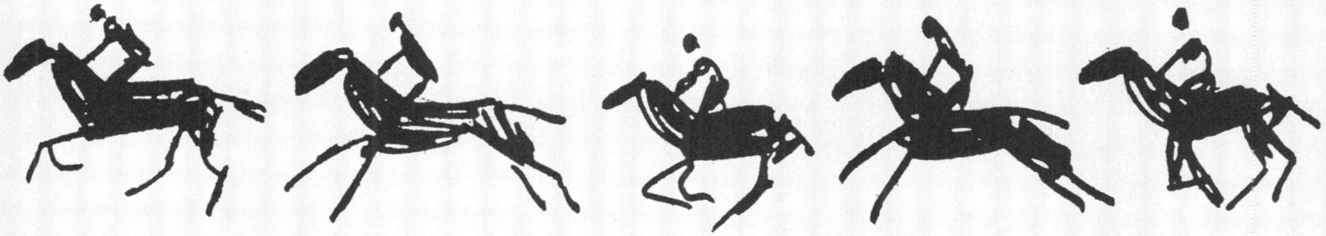

Racehorses on TV
(Pen and ink sketches)
The fleeting shapes of passing racehorses (*above*) must be captured with instantaneous vision. Whatever the results, the accumulation of notes will provide you with knowledge of how a horse moves.

Rabbit's skulls
(Pen and ink drawings)
You can sketch a rabbit more easily if you have examined and understood its anatomical forms (see *right*).

Horse in a field
(Pen and ink drawing)
The drawings (*below*), all of one horse, are incomplete, but the basic structure is well recorded.

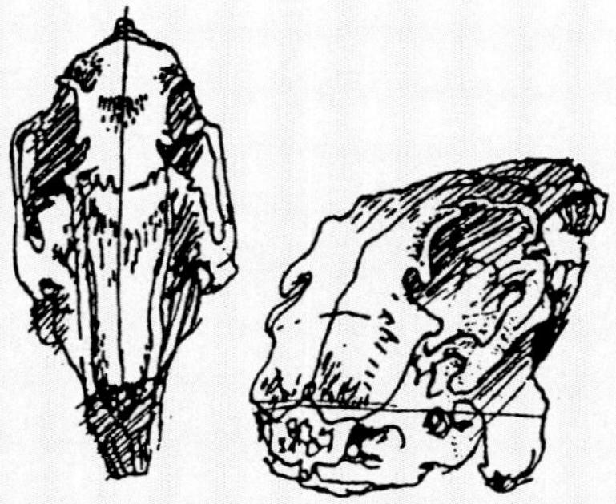

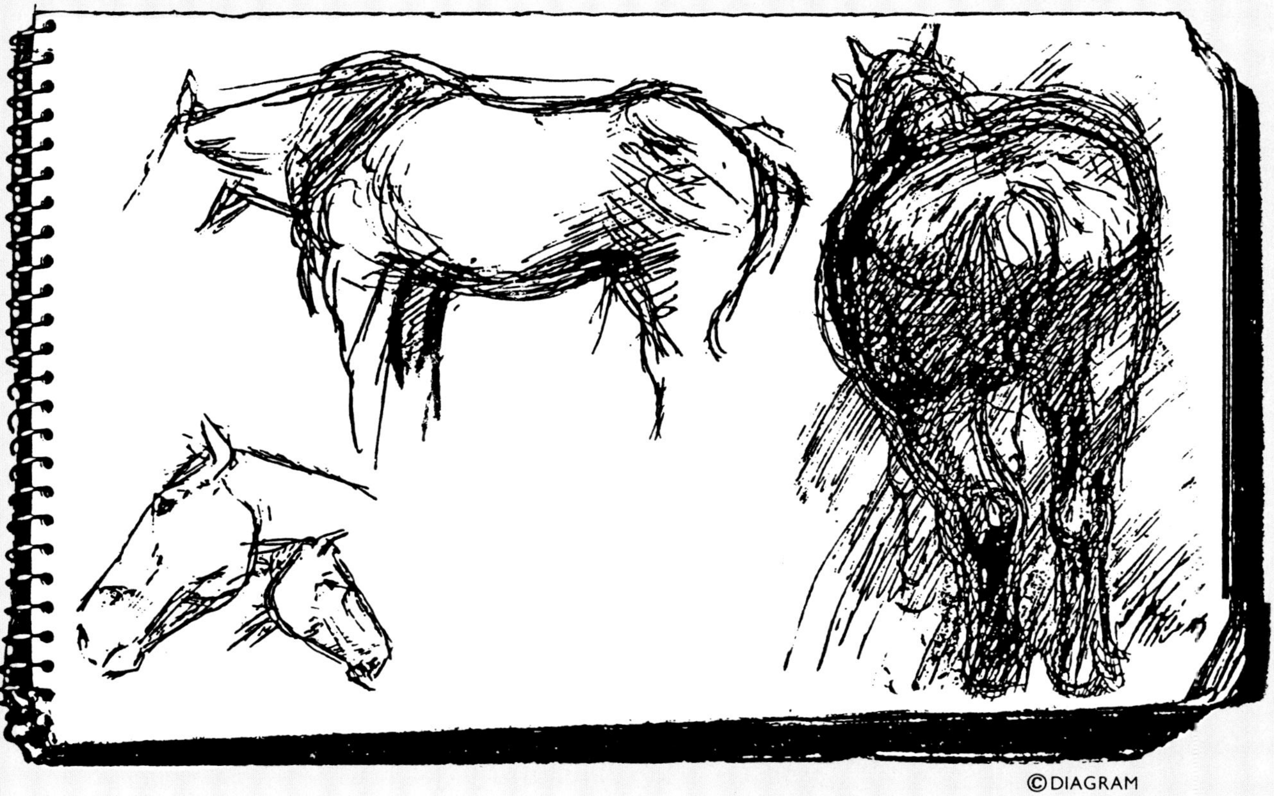

animals

Most of the drawings in commercial publications are done from photographs. The photographer captures the creature and you take your time over drawing it. Sketching from life requires powers of rapid observation and an ability to record information instantly; drawing from photographs enables you to study your subject carefully, even to make changes and to delete what you don't want – for instance, the background. But there are problems: your drawings may be over-realistic and may contain too much minute detail.
Remember you must interpret what you see: be selective; don't just copy all the tones.

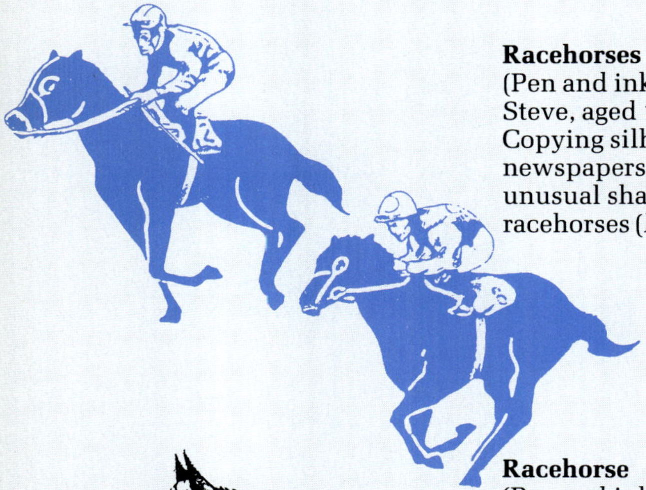

Racehorses
(Pen and ink drawings by Steve, aged 18)
Copying silhouettes from newspapers can produce unusual shapes, like the racehorses (*left*).

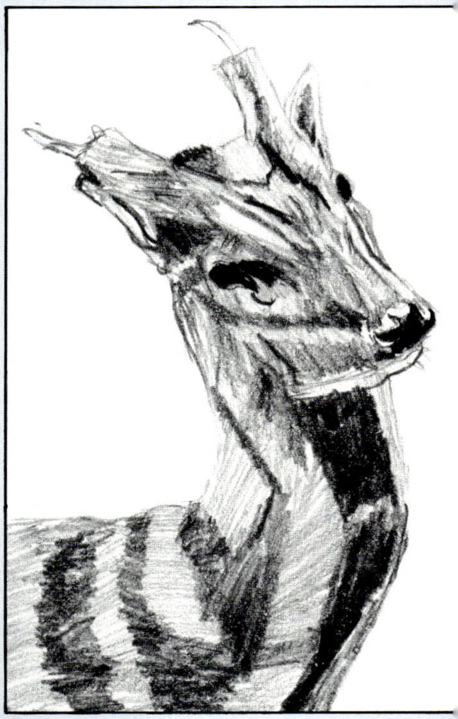

Antelope
(Pencil drawing by Steve, aged 18)
The antelope head (*above*), from a photograph, increased Steve's confidence in his drawing.

Racehorse
(Pen and ink study)
Without a photographic source, the detailed drawing of a racehorse (*below*) would have needed any number of studies.

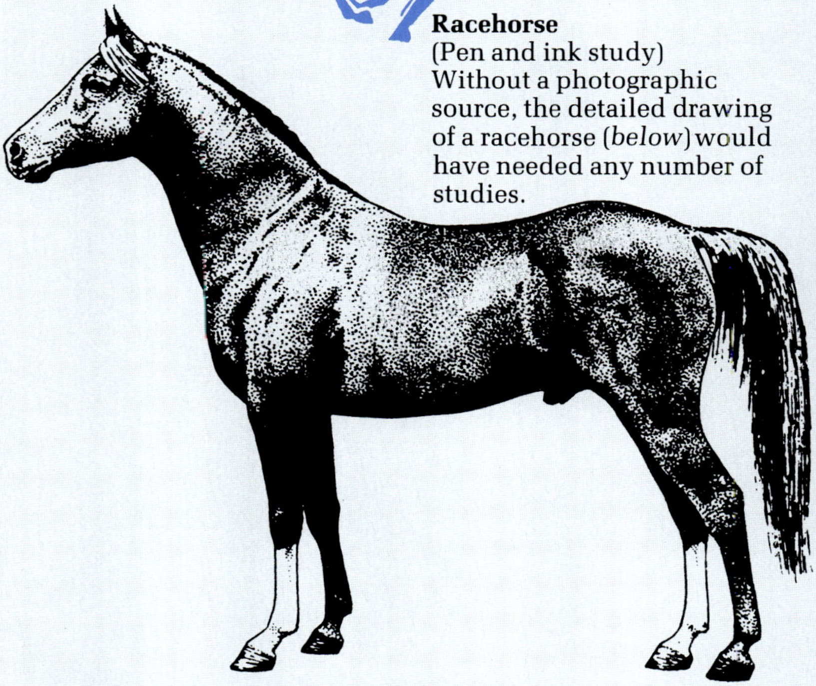

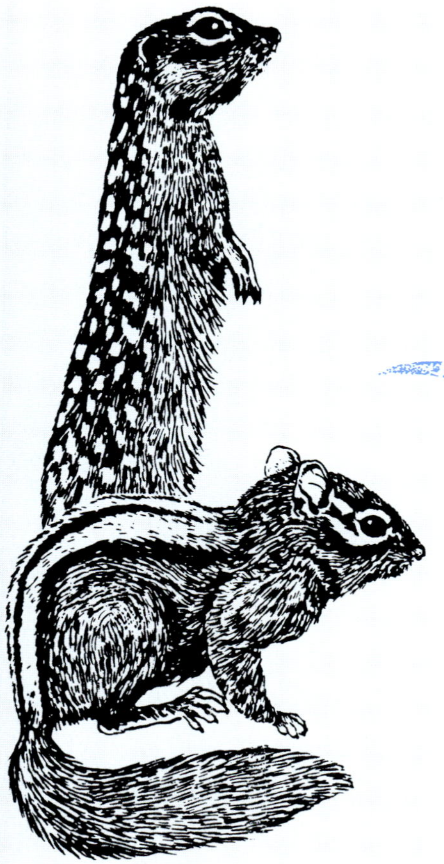

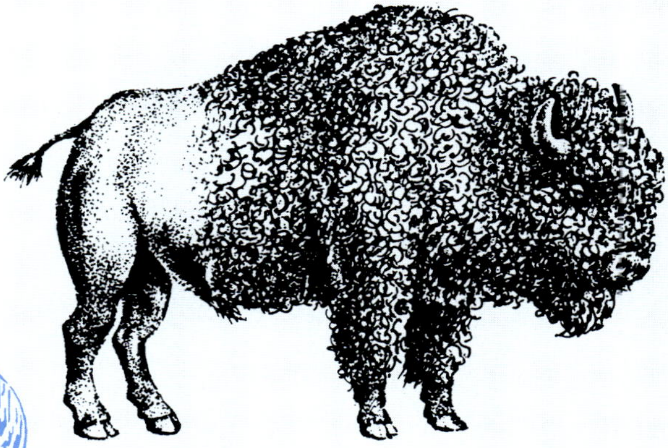

Buffalo
(Pen and ink drawing)
The inaccessibility of some creatures you may want to draw – when did you last see a lion or buffalo as illustrated (*above*) – often makes it necessary to use photographs, which are easily obtainable from books and magazines.

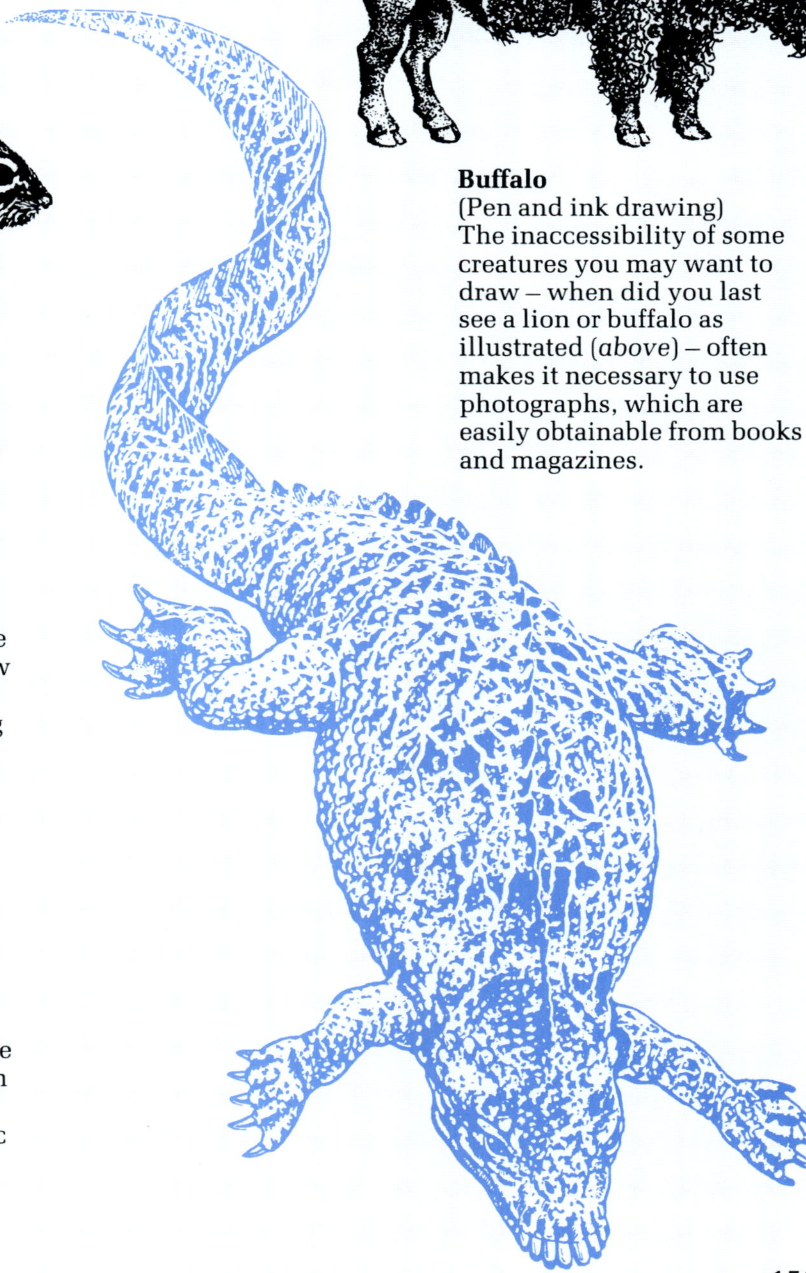

Squirrel and chipmunk
(Pen and ink drawings)
Drawing the characteristic gestures of any creature, like the chipmunk (*above*) – how it sits, twists, turns – can be done more easily by looking at a group of photographs. And it is hard to grasp their colours, textures and markings from life studies alone.

Placodont
(Pen and ink drawing)
The prehistoric marine reptile (*right*) is now extinct but the artist was able to draw it because of the knowledge he gathered from photographs of lizards, crocodiles and other aquatic reptiles.

animals

Animals are constantly on the move, and animal structures are unfamiliar to most of us. These two factors make drawing them from life very difficult. Whenever you have the chance, try to do some quick sketches of all kinds of animals, just outlining the basic shapes and gestures. Do not attempt more complete studies unless you think that your subject will stay still for some time. Choose tools that let you make marks rapidly, and be prepared to work fast.

Never compare your results with published studies – you do not know whether the drawings were done from photographs, stuffed animals, careful earlier studies, or from a profound knowledge of the subject.
Whatever results you produce, they are the fruits of your own work, and they add to your knowledge of the animal.

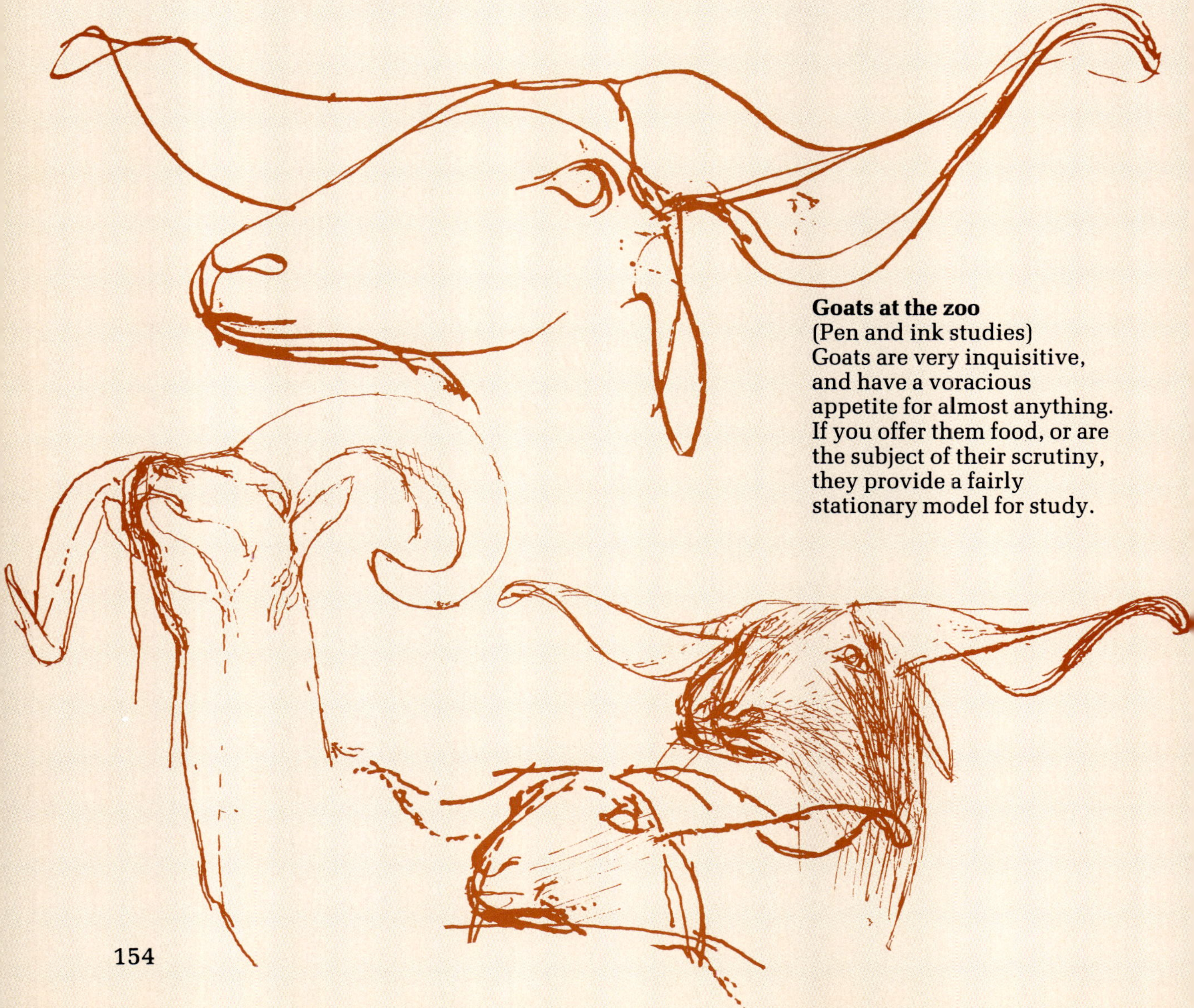

Goats at the zoo
(Pen and ink studies)
Goats are very inquisitive, and have a voracious appetite for almost anything. If you offer them food, or are the subject of their scrutiny, they provide a fairly stationary model for study.

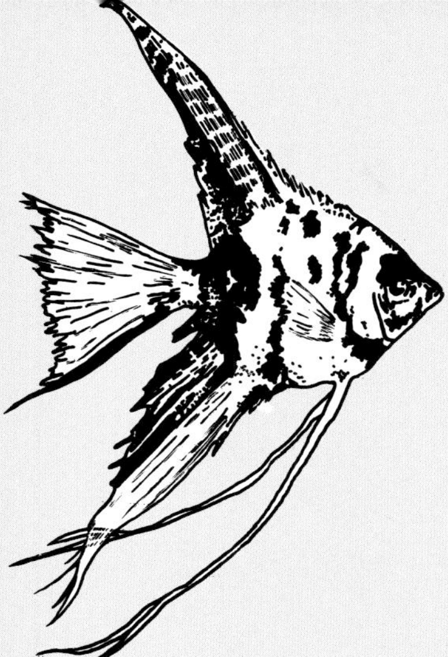

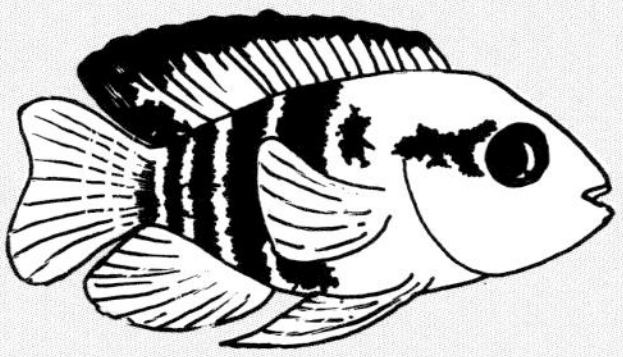

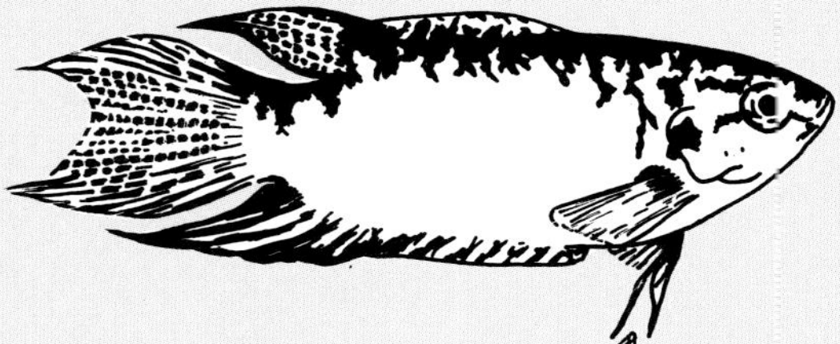

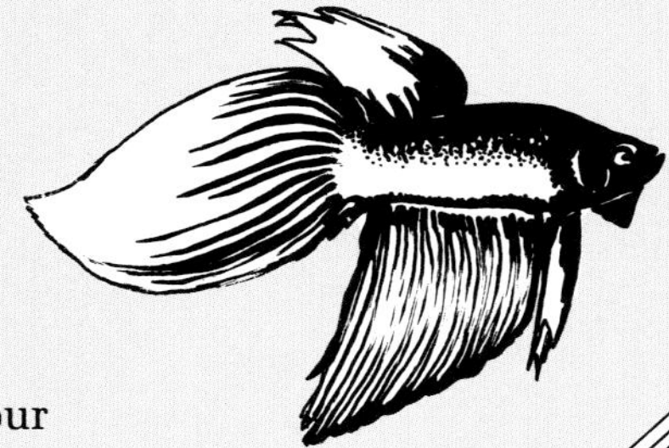

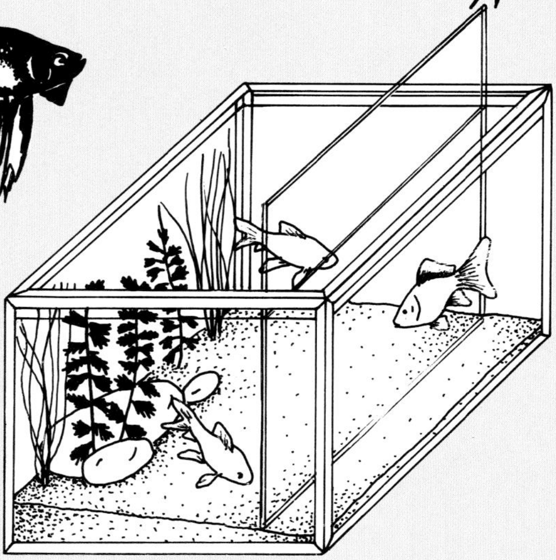

Aquarium studies
(Pen and ink drawings)
Limit the movements of your fish for easy study by penning them into an area of the tank with a glass pane (*right*).

Marine tank studies
(Pencil drawings)
Lobsters, crabs and beetles move much more slowly than fish, so can be investigated in more detail (*below*).

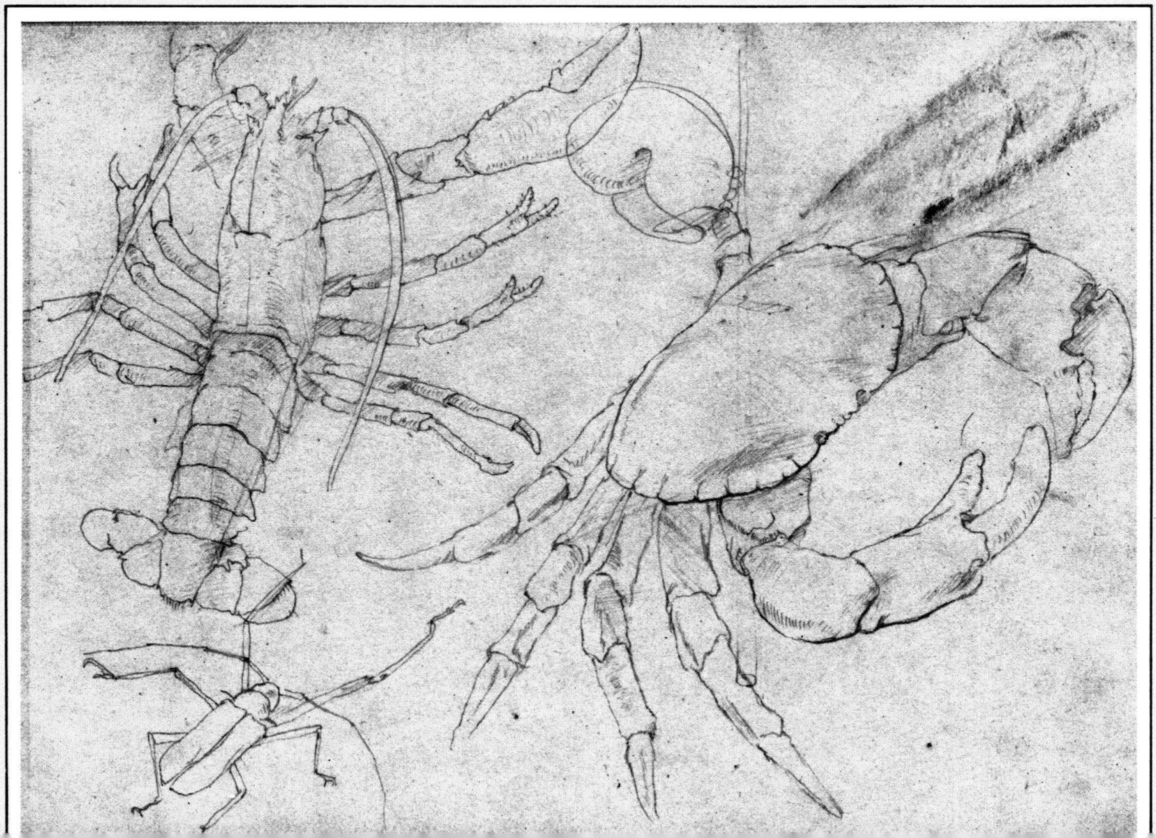

animals

The style of a drawing very much depends on how that drawing is to be used. It may be realistic – that is, it describes in a particular way the effects of light, colour and form; this can be in minute detail or sketchily. The drawing may be a cartoon in which the beast is shown as a personality. The animal may be drawn as a decorative device, in which case the patterning is of major importance. Or the creature may be reduced to a symbolic shape, a representative emblem. Whichever method you choose, it is advisable to know something about the real animal or your solution may be naïve and fail to encompass its distinctiveness.

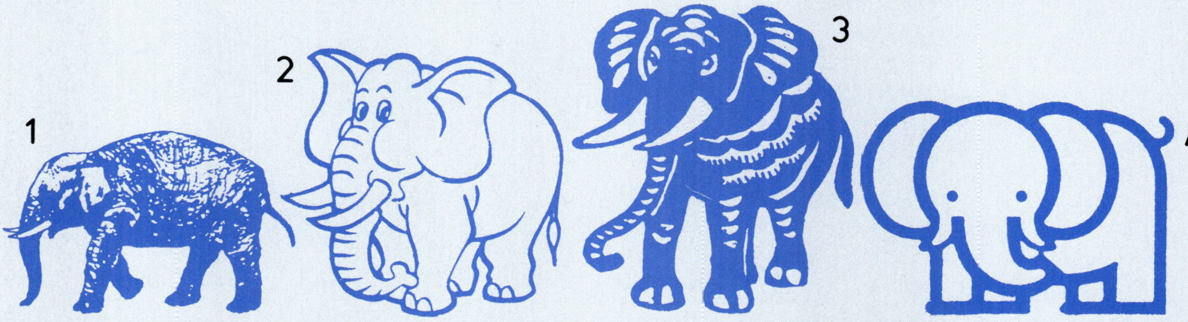

The four graphic methods
(Pen and ink drawings,*above*)
1 Realistic: light, texture and form described by lines.
2 Cartoon: the jumbo personality quickly depicted.
3 Decorative: white breaks up dark areas producing a pattern.
4 Symbolic: true anatomy is ignored, forms outlined and features simplified.

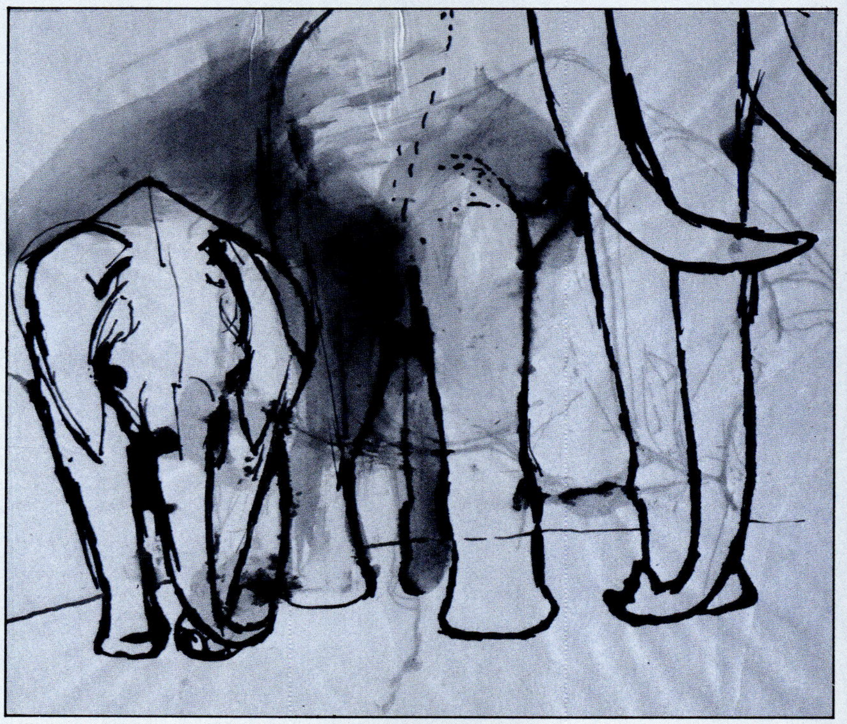

Realistic
(Pen and ink drawing)
The study (*right*) of a baby elephant in a zoo is an example of an enquiring drawing, one in which the artist is seeking knowledge about the elephant's structure, how the big forms interlock and how the shapes reflect the anatomy.

Cartoon
(Pen and ink drawings)
Cartoons include unrealistic elements. Elephants do not sit or walk as illustrated (*right*); they do not have eyelashes. Cartoons attribute to animals human characteristics and abilities.

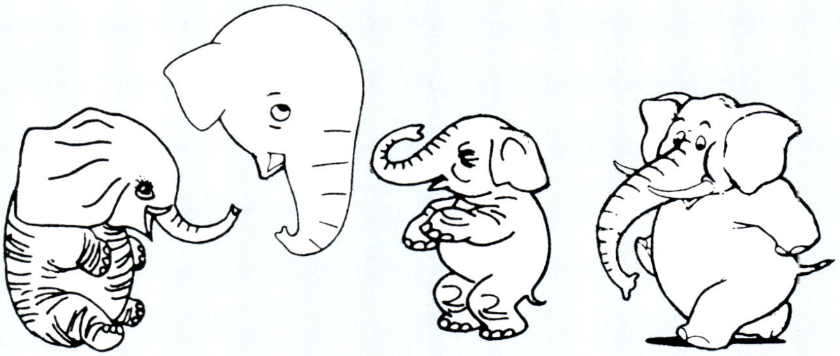

Decorative
(Pen and ink drawing)
The drawing (*right*) is from an Indian fabric design. All the shapes are reduced to even lines, and proportions, forms and textures are subordinated to the aim of producing a repetitive pattern.

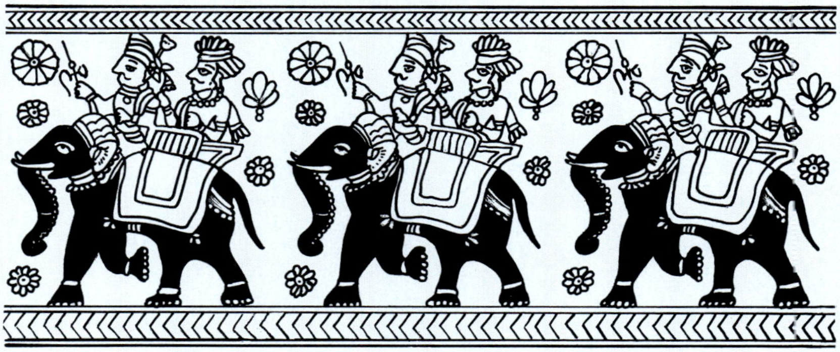

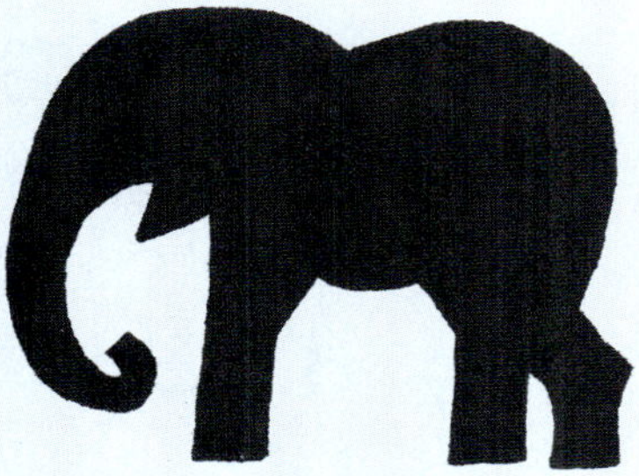

Symbolic
(Pen and ink studies)
A page of notes which transform and simplify information about the characteristic features of an elephant taken from photographs is shown (*right*). Each sketch tries to convey the elephant as emblem while keeping details to a minimum.

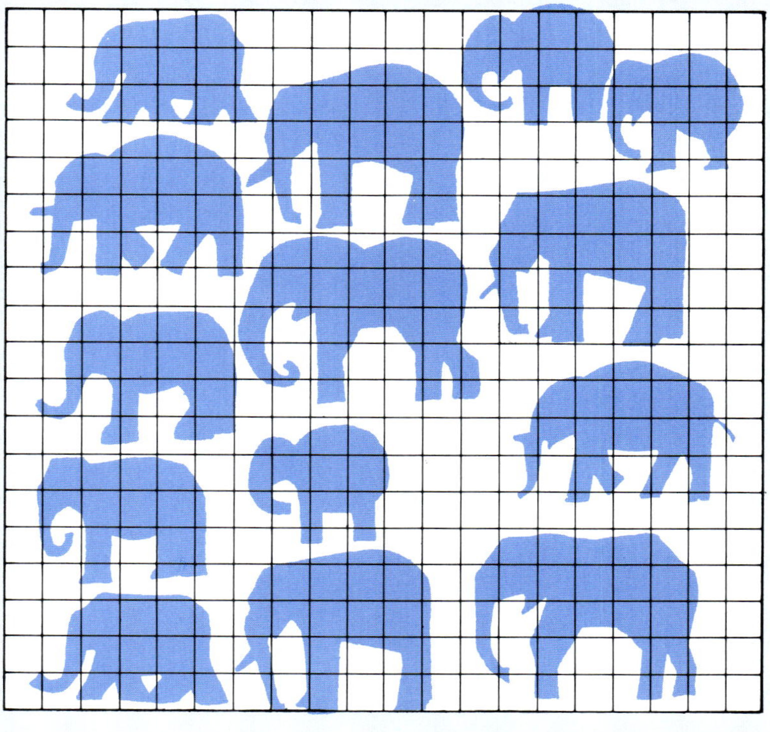

animals

Dogs come in all sorts of shapes, sizes and textures, from the enormous, shaggy Old English Sheepdog to the smooth-haired Dachshund. Nevertheless, although the features may change, the fundamental structure is always the same.
Practise drawing details of your dog, any dog – its nose, the tilt of its head – and build up a knowledge of its personality.

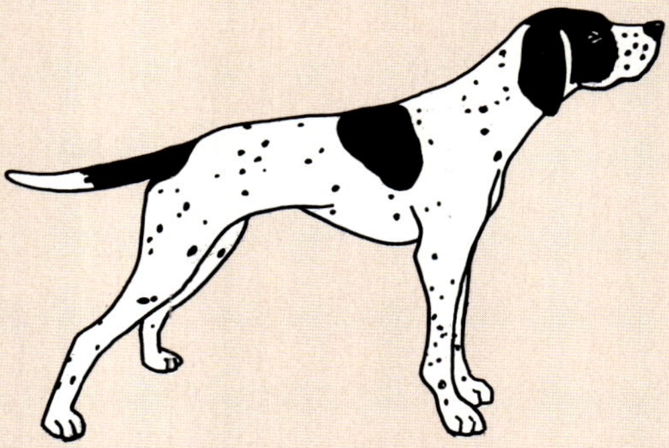

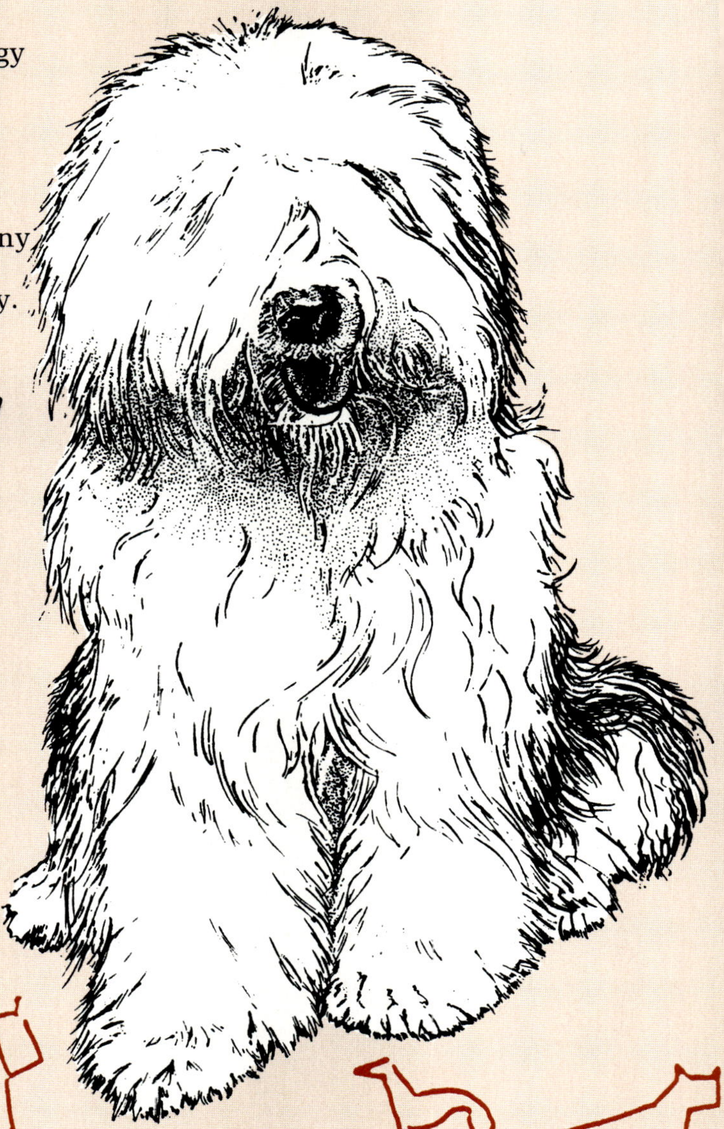

Pointer and English Sheepdog
(Pen and ink drawings)
The frame of the Pointer (*above*) is clear from its stance which also shows up its muscles; and its markings help to describe its form. In contrast, the Old English Sheepdog (*right*) disguises its form. You cannot detect the leg structure under the heavily draped hair.

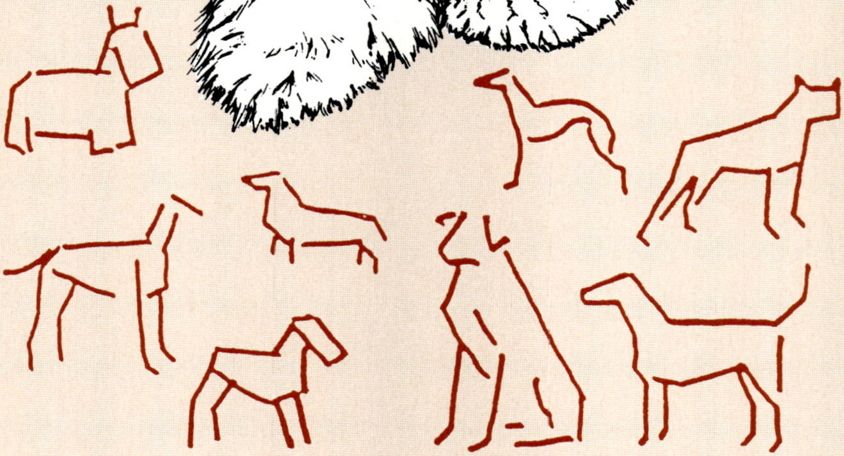

Basic dog structure
(Pen sketches)
The rectangularity of a dog's frame and its four legs are constant whatever its pose. Practise drawing matchstick dogs (*right*), so that you understand the changing shapes as they stand, sit or lie down.

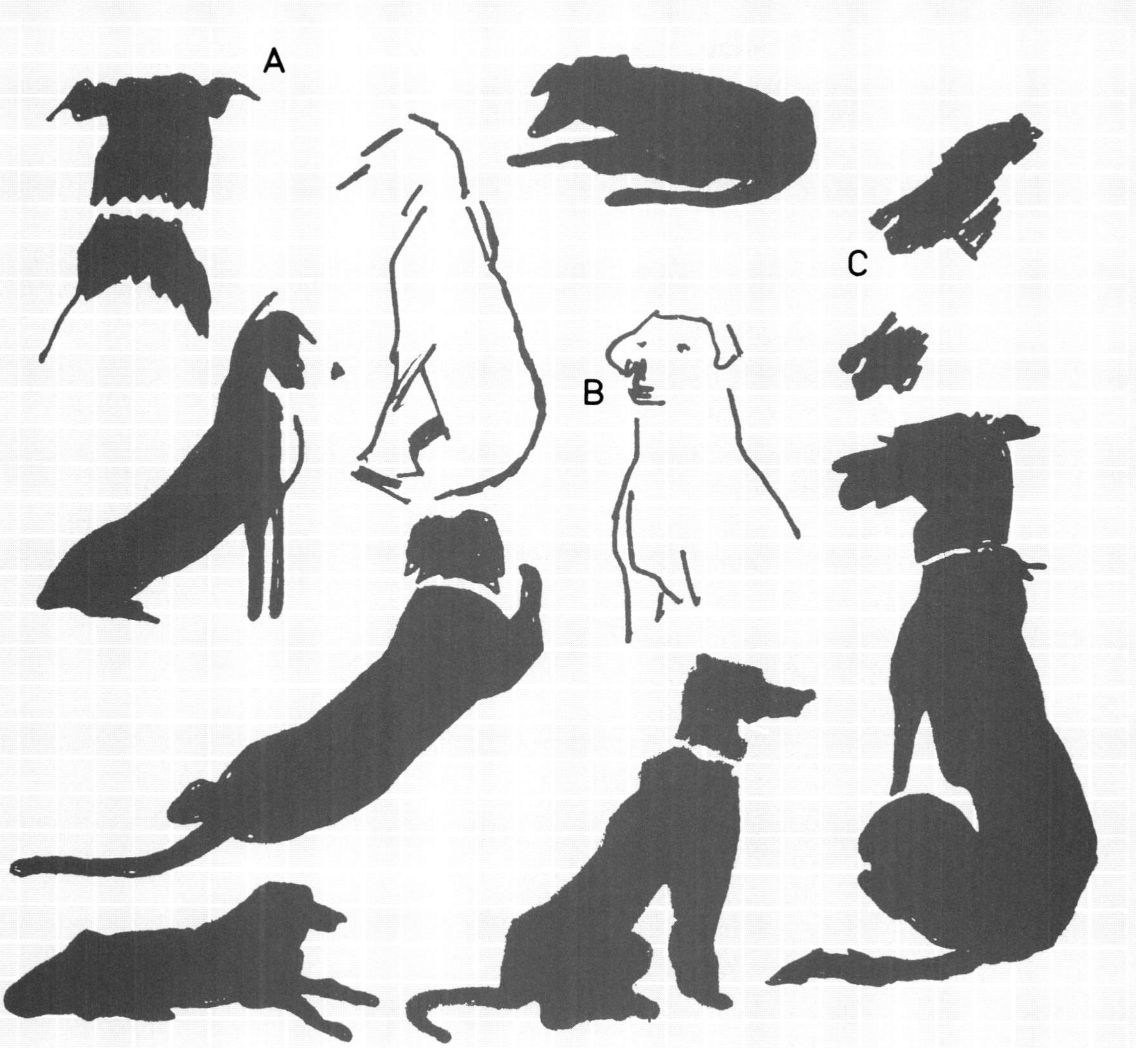

Hardy
(Pen and ink drawings, *above*)
Keep a sketch book to record some of your dog's unique features. Practise outlining the whole dog and searching out its personal quirks, like an upturned ear (**A**). If a drawing fails (**B**), just restart with a new pose. Difficult forms, such as the nose (**C**), need many studies

Hardy watching a fly
(Pen and ink drawing)
There can be unlimited pleasure and fun in catching just the right moment when your dog does something unexpected, like Hardy watching a fly (*right*).

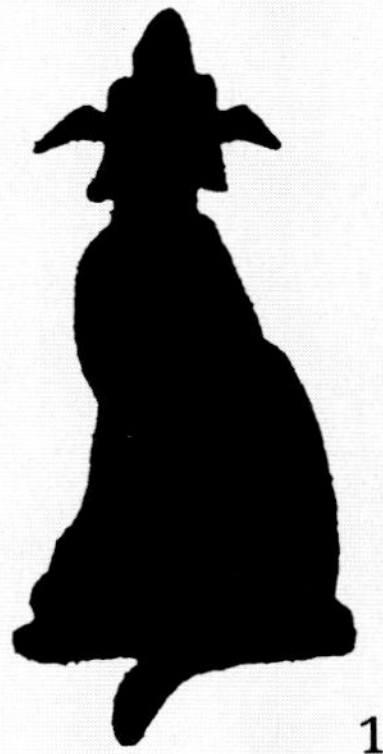

animals

Drawing cats successfully is extremely hard, and the beginner has difficulty in conveying their flexibility, their enquiring gestures and their personalities.
First practise on a sleeping animal or work from photographs. It is only the most obvious forms that are easily drawn, and they can be reduced to very simple outlines.

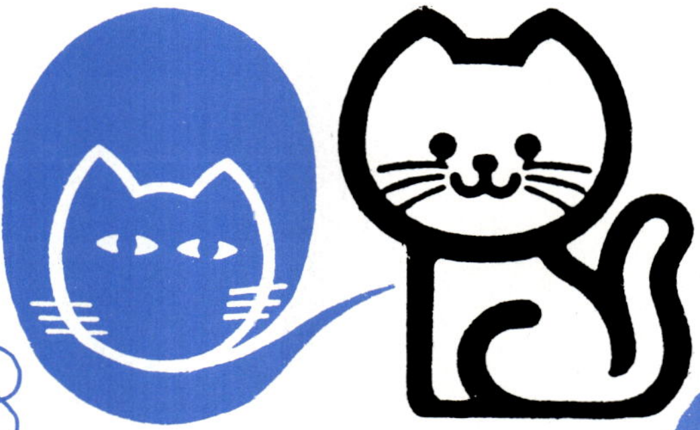

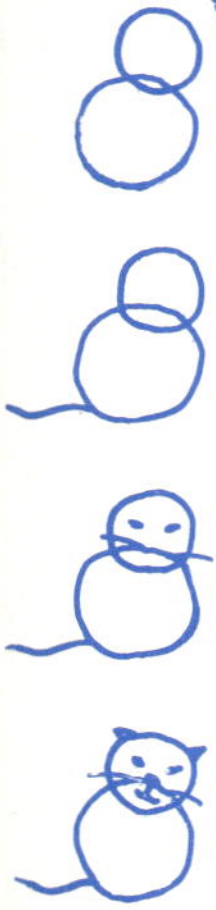

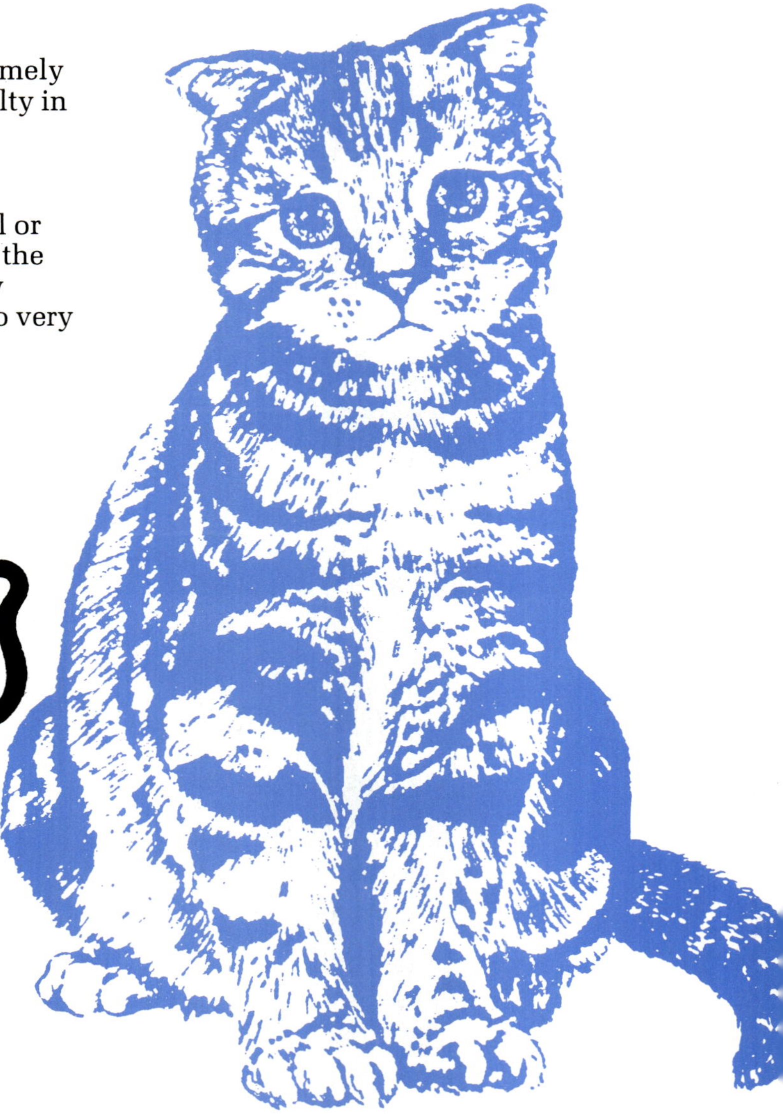

A cat's character
(Brush and ink drawings)
A cartoon can be achieved by drawing balls for the head and body; add a tail, eyes, whiskers, a lion nose – and you have an animated pussycat.

Cats on a wall
(Pen and ink drawings)
Go to the places frequented by cats – roofs or garden walls – and mentally photograph the variety of their shapes and movements, irrespective of form and colour (*right*).

Personality
(Pen and ink drawing, enlarged)
The wistful look of a tabby, with its enquiring tilt of the head was taken from a photograph (*above*).

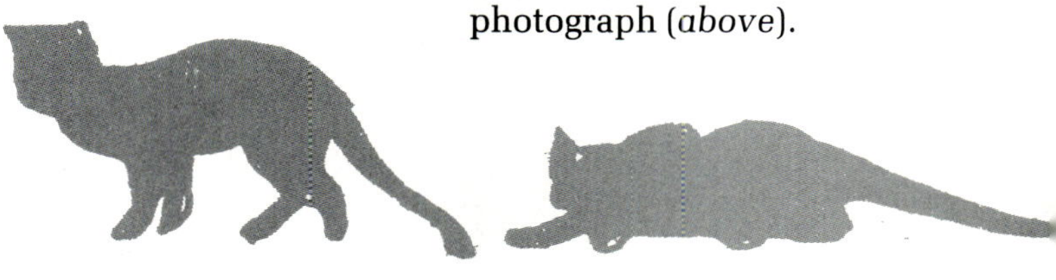

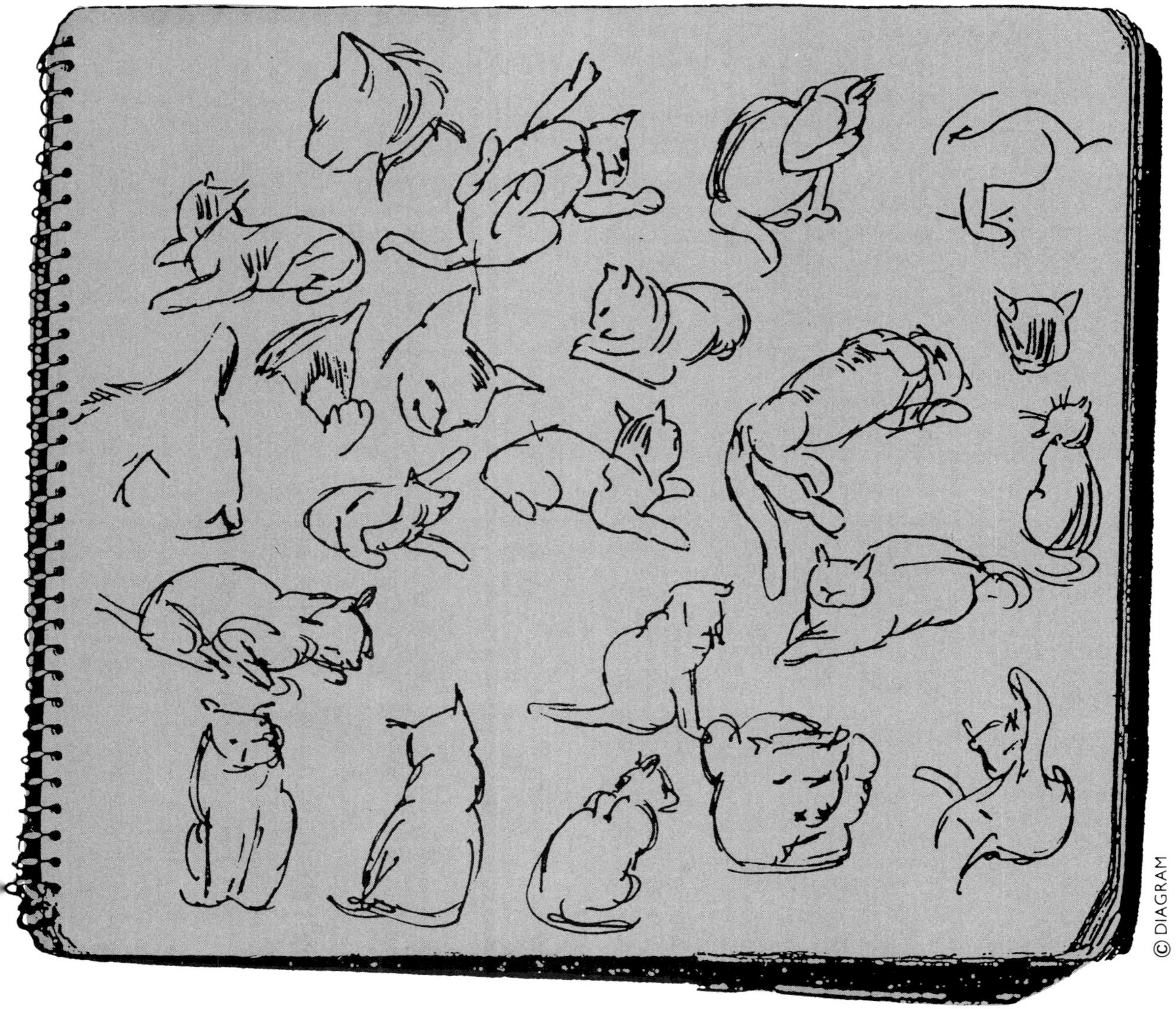

Cats playing
(Pen and ink sketches, *above*) Try to keep lots of sketches on the go, returning to an earlier, unfinished one as the cat adopts the same attitude. Don't be inhibited by what you think are failures – just transfer to another pose. You will acquire versatility if you observe all the ways a cat moves.

Part Five

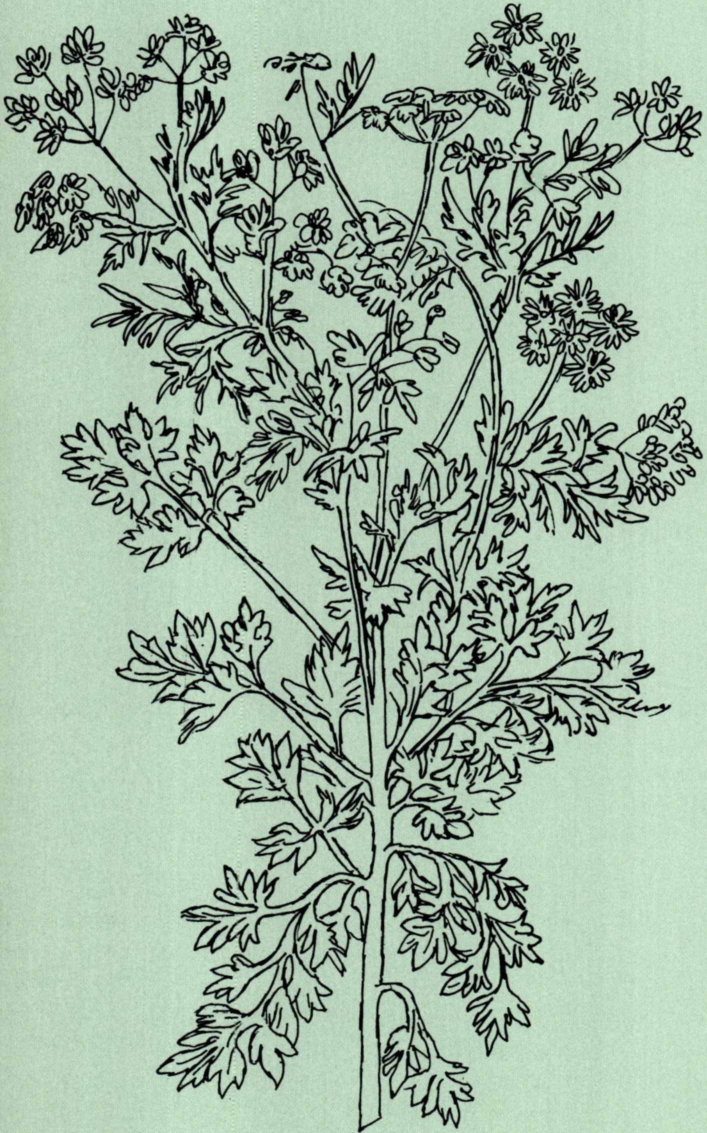

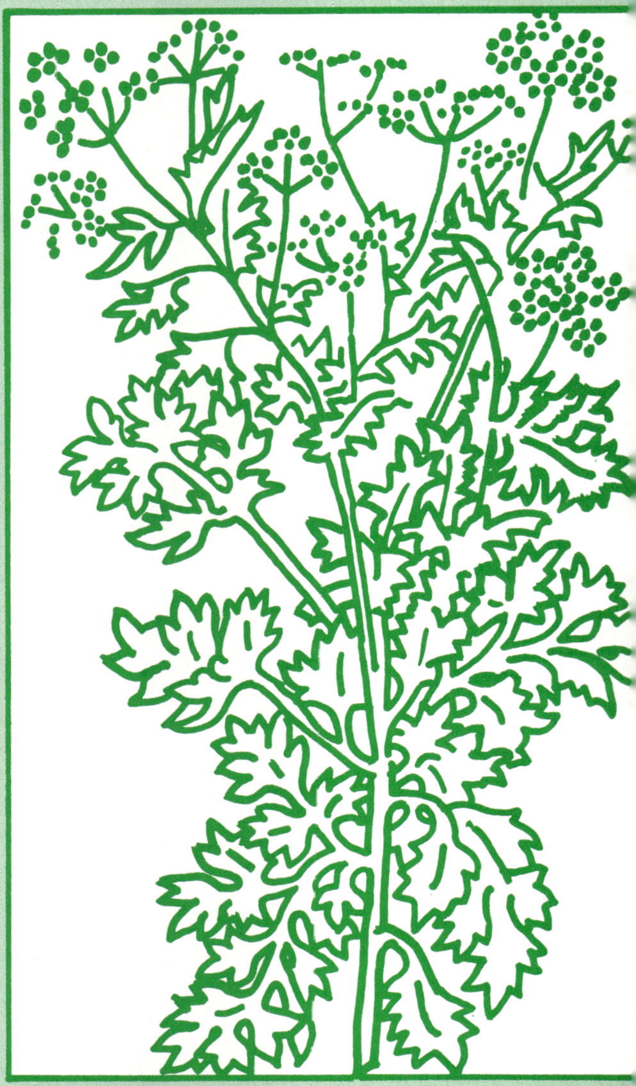

THE RESULT

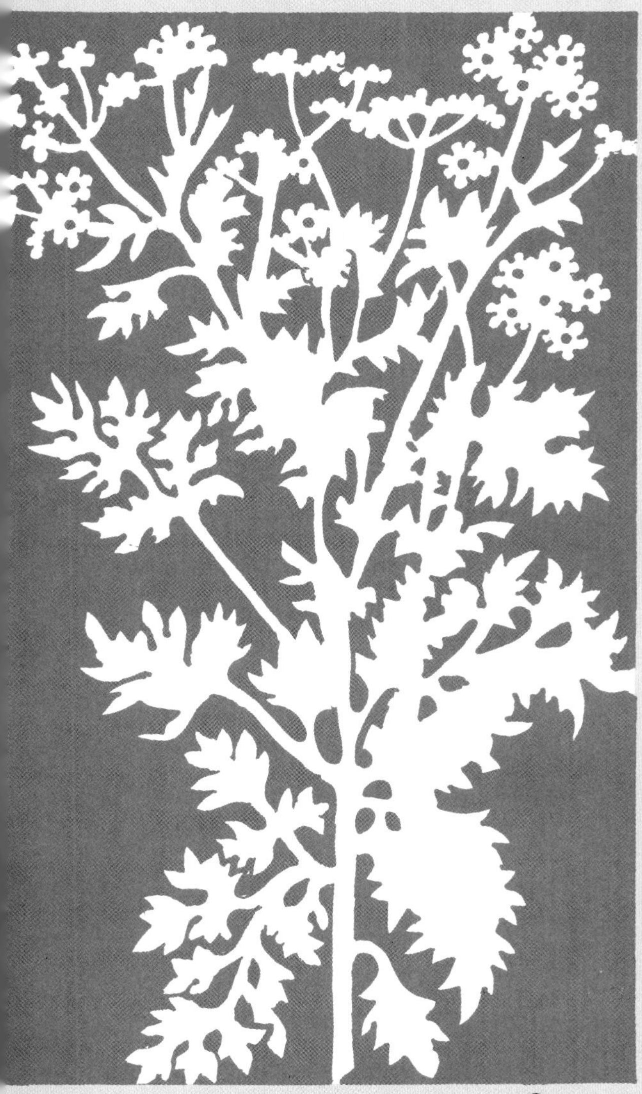

displaying your drawings

There are no rules for hanging your work; the guidelines should be your personal choice and what feels right – after all they add to the atmosphere of your home. Decide what you want from each picture – is it an icon, a thing to worship, to be admired by visitors, or is it a decoration to relate to other items in a room?

Where to put your drawings and how to frame them depends on many considerations; these and practical advice follow on the next eight pages. Feel proud of your drawings; they are your personal treasures, of greater value than any bought object.

Where to hang your work
Pictures can be hung in any part of the house, except for rooms which are liable to have condensation: kitchens and bathrooms. They can hang alone, be in groups or cover a wall. Avoid direct sunlight, which fades paper.

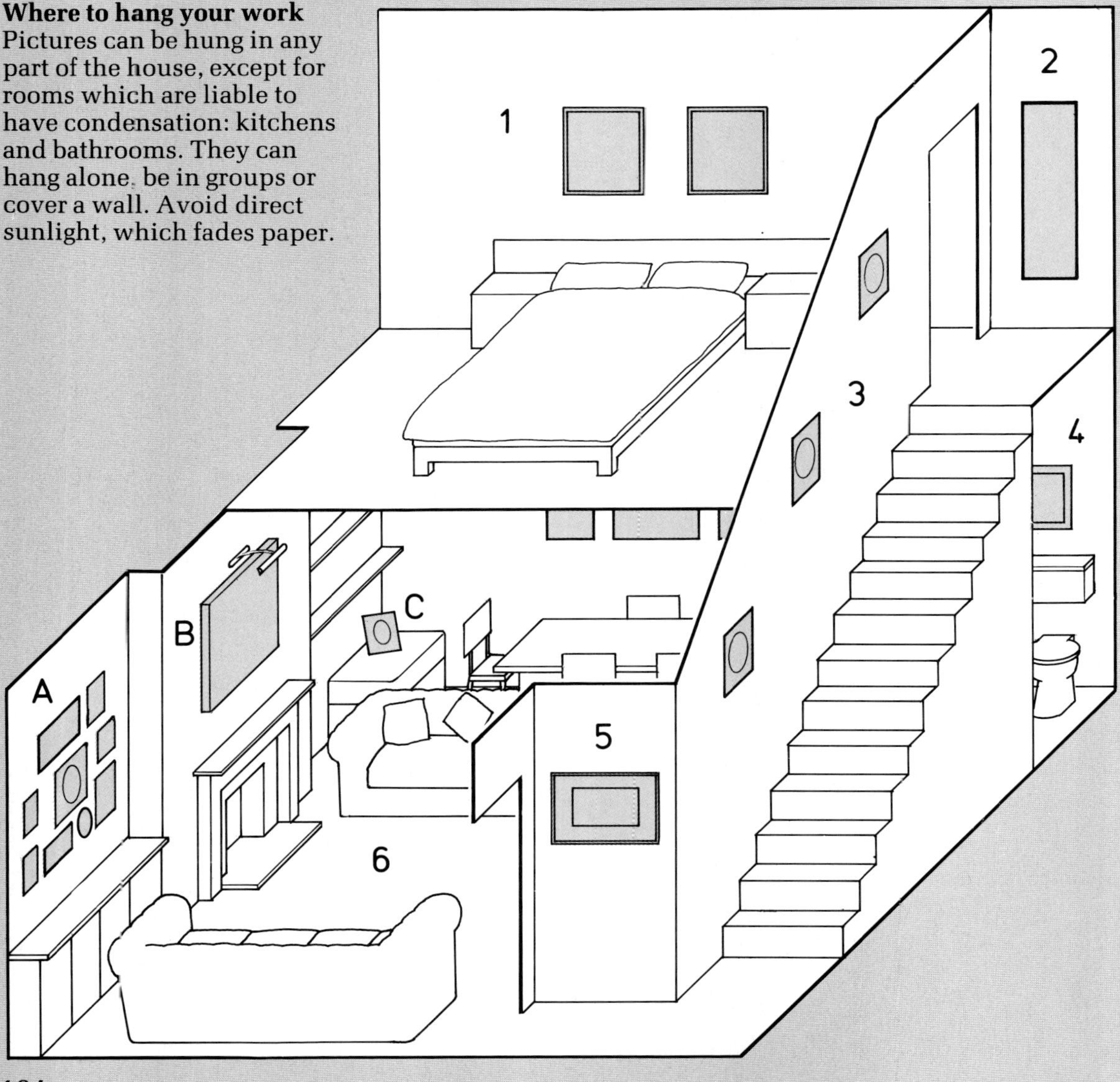

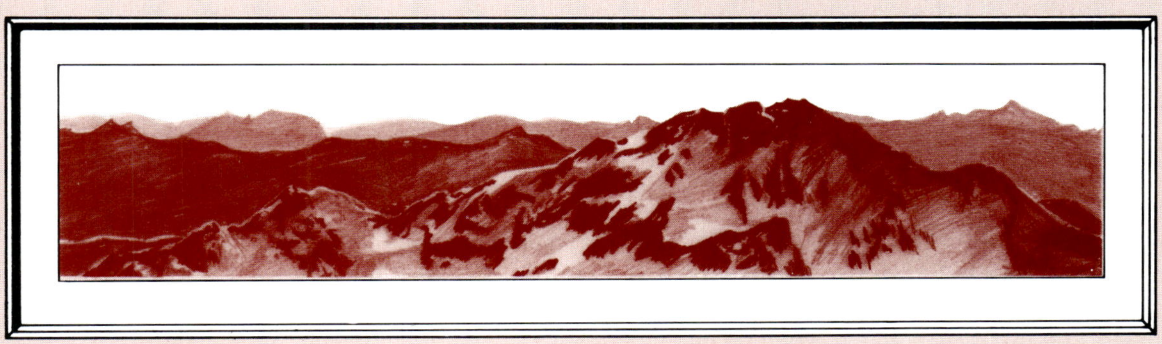

Locating pictures (*left*)
When thinking about the exact position for a drawing, consider a visitor's reaction on coming upon it unawares; or if you want it to be part of a larger scheme which will enhance a room.
1 Bedrooms: restful environments where you can hang personal drawings, or ones that will blend with wallpaper and fabrics.
2 Landings: ideal for small, intimate drawings which can change a space in which you move around into a background comment on your life.
3 Staircase: a lot of space for groups of drawings leading the attention upwards.
4 Toilets: excellent for drawings that can and should be studied.
5 Entrance hall: an opportunity to welcome your visitors with your ability.
6 Living room/dining room: Pictures may be grouped (**A**) to cover an entire wall; or be illuminated to catch attention (**B**) or framed on a table as a memento of your friends or of significant events (**C**).

Choosing pictures to hang
Your choice may be influenced by several factors – the beauty or charm of the drawing, or a reminder of an event in your life, a view from a holiday (*above*), or a child's drawing of his teddy bear (*right*). Build up a personal gallery which becomes a family heirloom.

Height of pictures
The best height for a picture is where the centre is at eye level, about 5 ft from the floor; but its surroundings – cupboards, windows, side tables, curtains nearby – will also have to be taken into account.

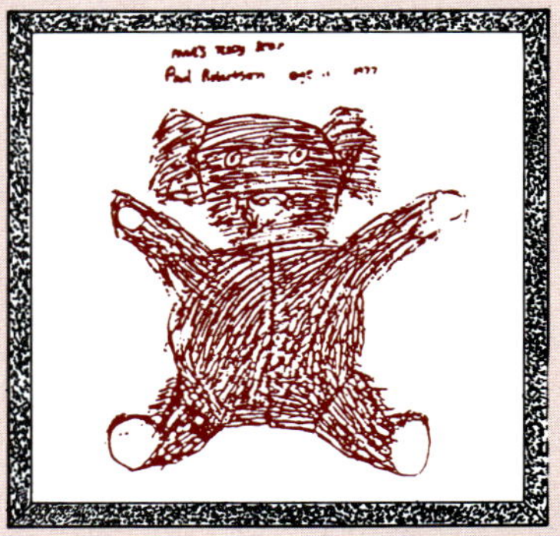

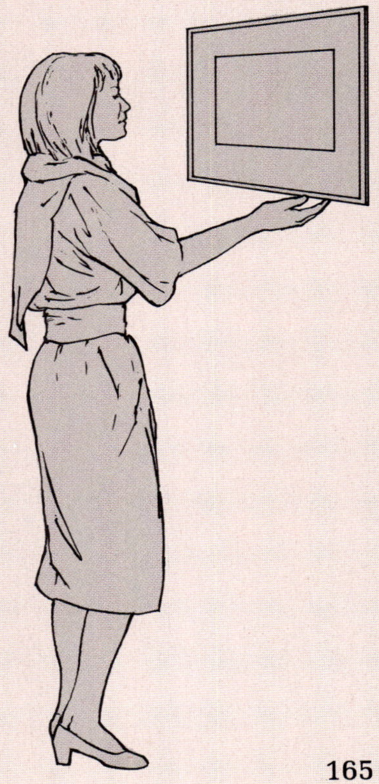

displaying your drawings

The best method for mounting your work depends on the condition of the paper and on whether the display is to be temporary or permanent. Don't stick drawings on to backgrounds that are firmer unless the paper is torn or fragile; the process itself can result in damage. For display, your work can be fixed down on backing card by using hinges or corner tabs or with tiny spots of gum or all-over adhesive. But it is better to display your drawings by using a window mount since the paper on which you have done your drawing is preserved unaltered. In addition, the frame will lead the viewer's eyes into the picture.

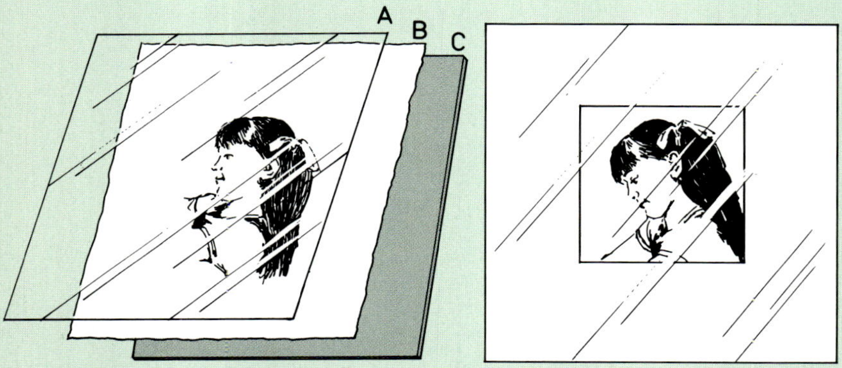

Direct mounting (*far left*) Your drawing should be trimmed to a regular shape and, for temporary mounting, fixed to a backing card, then covered with clear plastic, or, if on display, glass. But if it is stuck down firmly, the drawing will be impossible to remove without damage.

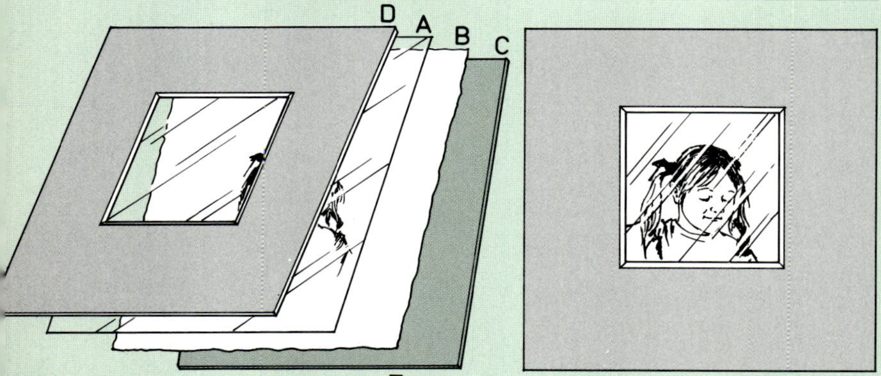

Window mounting (*far left*) Again for temporary mounting, your drawings can be very satisfactorily displayed in a frame made of card, although skill in cutting a clean hole in the overlay card is required. If you want to protect your work by a sheet of clear acetate, then put it under the mount.

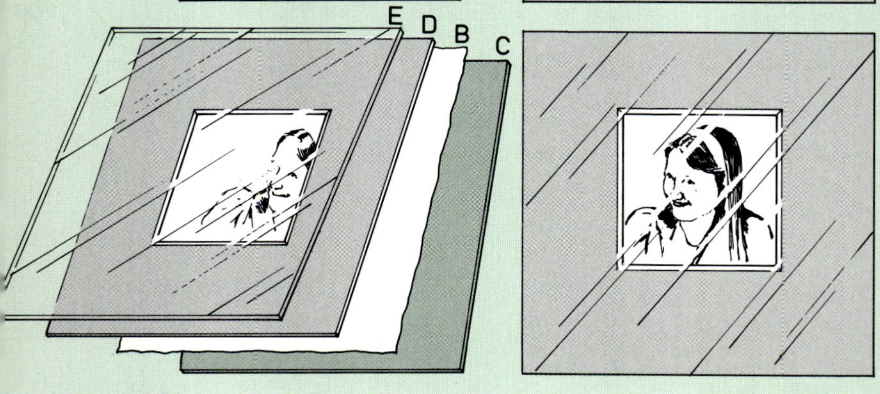

Window mounting for permanent display (*far left*) Using the same method as above, you can shield your drawing with glass. But clean plastic and glass carefully since both produce static electricity when rubbed.

A Clear acetate; **B** Drawing; **C** Backing card; **D** Window mount; **E** Glass.

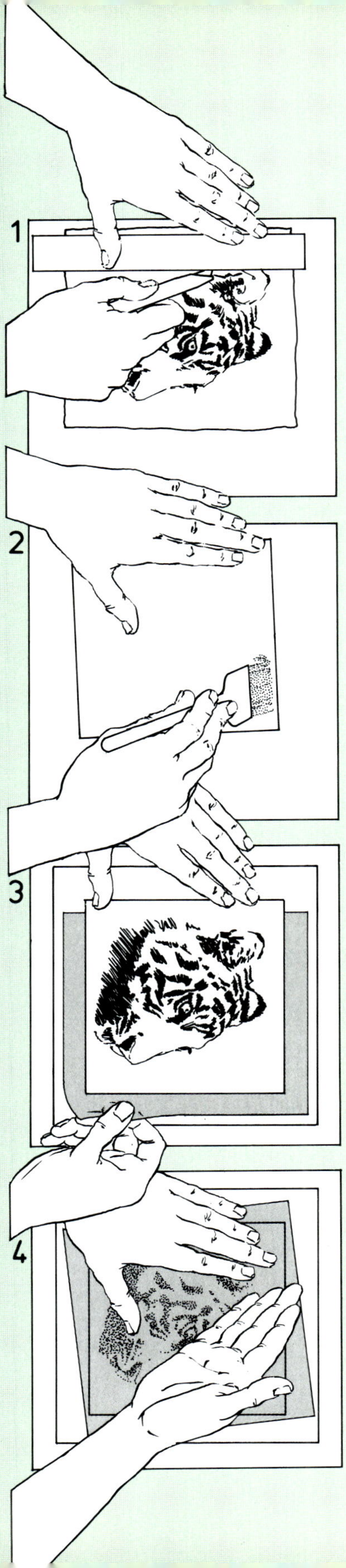

Permanent mounting
You can fix a drawing to a backing card by rubber gum or dry mounting.

Rubber gum mounting (*left*)
1 Trim the drawing to the correct size and lightly spread a thin layer of gum over the back of it and leave to dry.
2 Lightly spread a thin layer of gum over the surface of the backing card also and leave to dry.
3 Place tracing paper between the two gummed surfaces, locate the correct position for the drawing and slowly withdraw the tracing paper.
4 Press down the drawing onto the gummed surface through another sheet of paper. Work carefully, since it is very difficult to reposition your drawing.

Dry mounting (*right*)
You need a sheet of shellac slightly larger than your drawing; electric iron or heat tacker; protective sheet.
1 Put the drawing face down, shellac on top, and tack on the shellac by heat contact at the centre.
2 Trim shellac and drawing and position both on backing card.
3 Lift your drawing at the corners, and lightly heat fix the shellac to the backing.
4 Cover the drawing with a heat-resistant sheet and iron down on to the backing. Work evenly from the centre.

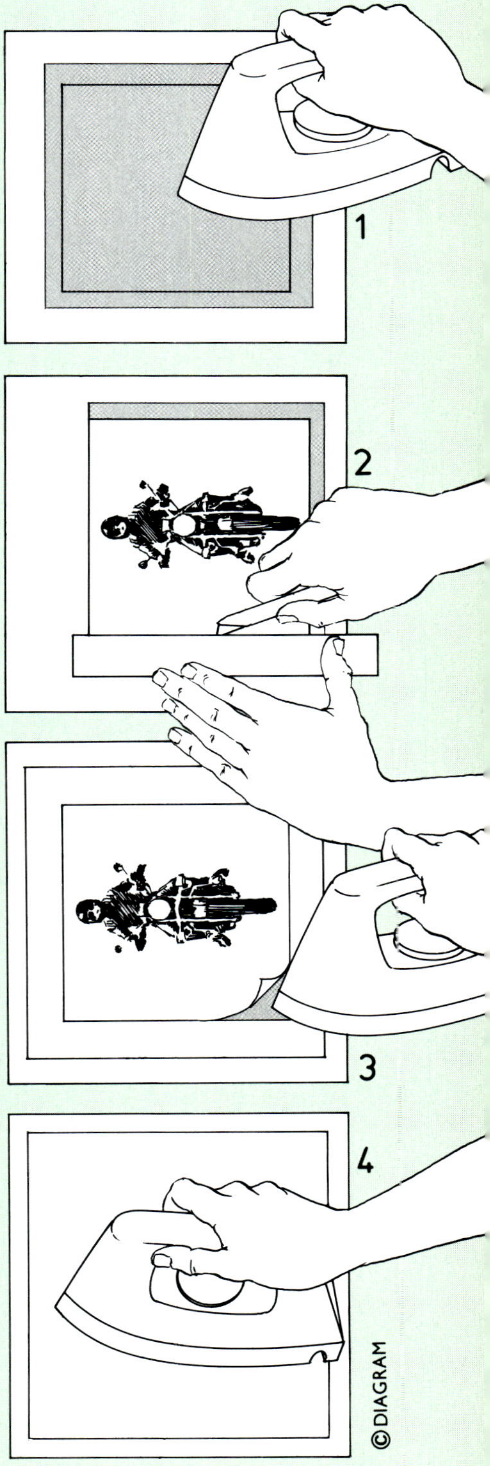

displaying your drawings

The surrounding frame or mount of a picture can greatly influence the effect of the drawing on the viewer. Dark backgrounds usually overpower; light ones are passive. Try placing your drawing on a range of backgrounds and judge the effects of different tones and colours. Normally, large surrounds make a drawing seem insignificant; small ones tend to make it appear expansive.

It is common practice to surround the window of the mount with finely drawn lines, but these may be hard for the beginner to do well.
The basic factors to consider are:
size of the surrounding mount;
shape of the window in the mount;
location of the drawing within the frame or mount;
style of the window edge.

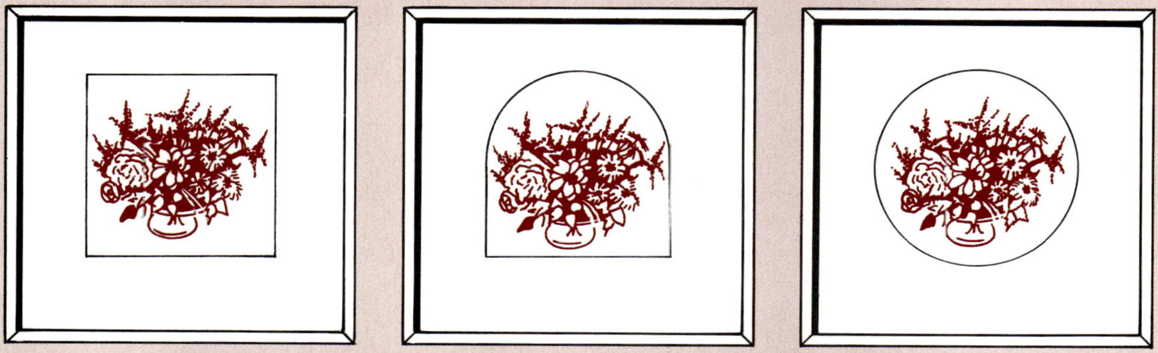

The shape of the frame (*above*)
Normally a rectangle is best suited to drawings but they can be shown off beautifully by oval, circular or arched frames. However, be warned that cutting curved edges requires a great deal of experience and skill.

The background (*right and below*)
The colour, tone and area of the surrounding mount or frame will affect the quality of your drawing. Try exploring what happens when you put it on different backgrounds.

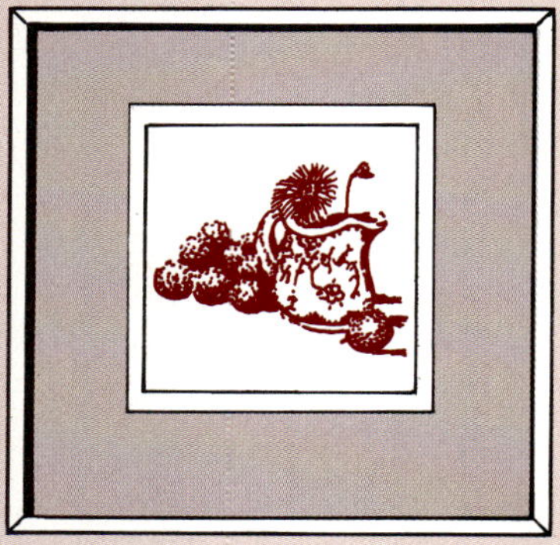

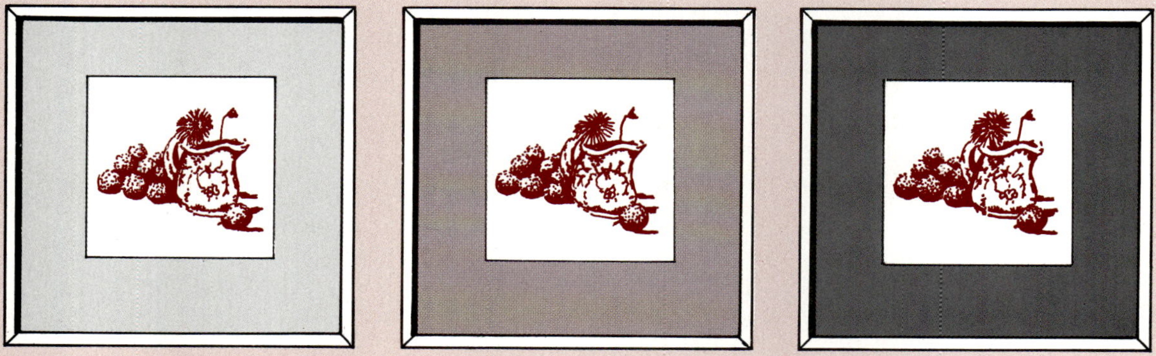

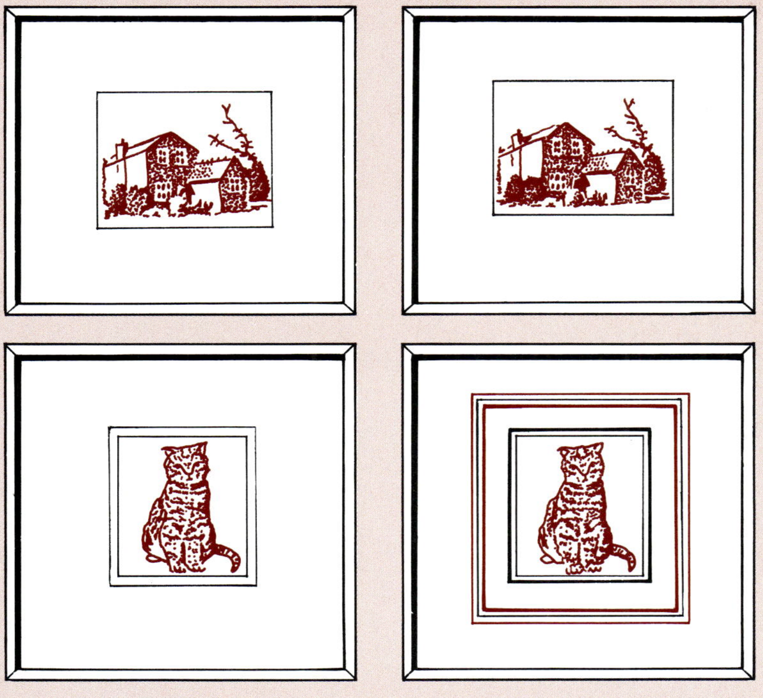

Positioning the drawing in the frame (*left*)
Normally a balanced effect is achieved by having the mount slightly deeper at the bottom than at the top. Try to keep the top the same depth as the sides. Remember that the mount or frame has to serve the drawing, not overpower it.

Lines around a mount (*left*)
Surrounding many mounts, close to the window, are fine rules or lines which emphasise the edges of the drawing and the frame. These are difficult to draw and should only be attempted after much practice.

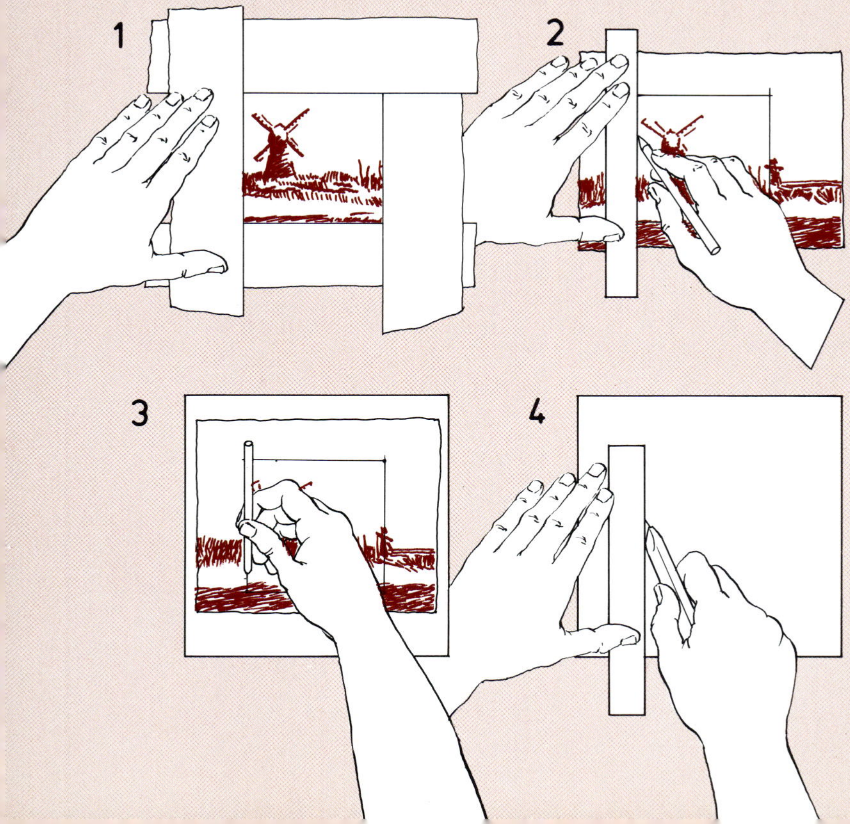

Cutting a window mount (*left*)
1 Having cut the mounting card to size, select the exact area of the drawing to be exposed.
2 Accurately outline the inside of the frame, ensuring the corners are square.
3 Prick a pin through at the corners to the mounting card.
4 Carefully cut out the inner edges of the frame on the mounting card. Always use a very sharp blade and a metal ruler.
Attach the drawing to the back of the mount with double-sided tape at the corners or small spots of glue. Do not use Sellotape. Do not attempt bevelled edges (edges at about 45°) without extensive practice.

displaying your drawings

Framing brings a drawing to life. What may appear as an insignificant sketch, once it is framed, becomes a wonderful record of a person, place or event. You may either consult a local frame-maker, who will be willing to recommend frames, or you can adapt ones you already have. There is an almost unlimited variety of decorative frames in different materials and textures, colours and mouldings, but it is wisest to use simple, narrow edges as elaborate borders tend to overpower drawings. Remember that paper and card are easily affected by damp and heat, whereas glass and wood are much more resilient to temperature and humidity changes. Always seal your drawing into the frame by closing all gaps in the back.

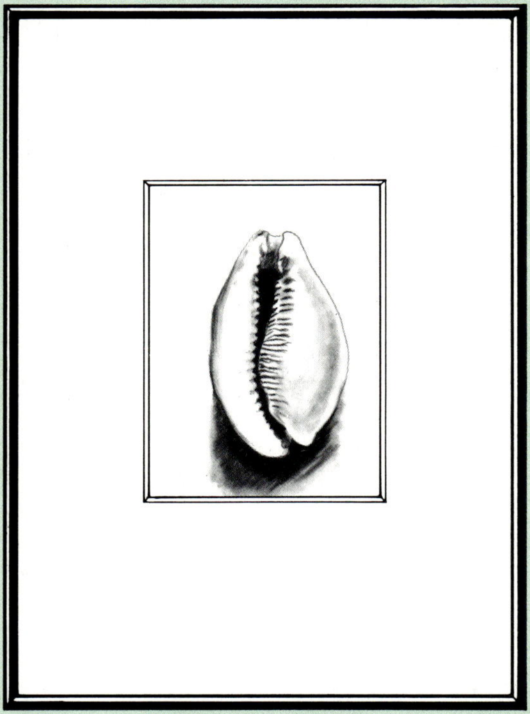

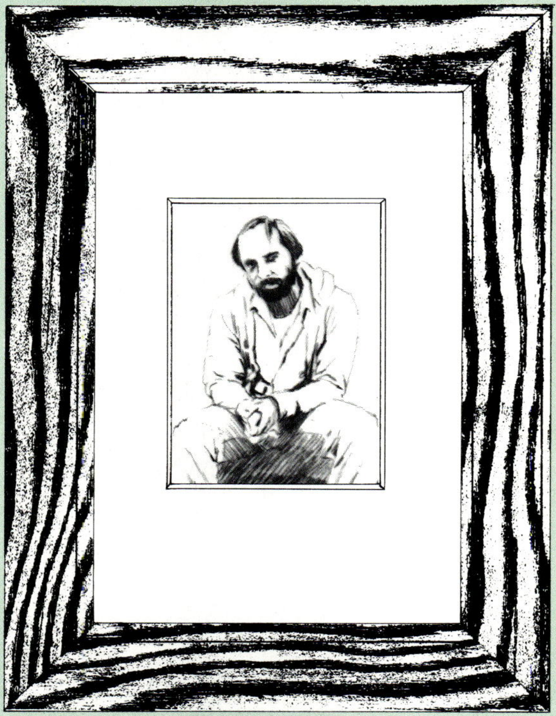

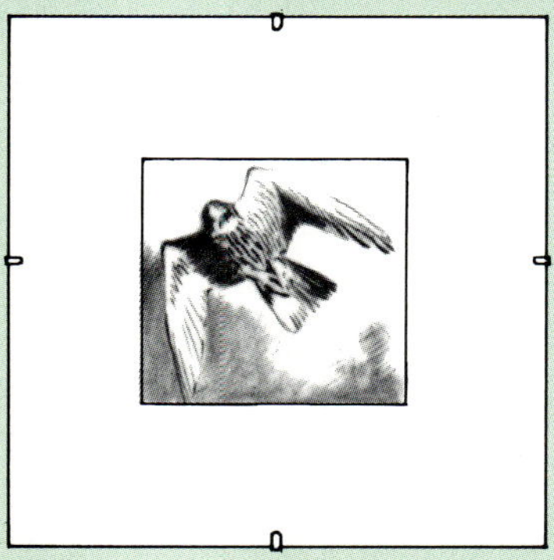

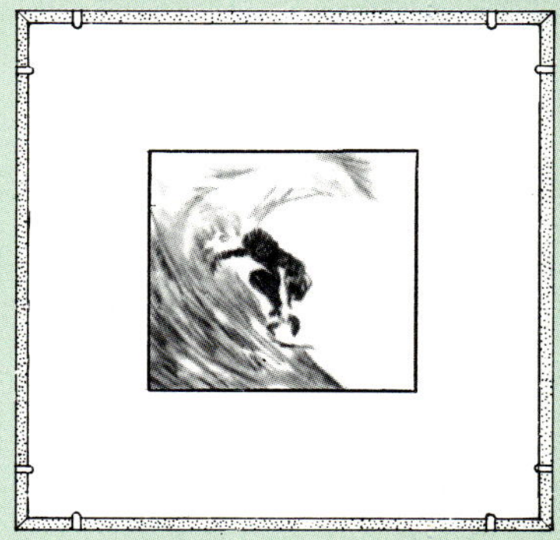

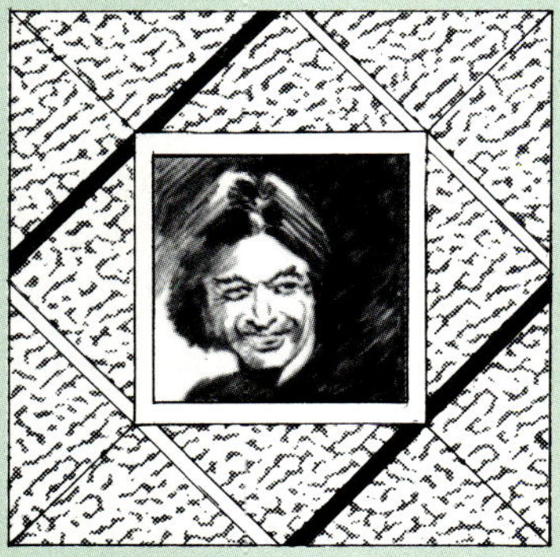

Selecting a frame (*below left*)
A narrow border, with a wide mount around your drawing, will enhance it much more than an overpowering antique frame.

Modern frames (*bottom left*)
Borderless mounts or modern frames made of coloured plastic can work very well with drawings.

Preparing the frame
1 Cutting the glass: First measure the rectangle to just 2 mm in each direction less than the picture area and mark the corners on the glass with a felt pen. Using a metal ruler, a set square and a glass cutter, score the glass and then gently snap off the excess at the edge of a table.
2 Clean the inside surface of the glass thoroughly and put it into the frame.
3 Position the drawing (already mounted) into the frame.
4 Pin the backing into the frame at the back with small panel pins, taking care not to apply too much force and risk breaking the glass.

The back (*right*)
Make certain the back of the frame is sealed to prevent the entry of dust and moisture. Stick gummed paper along the join between the backing and the frame. Do not use Sellotape.
On the back, record the subject, artist and date and anything else that might be of interest years later.

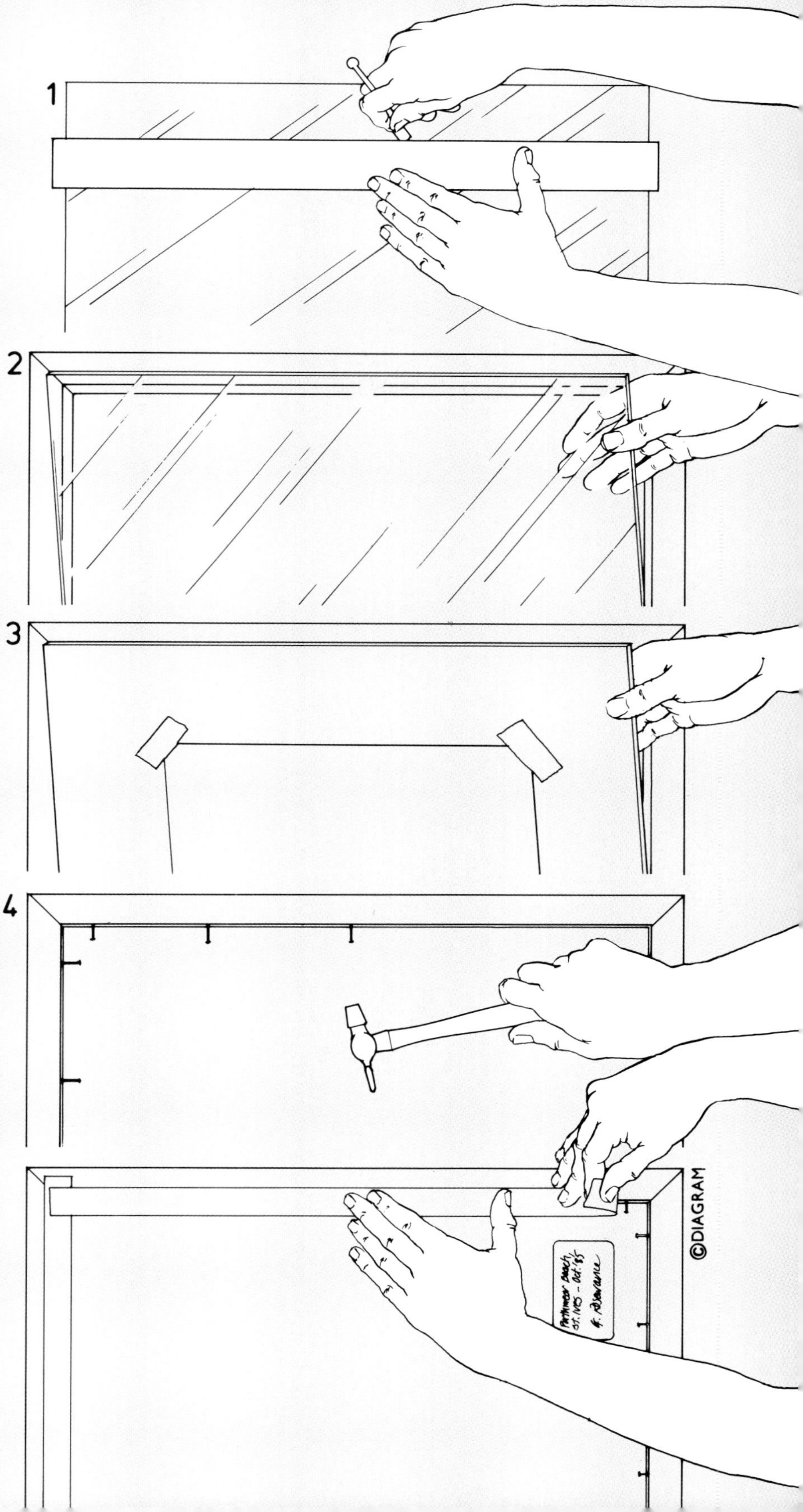

changing the size

Very often you may want to enlarge or reduce a drawing. The most satisfactory method is to pay for an inexpensive photocopy to the required size. If you want to use your drawing as a basis for another piece of work, then you may enlarge by squares or by using a pantograph or gain access to a commercial enlarging machine. As a rule of thumb, the diagonal of the enlargement will be an extension of the diagonal on your original, since the proportion of its length to that of the enlargement will be the same as the ratio of its height to that of the enlargement. To avoid enlarging with preconceptions about the image, begin drawing the larger version from the original put upside down.

Enlarging by squares (*right* and *below right*)
1 On an overlay, construct an accurate grid of squares covering your drawing.
2 Beside it align a duplicate grid enlarged to the correct scale.
3 Plot the contents of each square on to the larger and corresponding square.
4 To copy great detail subdivide into a smaller grid (*below*).

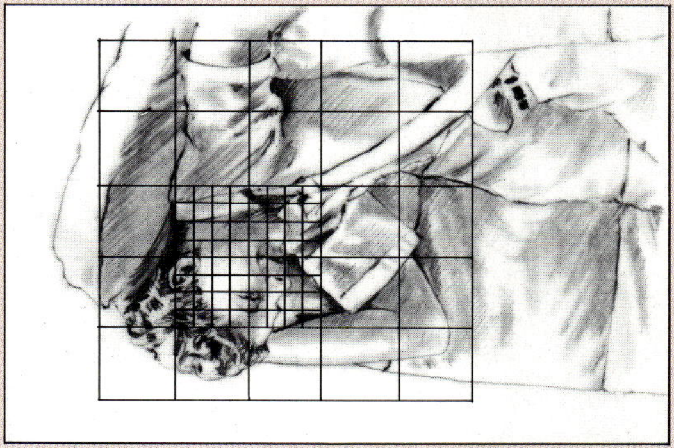

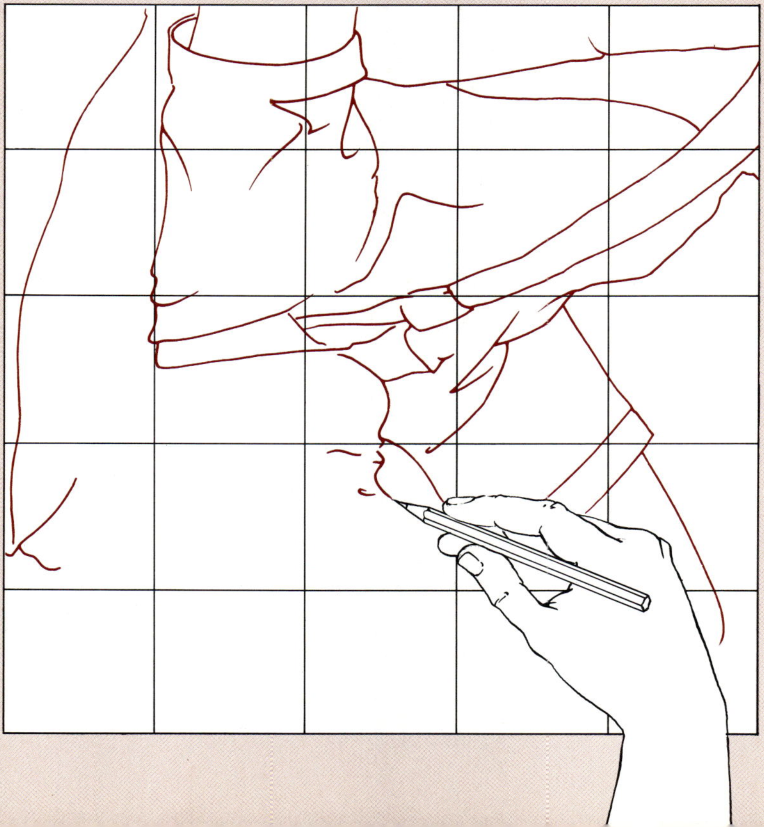

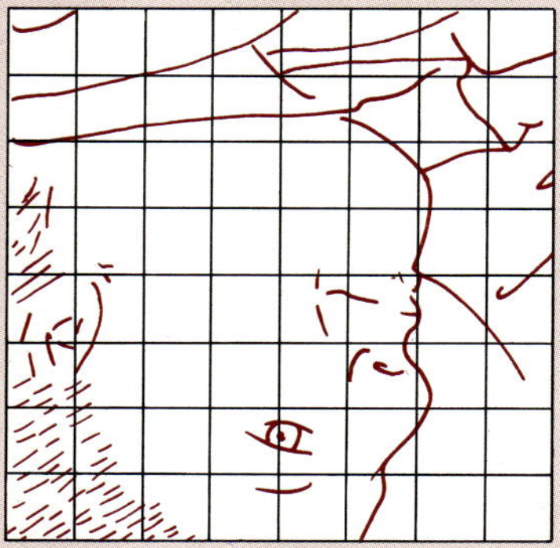

Enlarging and reducing by pantograph (*right*)
Having set the pantograph to enlarge to a simple ratio of, say 1 to 3, trace its point along the lines of your drawing. The pencil at the end of the arm will copy the track to the ratio required. For reduction, transpose the point with the pencil.

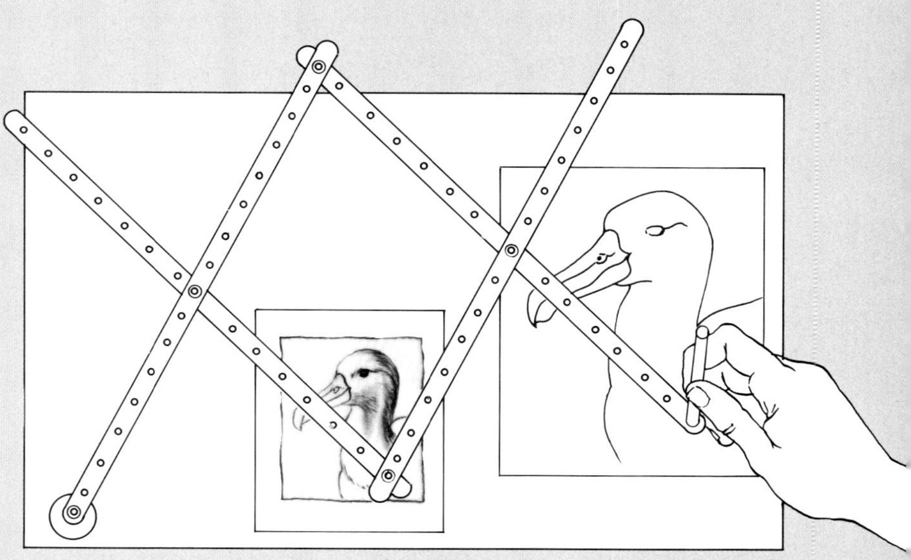

Enlarging by dividers (*right*)
Set a pair of simple dividers to a measurement on your drawing, then step the dividers the number of times that the enlargement should be. Proportional dividers can be set to a constant enlargement, the distance between the long legs being the required number of times longer than that between the short legs.

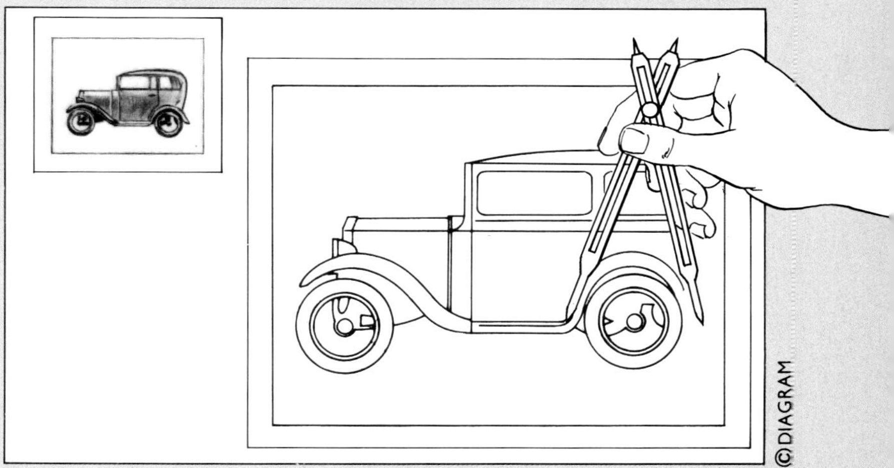

Enlarging, reducing machines (*right*)
Most professional artists have access to an enlarger which operates with a lens in a way that is similar to a vertical camera. The original is put on the adjustable base plate and a copy to the required scale can be traced on the upper viewing area.

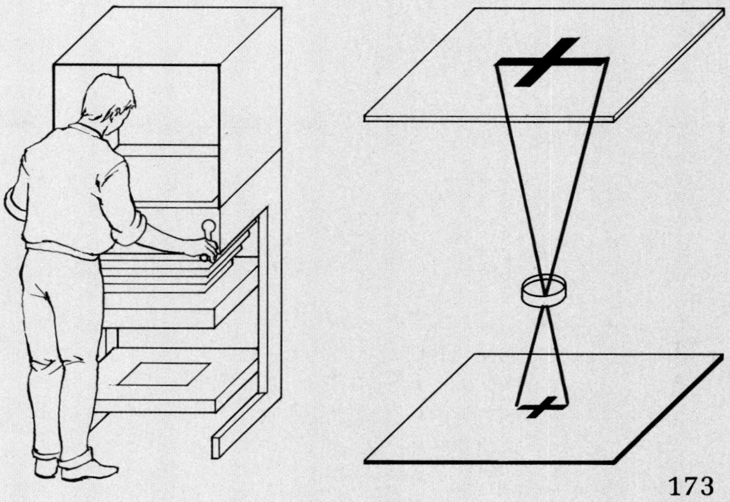

decorative drawing

Your drawing style is like your handwriting, a signature of your character. Whatever you draw will carry a consistent quality of line, and this may not always result in work which can be used in the way you want. Consider transforming your drawings into other styles, either by changing the technique or method of producing the marks, or by deliberately aiming for a drawing in a particular style. Such a conversion is most appropriate when you want to reproduce your work, since few methods of reproduction can normally be used on pencil studies or even on pen and ink drawings.

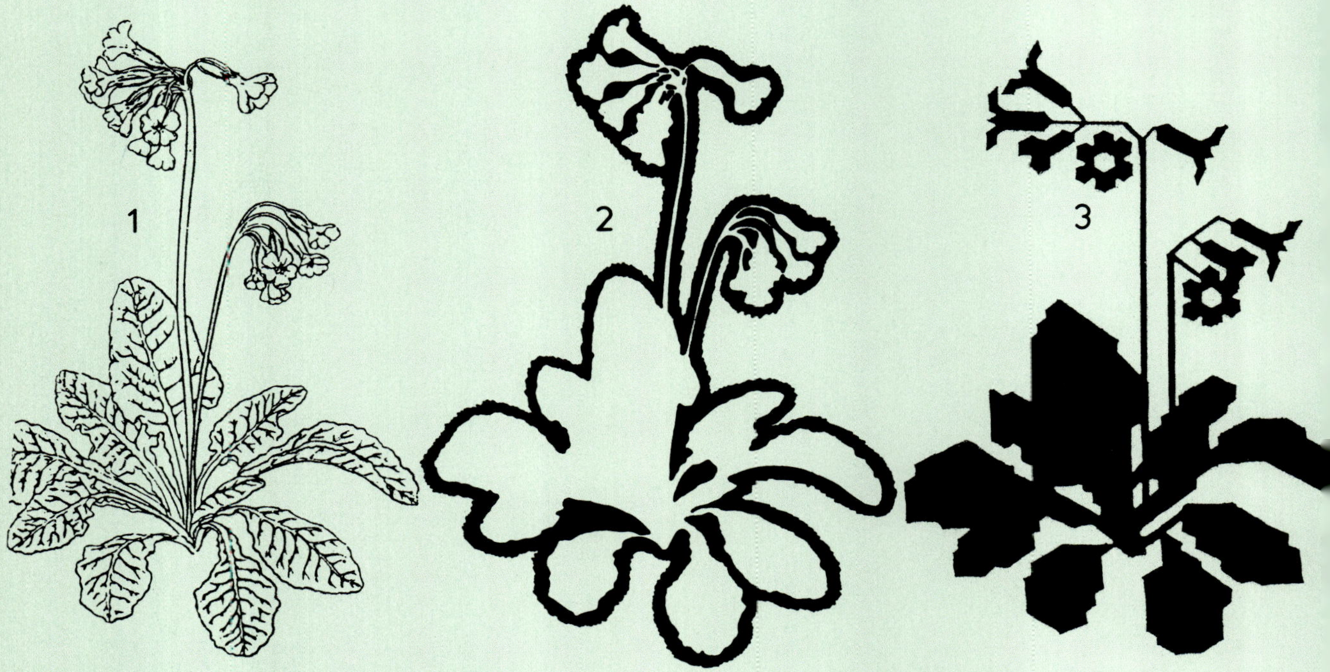

Studies in style
Cowslip
1 The careful pen and ink drawing (*above*) records the precise form of the cowslip. It is already selective, omitting any information on tone or colour; it is a map in which lines depict the edges and surface markings of flowers, stems and leaves.
2 The silhouette study beside it is produced by tracing around the original drawing. This offers wide possibilities for reproduction but the image carries less information.
3 Conversion to regular patterning: by interpreting the shapes against a grid (*right*), you can produce a formal design more suitable for application to fabric.

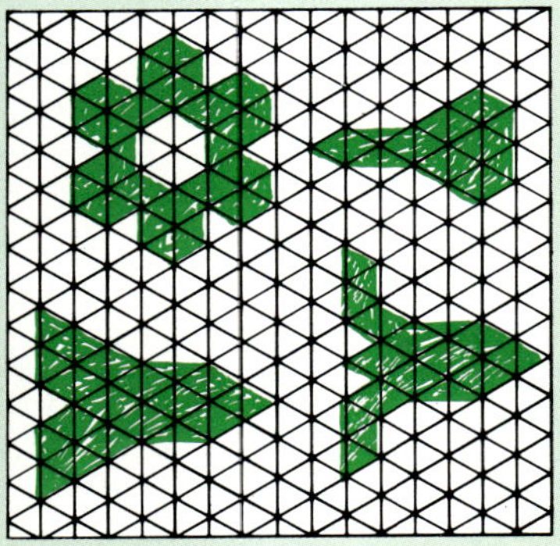

Comic book style
Bringing in the pudding
(Pen and ink drawing, *right*)
First sketch out the figure, either from a model or from imagination (**A**). Next draw the main trimmings on the costume in soft pencil (**B**). Finally, with a brush or pen, add the strong features in black and white. A suitable style for coarse reproduction (**C**).

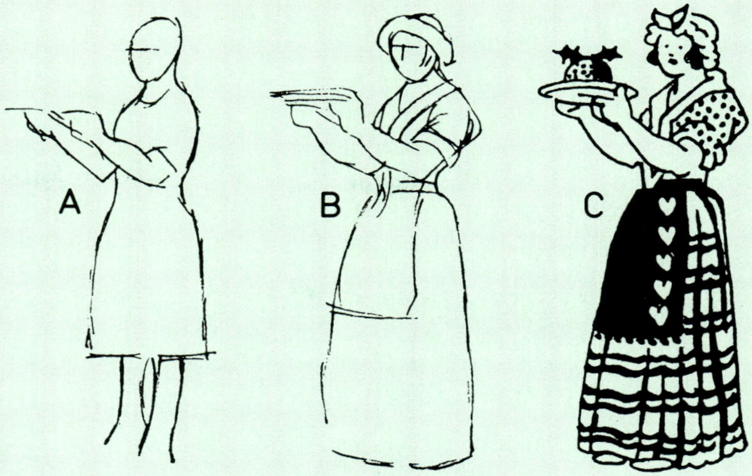

Pattern Style
Half an apple
(Pencil drawing, *right*)
Begin with a study from nature, then on tracing paper convert the main areas to either black or white. This simplistic result is ideal for decorative applications where details are not required.

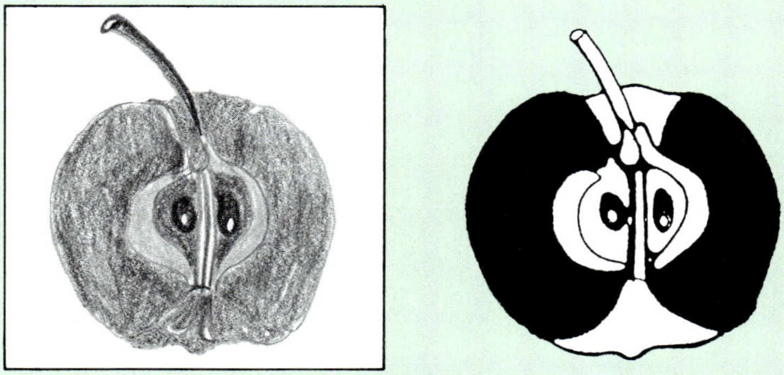

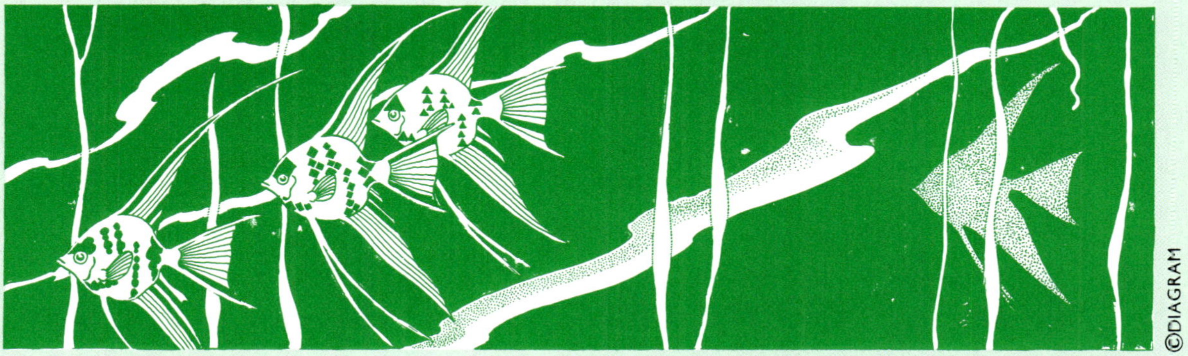

Period style
Aquatic motifs
(Brush and ink drawings)
To produce a pastiche of the style of any period in history or of any culture, choose a good book on that style and examine carefully its mannerisms and the ways in which artists of that culture saw the world. 1920's (*above*), Oriental (*right*).

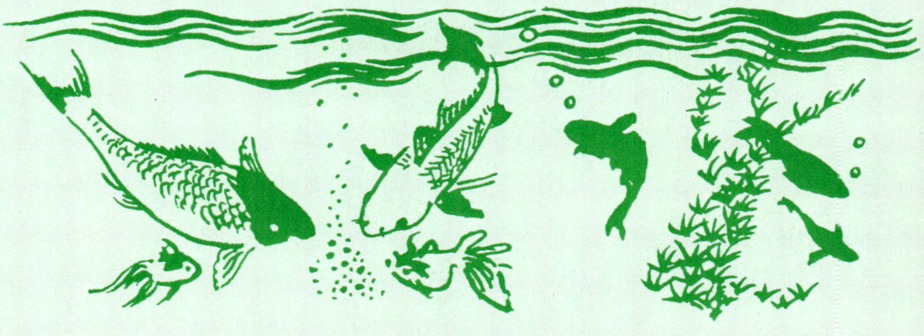

decorative drawing

Your drawings can be converted to simple black and white statements, with no tone and no internal drawing – just simple shapes against a background. This technique transforms your work into two-colour patterns which make excellent presents. The best results are achieved by blocking in large areas and concentrating on the accuracy of the finer features.

You can use grid paper to help you in establishing the overall arrangement and the details more accurately. When studying the shapes, try to see both the dark areas and the light areas as being of equal value, looking carefully to see how they interlock.

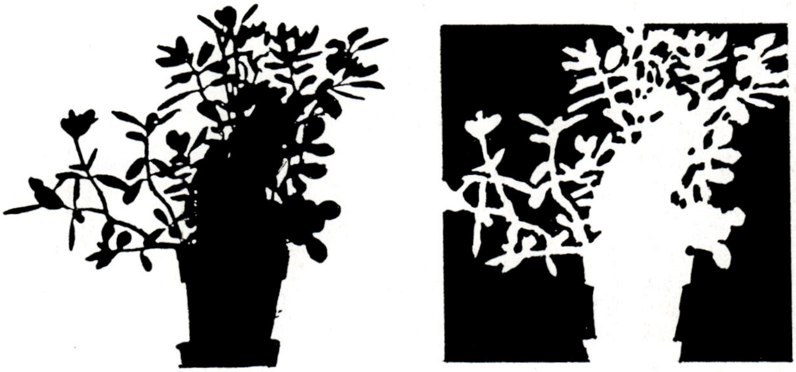

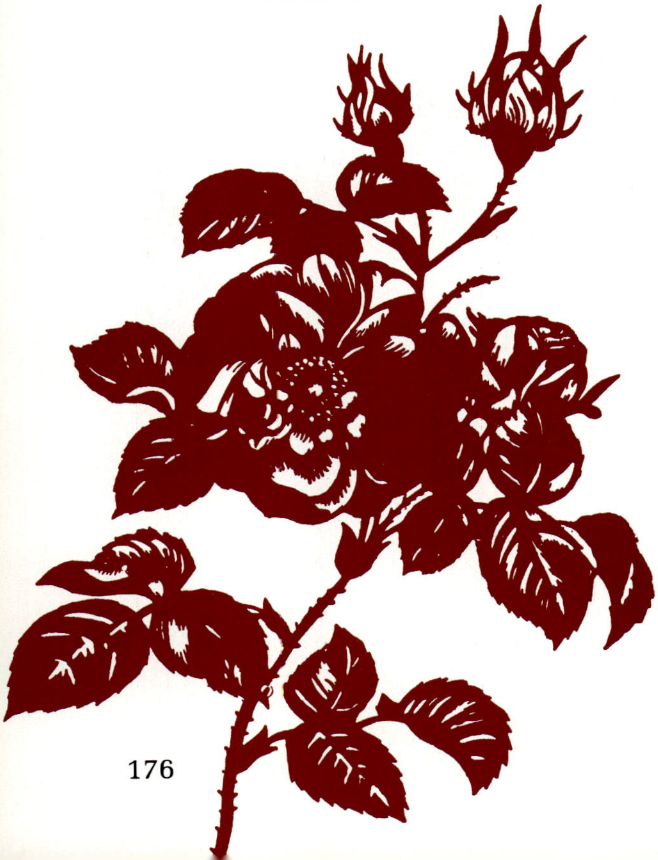

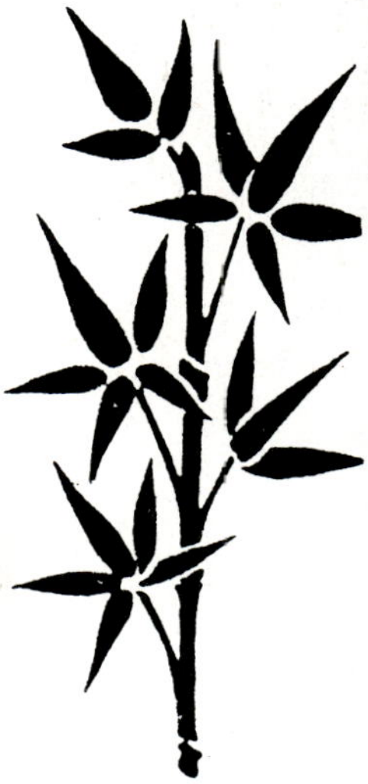

Positive or negative (*left*)
What is on the paper and what we think we see may not be the same. A drawing on white conveys a different impression from one on black: we tend to see black lines as the edges of forms but do not intepret white ones in the same way. Produce a silhouette, first black on white and then vice versa. Which is clearer?

Paper cuts (*far left*)
Converting your drawings to paper cuts requires constant practice. Make sure your cutting blade is very sharp and very fine, and try first on paper of normal thickness before attempting to cut thin tissue. If you do master the technique, you can use your drawings for gift cards and for decorative purposes.

Stencils (*left*)
To create a design for conversion to a stencil, remember: the image must be simplified. Construct white links between forms so there are no floating elements; allow no large open spaces that would be hard to ink evenly when stencilling.

Portrait silhouettes
There are two basic methods of producing silhouettes from a posing model; by lighting from the front, or from behind. For both you need a single, clear source of light.
Method 1: Rear lighting. Sit the subject between you and the light source and very carefully copy the shapes on to a drawing surface (*right*).
Method 2: Front lighting. This method enables you to trace precisely onto a drawing surface the shadow made when the light is between you and the subject (*right*).
In both cases it can be helpful to draw on a grid so that you can check vertical and horizontal alignments. When completed the outline can then be scaled down.

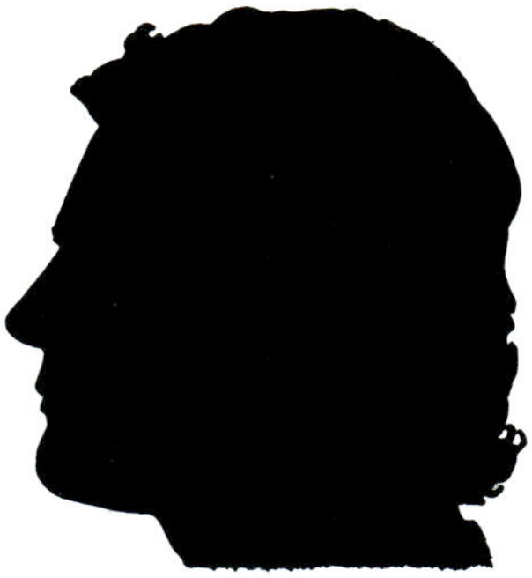

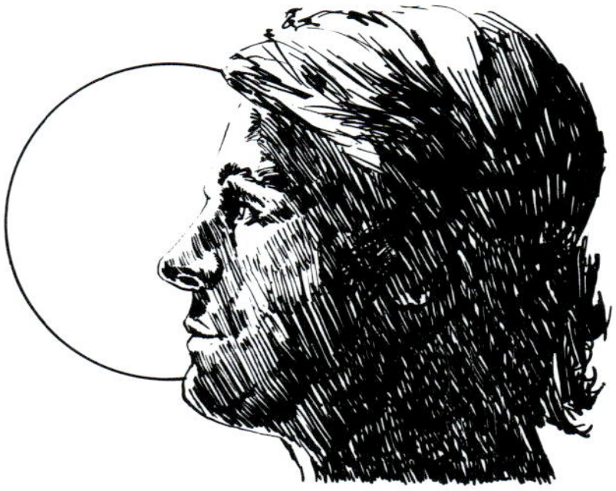

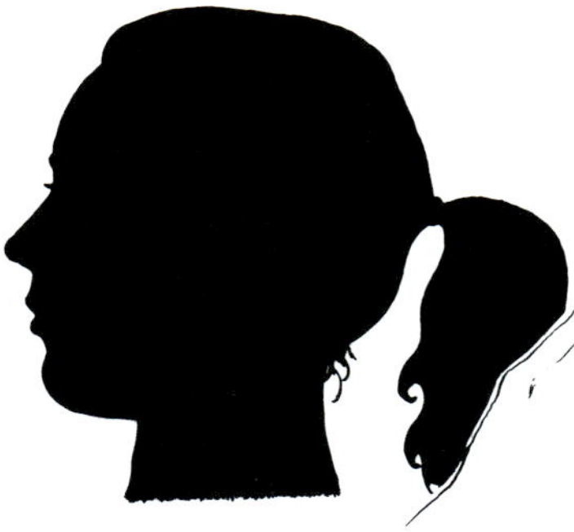

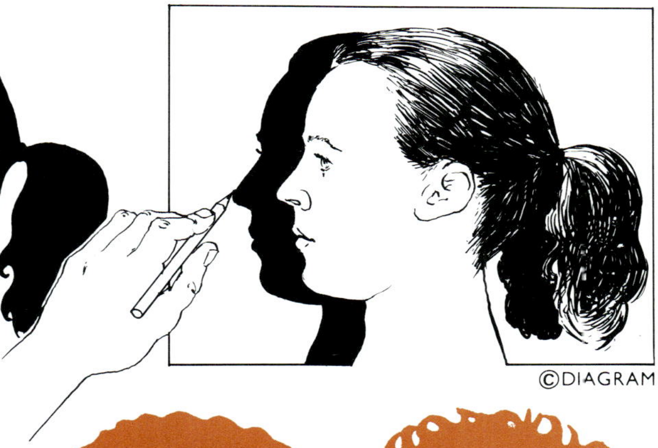

©DIAGRAM

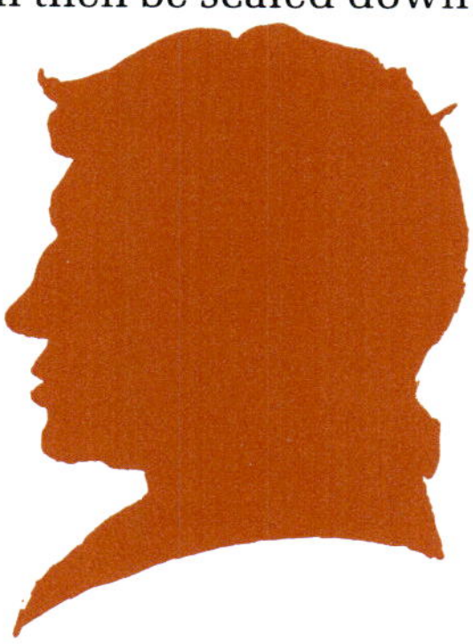

The silhouette portrait
Although the information conveyed is limited, a silhouette should identify the model because of its precise record of small particulars – the curve of a lip, the line of the hair, the shape of the nose.
You can check width and height before blocking in the whole head.

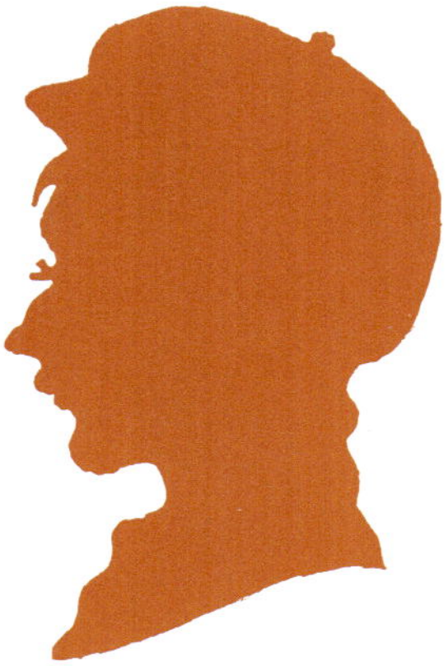

decorative drawing

If you want to create repeating patterns, drawings can produce exciting motifs for development. They can be reproduced by various methods – simple block or screen printing, stencilling, or tracing and hand painting for walls. Remember that if a design is to be repeated over a large area if must be simple.

1

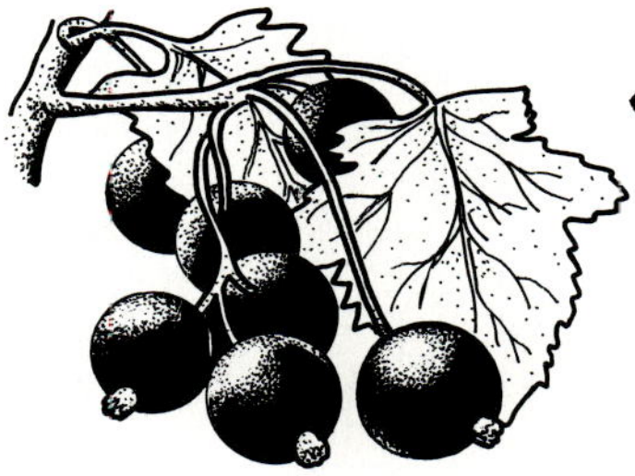

2

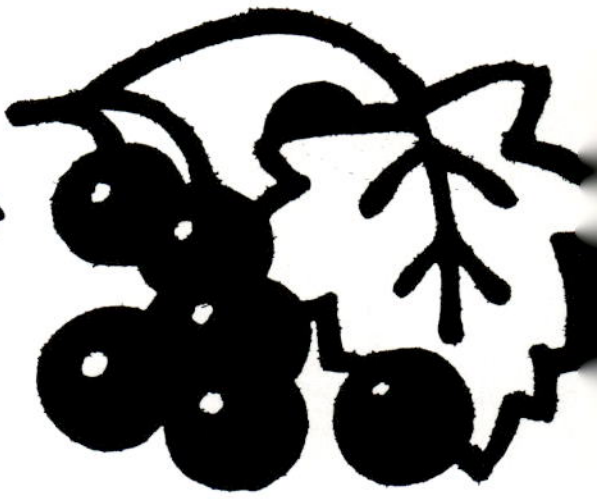

3

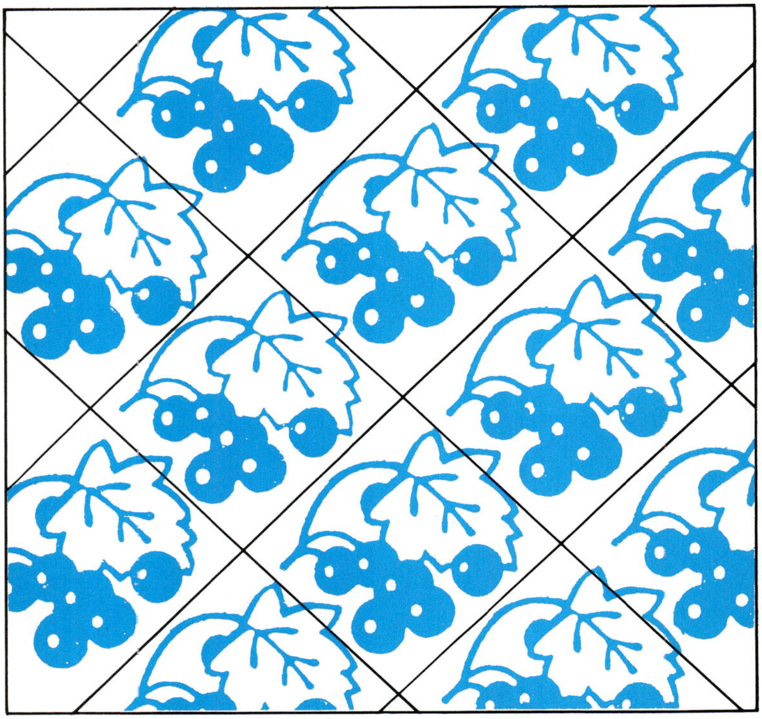

Blackcurrant patterns
(Pen and ink drawings)
1 First draw your subject (*above left*) either from life or from a photograph.
2 Convert it to a simple design, choosing the most characteristic features of the subject (*above right*).
3 Then divide up the area for decoration into regular squares into each of which you put your motif (*left*). A diagonal grid creates the most interesting effect.
4 By transposing your image from left to right, or top to bottom, you can achieve a symmetrical design very suitable for borders (*below*).
5 Using the original device you can also build up groups to form their own repetitive possibilities (*bottom*).

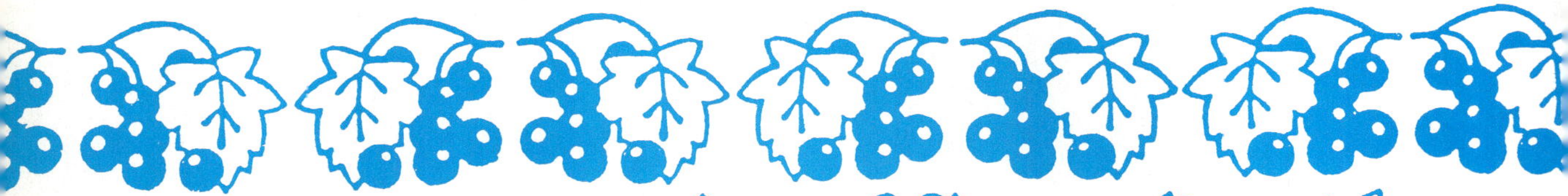

4

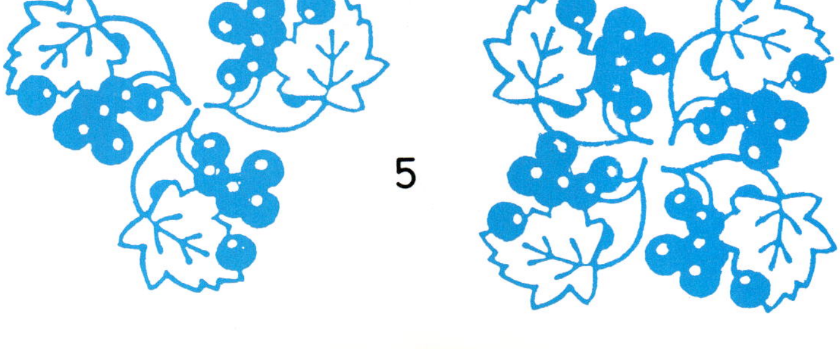

5

Repeat pattern technique
Perhaps you want to cover a large surface with a pattern which does not immediately reveal your motif. The drawings on this page show you how to do this by conversion of your design.
1 Put your motif in a square; cut it vertically into two sections, **A** and **B**, along edges in the design.
2 Transpose the sections and Sellotape them along their original outer edges.
3 Now cut the new design horizontally, again along edges of forms or unevenly across spaces.
4 Transpose these sections, sticking them along their old top and bottom edges. Make sure all four corners of the original square are together, the edges forming a cross inside your new shape, which now contains a blank space.
5 Insert into it a fresh design of similar elements to result in an even tone.

Now print copies of your converted design by any method you choose, carefully fitting together all the edges of the pattern. You will see that the repeat (**a**) includes parts of the original motif and that the assembly is hard to detach. The initial design (**b**) does not immediately stand out from the overall pattern.

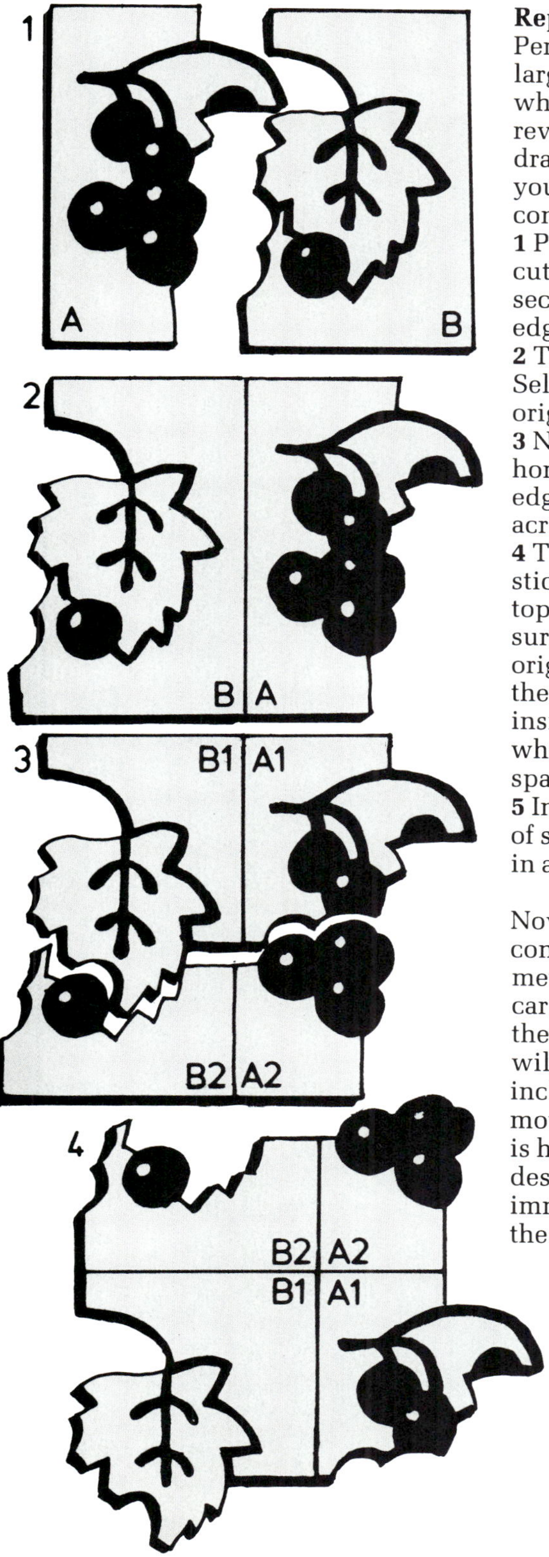

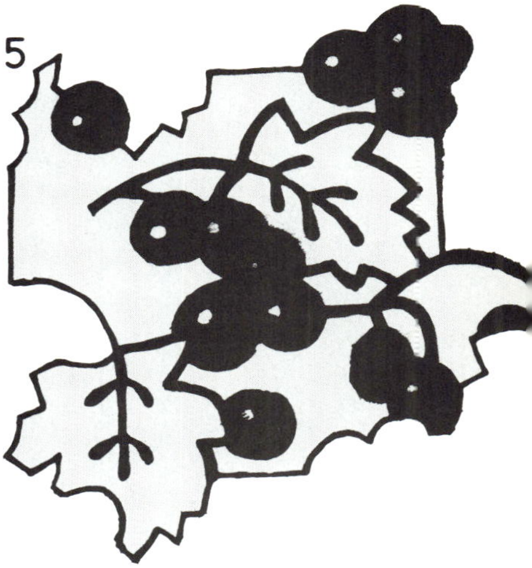

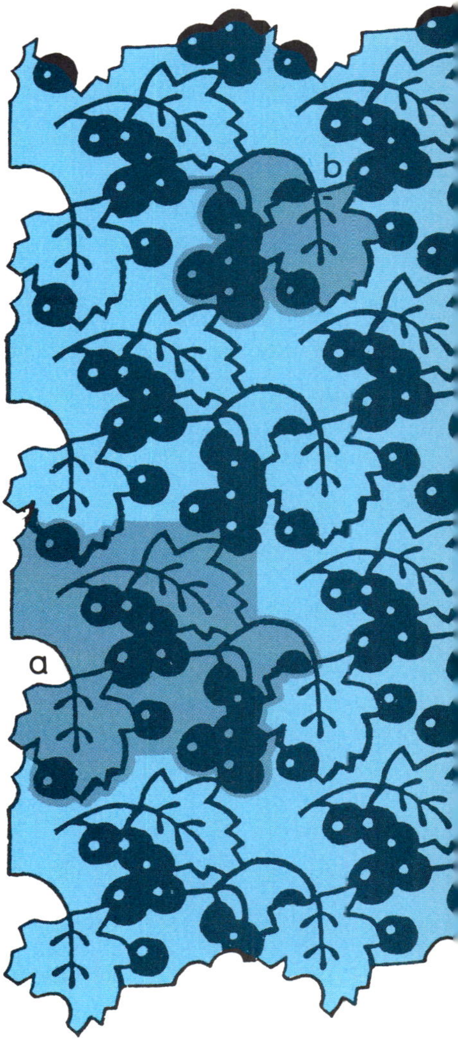

drawing for reproduction

The quality of a reproduced drawing depends on three factors: the method of photoreproducing the image; the method of printing; and the paper used in the printing.
Before you begin your drawing, consider how it will be altered by reproduction. Initially you will be unable to predict the results, but, gradually, if you work within the guidelines set out below and on the following pages, you will, by comparison between drawings and reproductions, develop a sense of what type of artwork will reproduce best. A warning: experimenting can be costly, so draw what you think will come out well.

Selecting the method
1 Line: Everything is black or white.
2 Screen: Lines are made up of dots and appear grey.
3 Line and tone: 1 and 2 combined.
4 Half-tone: Entire image is made up of a screen of dots.
5 Duotone: Overprinting of image already screened with a second colour.

Line reproduction (*right*)
Lines and all tonal values are produced by lines only. There are no greys, only black or white.

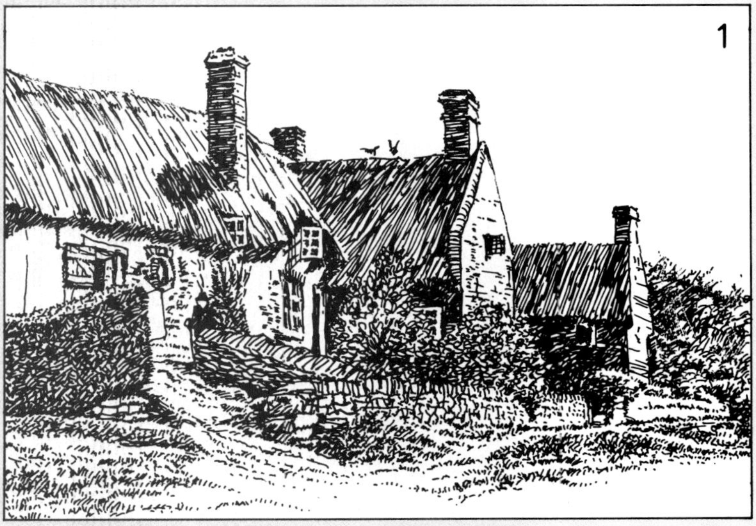

Screen reproduction (*right*)
Lines, which appear grey, are produced by a fine screen. Close examination (see *below*) reveals marks are composed of small connected dots in lines.

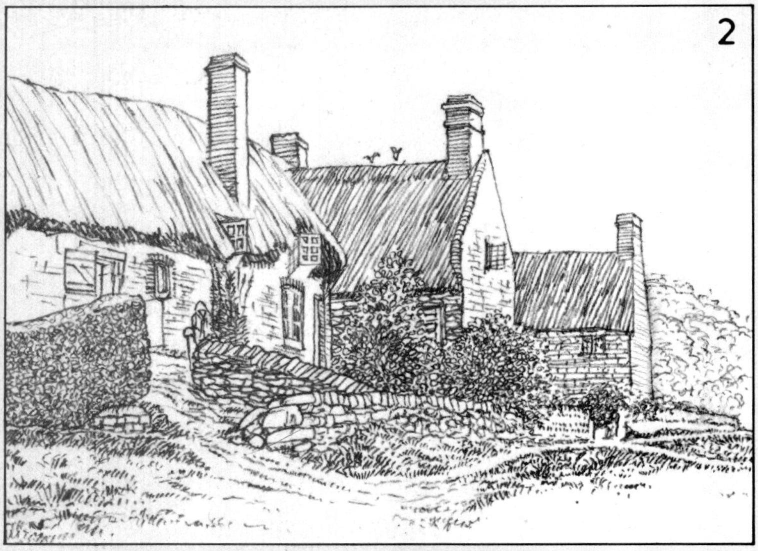

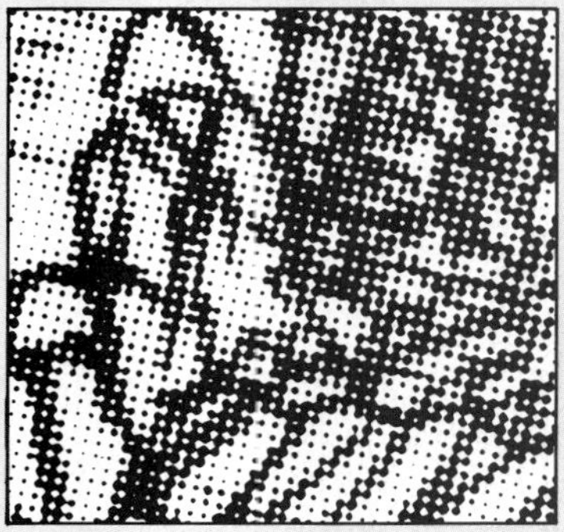

Line and tone reproduction
(*right*)
Tones are made up of a screen of dots and the lines by solid black. The result (*right*) is a combination of line and tone.

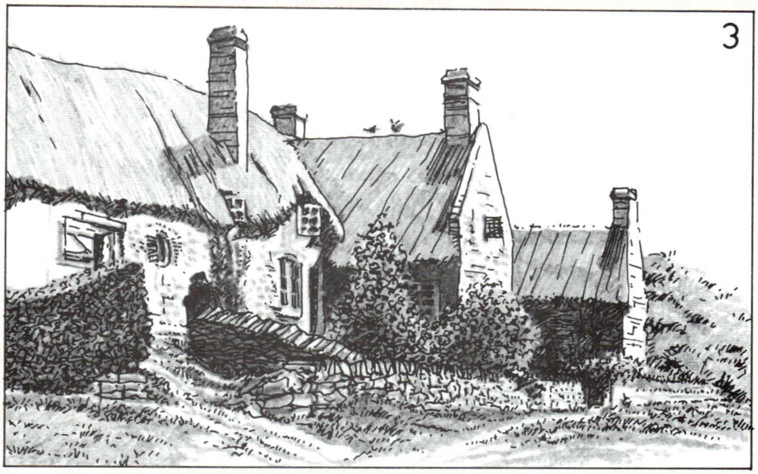

Half-tone reproduction
(*right*)
The entire surface of the image is composed of a fine screen of dots which record a wide range of tones. This method is not suitable for reproduction on coarse paper unless the screen is coarse.

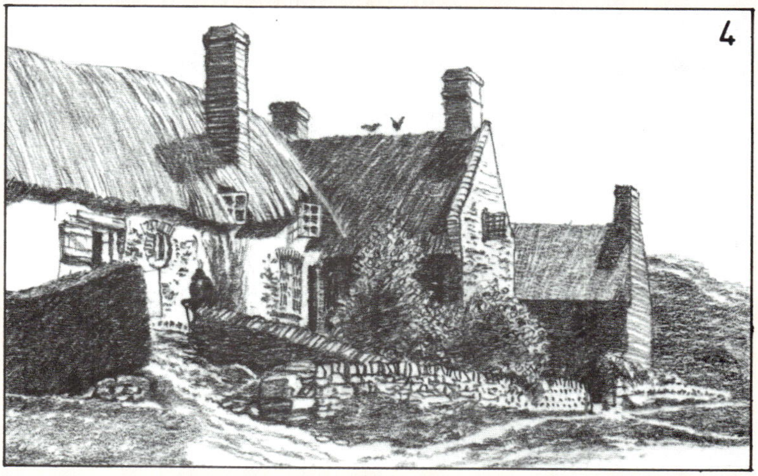

Duotone reproduction
(*right*)
The image is reproduced by overprinting a second colour, both printings using the same size screen of dots. The result is a rich range of tones, and it allows for the introduction of a second colour.

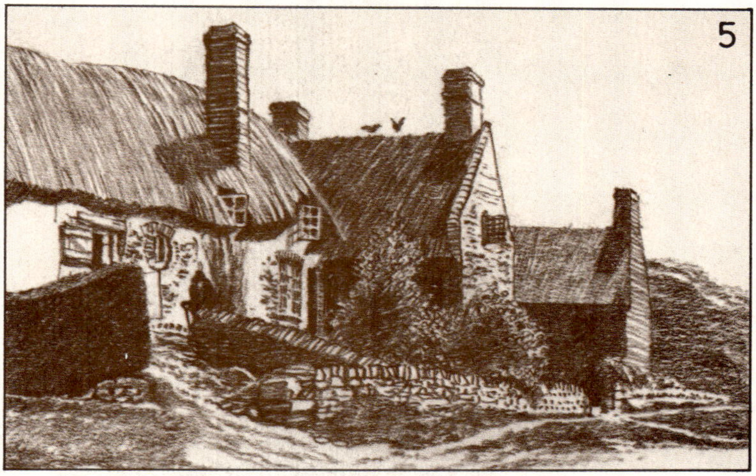

drawing for reproduction

Line images present fewer problems for a printer than tonal drawings; the camera records only black and white marks. They offer a wide choice of processes for reproduction, although some may be crude. They can be reduced in size particularly well, as the lines are simply printed more finely and closer together. And line drawings can be free shapes, not circumscribed by a tone background. The sharp contrast between black and white produces a powerful image.

The great disadvantage of the line image is that it does not portray reality very accurately. Subtle shades are hard to convey since the line drawing must be confined to black and white marks. This means you must interpret the subject matter, and you cannot describe colour, textures and tones with the same facility as in a tonal drawing.

Reducing artwork
Drawings in line are well suited to reduction. Tonal drawings change in their effect, but line sketches become crisper (unless excessively reduced). The detail (*right*) of a drawing on page 180, was reproduced actual size. The reduction beside it retains all the information in the original.

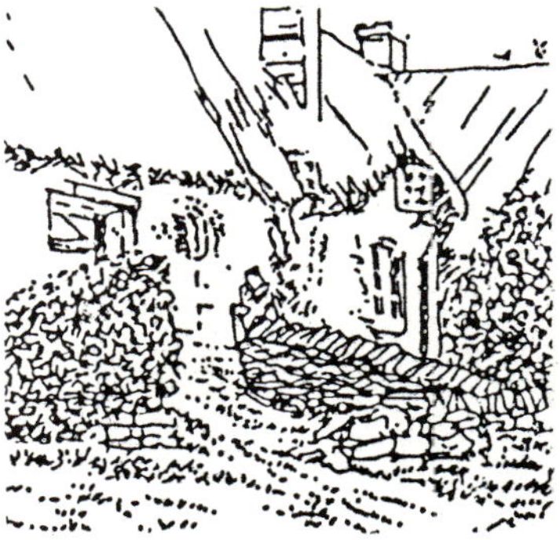

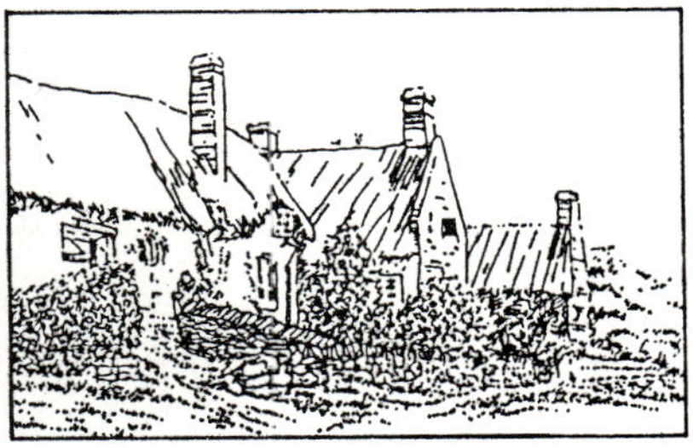

Preparing line drawings (*right*)
The final printed image will be in black and white only, so you must reduce all the information to black and white. Construct your drawing in soft pencil, then work in black ink (adding white where needed). Clean off pencil marks, or work initially in blue pencil which does not come out in photographs.

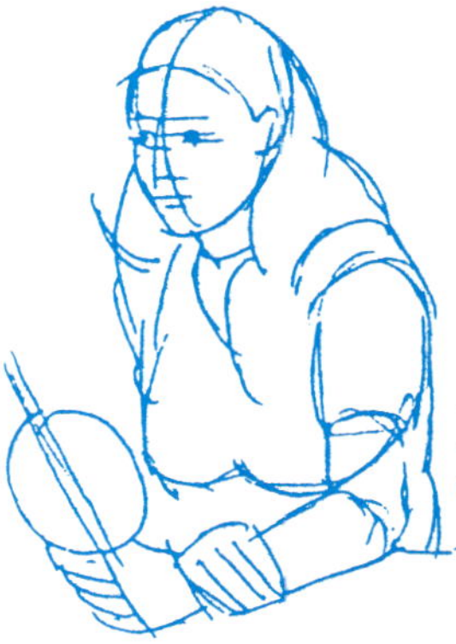

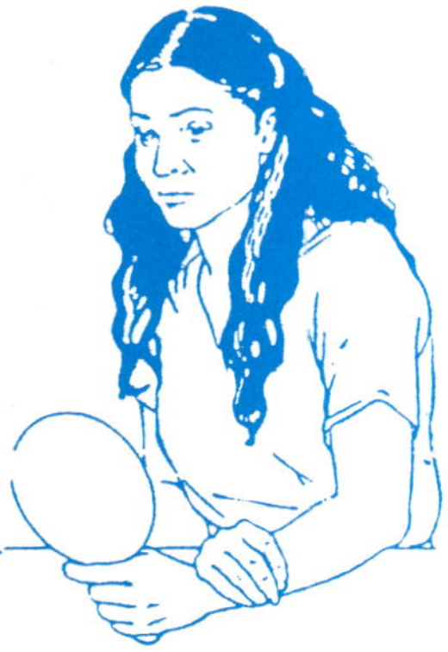

Suitability of line drawings
The coarser reproduction methods cope well with line. Illustrated (*right*) are two drawings from newsprint, notoriously poorly printed. The simpler reproduction processes can more easily convey the marks of a line drawing than of a tonal drawing.

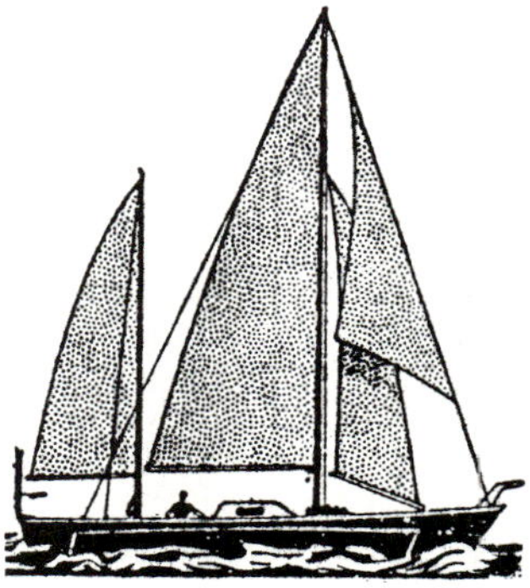

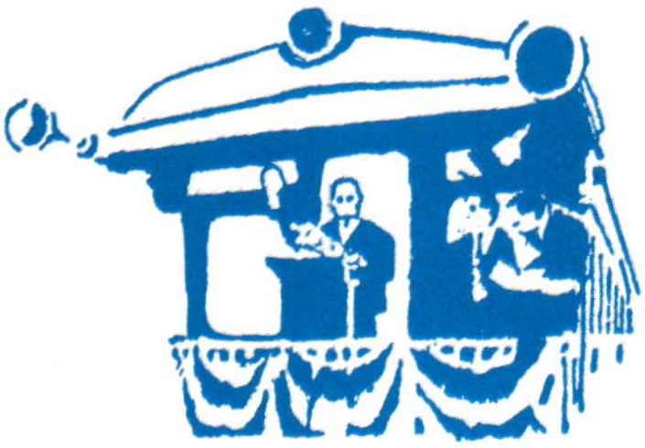

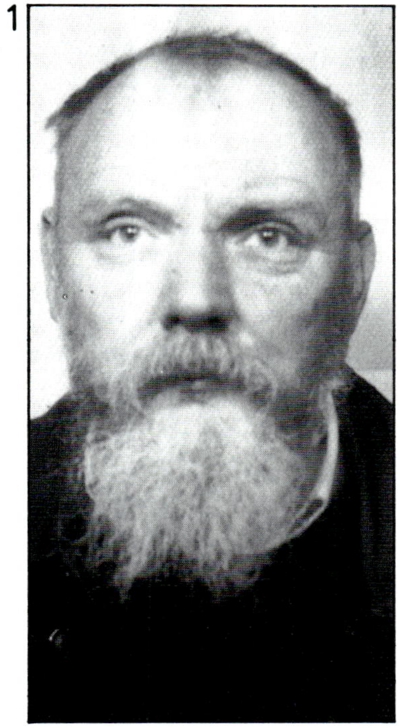

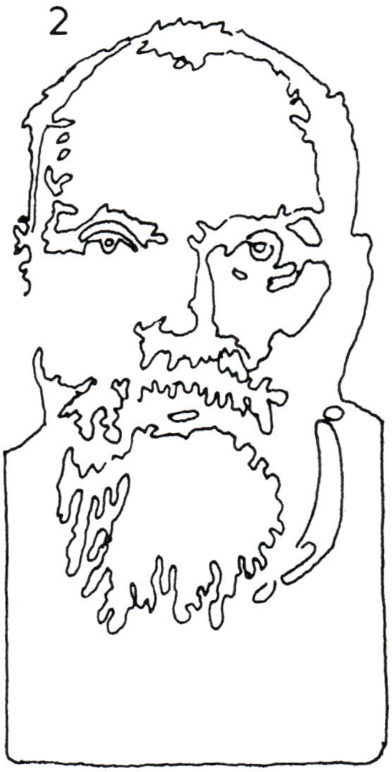

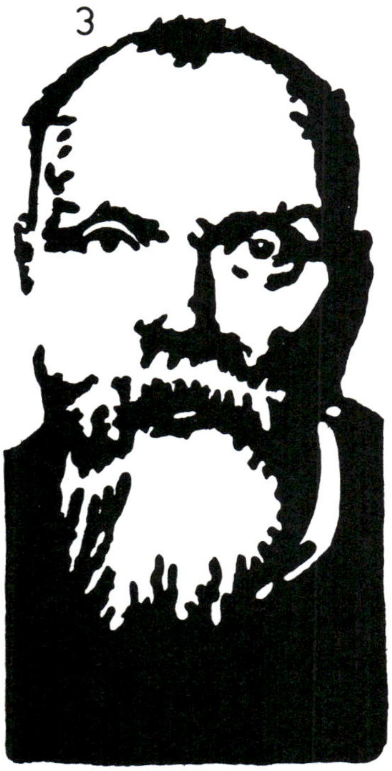

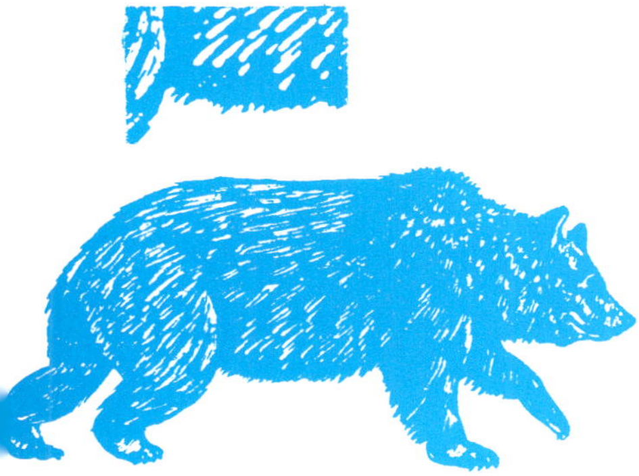

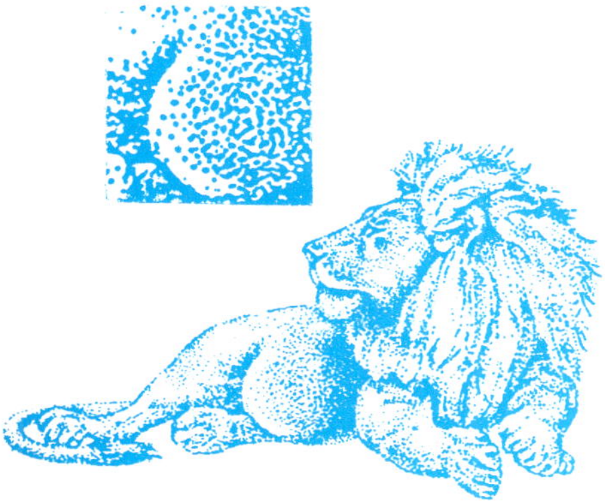

Working backwards

The drawing of the bear (*left*) is reproduced here the size it was drawn. The inset (greatly enlarged) reveals that the artist worked in the detail by scratching out, i.e. drawing in white. Line reproduction favours images that have clear contrasts of black and white.

Building up

The drawing of the lion (*left*) is reproduced here the size it was drawn. The inset (greatly enlarged) reveals that the artist worked in the detail by adding hundreds of tiny dots. Great care must be taken to control the tone of the assembly of dots.

Conversion technique

(*above*)
The simplest way to produce a line drawing for reproduction from a tonal image is to work from a picture with tones.
1 A photograph (reproduced by half tone) containing a wide range of tonal values.
2 Cover the original with tracing paper and outline the edges of the darker tones. Aim to indicate the smallest possible areas of darkness.
3 Fill in the dark patches to produce an image with sharp contrasts. Afterwards you will have to adjust it by adding small touches of white in the black, or, if necessary, inserting some detail in the white.

drawing for reproduction

Most of your drawings are a combination of lines and tones, even if the tones are indicated by applying groups of lines. Only by experience will you be able to judge the effects of having your work reproduced. And how you apply tone will depend upon which reproduction process you choose.

In printing, tone is achieved by the application of a mechanical screen which converts the various grades of tone to groups of very tiny dots. These can be widely spaced and large (coarse-screen reproduction) or very close together and very small (fine-screen reproduction).

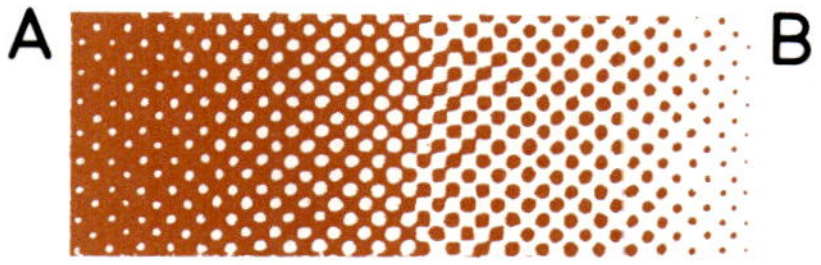

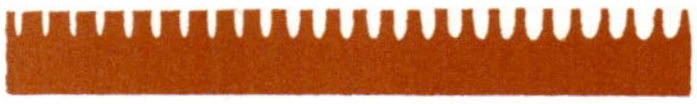

Section of a half-tone

Half-tone screen
Relief printing, in which the raised surfaces of the printing block carry the ink (see *immediate right*), achieves gradation of tone by altering the diameter of the dots and the distances they are apart. Big, close dots produce dark areas (**A**); small, spaced dots produce light areas (**B**) (*above right*).

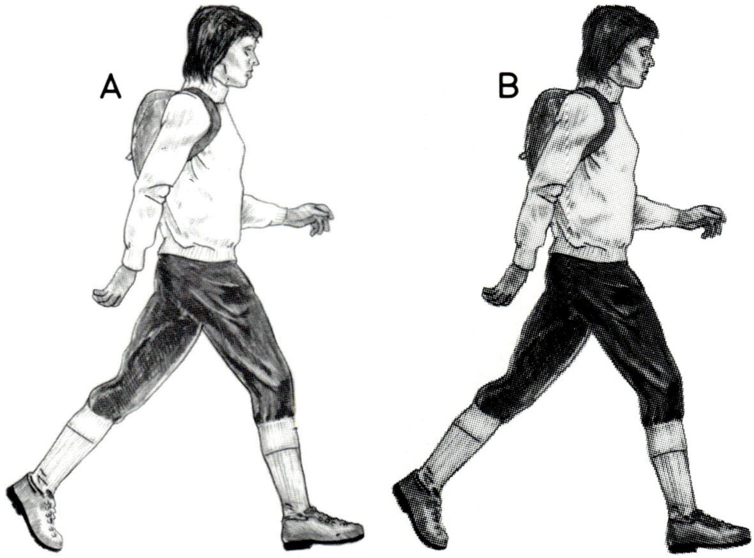

Screen scale
(Pencil drawing of hiker)
An identical drawing is reproduced twice (*right*) by (**A**) a very fine screen of dots, and (**B**) a very coarse screen of dots. You can see that a greater range of tones is produced with the finer screen.

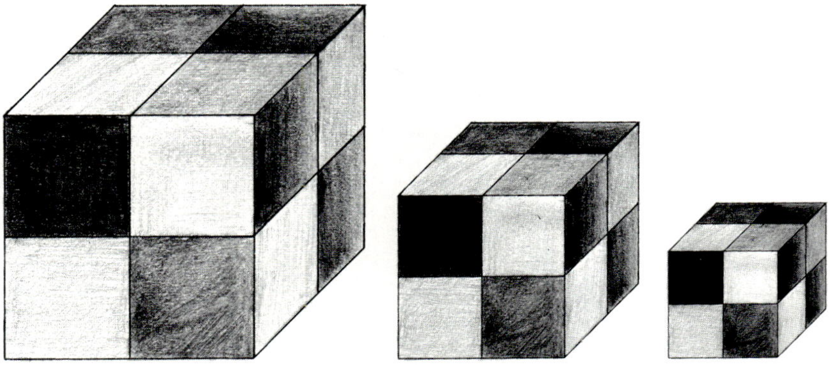

Scale effects
(Pencil drawing of a cube)
Your drawing is changed when it is reduced in print. Normally very large reductions darken the tones. This can be shown by reproducing a simple design containing constant weights of tone. In reduction these appear much darker (*right*).

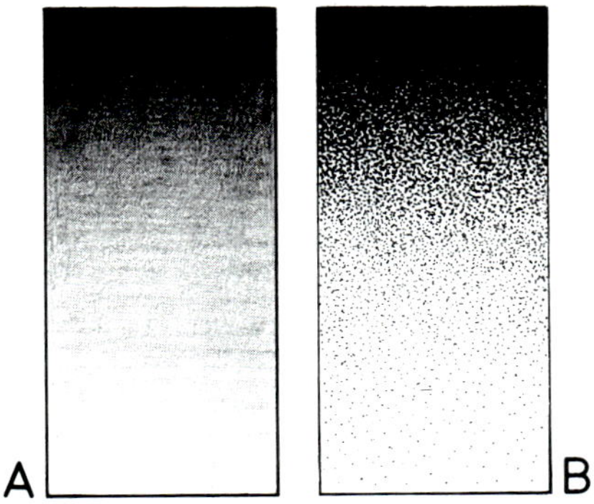

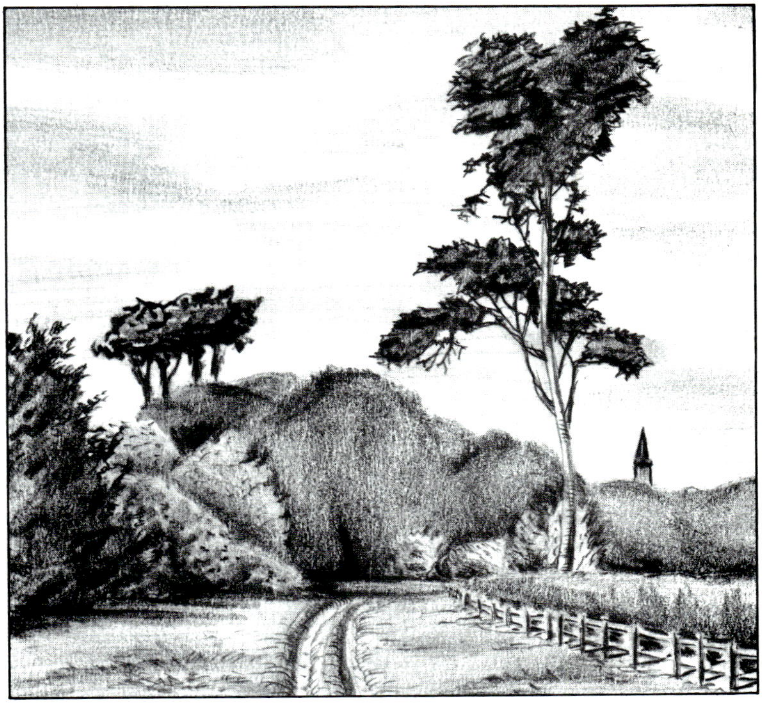

Tonal range
A pencil or brush drawing can produce a wide range of tonal values when reproduced by the half-tone process: (**A**) (*above left*). A pen and ink drawing reproduced by the line process achieves the same effect, but it is harder to keep an even gradation of tone: (**B**) (*above right*). The pencil drawing of a forest (*right*) has been reproduced as a half-tone.

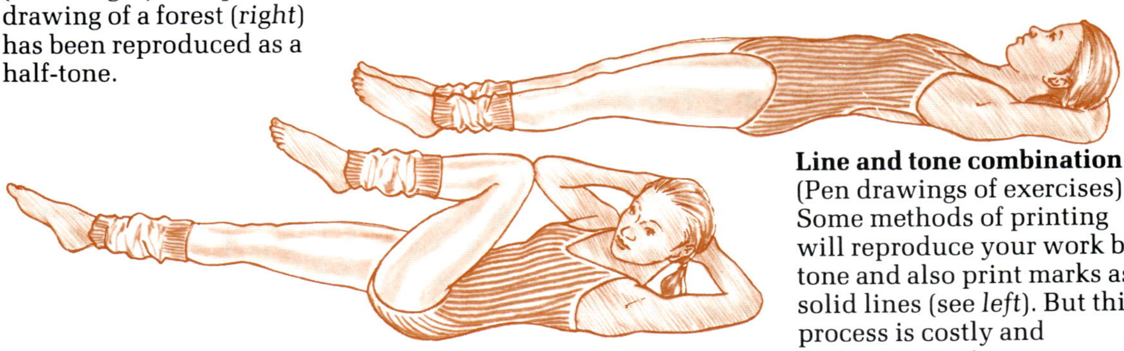

Line and tone combination
(Pen drawings of exercises)
Some methods of printing will reproduce your work by tone and also print marks as solid lines (see *left*). But this process is costly and requires experience.

Lithographic printing
(Pencil drawing of foot)
The foot (*right*) is printed by a screen process but this whole book is printed by lithography – that is, the dots appear on the surface of the printing plate but not in relief.

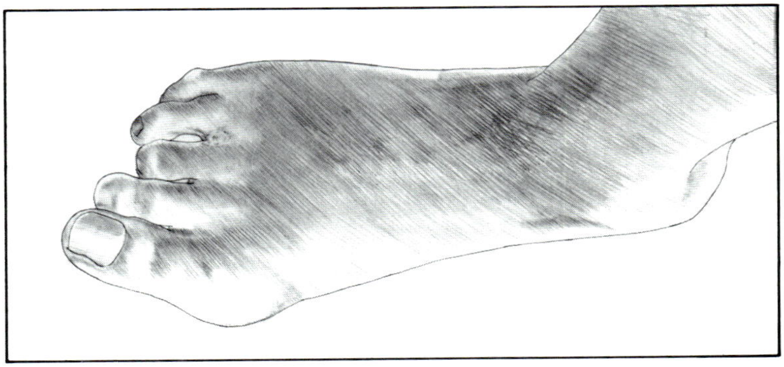

drawing for reproduction

Converting your drawings to a medium from which copies can be made greatly widens the scope of your work. Making a linocut or woodcut is not difficult and requires very few specialised tools, available from most art suppliers. Remember that your drawing will be in reverse when printed; you may either reverse it during the planning stage or accept the change.

Linocuts are simpler to make as the surface is soft and the materials are easy to buy. Woodcutting requires more skill and the results can be finer, but the quality of the lines printed may be affected by the hardness of the wood. You should obtain about fifty prints before the surface begins to deteriorate. Never forget to clean all your tools and the inking surfaces of the blocks.

Making a linocut (*right*)
1 Transferring the original drawing: First paint the lino surface white; then, using red chalking down paper or carbon paper, transfer down the basic design.
Remember the drawing will be reversed when printed. Either accept this reversal or correct it by using a mirror reflection.
2 Cut away the larger areas that should appear white.
3 Cut away the finer detail – again the marks that will be white.
4 Ink the remaining raised surfaces.
5 Lay paper over the lino block and rub evenly with the back of a comb or a clean cloth. Work outwards from the centre.
Always clean the lino block after use.

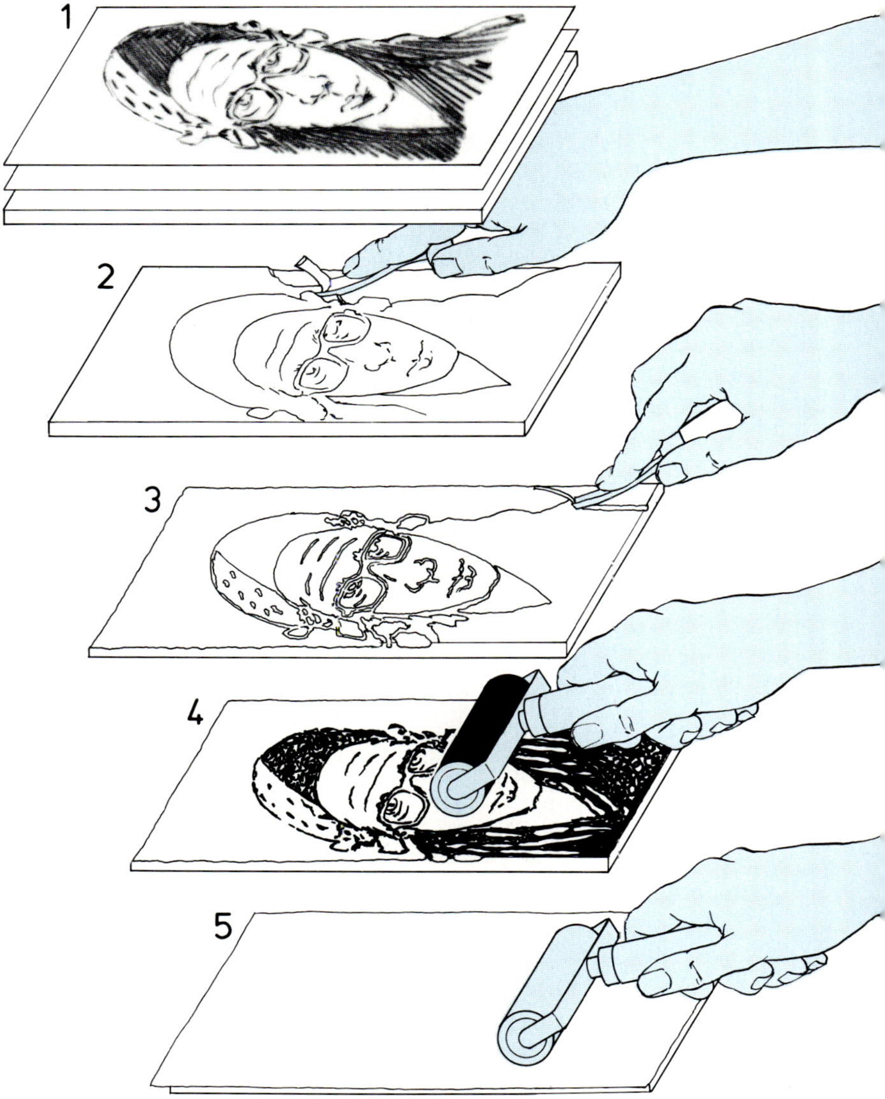

©DIAGRAM

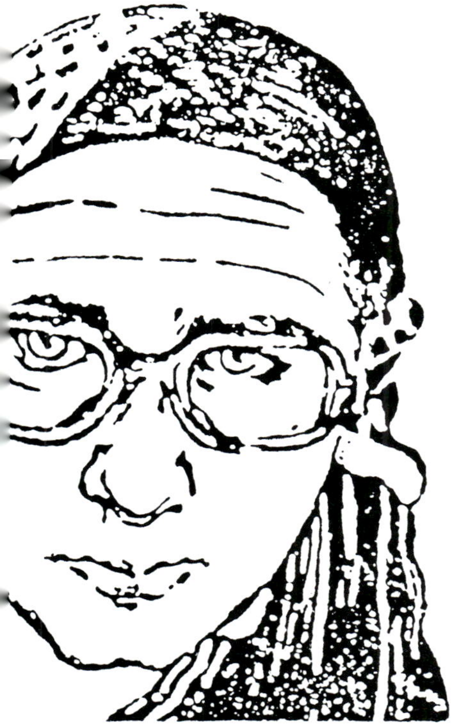

Self portrait of Kathleen
(Linocut)
The portrait (*left*) was produced by Kathleen by observing herself carefully in a mirror, and was reproduced by a linocut. Lino is brittle and cannot support fine lines, so the process should not be used to print tiny detail.

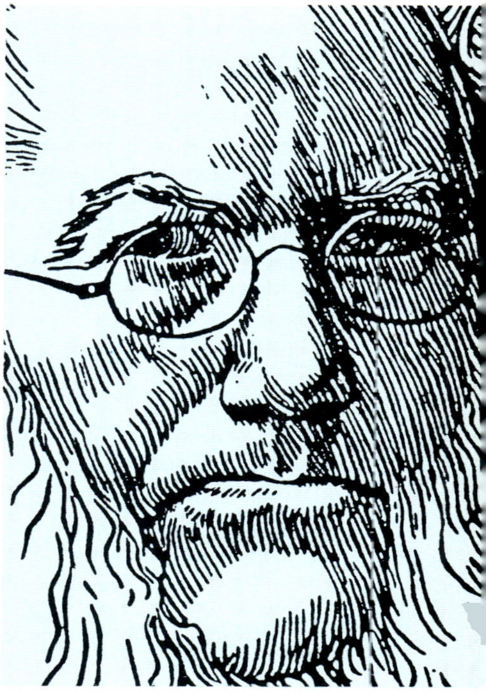

Portrait of a 19th century dignitary
(Enlargement of a woodcut)
The surface of a block of wood can be incised to produce finer detail than a piece of lino. The enlargement (*right*) shows how closely a woodcut can resemble the lined surface of a pen and ink drawing.

Portrait of George
(Detail of woodcut by Thomas Durham)
The drawing (*right*) uses the uneven surface of a woodblock; the harder strips of the grain pick up tone, the softer areas print grey. This apparent defect can be used to great advantage: it gives the woodcut greater force than pure blocks of black or white would achieve; and it permits the artist to incorporate larger black areas which would otherwise be difficult to ink evenly.

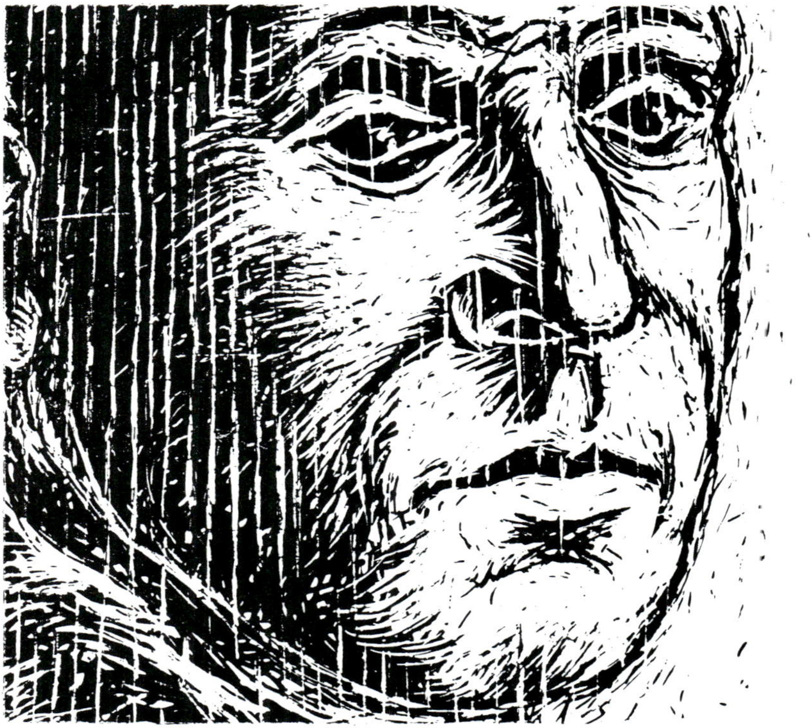

using your drawings

One of the greatest joys of drawing comes when you see the effect on your friends of your best work reproduced on cards, stationery and posters, in magazines and for making patterns. You may be able to convert your drawings yourself and print the results, or you can go to a professional printer. But whichever method you choose, don't be surprised when the reproduction is different from the original drawing – accept the finished work as it is. When you have decided to start to convert your drawings yourself, begin with simple, clear, clean designs, and continue to develop your abilities and build up experience gradually over a period of time.

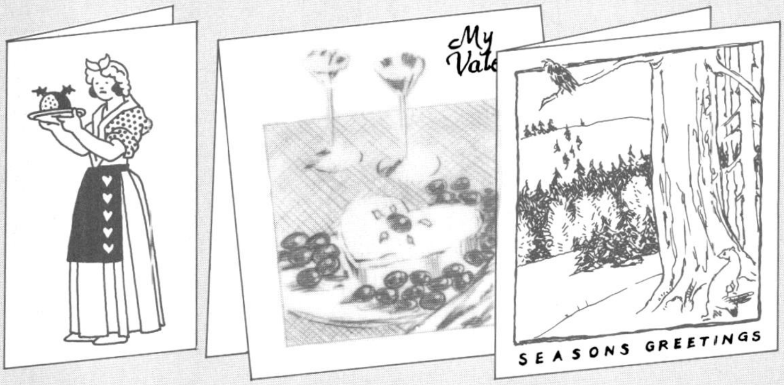

Greetings cards
By producing your own cards, you make them personal, far more valuable than any you can buy. Your individual designs for Christmas and birthday cards will give immense pleasure to those who receive them and great pride to you.

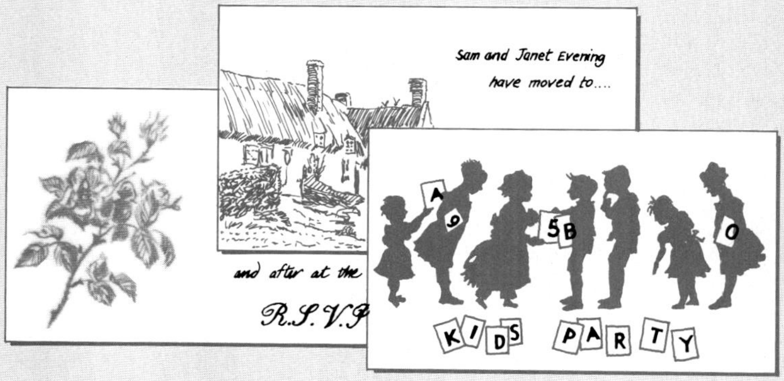

Invitations
All the anticipated excitement of those special events in your life – parties, weddings, births, house moving – will be conveyed to your friends and relations in your own designs. Remember to include all the information you want to pass on.

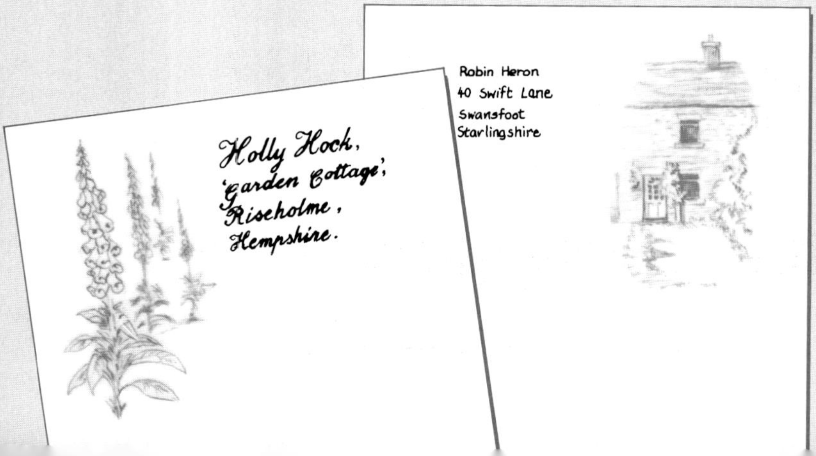

Stationery
Design your own letterheading, including one of your own drawings to describe the nature of your business. Or reveal a little of your character on your personal stationery with your choice of one of your drawings.

Magazines
Drawings enliven any page of text, whether reproduced by an office copier or by sophisticated commercial printing techniques (see *right*). In any magazine the illustrations set the style and tone of the pages. They catch the attention of the reader and inform him at a glance of the content. Keep the illustrations decorative and subservient to the words; too many pictures are confusing and dominating.

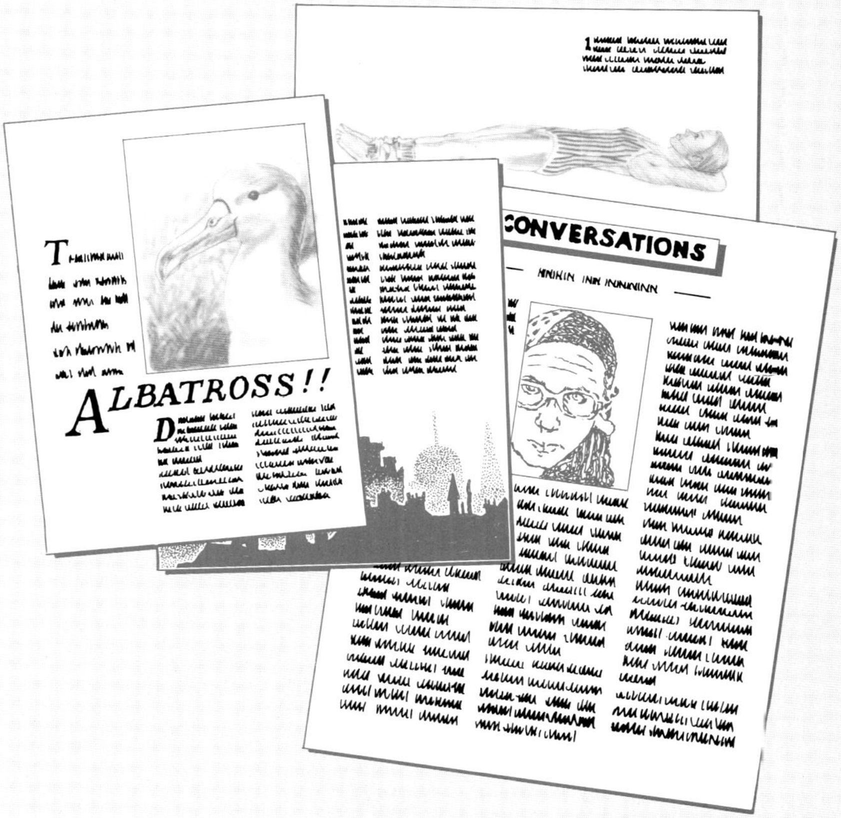

Posters
A poster is a perfect medium for drawings, a direct and powerful appeal to the viewer (see *right*). Simple, clear images are stronger than complex (and confusing) groupings and wide tonal variations.
A permanent record of your artistic development, your posters will be a reminder through the years of your achievements.

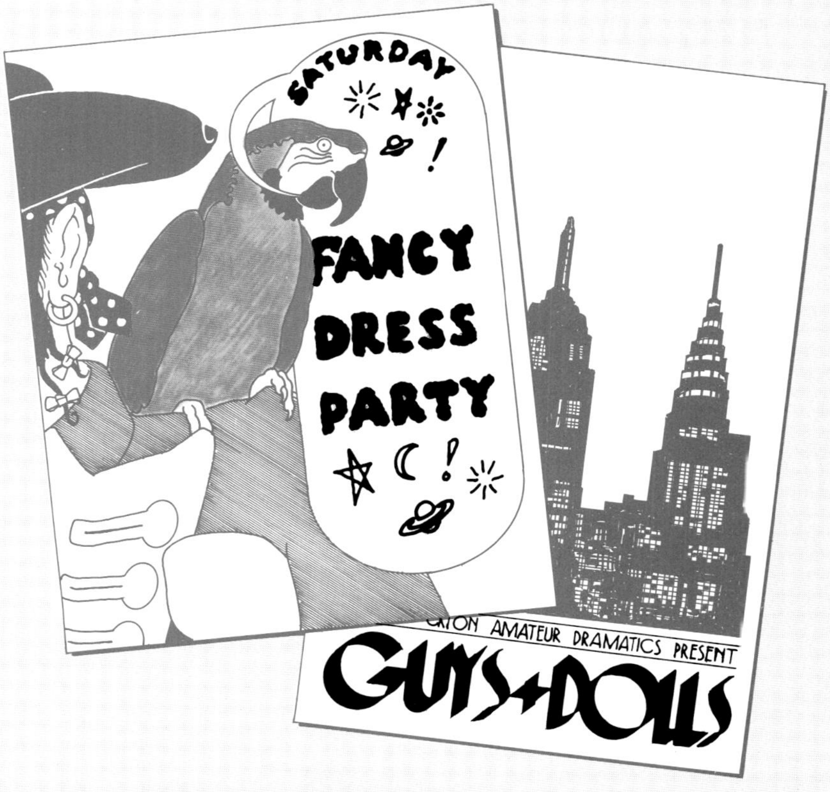

index

index